successful advertising research methods

successful advertising research methods

Jack Haskins & Alice Kendrick

NTC Business Books

a division of *NTC Publishing Group* • Lincolnwood, Illinois USA

Library of Congress Cataloging-in-Publication Data

Haskins, Jack B., 1922-
    Successful advertising research methods / Jack B. Haskins. Alice Gagnard Kendrick.
      p.   cm.
    Includes index.
    ISBN 0-8442-3189-4
    1. Advertising—Research—Methodology.   I. Title.
HF5814.H38 1991
659.1'072—dc20

91-9009
CIP

Published by NTC Business Books, a division of NTC Publishing Group,
4255 West Touhy Avenue, Lincolnwood (Chicago), Illinois 60646-1975 U.S.A.
© 1993 by Jack Haskins and Alice Kendrick.

2 3 4 5 6 7 8 9 0 VP 9 8 7 6 5 4 3 2 1

Contents

While the authors read and commented on each others' work, Professor Haskins had the primary responsibility for the writing of Chapters 1, 2, 5, 7, 9, and 19. Professor Kendrick was responsible for Chapters 3, 4, 6, 8, 10–11, and 20–23. All other chapters were a collaborative effort between the two authors.

Part 1

Before
Research
Begins

Chapter 1   The Advertising Process

Chapter 1

A Systematic Approach to Advertising

The first step toward effective advertising research is to acquire some understanding of the processes through which advertising decisions are made. Many companies and advertising agencies are still surprisingly unsystematic in the ways they choose to advertise. Their advertising may, for example, be led by personal preferences, traditions, emotional reactions, or simply convenience. Take, for example, company presidents who advertise only in magazines that their families and friends like to read, whose advertising expenditure is based on funds left over after other company expenses have been taken care of, or who insist that their advertising contain irrelevant accounts of company history or their own business philosophy. The advertising that results may be satisfying on a personal level to the sponsor, but it is unlikely to produce the maximum possible sales for the product. Decisions may also be influenced by the wrong people. For example, an advertising agency might tend to recommend larger than necessary advertising budgets to its clients, because agency fees are geared to a percentage of the client's spending. Or the choice of agency might be based on the congeniality of account executives rather than on the quality of services provided.

The end result of unsystematic decisions like these ranges from, at best, wasting money on ineffective advertising to, at worst, alienating the public and producing fewer sales than if no advertising had been done at all. And there are documented cases where such advertising has had not just neutral, but disastrous effects.

It is, then, important to be systematic and to be objective when making advertising decisions. The approach we recommend is based on four simple decision-making questions:

- What and who is the **market** for a product or service?

- Which **media** are best for advertising to that market?

- How much **money** should be spent on advertising a product or service?

- Which advertising **messages** should be placed in the chosen media?

These four questions constitute a systematic approach to advertising decision making. Coincidentally, they can be remembered as the four *M*s: *m*arkets, *m*edia, *m*oney, and *m*essages. Note that the decisions are not necessarily made in this order. The *market* decision certainly comes first, and the *messages* decision usually comes last, but, as you will see, making decisions on media, money, and messages is an interactive process—the decision you make on one will often dictate or influence your decisions on the others.

What and Who Is the Market for a Product or Service?

The market for a product or service is made up of those people who are its intended prospective purchasers. Who are the people to whom you want to advertise? How many of them are out there? What are their characteristics, motivations, behaviors, and purchasing patterns? Consumer research can answer these questions.

The aim of consumer research is to define a market. This can mean one of two things: finding a market for an existing product, or finding a product to suit an existing market. To understand this dual purpose, think of the difference between marketing and selling. *Marketing* is finding out what people want and giving it to them; *selling* is convincing people to buy what you have to offer. In the recently exploited "seniors" market—the growing number of people over age 50 who have high disposable incomes and who collectively control a disproportionate fraction of the nation's financial assets—marketers are busily researching current buying habits and unmet needs so that new products or services can be tailor-made to the market's requirements. In contrast, Henry Ford I, reported to have been willing to sell people any car they wanted so long as it was his black Model T, was speaking as a salesman, not a marketer. Thus, consumer research is aimed at either defining the market for "the product looking for a market" or defining the product for "the market looking for a product."

Which Media Are Best for Advertising to that Market?

The media are the channels of communication through which advertising reaches its target markets. The major media are TV and radio broadcasting, newspapers, magazines, outdoor billboards, and direct mail. The media decision depends on finding out which of these channels will be most efficient at both reaching and attracting the attention of your prospects. There are literally thousands of TV and radio stations and many more magazines, newspapers, and other media available, and no one can afford the shotgun approach of buying into them all. How do you decide which ones to use?

The answer is, through media research. The aim of media research is to determine the cost-effectiveness of advertising in various media, singly or in combination, to reach your target markets. Media research will tell you which TV programs your prospects tune to, which magazines and newspapers they receive, and which they pay attention to. It will also tell you how many members there are in the households that receive different media and how often they are exposed to those media.

How Much Money Should Be Spent on Advertising a Product or Service?

Money research is not limited to deciding how much to spend. It is also concerned with how best to spend that money in terms of time, place, and competitive strategy. How should money be allocated over the year, or during a month, to get the most "bang for your buck"? In which parts of the country or in which areas of a state do you get the most sales per advertising dollar? Should you advertise in the same places and at the same times as your competitors (the hand-to-hand combat strategy), or should you "hit 'em where they ain't"? Should you put your money into markets that are already strong buyers of your product or brand, or should you play missionary in weaker markets?

Decisions on advertising budget setting and spending should not be made by the seat of the pants but by careful research. A systematic, objective approach will provide you with facts rather than guesswork on which to base the money decision.

Which Advertising Messages Should Be Placed in the Chosen Media?

A message can be defined as any individual advertisement intended for placement in the media. A campaign is a systematic series of messages.

The message, or copy, decision can be the most difficult one of all. Why? Because there are an infinite number of things you can say or show in advertisements, only a fraction of which will turn people on to your product or service. Most possible advertising messages have either no effect or a negative effect. Those that have no effect are simply a waste of money. Those that have negative effects can mean losing sales that might have been made without the advertising. They can turn customers and prospects off your product or service. All other advertising decisions may be perfect, but if the message decision is wrong—disaster.

Stages of the Advertising Research Process

The systematic approach to advertising may be clarified further by describing the stages that an advertisement must go through to reach its target and have the desired effect.

After a product or service and its market have been defined, an advertisement must pass through a six-stage research process in order to be successful.

1. **Media distribution.** The circulation of a magazine or the number of sets tuned to a particular TV channel.

2. **Media exposure.** The number of people who are exposed to the magazine or TV set.

3. **Advertisement exposure.** The number of people exposed to a particular advertisement printed in the magazine or aired on the TV set.

4. **Advertisement perception.** The number of people who give some degree of cognitive attention to the advertisement.

5. **Advertisement communication.** The number of people whose responses to the product are in some way affected by the advertisement.

6. **Behavioral response.** The number of people who respond to the advertisement with some sort of behavior.

To place these six research stages within our advertising decision-making framework, note that the first three are elements of media research, and the last three are elements of message, or copy, research. Let's look at each of the six stages in a little more detail.

Media Distribution

Media distribution is the number of physical units of a given medium through which an advertisement can be delivered. A magazine's circulation, for example, will tell us the number of copies of a particular issue (or the average number per issue) delivered to subscribers and other receivers. Notice that circulation is not equivalent to the number of copies printed, because not all printed copies will be distributed and delivered. In the case of television, media distribution refers to the number of sets tuned to a particular station or program. Take a local TV station's 6 p.m. news show: its distribution is not the number of TV sets in the station's coverage area, nor even the number of sets turned on, but the number of sets tuned to that program at that time (or an average weekly number for the program). Outdoor advertising distribution is the number of billboards carrying the advertising message. Direct mail distribution is the number of catalogs delivered to residences, for example.

Media distribution is the very roughest measure of a medium's value in disseminating advertising. It specifies only the number of physical units carrying the message and says nothing about the number of people exposed to or affected by it. However, in the absence of more precise data, measuring media distribution provides a rough numerical basis for comparing one medium with another.

Media Exposure

A single copy of a magazine delivered to a home may be read by several persons, by one person, or by no one. Similarly, a TV set tuned to a particular program may have no viewers or it may have several. Obviously, someone must be exposed to a media unit for it to have any value to the advertiser, which explains why media exposure is a better measure of advertising effectiveness than media distribution.

A medium's audience size can be quite different from its distribution size. A woman's magazine, for instance, may have only one reader per copy, while a general family magazine may have three or more readers per copy. It's also possible for audience size to be smaller than distribution. There may be an average of less than one reader per magazine copy, or, though a large number of TV sets are tuned to a particular station, there may be no one in the same rooms as the sets. It's not difficult to think of examples of two or more media with the same distribution but different audience sizes.

Although media exposure or audience size is a more useful measurement than distribution, it is also more difficult to define. A great deal of media research is aimed at clarifying precisely what is meant by exposure, in terms that will permit comparisons between different media.

To measure media exposure, then, is to measure the number of people within sight or sound of a particular medium. To get an idea of how difficult this measurement is, consider a single copy of a magazine, let's say, the latest issue of *Reader's Digest*. Which of the following can you count as an exposure?

- A person who has seen the magazine lying on a table from a distance

- A person who has glanced idly at the cover

- A person who has picked up *Reader's Digest* while going through a stack of magazines

- A person who has riffled through the pages but hasn't read anything

- A person who has read at least one item completely

- A person who has spent at least five minutes with the magazine in hand

- A person who can correctly identify something from the magazine

The same problem arises in measuring exposure to broadcast advertisements, for example, last night's 6:30 p.m. NBC news. Which of the following constitutes an exposure?

- A person who hears snatches of the show from another room while doing something else

- A person who walks through the room while the show is playing

- A person who is in the room but talks throughout the program

- A person seated in front of the TV set throughout the show but who reads a book

- A person who watches and listens to the program for a few seconds or one minute or five minutes

- A person who can remember, unaided, at least one item from the program

Or consider an outdoor billboard. Which of the following is an exposure?

- A person walking or driving by in either direction

- A person walking or driving by in the direction facing the advertisement

- A person driving with eyes on traffic

- A person who happens to glance at the billboard

- A person who is able to recall what was on the billboard

These may seem like trivial questions until you are faced with the decision of which of three media is best for advertising a product or service: a magazine claiming an average of 20,000,000 exposures per issue (defined as the number of people who have held it in their hands); a TV program claiming an average of 20,000,000 exposures (defined as the number of people who are in the same room for at least five minutes during the show); or a billboard claiming 20,000,000 exposures (defined as the average number of people who walk or drive by each month).

One job of media research is to decide which type of exposure is most valid for each media type. Another, even knottier problem is to determine how these exposures can be compared. Even assuming that exposure to a magazine can be defined and measured and that the same can be done for a TV program, how can the buyer be sure that one exposure in a magazine has the same value as one exposure on television?

So far, media exposure has been described as the total number of people exposed to a media unit. Another important factor is the number of exposures per person—two exposures by the same person are, in most cases, more valuable than one each by two different people. Different media may have the same audience size but may differ greatly in terms of the number of exposures per person. If Magazine *A* has 20,000,000 exposures (10,000,000 people exposed two times each), and Magazine *B* has 20,000,000 exposures (20,000,000 people each exposed once), are the two of equal value to the advertiser?

Media exposure, then, can refer both to the number of people who are exposed (audience size), and the total number of exposures (the audience size multiplied by the average number of exposures per person).

Advertisement Exposure

Advertisement exposure is the number of people who are within sight or sound of a particular advertising message. It is a much more exact measure of advertising effectiveness than media exposure, because it eliminates those persons who were exposed to the medium but not to the advertisement itself.

As in the case of media exposure, advertisement exposure can be specified in terms of either the number of people exposed or the total number of exposures. Measurement is even more difficult. How can the researcher determine whether a person saw a particular magazine advertisement? How can we be sure it was seen in the particular medium under evaluation and not elsewhere? Similarly, assuming a person recalls seeing a particular TV commercial, how can we determine where and when it was seen?

Measures of advertisement exposure provide the most direct index to describe how well a medium delivers an advertising message. However, none of these first three stages—media distribution, media exposure, and advertisement exposure—says anything about the quality or effectiveness of the advertising message itself.

Advertisement Perception

One is on fairly firm ground in talking about media distribution, media exposure, and advertisement exposure; they can be defined and measured in fairly objective terms. Advertisement perception, however, is entirely different, as it deals with individual responses to messages.

Perception is defined as conscious awareness through the senses of objects or other data. For our purposes, perception includes awareness of, attention to, and liking for an advertisement.

The table below highlights the difference between advertisement exposure and advertisement perception.

	Advertisement Exposure	Advertisement Perception
Television	A person in the same room with a TV set turned on, but who doesn't hear or see a commercial when it comes on because of daydreaming, conversation, or other activities.	A person who is aware of the sound or picture or both from a TV commercial, even though deliberately trying to screen it out (as in the case of some annoying commercials).
Magazine	A person idly flipping through the pages of a magazine while thinking of something else but who doesn't see the advertisement even though it passed in front of his or her eyes.	A person flipping through the pages of a magazine who sees or reads a part of the advertisement.

People exposed to a newspaper page provide an interesting example of this distinction. Eye-movement cameras have been used to photograph all the places on a newspaper page over which a person's vision has wandered. Tests show that a person's gaze will generally pass over or scan almost every item on the page, no matter how small. When asked to go back over the same page with an interviewer and point out what they have seen, however, people can report seeing only a fraction of the items; some of them they are not at all aware of having seen. In this case, exposure has occurred on all the items scanned, but perception has occurred only on those items that the person is at least aware of having seen. One magazine study has found that about two out of three exposures result in measurable perception. "Aided recall" and "recognition" scores are measures of perception commonly used by the print media.

In addition to simple awareness of an advertisement's existence, advertisement perception also includes interest in, recall or recognition of, knowledge of, and attitude toward the advertisement. Perception is important to the advertiser because, as long as it can be clearly defined and measured, it can provide a means of determining the effect of advertising.

Advertising Communication

One distinction between perception and communication is that the former refers to *advertisement* responses and the latter to *product* responses. If an advertisement adds to a person's product *knowledge*, affects product *attitude*, or stimulates a desire to take some product *action* (action-arousal), then it has communicated. Conversely, if a person reports having seen an advertisement, but there is no evidence of increased product knowledge, attitude change, or action-arousal, then it has been perceived but has not communicated.

Awareness and factual recall of the product or its attributes do not necessarily result in a change of attitude. Attitude generally refers to the overall liking or disliking for a whole product. But when one speaks of feelings about some aspect, trait, or attribute of a product rather than the whole product, this is referred to as *product image*. With cause, for example, attributes might be power, attractiveness, economy, durability, ease of maintenance, and so on. An advertisement may change some aspect of product image without necessarily changing overall attitude toward the car. If an advertisement stresses the car's horsepower, the consumer may become more convinced that the car is powerful, but if increased power is unimportant to that consumer, his or her attitude will not change.

Even though an advertisement may change product knowledge or product attitude, this may not be sufficient to produce action-arousal—a strong motivation or desire to take some action regarding the product. After seeing a car advertisement, for example, action-arousal might be evident in a desire to visit a showroom, a desire to test-drive the car, or a strong intention to purchase the car.

Action-arousal is, then, the strongest form of advertising communication. Even so, it will not necessarily result in action; other things may intervene to prevent the action or behavior from taking place, even though the motivation is there.

In summary, then, successful communication may be measured by an increased awareness of or knowledge about a product, by a change of attitude or product image, by a desire to take some sort of action regarding the product, or by a combination of these responses. There is much disagreement among researchers as to which of these is the best measure of advertising communication. It is probably safest to say that they all measure some aspect of communication effectiveness, but it is unclear which one is most important or if they're equally important. Logic, however, indicates that attitude change and action-arousal are probably closest to the ultimate goal of advertising—persuading prospects to purchase the product.

Behavioral Response

Behavioral response to advertising refers to any sort of observable behavior stimulated by advertising. This can take many forms. The ultimate and most desirable behavior is, of course, purchase of the product, but various intermediate behaviors may be necessary or desirable before this happens: talking about the product, visiting a retail outlet to see or touch it, borrowing or otherwise trying out the product, requesting more information about it, and so on.

Behavioral response—particularly the purchase response—has two important advantages over such psychological responses as perception and communication. The first is that it measures exactly the effect advertising wants to achieve. One might quarrel with the notion that an advertisement needs to communicate product facts that stick in the consumer's memory, but no one can deny that a purchase of the product is desirable. The second advantage, especially to the researcher, is that behavior is often easy to measure. Behavior is something that can be seen, pointed at, and counted, whereas perception and communication cannot be observed in the same way and generally must be inferred from what the consumer *says* was perceived or communicated. However, a single advertisement is usually not sufficient to bring about a purchase, except in special cases; therefore, the effects of advertising can usually be detailed only for campaigns and not for individual advertisements.

One difficulty with using behavior response, such as the purchase response, as a measure of advertising effectiveness is that it is often difficult to separate the effect of advertising from the numerous other factors that influence purchase. The purchase may result from product quality, previous experience with the product, the proximity of a retail outlet that stocks the product, money or credit availability, or the absence of deterring factors, such as a veto by a family member or a cut-rate campaign for a competitive product.

It's easy to see that a purchase can take place without advertising, or despite poor advertising. Conversely, even though advertising might be excellent, the overriding influence of other factors might prevent a purchase from taking place. To overcome the difficulty of separating the influence of advertising from other influences on behavior, researchers have developed controlled field experiments— a topic that will be covered in detail later in this book.

Review

In this chapter we saw that:

- A systematic approach to effective advertising demands the following:
  - A product's market or potential customers must be defined and described by consumer research.
  - Advertising media that are efficient in reaching that market must be selected.
  - These efficient media must be distributed to the market.
  - The market must be exposed to the media.
  - The market must be exposed to the advertising within the media.
  - The advertising must be perceived by the market.
  - Some form of product communication must take place.
  - The behavioral goal of a purchase must be reached.
- Media distribution, media exposure, and advertisement exposure are generally considered to be the responsibility of the medium in which the advertising is carried. The evaluation and comparison of media fall within that category of advertising research called *media research*.
- Advertisement perception and communication are generally considered to depend on the advertising message. The evaluation and testing of advertisements is another category of advertising research called *message, or copy, research*.
- Media distribution, media exposure, and advertisement exposure are relatively easy to define and can be measured fairly objectively, but they represent only intermediate steps toward the advertiser's ultimate goal.
- Advertisement perception and communication are difficult to define and usually are not amenable to direct measurement, because the researcher must generally rely on the consumer's subjective report, which may or may not be accurate.
- Of all the possible responses to advertising, the purchase response is the most desirable and most directly measured. The principal drawback is the influence of non-advertising factors on the purchase decision. This difficulty can be surmounted through the use of rigorous research methods, principally through controlled field experiments.

Chapter 2 The Research Process

Just as there is an advertising process, so is there a research process—an orderly model of how research works. This involves a scientific approach to problem solving, described in this chapter as an orderly procedure of steps to be followed in planning and implementing any research project.

A Scientific Approach to Advertising Research

The creation of effective advertising is the result of two kinds of thinking: logical and creative. In advertising, most people are good at either one or the other. Though the public image of the advertising executive is one of a sophisticated, persuasive, dynamic, glib, and businesslike person with a satchel full of eye-catching and imaginative ads, a business mind and a creative mind are rarely found in the same person. The business mind is concerned with the practical and tangible aspects of running a business, with marketing products, and with making profits. The creative mind is more interested in ideas and the intangible aspects of communication.

Traditionally, advertising has thrived through the combined efforts of the two. In recent years, however, there has been a growing feeling among advertisers that the industry should become even more business oriented. They would like to see a more objective approach to both creating advertising and measuring its effectiveness. As the old saying goes, "I know that half my advertising is wasted, but I don't know which half." In short, without understanding the general principles of how and why advertising succeeds or fails, and without an objective measure of advertising effects, it is impossible to know whether the money we plan to invest in advertising will be well-spent or wasted. Like a hunter with an expensive, high-powered rifle, the unscientific advertiser fires madly at a group of moving targets, then moves on complacently without bothering to see whether the targets have been hit, satisfied simply that the gun has been firing away. We fire as many ads through as many media as possible and at great cost, hoping that some will reach our target markets and have the effects we want.

The missing ingredient is the scientific approach, an orderly, objective procedure of gathering and verifying facts that will add to our knowledge, understanding, and control over future advertising activity. Advertising is certainly not a science in the traditional sense of the word, but it is nevertheless possible to use a scientific approach to aid problem solving and decision making.

Characteristics of the Scientific Approach

Procedures are explicit.

The methods used for collecting information, solving problems, and communicating results must be clearly described, and other advertising and non-advertising professionals must be able to read the research report and replicate its procedures. The description must be honest and minutely detailed.

Data collection is objective.

Research must be conducted and reported objectively. Whatever predictions are made prior to research, these must not be allowed to influence procedures or results.

Research is systematic and cumulative.

Though research may be initiated to find the answer to a specific and immediate problem, the researcher's scope should not be too narrow. The researcher should aim to build up whole bodies of knowledge, verified facts, generalizations, and principles in each research field. *Applied research* concentrates on specific problems, whereas *basic research* is cumulative. The researcher should carry out applied and basic research simultaneously.

The researcher is both open-minded and skeptical.

Researchers must be open-minded about accepting alternatives to their own preconceived notions or to commonsense answers. They must look critically at traditional methods and cherished assumptions, think of alternatives, and admit that new hypotheses may be correct. At the same time, researchers must be extremely skeptical, reluctant to accept anything as fact until it is proven.

The objectives of research are explanation, understanding, and control.

Research should show and explain not only *what* has happened, but also *why* and *how* it happened. Research must discover and report causes and effects, not just correlations. Control then can be exercised by taking action.

Findings are replicable.

Results must be verifiable. If the same procedures are used, other researchers should arrive at the same conclusions. Intuition, sensitivity, and insight are not sufficient to establish a point of fact. Those who agree with your results usually won't try to verify them; those who disagree will try to prove you wrong.

Taking a scientific approach to advertising research is a practical measure to ensure against advertising failures and to improve the probability of success. The scientific approach also provides the theoretical basis on which a structured research program can be built. One way to establish such a structure is to break the research process into ten distinct steps. The following section examines each of these steps.

Ten Steps for Planning and Executing an Advertising Research Project

Once advertising research is viewed as a systematic and objective process, planning and executing each project to solve a specific advertising problem becomes an easier task. Here is a simple, ten-step checklist that takes the researcher from the early planning stages to actual problem solving.

1. Become aware of an advertising problem.
2. Define and clarify the problem.
3. Secondary research: review existing knowledge.
4. Primary research: define one specific problem.
5. Prepare a detailed research plan.
6. Implement the research plan and gather data.
7. Process the data.
8. Interpret the data.
9. Communicate the results.
10. Apply the results to solve the advertising problem.

This outline is broad enough to be applied to any advertising or marketing decision that requires research. Let's look at each of the ten steps in a little more detail.

1. Become Aware of an Advertising Problem

An advertising problem can be as complex as a decision on a complete change in strategy, or as simple as a practical "how to do it" question. It may concern an idea or hypothesis you want to test out, or it may involve the choice of one of several options. And let's not rule out simple curiosity: "I wonder what would happen if . . . ?" Problems may be specific to one decision, or they may affect several different decisions or business activities.

Most advertising problems come to the researcher from those responsible for making advertising decisions, perhaps from the business, media, or creative people within an agency. Problems usually stem from broad and vague questions, such as "Are we getting any results from our TV advertising?" or "Why isn't our market share increasing as quickly as we planned?" The first step for the researcher is to identify the nature of the problem in terms of how it might be solved through research.

2. Define and Clarify the Problem

No matter how simple or clear the original problem seems, it can almost always be broken up into several related problems, questions, and possibilities. As an example, look again at the broad advertising problem, "Are we getting any results from our TV advertising?" Before tackling this major issue, the researcher needs to define and clarify the question into more precise, researchable components such as:

- What is the net change in attitudes and sales resulting from the September-June spot-commercial campaign on NBC?
- Are there any differences in effects between current users of our brand, users of other brands, and non-users?

And so on. Any single research project usually can handle only one of these questions at a time. Related questions like these emerge as the researcher thinks through the advertising problem and discusses it with colleagues. Clarify the problem by asking as many related questions as possible. What market is the advertising trying to reach? What are its overall goals? Who is the person requesting the problem-solving information? Who will use it once the results are produced? What decisions will be based on the results? What information is already available on the problem? Are there other, related problems? Exploring the original problem in this way will help the researcher identify those aspects that research can solve. The researcher and those who originally posed the problem to be carried out should agree on a list of researchable questions. It is important that everyone has the same understanding of what information is needed to solve the problem.

3. Secondary Research: Review Existing Knowledge

Although it is certainly the fastest and most cost-effective kind of research to conduct, secondary research is strangely neglected by advertisers and marketers. Impatience leads us to reinvent the wheel rather than review existing information to find out whether a problem has previously been analyzed. Even if no specific answers can be found, a review will help to define the problem further and clarify the research procedures to be used.

Here are just a few of the many readily available sources of marketing and advertising research information:

- Your own company and agency research files.
- Libraries: books, trade journals, periodicals, specialized computer databases and other information services.
- Professional advertising and marketing organizations.
- Commercial research firms.
- Research consultants, college professors.
- Research conferences.

4. Primary Research: Decide on One Specific Problem

As we have seen, several researchable questions usually arise during the first three steps in the process. Discussions with colleagues may have answered some questions, and secondary research may have helped with others. Perhaps the problem can even be solved without further research. If unanswered questions remain, however, the next step is to decide which one should be investigated first.

Problem selection is considered by many researchers to be the most important—and often the most difficult—stage of the research process. There are no hard-and-fast rules. In fact, problem selection usually comes down to a judgment call, a subjective choice of one alternative over the others. The decision usually rests with the person who identified the original problem and who must take action, although the advice and agreement of researchers and other affected decision makers is important.

5. Prepare a Detailed Research Plan

The word *plan* is used here in its broadest sense. The research plan includes the overall pattern, or *design,* and the techniques, or *methods,* that are to be used.

Design.

Research design depends on the purpose of the study. In brief, the study may be purely *descriptive* of a particular state of affairs, or it may be *predictive* of the future. It may be *correlational,* where the purpose is to determine relations among variables, or it may be *causal,* where the purpose is to determine the precise causes of certain effects. The objectives of the research will, then, influence the design it takes.

A *one-shot* design is used for simple, descriptive studies and provides a snapshot of a particular situation at a particular point in time.

A *longitudinal* design is made up of a series of individual, one-shot studies, conducted in the same way but at various different times to measure change. Though still largely descriptive, a longitudinal design can be predictive of the future.

A before-and-after or *pretest-posttest* design can determine the changes that accompany a particular action.

A *laboratory experiment* design can be used to measure cause and effect in a controlled, artificial environment.

A field experiment, another example of *experimental* design, is used to determine causation in real market conditions. You would use a field experimental design, for example, to determine the impact of a campaign (cause) on sales (effect).

To sum up, research designs can be classified as follows:

- Non-experimental: Research that can describe, correlate, and predict but cannot determine causation.

- Quasi-experimental: Research that can approximate causation when experiments are not possible.

- Experimental: Research that can determine causation in real-life conditions.

Methods.

The techniques selected for data collection—the backbone of most research projects—depend on the objectives of the study. The details of these techniques will be covered in later chapters; we address here how to select among techniques. To research buyer behavior in supermarkets, for example, direct observation and video-camera observation might be among the data collection methods used. A comparative study of advertising trends among competitors, on the other hand, might call for data collection through content analysis techniques. Methods of data collection are many and varied. The most frequently used is the survey method. Data can be gathered through personal or group interviews, mail questionnaires, telephone interviews, and interviews conducted in the home or at mall-intercept locations. A major distinction in survey methods is between *random* surveys, which take a representative sample of a larger group of people, and *non-random* surveys, which target particular groups. Other data collection methods include focus group studies, panel studies, physiological testing (measuring physical responses such as heart rate, brain waves, or galvanic skin response), and mechanical data collection (e.g., computerized checkout devices in stores or "people-meters" installed on TV sets). As you can see, there are many, many data collection methods available, and the research plan must include a decision about which ones will be used in any specific study.

Other method decisions that need to be made during the planning process concern the following questions:

- Population definition: What group or groups of people should be measured?

- Sampling techniques: How will a valid population sample be arrived at?
- Data-gathering techniques: How will data be gathered and compared?
- Measurement techniques: What measures will be used?
- Research "environment": What elements in the research setting might impede or aid the study? Can the setting be improved?
- Use of statistical tests: Are the data mathematically valid, and what is the margin of error?
- Research timetable: How much time is available, and how should the research stages be scheduled?
- Research personnel: What kinds of people are needed at every stage of the process?
- Research costs: How much money is available, and how should it be allotted among the research steps?

6. Implement the Research Plan and Gather Data

Putting the research plan into action involves collecting and processing data using the methods selected in step 5. This field work is often contracted out to commercial research firms whose staff are trained in professional research techniques.

Note that although the advertising researchers may delegate or contract some stages of the work, he or she should never delegate the planning and interpretation stages of the research process.

7. Process the Data

Processing the data involves five activities:

- *Cleaning up the data*: Editing raw data or questionnaires and transferring all the relevant information into a form suitable for analysis.
- *Verifying the data:* Checking the accuracy and consistency of interviewers and others who gathered the data.
- *Coding the data:* Coding verbal or written responses into numbers suitable for computer or mathematical analysis.
- *Data entry:* Transferring the data onto cards, tapes, or computer disks.
- *Tabulation:* Tabulating (massaging) the data by hand, computer, or mechanical means.

Data processing usually results in a set of tables, statistics, or other numerical information that can be easily understood and evaluated. Remember, however, that tables and statistics in themselves tell us nothing of the *meaning* of the data.

8. Interpret the Data

Tables, statistics, and other quantitative data are not as objective as they may seem. Give a table of numbers to three different people, ask for interpretations, and you will usually get three different conclusions. No matter how objective the data, individuals will bring their personal opinions to it. Though we may try to be dispassionate and unbiased, our own hopes, likes, and dislikes can influence the way we interpret "hard" numbers. This happens in advertising, just as it happens in other fields. Though we are using scientific methods, advertising is an art, not a science.

So how can you remain objective when interpreting data? Here are a few guidelines.

- Go through each table or set of statistics or data in detail and write down your own conclusions.
- Get one or more other disinterested persons to interpret the same data. If they do not reach the same conclusions, incorporate the various possible interpretations into your report.
- Go back to the primary research problem (step 4) and frame the most direct answer you can from the data. This is your action recommendation.
- Write three separate statements, consisting of your *findings,* your *conclusions,* and your action *recommendation.*

In this way, you will achieve as objective as possible an interpretation of the data. The researcher is obligated to deliver the raw data. He or she is also expected to provide an objective interpretation of that data. If an action recommendation is made, it should be clearly separate from the actual results. The researcher should also indicate that there are other possible action recommendations that might be made from the same data.

9. Communicate the Results

Researchers often mistakenly assume that if they deliver a thick report on a project, they've done their job. But pages of tables and quantitative data are of little use to decision makers. Research results need to be communicated in as many different ways as possible to as many relevant people as possible. Most often, results are reported through written reports; oral group presentations, complete with audio-visual aids; and individual discussions with decision makers. Where research topics or the techniques used are of interest to other advertising or research professionals, results are often reported at advertising and research conferences or are published in trade and research journals.

10. Apply the Results to Solve the Advertising Problem

A great deal of money is spent each year on research that is never used, and unused research is useless. Though not strictly speaking the responsibility of the researcher, applying results to solve a problem is the only reason for conducting research in the first place. To improve the chances of your research results being used, try to involve decision makers as closely as possible in the whole research process. And take care to communicate your results clearly—if they are easily understood, they can be more easily applied by the decision makers.

The ten steps discussed here form a structure on which a scientific, practical, and useful research project can be built. The ten steps may overlap in some cases, but the careful researcher will not omit any of the steps. Keep the overall planning process in mind as you learn more about the individual steps in future chapters.

Review

In this chapter we saw that:

- The scientific approach to problem solving helps advertisers plan and invest objectively and measure effectiveness of advertisements accurately.
- The characteristics of the scientific method are explicit procedures, objective data collection, systematic and cumulative research, open-minded and skeptical researchers, goals of explanation, understanding and control, and replicable findings.
- The ten steps of planning and executing a research plan can be applied to any advertising or marketing problem:
    1. Become aware of an advertising problem.
    2. Define and clarify the problem.
    3. Secondary research: review existing knowledge.
    4. Primary research: decide on one specific problem.
    5. Prepare a detailed research plan.
    6. Implement the research plan and gather data.
    7. Process the data.
    8. Interpret the data.
    9. Communicate the results.
    10. Apply the results to solve the advertising problem.

Chapter 3 Pre-Research Strategies

To view research strategically is to see that it is one part of a larger advertising plan. The researcher should always focus on what the research process can contribute to overall advertising objectives. Only in this way can research be successfully integrated into the larger business activities of an agency or advertiser.

In this chapter, we introduce several pre-research methods and models through which this integration can be achieved. Among these pre-research strategies are the FCB Grid, which is an example of *perceptual mapping;* the DAGMAR system for determining advertising objectives and measuring their effectiveness; positioning strategies; and target market definition.

We will also look at the role that advertisers and agencies play in conducting research and explain how the research effort can best be coordinated to benefit from available expertise from both inside and outside the agency.

Research as a Marketing Tool

Research is primarily a tool that is used to help the overall marketing effort. Alone, it is of no use. To be of value it must fit within the advertiser's or the agency's advertising and marketing strategies. To discover the precise roles research plays, we will look at it within the broader contexts of consumer involvement, advertising objectives, positioning, and target market definition. We will also discuss techniques researchers can use to place their activities within each of these larger advertising and marketing concerns.

Consumer Involvement: The FCB Grid

In an effort to provide structure and direction to strategic planning and creative development of its client's brands, Foote, Cone & Belding created what has come to be known as the FCB Grid. The grid is one of several models that can be

---

Figure 3–1
FCB Grid

Source: Richard Vaughn, "How
Advertising Works: A Planning
Model Revisited," *Journal of
Advertising Research,* February/
March 1986, pp. 57–65.

	THINK	FEEL
	1	**2**
LOW INVOLVEMENT	**INFORMATIVE** (Economic) Learn—Feel—Do	**AFFECTIVE** (Psychological) Feel—Learn—Do
	3	**4**
HIGH INVOLVEMENT	**HABITUAL** (Responsive) Do—Learn—Feel	**SATISFACTION** (Social) Do—Feel—Learn

used to explain consumer *involvement* with particular products or services. Using *perceptual mapping,* the grid provides a visual representation of consumer involvement. As you can see in Figure 3–1, the FCB Grid is composed of two axes. The horizontal axis represents rational versus emotional involvement with the words "think" and "feel" (the classic "left-brain versus right-brain" distinction). The vertical axis indicates the degree of involvement on a simple scale of "high" to "low." The axes intersect to form four quadrants, each of which represents a consumer approach to decision making.

The classic models of consumer response to advertising proposed "hierarchies" of communication effects, which typically suggested that a person moves from awareness of something to knowledge about it, then formulates an attitude toward it, and finally might act on it, usually by making a purchase decision. As more was learned about consumer behavior, such models did not adequately reflect the range of consumer response to communication. Researchers discovered that not everyone moves through the hierarchal order. Many actually skip steps.

The FCB Grid and other models like it reflect the range and order of elements of consumer response. Each quadrant of the FCB Grid is labeled with each of four advertising planning strategies, based on the ordering of consumer response.

The Information Strategy (Quadrant 1) is for highly involved big-ticket purchases that require thinking and economic considerations. This strategy best parallels the classic hierarchy of effects and is labeled "learn-feel-do." Examples of products and services in this quadrant are automobiles, insurance, large appliances, and choice of universities.

The Affective Strategy (Quadrant 2) is appropriate for purchases that are highly involving and feeling, such as those that enhance self-esteem or are ego-related. Cosmetics, jewelry, and fashion clothing are examples. Emotional communication is required for products in this quadrant, because consumers exhibit a "feel-learn-do" sequence.

The Habitual Strategy (Quadrant 3) is for products such as gasoline and household cleaners, which require little emotion or thinking. Often such products are purchases first for trial, after which learning takes place. The routinized behavior of consumers in this quadrant can be described as "do-learn-feel."

The Satisfaction Strategy (Quadrant 4) involves a social model of "do-feel-learn," as consumers purchase pleasure items such as beer, cigarettes, and candy. The product experience (do) is considered almost inextricably linked to the communication process.

Operationalization of the axes on the grid was accomplished by the use of eight bipolar scales:

Involvement

- Very important/unimportant decision
- Lot/little to lose if you choose the wrong brand
- Decision requires lot/little thought

Think

- Decision is/is not mainly logical or objective
- Decision is/is not based mainly on functional facts

Feel

- Decision is/is not based on a lot of feeling
- Decision does/does not express one's personality
- Decision is/is not based on looks, taste, touch, smell, or sound (sensory effects)

By using consumer scores on eight scales, researchers are able to map major product categories in appropriate quadrants, as shown in Figure 3–2. The grid system has been used both to chart the results of previous consumer research and to plan advertising strategy.

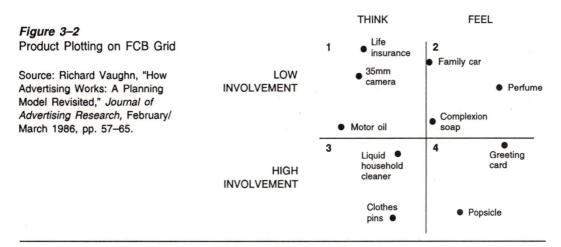

Figure 3–2
Product Plotting on FCB Grid

Source: Richard Vaughn, "How Advertising Works: A Planning Model Revisited," *Journal of Advertising Research*, February/March 1986, pp. 57–65.

Advertising Objectives: DAGMAR

Russell Colley's *Designing Advertising Goals for Measured Advertising Results* (DAGMAR), has become a classic in advertising planning, implementation, and evaluation.[1] It introduces a structured approach to overseeing advertising activities. DAGMAR consists of a checklist of questions designed to specify the objectives of the advertising campaign. It also provides the criteria by which the advertising effort later can be judged. Unlike the FCB Grid, which relies on *consumer* evaluation of a brand or product, DAGMAR requires *those who plan the advertising* to declare what the advertisement is supposed to achieve.

Recognizing the multitude of factors in addition to the quality of the advertising itself that can affect the success or failure of an overall marketing effort, Colley stressed the importance of making a distinction between marketing goals and advertising goals. As can be seen from the example below, the advertising goal is a statement of the communication aspects of the marketing goal. Colley also recommended that goals be stated in terms that are objective and quantitative. This makes the later task of measurement and evaluation considerably easier than it would be if no evaluative criteria had been set in advance.

Example.

Marketing goal: To increase sales of Brand X cookies 10 percent in the next 12 months. Advertising goal: To raise awareness levels of Brand X cookies in the target market from 30 percent to 80 percent in the next 12 months.

According to Colley, the best time to sound out all of the players in the advertising and marketing process about their views on the purpose of an upcoming advertising campaign is *before* the planning for the campaign begins. The responses to the DAGMAR questions then become the basis for discussion among those involved in the setting of objectives. The DAGMAR checklist is shown in Figure 3–3.

Figure 3-3
Advertising Task Check List

(This check list is a "thought starter" in developing specific advertising objectives. It can be applied to a single ad, a year's campaign for each product, or it can aid in developing a company's entire advertising philosophy among all those who create and approve advertising.)

To what extent does the advertising aim at closing an *immediate sale?*

1. Perform the complete selling function (take the product through all the necessary steps toward a sale)
2. Close sales to prospects already partly sold through past advertising efforts ("Ask for the order" or "clincher" advertising)
3. Announce a special reason for "buying now" (price, premium, etc.)
4. *Remind* people to buy
5. Tie in with some special buying event
6. Stimulate impulse sales

OTHER TASKS:

_____

_____

	SCALE OF IMPORTANCE					
	Not Important				Very Important	
	0	1	2	3	4	5
1.						
2.						
3.						
4.						
5.						
6.						

Does the advertising aim at *near-term* sales by moving the prospect, step by step, closer to a sale (so that when confronted with a buying situation the customer will ask for, reach for or accept the advertised brand)?

7. Create awareness of existence of product or brand
8. Create "brand image" or favorable emotional disposition toward the brand
9. Implant information or attitude regarding benefits and superior features of brand
10. Combat or offset competitive claims
11. Correct false impressions, misinformation and other obstacles to sales
12. Build familiarity and easy recognition of package or trademark

OTHER TASKS:

_____

_____

	SCALE OF IMPORTANCE					
	Not Important				Very Important	
	0	1	2	3	4	5
7.						
8.						
9.						
10.						
11.						
12.						

Does the advertising aim at building a "long-range consumer franchise?"

13. Build confidence in company and brand which is expected to pay off in years to come
14. Build customer demand which places company in stronger position in relation to its distribution (Not at the "mercy of the market-place")
15. Place advertiser in position to select preferred distributors and dealers
16. Secure universal distribution
17. Establish a "reputation platform" for launching new brands or product lines
18. Establish brand recognition and acceptance which will enable the company to open up new markets (geographic, price, age, sex)

OTHER TASKS:

	SCALE OF IMPORTANCE					
	Not Important				Very Important	
	0	1	2	3	4	5
13.						
14.						
15.						
16.						
17.						
18.						

_____

_____

Specifically, how can advertising contribute toward increased sales?

19. Hold present customers against the inroads of competition?
20. Convert competitive users to advertiser's brand?
21. Cause people to specify advertiser's brand instead of asking for product by generic name?
22. Convert non-users of the product type to users of product and brand?
23. Make steady customers out of occasional or sporadic customers?

Increase consumption among _present users_ by:

24. Advertising new uses of the product?

	SCALE OF IMPORTANCE					
	Not Important				Very Important	
	0	1	2	3	4	5
19.						
20.						
21.						
22.						
23.						
24.						

25. Persuading customers to buy larger sizes or multiple units?
26. Reminding users to buy?
27. Encouraging greater frequency or quantity of use?

OTHER TASKS:

_____

_____

	Scale of Importance					
	Not Important			Very Important		
	0	1	2	3	4	5
25.						
26.						
27.						

Does the advertising aim at some specific step which leads to a sale?

28. Persuade prospect to write for deceptive literature, return a coupon, enter a contest
29. Persuade prospect to visit a showroom, ask for a demonstration
30. Induce prospect to sample the product (trial offer)

OTHER TASKS:

_____

_____

	Scale of Importance					
	Not Important			Very Important		
	0	1	2	3	4	5
28.						
29.						
30.						

How important are "supplementary benefits" of end-use advertising?

31. Aid salesmen in opening new accounts
32. Aid salesmen in getting larger orders from wholesalers and retailers
33. Aid salesmen in getting preferred display space
34. Give salesmen an entree
35. Build morale of company sales force
36. Impress the trade (causing recommendation to their customers and favorable treatment to salesmen)

OTHER TASKS:

_____

_____

	Scale of Importance					
	Not Important			Very Important		
	0	1	2	3	4	5
19.						
20.						
21.						
22.						
23.						
24.						

Is it a task of advertising to impart information needed to consummate sales and build customer satisfaction?

37. "Where to buy it" advertising
38. "How to use it" advertising
39. New models, features, package
40. New prices
41. Special terms, trade-in offers, etc.
42. New policies (guarantees, etc.)

OTHER TASKS:

	SCALE OF IMPORTANCE					
	Not Important				Very Important	
	0	1	2	3	4	5
37.						
38.						
39.						
40.						
41.						
42.						

To what extent does the advertising aim at building confidence and good will for the corporation among:

43. Customers and potential customers?
44. The trade (distributors, dealers, retail sales people)?
45. Employees and potential employees?
46. The financial community?
47. The public at large?

OTHER TASKS:

	SCALE OF IMPORTANCE					
	Not Important				Very Important	
	0	1	2	3	4	5
43.						
44.						
45.						
46.						
47.						

Specifically what kind of images does the company wish to build?

48. Product quality, dependability
49. Service
50. Family resemblance of diversified products
51. Corporate citizenship
52. Growth, progressiveness, technical leadership

OTHER TASKS:

	SCALE OF IMPORTANCE					
	Not Important				Very Important	
	0	1	2	3	4	5
48.						
49.						
50.						
51.						
52.						

Source: Russell H. Colley, *Defining Advertising Goals for Measured Advertising Results,* Association of National Advertisers, Inc. New York, 1961, pp. 62–68.

Positioning

With the proliferation of brands and the increased competition for consumers' attention and purchasing dollars, advertisers must pay special attention to the status their brands occupy both in the marketplace and in the individual consumer's mind. In *Positioning: The Battle for Your Mind,* Al Ries and Jack Trout define positioning as "an organized system for finding a window" in the consumer's mind.[2] They contend that consumers maintain "ladders" in their heads, the rungs of which are occupied by various competitors in a product category. The advertising challenge is to establish a position that is meaningful, durable, and profitable.

Positioning strategy can exert considerable influence on consumer perception of an advertiser's brand and that of the competition. Think of the success of such campaigns as Miller Lite beer—"We Try Harder"—as second to Hertz; and the "repositioning" of products such as Johnson's Baby Powder to an adult market and Arm and Hammer baking soda as an agent to fight household odors and clean laundry.

The Value of Research in Product Positioning

Some very effective positioning strategies are, admittedly, made very subjective and are based on intuition or the advertiser's "feel" for the market or competition. However, chances of success are higher if a systematic approach is used to determine a product's current position, analyze the competition's position, and home in on the product characteristics that appeal to a particular market. Research is central to this approach; it can shed light on current positions, the possible effects of new positioning messages on consumers, and alternative promising courses of action before positioning decisions are made. Research can also provide the means of measuring achievement of positioning objectives.

Aaker's Six Approaches to Positioning Strategy

In a classic article, David Aaker identified six approaches to positioning strategy: by attribute, by price quality, by use or application, by product user, by product class, and by competition.[3]

Positioning by attribute.

This strategy emphasizes one or more product characteristics. Decisions here involve determining which characteristics are unique to the brand in question; whether those characteristics are important to the consumer; and, if there are several important characteristics, how many should be stressed. Many new products use a strategy that stresses characteristics of a product not previously exploited by the competition.

Positioning by price quality.

Some brands use high price to suggest quality and superior service; others use a low price/value strategy. These positioning strategies based on price give a brand or retail store an image that is not easily changed in the consumer's mind. The difficulties Sears has had in attempting an image change in the past few years is a good example of the effects of positioning by price.

Positioning by use or application.

The term *repositioning* often means that an additional use for the product has been emphasized, thus expanding its market. Examples are the positioning of orange juice as a non-breakfast beverage and Cheez Whiz as a microwavable cheese topping.

Positioning by product user.

Products are often introduced to entirely new market segments. For example, Johnson's baby shampoo is advertised for adults, and antacid tablets are marketed to women as a source of calcium. A celebrity or other spokesperson who appears in an advertisement also can suggest characteristics of the targeted consumers. Such was the case with Miller Lite in its "famous ex-athletes" campaigns.

Positioning by product class.

It is human nature to relate new information to that which we already know. Consumers tend to remember products in categories and find a suitable place to "file" a new piece of information about an existing brand.

In marketing, it is very important that a clear product or class position be established for a brand. Otherwise, consumers have no place to file it. Labeling 7-UP as the "un-cola" is a classic example of positioning a product as an appealing alternative to a successful product class (colas).

Positioning by competition.

It is estimated that about 35 percent of all advertising is comparative, making either direct or implied comparisons with another brand. This type of advertising is particularly beneficial to the underdog brand, as it takes advantage of the established identity and image of the leader. Comparative advertising is one way of establishing a frame of reference for the consumer.

Crush lemon-lime soda used a direct comparison to suggest that it had a bolder taste than 7-UP. The use of 7-UP as the named competitor suggested a competitive frame for the consumer. The Avis versus Hertz campaign, in which Avis positioned itself as Number Two in car rentals, is a classic example of comparative advertising.

Research Methods Used in Determining a Positioning Strategy

Aaker outlined six steps for developing and maintaining a positioning strategy.[4] They are:

1. Identify the competitors.
2. Determine how the competitors are perceived and evaluated.
3. Determine the competitor's positions.
4. Analyze the customers.
5. Select a position.
6. Monitor the position.

Several research techniques are available to the advertiser for acquiring information for the positioning strategy. These methods can be used at various points in Aaker's six-point sequence.

Evoked set technique.

An evoked set is a group of brands or products a consumer identifies when asked a question about a product category. Asking a consumer to name the top three brands of imported chocolate candy would elicit a listing and a ranking, if desired, of the brands that come to mind. This technique can be used both to identify competitors and to determine the perception and evaluation of a brand against its competitors (steps 1 and 2 above).

Word/thought association.

Respondents can be asked what appropriate uses come to mind for a particular brand and its competitors. They also can be asked to associate specific words or thoughts with the individual brands and brand images. This information can be used in a number of ways in the first three steps above.

Multidimensional scaling.

A researcher can measure intensity of consumer response with the use of scaled questions. For example, a consumer could be asked to check one of seven equidistant points appearing on a continuum between the words "interesting" and "uninteresting" as they relate to a particular brand or service (see example below):

Please rate XYZ Bank on the following items by placing a check in the space that best describes XYZ.

| Big | ___ ___ ___ ___ ___ ___ ___ | Small |
| Friendly | ___ ___ ___ ___ ___ ___ ___ | Unfriendly |

Interesting	__ __ __ __ __ __ __	Uninteresting
Innovative	__ __ __ __ __ __ __	Not innovative
Best	__ __ __ __ __ __ __	Worst
Good	__ __ __ __ __ __ __	Bad

Focus groups.

Structured group interviews with target consumers provide an excellent forum for the discussion and dissection of the image of a brand and that of its competitors. Participants also can be asked to profile an "ideal brand" of a specific product. This is very useful in selecting a product position.

Tracking studies.

The final step involves monitoring the brand's position. This is critical to the continuity and success of the advertising program. Surveys using either independent random samples of consumers, panels of users, or other samples can be implemented at this stage. If a questionnaire is used as a tracking device, it should measure whether the intended position on the specific dimension required has registered with the consumer. These dimensions include product attribute, product use or application, product class, product user, etc.

Target Market Definition

The objective of market segmentation is to *identify people* who are most likely to be influenced by the marketing and advertising efforts on behalf of a product. This both reduces the risk associated with marketing a product and increases the efficiency of marketing activities, which can be directed toward only a narrow segment of the entire population.

Theoretically, any single attribute of a population—hair color, age, freckles, etc.—could be used to divide it into segments. The marketing challenge is to classify consumers meaningfully with respect to a particular product or product category. Market segmentation, in its essence, lays the foundation on which a group or groups of consumers will be targeted in the advertising effort.

Demographics, or "census-like" characteristics of age, sex, size of household, etc., historically have been the building blocks of target market definitions. More recently, geographic segmentation has become the marketing focus of national advertisers, as such phenomena as "regional tastes" have been the basis for product development or modification (such as spicy flavor) and target marketing. *Psychographics,* first defined in the 1970s as life-style indicators, have continued to play a major role in target market definition. Other means of segmenting target markets are based on consumer attitudes toward the product and also on product usage. Some of the major typologies for segmenting target audiences are described in detail below.

Demographics

Traditionally, advertisers describe a target market's demographics, including age, gender, race, employment status, income, size of household, and other such variables. This information allows market descriptions such as "women age 35–49 with children living at home." A primary reason such a tradition persists is that demographic characteristics are easy to collect, and segmentation based on demographic characteristics has provided a meaningful and useful method of dividing the world of consumers for a variety of products.

Figure 3–4 contains sample demographic questions for a telephone survey of prospective home buyers. The American Association of Advertising Agencies compiled a set of guidelines for collecting demographic information about the audiences of individual media vehicles. This is reproduced in Chapter 12.

Figure 3–4
Sample Demographics for Telephone Survey of Prospective Home Buyers

16. Lastly, a couple of questions for statistical purposes. Which of the following groups includes your age? (READ LIST)

Under 25 1
25 to 34 2
35 to 44 3
45 to 54 4
55 to 64 5
65 or older 6
(DO NOT READ) Refused 7

17. And what is the highest level of education you have completed? (DO NOT READ)

Some high school or less 1
High school graduate 2
Some college 3
College graduate 4
Postgraduate degree/work 5
(DO NOT READ) Refused 6

18. And how many children under 18 years of age are currently living in your household?

_____

19. (IF HAVE CHILDREN UNDER 18) And are the children in your household ... (READ LIST)?

Less than a year old 1
From 1 to 3 years old 2
From 4 to 5 years old 3
From 6 to 10 years old 4
From 11 to 14 years old 5
From 15 to 17 years old 6

20. And are you currently ... (READ LIST)

Married 1
Single & have never been married 2
Single & was formerly married 3

21. And which of these categories includes your total annual household income? (READ LIST)

Under $20,000 1
$20,000 but less than $30,000 2
$30,000 but less than $40,000 3
$40,000 but less than $50,000 4
$50,000 but less than $60,000 5
$60,000 but less than $75,000 6
$75,000 but less than $100,000 7
$100,000 or more 8
(DO NOT READ) Refused 9

RECORD SEX WITHOUT ASKING: _____ MALE _____ FEMALE

Psychographics

Psychographics provide insight into consumer motivation by analyzing such variables as personality type, political preference, lifestyle, interests, and personal and social aspirations. In 1971, William Wells and Douglas Tigert introduced the notion of attitudes, interests, and opinions (AIO) as a basis for segmenting market groups. (See Figure 3–5.)

Figure 3–5

Items from Early Activities, Interests, and Opinion Studies,
Precursors of Psychographic Segmentation

Price Conscious

I shop a lot for "specials."

I find myself checking the prices in the grocery store even for small items.

I usually watch the advertisements for announcements of sales.

A person can save a lot of money by shopping around for bargains.

Fashion Conscious

I usually have one or more outfits that are of the very latest style.

When I must choose between the two I usually dress for fashion, not for comfort.

An important part of my life and activities is dressing smartly.

I often try the latest hairdo styles when they change.

Child Oriented

When my children are ill in bed I drop most everything else in order to see to their comfort.

My children are the most important thing in my life.

I try to arrange my home for my children's convenience.

I take a lot of time and effort to teach my children good habits.

Compulsive Housekeeper

I don't like to see children's toys lying about.

I usually keep my house very neat and clean.

I am uncomfortable when my house is not completely clean.

Our days seem to follow a definite routine such as eating meals at a regular time, etc.

Dislikes Housekeeping

I must admit I really don't like household chores.

I find cleaning my house an unpleasant task.

I enjoy most forms of housework. (Reverse scored)

My idea of housekeeping is "once over lightly."

Sewer

I like to sew and frequently do.

I often make my own or my children's clothes.

You can save a lot of money by making your own clothes.

I would like to know how to sew like an expert.

Homebody

I would rather spend a quiet evening at home than go out to a party.

I like parties where there is lots of music and talk. (Reverse scored)

I would rather go to a sporting event than a dance.

I am a homebody.

Community Minded

I am an active member of more than one service organization.

I do volunteer work for a hospital or service organization on a fairly regular basis.

I like to work on community projects.

I have personally worked in a political campaign or for a candidate or an issue.

Credit User

I buy many things with a credit card or a charge card.

I like to pay cash for everything I buy. (Reverse scored)

It is good to have charge accounts.

To buy anything, other than a house or a car, on credit is unwise. (Reverse scored)

Sports Spectator

I like to watch or listen to baseball or football games.

I usually read the sports page in the daily paper.

I thoroughly enjoy conversations about sports.

I would rather go to a sporting event than a dance.

Cook

I love to cook.

I am a good cook.

I love to bake and frequently do.

I am interested in spices and seasonings.

Self-Confident

I think I have more self-confidence than most people.

I am more independent than most people.

I think I have a lot of personal ability.

I like to be considered a leader.

Self-Designated Opinion Leader

My friends or neighbors often come to me for advice.

I sometimes influence what my friends buy.

People come to me more often than I go to them for information about brands.

Information Seeker

I often seek out the advice of my friends regarding which brand to buy.

I spend a lot of time talking with my friends about products and brands.

My neighbors or friends usually give me good advice on what brands to buy in the grocery store.

New Brand Tryer

When I see a new brand on the shelf I often buy it just to see what it's like.

I often try new brands before my friends and neighbors do.

I like to try new and different things.

Satisfied with Finances

Our family income is high enough to satisfy nearly all our important desires.

No matter how fast our income goes up we never seem to get ahead. (Reverse scored)

I wish we had a lot more money. (Reverse scored)

Canned Food User

I depend on canned food for at least one meal a day.

I couldn't get along without canned foods.

Things just don't taste right if they come out of a can. (Reverse scored)

Dieter

During the warm weather I drink low calorie soft drinks several times a week.

I buy more low calorie foods than the average housewife.

I have used Metrecal or other diet foods at least one meal a day.

Financial Optimist

I will probably have more money to spend next year than I have now.

Five years from now the family income will probably be a lot higher than it is now.

Wrapper

Food should never be left in the refrigerator uncovered.

Leftovers should be wrapped before being put into the refrigerator.

Wide Horizons

I'd like to spend a year in London or Paris.

I would like to take a trip around the world.

Arts Enthusiast

I enjoy going through an art gallery.

I enjoy going to concerts.

I like ballet.

Source: William Wells and Douglas Tigert, "Activities, Interests and Opinions," reprinted in "Advertising Research Classics," *Journal of Advertising Research,* September 1982, pp. 30–38.

Wells and Tigert characterized this approach as an attempt to "draw recognizable human portraits of consumers."[5] AIO was, in part, a reaction to an earlier era of motivation research (MR), which saw an overuse of projective techniques and psychoanalytical methods and drew wide criticism from the research establishment. The AIO classifications were the precursors of psychographic studies. An example of the statements that formed AIO "types" is included in Figure 3–5.

Several classifications or typologies of consumer groups have since been compiled for use in describing and targeting consumer segments. Two of these typologies—VALS and PRIZM—are discussed below.

VALS.

The Values and Lifestyles System (VALS), created by SRI International in 1978, combined demographics and consumer lifestyle characteristics to describe buying patterns. Three major consumer categories of need-driven (11 percent of adults), outer-directed (67 percent) and inner-directed (22 percent) reflected the psychological motivation of consumers. Need-driver consumers made purchases necessary for survival, the outer-directed purchased to "keep up with the Joneses," and the inner-directed bought products that reflected their independent personalities and lifestyles.

In the late 1980s, VALS 2 was developed to update the VALS system and to further reflect the psychological foundations of consumer decision making. Most consumers fall into one of the three major categories of the new VALS system with respect to their self-orientation: principle-oriented, status-oriented, and action-oriented. Self-orientation is defined as "patterns of attitudes and activities that help people reinforce, sustain, or even modify their social self-image." In addition to expressing self-image through choice of career, relationships, and community role, people also express themselves by buying products that are consistent with their image of themselves:

- **Principle-oriented** consumers make their behavior consistent with their views of how the world is or should be.

- **Status-oriented** consumers seek a secure place in a valued social setting; they look to others for what they should do and be.

- **Action-oriented** consumers like to have an effect on their environment, becoming intensely involved in their activities at home and work.

In addition to self-orientation, VALS 2 describes the resources consumers can use to act on their desires and decisions. Resources are defined as "the full range of psychological, physical, demographic, and material means and capacities consumers have to draw on. It encompasses education, income, self-confidence, health, eagerness to buy, intelligence, and energy level." Categories and subgroups are ranked on a continuum from "abundant" to "minimal" resources. The VALS 2 system contains eight subgroups, six of them within the three major self-orientation categories and two, Actualizers and Strugglers, which fall into categories by themselves. An explanation of the VALS 2 subgroups appears in Figure 3–6.

Figure 3–6
VALS 2 Subgroups

Actualizers

Actualizers are successful, sophisticated, active, "take-charge" people with high self-esteem and abundant resources. They are interested in growth and seek to develop, explore, and express themselves in a variety of ways—sometimes guided by principle, and sometimes by a desire to have an effect, to make a change. Image is important to Actualizers, not as evidence of status or power, but as an expression of taste, independence, and character. Actualizers are among the established and emerging leaders in business and government, yet they continue to seek challenges. They have a wide range of interests, are concerned with social issues, and are open to change. Their lives are characterized by richness and diversity. Their possessions and recreation reflect a cultivated taste for the finer things in life.

Principle-Oriented

Principle-oriented consumers seek to make their behavior consistent with their views of how the world is or should be.

Fulfilleds are mature, satisfied, comfortable, reflective people who value order, knowledge, and responsibility. Most are well educated, and in, or recently retired from, professional occupations. They are content with their careers, families, and station in life; well-informed about the world and national events; and alert to opportunities to broaden their knowledge. Their leisure activities tend to center around their homes. Fulfilleds have a moderate respect for the status quo, institutions of authority, and social decorum, but are open-minded about new ideas and social change. They tend to base their decisions on strongly held principles and consequently appear calm and self-assured. While their incomes allow them many choices, Fulfilleds are conservative, practical consumers; they are concerned about functionality, value, and durability in the products they buy.

Believers are conservative, conventional people with concrete beliefs based on traditional, established codes: family, church, community, and the nation. Many Believers express moral codes that are deeply rooted and literally interpreted. They follow established routines, organized in large part around their homes, families, and social or religious organizations to which they belong. As consumers, they are conservative and predictable, favoring American products and established brands. Their education, income, and energy are modest but sufficient to meet their needs.

Status-Oriented

Status-oriented consumers have or seek a secure place in a valued social setting. Strivers look to others to indicate what they should be and do, whereas Achievers seek recognition and self-definition through achievements at work and in their families.

Achievers are successful career and work-oriented people who like to, and generally do, feel in control of their lives. They value structure, predictability, and stability over risk, intimacy, and self-discovery. They are deeply committed to their work and their families. Work provides them a sense of duty, material rewards, and prestige. Their social lives reflect this focus and are structured around family, church, and business. Achievers live conventional lives, are politically conservative, and respect authority and the status quo. As consumers, they favor established products and services that demonstrate their success to their peers.

Strivers seek motivation, self-definition, and approval from the world around them. They are striving to find a secure place in life. Unsure of themselves and low on economic, social, and psychological resources, Strivers are deeply concerned about the opinions and approval of others. Money defines success for Strivers, who don't have enough of it, and often feel that life has given them a raw deal. Strivers are sensitive to the tastes and preferences of the persons with whom they live and socialize. They may try to emulate those who own more impressive possessions, but what they wish to obtain is often beyond their reach.

Action-Oriented

Action-oriented consumers like to affect their environment in tangible ways. Makers do so primarily at home and at work, Experiencers in the wider world. Both types tend to become intensely involved in their activities.

Experiencers are young, vital, enthusiastic, impulsive, and rebellious. They seek variety and excitement, savoring the new, the offbeat, and the risky. Still in the process of formulating life values and patterns of behavior, they quickly become enthusiastic about new possibilities but are equally quick to cool. At this stage in their lives, they are politically uncommitted, uninformed, and highly ambivalent about what they believe. Experiencers combine an abstract disdain for conformity and authority with an outsider's awe of others' wealth, prestige, and power. Their energy finds an outlet in exercise, sports, outdoor recreation, and social activities. Experiencers are avid consumers and spend much of their income on clothing, fast food, music, movies, and video.

Makers are practical people who have constructive skills and value self-sufficiency. They live within a traditional context of family, practical work, and physical recreation and have little interest in what lies outside that context. Makers experience the world by working on it—building a house, raising children, fixing a car, or canning vegetables—and have sufficient skill, income, and energy to carry out their projects successfully. Makers are politically conservative, suspicious of new ideas, respectful of government authority and organized labor, but resentful of government intrusion on individual rights. They are unimpressed by material possessions other than those with a practical or functional purpose (e.g., tools, pickup trucks, or fishing equipment).

Strugglers

Strugglers' lives are constricted. With limited economic, social, and emotional resources, and often in poor health, Strugglers experience the world as pressing and difficult. Because they are so limited, they show no evidence of a strong self-orientation, but are focused on meeting the urgent needs of the present moment. Strugglers are cautious consumers. They represent a very modest market for most products and services, but are loyal to favorite brands.

Source: Values and Lifestyles Program, SRI International, Menlo Park, California.

Applications of the VALS 2 segmentation system range from description of audiences for magazines and other media, to target market definition for a new or existing product, to creative development, to name a few. Merrill Lynch applied VALS analysis to convey the image of an investor as an Achiever by using an image of a bull and the slogan "a breed apart" in its advertising. Through special services available to VALS 2 subscribers, the VALS 2 segments can be combined with a variety of syndicated research services such as Simmons Market Research Bureau, Mediamark Research, Inc., PRIZM, and others.

Geo-demographics: the PRIZM system.

PRIZM, a market segmentation system based on "geo-demographics," was pioneered by the Claritas Corporation of Alexandria, Virginia, in the 1970s. PRIZM is based on the principle that people of similar means, backgrounds, and buying patterns—birds of a feather—tend to gravitate to each other in neighborhoods. Though the PRIZM system is based on geographics and demographics, and hence is called a geo-demographics segmentation, the labels given the individual groups and their descriptions suggest a life-style and value orientation as well.

Using data from the U.S. Census Bureau, as well as socioeconomic and consumer-behavior information, PRIZM assigns one of 40 life-style classifications to each of more than a half-million U.S. neighborhoods. Three levels of geography are used in defining "neighborhoods" and assigning them to clusters:

- Census block group (approximately 350 households)

- Census tract (approximately 1,270 households)

- Postal zip code (approximately 2,320 households)

The 40 PRIZM classifications are grouped from most affluent to least affluent in 12 major social groups (see Figure 3–7). These groups are labeled with an "S" for suburban, a "U" for urban, a "T" for town, or an "R" for rural, to indicate the primary location of the respective populations.

A closer look at one PRIZM classification (Cluster 39, Gray Power) reveals the following cluster description. Gray Power represents nearly two million senior citizens who have chosen to pull up their roots and retire near their peers. Primarily concentrated in Sunbelt communities of the South Atlantic and Pacific regions, these are the nation's most affluent elderly, retired, and widowed neighborhoods with the highest concentration of childless married couples, on nonsalaried incomes, living in multi-unit dwellings, condos, and mobile homes. Gray Power is one of three clusters grouped in social group 4 (S4), which is labeled "middle-class, post-child families in aging suburbs and retirement areas," and also includes the "Levittown, U.S.A." and "Rank & File" clusters.

	What they like . . .	**. . . and don't like.**
Automobiles	Cadillac	Subaru
Investments	Discount brokers	Keogh
Leisure/sports	Power boats	Skiing
Package goods	Frozen entrees	Cake mixes
Vacation/travel	Cruise ships	Rental cars

Source: Claritas Corporation.

Figure 3–7
PRIZM Segmentation Scheme

P · R · I · Z · M

Market Segmentation & Targeting by Neighborhood Life-Style Clusters

THE 40 CLUSTER SYSTEM

THE TWELVE SOCIAL GROUPS			THE FORTY LIFE-STYLE CLUSTERS		PERCENT 1985 U.S. HOUSEHOLDS						COUNT OF COMPILED LIST NAMES			
					Block-Cluster Model		Tract-Cluster Model		ZIP-Cluster Model		List A: Micro Model		List B: Carrier Route Model	
Codes	Descriptive Titles	Numbers	Nicknames	One-Liners	Groups	Clusters	Groups	Clusters	Groups	Clusters	Groups	Clusters	Groups	Clusters
S1	Educated, Affluent Executives & Professionals in Elite Metro Suburbs	28	Blue Blood Estates	DEN5 SUBS DOM FAM 4/3 CG WC S-U Q 1		1.12		0.84		0.84		739,876		824,144
		8	Money & Brains	DEN7 SUBS DOM F/S 4/5 CG WC S-U Q 2		0.94		0.99		1.14		624,556		684,973
		5	Furs & Station Wagons	DEN5 SUBS DOM FAM 3/4 CG WC S-U Q 3	5.22	3.16	4.70	2.87	4.21	2.44	3,427,298	2,062,627	3,926,489	2,417,372
S2	Pre & Post-Child Families & Singles in Upscale White-Collar Suburbs	7	Pools & Patios	DEN6 SUBS DOM CPL 5/4 CG WC S-U Q 5		3.41		3.66		3.28		2,254,940		2,668,728
		25	Two More Rungs	DEN8 SUBS MIX F/S 6/5 CG WC M-U Q 6		0.74		0.85		1.03		465,795		482,496
		20	Young Influentials	DEN7 SUBS DOM F/S 1/2 CG WC M-U Q 7	7.00	2.85	7.13	2.62	7.33	3.02	4,349,482	1,628,747	4,984,045	1,832,821
S3	Upper-Middle, Child-Raising Families in Outlying, Owner-Occupied Suburbs	24	Young Suburbia	DEN5 SUBS DOM FAM 3/2 CG WC S-U Q 8		5.33		5.45		5.64		3,156,887		4,112,750
		30	Blue-Chip Blues	DEN5 SUBS DOM FAM 3/2 HS BW S-U Q10	11.33	6.00	11.58	6.13	10.83	5.19	6,636,825	3,479,938	8,622,406	4,509,656
U1	Educated, White-Collar Singles & Couples in Upscale, Urban Areas	21	Urban Gold Coast	DEN9 CITY MIX SGL 2/6 CG WC M-U Q 4		0.47		0.49		0.45		315,792		72,690
		37	Bohemian Mix	DEN9 CITY MIX SGL 2/1 CG WC M-U Q11		1.14		1.16		0.81		629,608		465,473
		31	Black Enterprise	DEN7 CITY DOM F/S 3/4 SC WC 2-9 Q14		0.76		0.75		1.21		365,000		563,984
		23	New Beginnings	DEN7 CITY MIX F/S 2/1 SC WC M-U Q15	6.67	4.30	7.52	5.12	7.25	4.77	3,591,473	2,281,073	3,711,827	2,609,680
T1	Educated, Young, Mobile Families in Exurban Satellites & Boom Towns	1	God's Country	DEN2 TOWN DOM FAM 3/2 CG WC S-U Q 9		2.70		2.37		2.97		1,788,911		2,103,285
		17	New Homesteaders	DEN3 TOWN DOM FAM 1/2 SC BW S-U Q17		4.15		4.76		5.08		2,328,851		3,002,295
		12	Towns & Gowns	DEN3 TOWN DOM SGL 1/2 CG WC S-U Q19	8.02	1.17	8.53	1.39	10.23	2.18	5,019,099	901,337	6,128,236	1,022,656
S4	Middle-Class, Post-Child Families in Aging Suburbs & Retirement Areas	27	Levittown, U.S.A.	DEN6 SUBS DOM CPL 5/6 HS WC S-U Q12		3.05		3.29		4.51		2,092,051		2,635,103
		39	Gray Power	DEN5 SUBS DOM CPL 6/5 SC WC M-U Q13		2.90		2.04		2.26		2,036,633		1,899,979
		2	Rank & File	DEN6 SUBS MIX CPL 5/6 HS BC 2-9 Q20	7.37	1.42	6.71	1.37	7.84	1.07	4,980,474	851,790	5,600,477	1,065,395
T2	Mid-Scale, Child-Raising Blue-Collar Families in Remote Suburbs & Towns	40	Blue-Collar Nursery	DEN2 TOWN DOM FAM 3/2 HS BC S-U Q16		2.24		2.41		1.70		1,056,574		1,287,202
		16	Middle America	DEN4 TOWN DOM FAM 5/4 HS BC S-U Q21		3.19		3.54		4.76		1,877,443		2,484,258
		29	Coalburg & Corntown	DEN2 TOWN DOM FAM 6/3 HS BC S-U Q23	7.39	1.96	7.98	2.02	9.01	2.56	4,234,831	1,316,814	5,453,058	1,681,589
U2	Mid-Scale Families, Singles & Elders in Dense, Urban Row & Hi-Rise Areas	3	New Melting Pot	DEN9 CITY MIX F/S 6/5 EX WC M-U Q18		0.91		0.96		1.33		474,280		369,250
		36	Old Yankee Rows	DEN7 CITY MIX F/S 6/5 HS BW 2-9 Q22		1.60		1.84		1.80		895,419		926,606
		14	Emergent Minorities	DEN7 CITY DOM S/S 1/2 SH BS 2-9 Q27		1.73		1.78		2.07		715,026		1,066,709
		26	Single City Blues	DEN8 CITY MIX SGL 1/2 SC BW M-U Q28	7.58	3.34	7.33	2.75	7.27	2.08	3,789,714	1,704,989	4,033,694	1,671,129
R1	Rural Towns & Villages Amidst Farms & Ranches Across Agrarian Mid-America	19	Shotguns & Pickups	DEN1 TOWN DOM FAM 3/4 HS BF S-U Q24		1.87		1.84		2.53		1,607,859		1,683,907
		34	Agri-Business	DEN1 FARM DOM FAM 6/5 EX BF S-U Q26		2.13		2.62		4.28		1,711,296		2,005,501
		35	Grain Belt	DEN0 FARM DOM FAM 6/5 HS BF S-U Q33	5.27	1.27	5.69	1.23	8.24	1.43	4,354,527	1,037,572	4,766,625	1,077,217
T3	Mixed Gentry & Blue-Collar Labor in Low-Mid Rustic Mill & Factory Towns	33	Golden Ponds	DEN3 TOWN DOM CPL 6/5 EX BW S-U Q25		5.24		5.03		3.06		3,110,930		3,502,241
		22	Mines & Mills	DEN3 TOWN DOM FAM 5/4 HS BC S-U Q29		2.84		2.60		1.85		1,641,671		1,830,216
		13	Norma Rae-Ville	DEN3 TOWN MIX FAM 1/4 SH BC S-U Q31		2.32		2.75		2.95		1,133,514		1,591,408
		18	Smalltown Downtown	DEN8 TOWN DOM F/S 5/1 HS BW 2-9 Q32	12.86	2.46	13.13	2.76	9.81	1.95	7,340,135	1,454,020	8,610,066	1,686,201
R2	Landowners, Migrants & Rustics in Poor Rural Towns, Farms & Uplands	10	Back-Country Folks	DEN1 TOWN DOM FAM 6/5 SH BC S-U Q30		3.42		3.16		4.29		2,023,110		2,577,307
		38	Share Croppers	DEN1 TOWN MIX FAM 6/5 GS BF S-U Q35		4.00		3.78		3.65		2,339,974		2,827,114
		15	Tobacco Roads	DEN0 TOWN DOM F/S 6/5 GS BF S-U Q38		1.22		1.08		0.96		571,598		897,081
		6	Hard Scrabble	DEN0 FARM MIX FAM 6/5 GS BF S-U Q39	10.15	1.51	9.06	1.05	9.92	1.03	5,651,854	717,172	6,143,158	841,656
U3	Mixed, Unskilled Service & Labor in Aging, Urban Row & Hi-Rise Areas	4	Heavy Industry	DEN7 CITY MIX F/S 6/5 SH BC 2-9 Q34		2.75		2.52		1.95		1,411,722		1,727,261
		11	Downtown Dixie-Style	DEN6 CITY DOM S/S 1/6 SH BS 2-9 Q36		3.39		3.51		2.30		1,455,892		1,966,047
		9	Hispanic Mix	DEN8 CITY DOM F/S 1/2 GS BC M-U Q37		1.68		1.94		1.62		659,679		862,099
		32	Public Assistance	DEN8 CITY DOM S/S 1/6 GS BS M-U Q40	11.13	3.12	10.85	2.87	8.07	2.30	4,645,865	1,118,772	5,853,036	1,297,629
					Total U.S.	100.00		100.00		100.00	Total	57,955,449		66,843,118

KEY TO ONE-LINERS
Example (Cluster No. 16 — Middle America)

Demographic Highlights	1	2	3	4	5	6	7	8	9
One Liner Abbreviations	DEN4	TOWN	DOM	FAM	5/4	HS	BC	S-U	Q21

1. Average Density Decile
DEN0 (Household Density
DEN9 Per Square Mile,
Lowest to Highest)

2. Predominant Area Type
CITY (Dense Urban Row & Hi-Rise Areas)
SUBS (Suburban Fringe Residential Areas)
TOWN (Ex Urban Towns & Satellite Suburbs)
FARM (Farms, Ranches & Other Rural Areas)

3. Ethnic Diversity
DOM (Dominant Ethnic Group)
MIX (Mixed Ethnic Groups)

4. Predominant Family Type
FAM (Married Couples w/Children)
CPL (Married Couples, Few Children)
F/S (Families w/Singles Elements)
SGL (Singles, Couples, Few Children)
S/S (Solo-Parent Families & Singles)

5. Relative Importance of Adult Age Groups
1 (18-24 Yrs) 4 (45-54 Yrs)
2 (25-34 Yrs) 5 (55-64 Yrs)
3 (35-44 Yrs) 6 (65 + Years)
First/second-highest indexed age groups are indicated by numbers separated by a slash.

6. Key Education
CG (College Grad & Above)
SC (Some College)
HS (High School Grad)
SH (Some High School)
GS (Grade School)
EX (Exception, Flat or Bi)

7. Key Employment Level
WC (White Collar)
BC (Blue Collar)
BW (Blue/White Mix)
BS (Blue Collar/Service)
BF (Blue Collar/Farm)

8. Key Housing Type
S-U (Single-Unit Housing)
2-9 (2-9 Unit Housing)
M-U (Multi-Unit 10+ Housing)

9. Social Rank
Q1 (Neighborhood Quality
Q40 Highest to Lowest Based on Weighted Composite of Socioeconomic Variables)

Source: Claritas Corporation.

PRIZM applications.

Figure 3–8 presents an example of how to use PRIZM. Other applications are for direct mail, media planning, and retail targeting.

Figure 3–8
Using PRIZM to Target Media Buys

Targeting Spot TV News in Dallas

Source: Claritas Corporation.

Direct Mail. Because the PRIZM database is address-driven, targets can be selected by PRIZM for direct-mail campaigns. In addition, separate sales messages can be tailored to the various PRIZM segments identified on the marketer's list.

Media Planning. Audience data from the major media measurement companies, including A. C. Nielsen, Arbitron, Simmons Market Research Bureau, Mediamark Research, and others, can be combined with the PRIZM database to identify the media that best reach target prospects. Also, by combining syndicated media data with PRIZM, each PRIZM target cluster can be analyzed in terms of most-used and least-used media vehicles.

Retail Targeting. The sales potential of various neighborhoods can be assessed using PRIZM analysis. This process involves matching PRIZM targets with census tract clusters containing high concentrations of potential customers for the marketer's product.

VALS, PRIZM, and other psychographic market segmentation services are subscribed to by advertisers and agencies who wish to use general and specialized information for their marketing efforts. But some companies prefer to produce their own segmentation research rather than pay for someone else to do it. One researcher contends that any company or agency, even those without a research department, can produce its own psychographic market segmentation study relatively inexpensively using available measurement instruments and a statistical consultant to analyze the data.[6]

Attitude toward Product Benefit Segmentation

Consumer attitudes toward product benefits or attributes can be used as a means of market segmentation. The underlying theory here is that consumers have different reasons for choosing a certain brand. Often those reasons are related to personal values toward a product category or the salient attributes of a specific product. Both of these factors—values and salient product characteristics—can form the basis for market segmentation. Information on such consumer preferences can be gathered by use of a preference questionnaire that includes items asking respondents to rank both values and product characteristics they consider important.

In a 1981 study by Boote, patrons of two competing restaurant chains in six major cities were interviewed in their homes.[7] Based on a factor analysis of answers to 45 scaled value statements, three "general values" categories were found to describe the restaurant patrons. Consumers then were ranked on their responses to each general value category.

1. **Food orientation**

   Eating only the best-quality foods

   Eating foods with the highest-quality ingredients

   Having leisurely, relaxed meals

2. **Rational orientation**

   Having a familiar routine for getting tasks done

   Having an orderly way of life

   Having things tidy and neat

   Scheduling each week in advance

   Doing things the best way, even if it takes longer

3. **Leisure orientation**

   Being able to relax for a few hours every day

   Having a lot of leisure time to myself

Responses to a scaled question asking female respondents which they preferred of Restaurant A and Restaurant B were compared with value orientation to yield the following data:

Value Segment	*n*	Prefer A (%)	Prefer B (%)
Food orientation	60	42	58
Rational orientation	37	65	35
Leisure orientation	33	45	55

Respondents then were asked to rate 47 separate product and service attributes for the restaurants on a five-point scale. Factor analysis reduced the 47 items to 10 general product attributes:

1. Generic product characteristics

2. Menu variety

3. Take-out service

4. Menu appeal

5. Value-price

6. Parking courtesy

7. Major entrees

8. Comfort

9. Lunches and snacks

10. Accommodations

Brand preference (as determined by the scaled question asking respondents which restaurant they preferred), mean ratings of restaurants on each of the product attributes, and the product attribute's average importance score were analyzed to determine product attribute salience. Results for female respondents were as follows:

Value Segment	Salient Product Attributes
1. Food orientation	Product
	Major entree
2. Rational orientation	Major entree
	Menu variety
3. Leisure orientation	Menu variety

Interestingly, no significant differences in restaurant preference were revealed using traditional major demographic factors of sex, age, or race. Such a lack of brand-preference differentiation suggested that other factors, in this case consumer values and salient product attributes, would be more powerful predictors of restaurant preference than demographics. Results had major implications for subsequent advertising for Restaurant A, the sponsor of the study. Restaurant A was advised to actively pursue customers in the food-orientation segment, the majority of whom favored the competitor. Further, it was suggested that the advertising should incorporate the values of the major consumer segments and emphasize the appropriate salient characteristics, such as cleanliness, food packaging, major menu items, etc.

Product Usage

The expression "20 percent of my customers buy 80 percent of my product" illustrates the efficiency of focusing the marketing effort on those who consume the most of a certain product. By collecting purchase data on a variety of consumers, a range of consuming types—heavy users, medium users, light users, and non-users of the product—will emerge. Other consumer characteristics, particularly demographics, life-styles, and media usage patterns, can be studied in an effort to utilize appropriate media to reach hot prospects for a product.

Two major syndicated sources of information combine data on consumer demographics, purchase behavior, and media usage. The Simmons Market Research Bureau (SMRB) *Study of Media and Markets* and Mediamark Research Inc. (MRI) provide figures for overall product and service categories and further classifies them by major national brand. For most products, consumers are divided among all users, heavy users, medium users, and light users. An example of an MRI table appears in Chapter 10.

Coordinating the Research Effort—Working Together

The advertising research process involves a variety of participants who plan, approve, execute, or make use of research information. Marketing departments of client firms usually have their own research staff with responsibility for product development research, as well as other areas, such as campaign tracking. Advertising agencies with research departments are primarily involved with defining target markets and, of course, testing creative materials, strategies, and executions. (See Figure 3–9—research activities of agencies and client companies.) Other players in the research scenario include suppliers who provide a variety of specialized services, and consultants and academics with valuable expertise and experience. Each of these participants is described in detail below.

Figure 3–9
Types of Research Conducted by Advertisers and Their Agencies

Product research	Positioning research
Sales trends	Brand recognition research
Market research	Concept development research
Competitive strategy analysis	Pre-campaign copy evaluation
Competitive spending analysis	Pilot campaign copy evaluation
Target market research	Post-campaign copy evaluation
Test market research	Campaign tracking

Client Company

Corporate management.

Top management of client companies often are involved at the beginning and the end of the research process. Typically a research program, whether conducted in-house or by an agency or outside firm, requires the company executives or board of directors to approve the allocation of resources for a research proposal. Corporate management is also one of several end-users of the research and often relies on its findings for direction in company decision making.

Brand personnel/advertising personnel.

An employee responsible for the marketing and advertising of a particular brand or service can hold a variety of titles within the organization. Referred to here as the advertising manager, this person represents the company's marketing and advertising interests. In addition to being an end-user of research, the advertising manager is responsible for choosing, working with, and evaluating advertising agencies for the brand.

Research department.

Among the duties of corporate research personnel are coordinating, gathering, and disseminating information on all aspects of the marketing activities for a brand. The corporate research team is involved with product research and consumer research, as well as with tracking the effectiveness of an advertising campaign. When a client company uses the services of an advertising agency, coordination must take place between the two firms so that efficiency is maximized. This is achieved in different ways for different brands, but it is advisable to have in place a "research charter" or research plan that spells out which research activities each organization will handle.

Advertising Agency

Research department.

Full-service advertising agencies in the United States generally have what is called a "research department." The British concept of account planning has infiltrated several American agencies, however, resulting in the renaming of some units using such titles as "account planning department" or "consumer planning department." (Account planning will be discussed in greater detail later in this chapter.)

Whatever the title, the agency research department is charged with serving the other agency departments, as well as advising and coordinating with the advertising and research departments of the client company. Among the agency researcher's possible job activities are product research, consumer research, market research, copy testing, and campaign evaluation. Generally speaking, though, the agency research department concentrates its efforts on providing information to develop and to study the effectiveness of the advertising message itself. It also interacts with various suppliers of specialty research services.

Often in the case of a new business pitch, the research department may be called on to supply necessary background on a prospective client company or band and its competition. Using secondary research, the agency can come up with an industry analysis that acts as a backdrop against which to view the problems and opportunities of the prospective business partner.

Account service.

The account service or account management team is responsible for coordinating the agency's activities on behalf of the client and acting as the link between the agency and client companies. In preparing the marketing and advertising plan for a particular brand, the account executive draws on the agency's own research and a variety of research information provided by the client. The account manager is also an end-user of research generated by the agency to test the effectiveness of creative ideas and their execution.

Media department.

The media department is both an end-user and, sometimes, a producer of research. It plans and allocates the client's advertising dollars for various media. Media planners use information compiled from a variety of sources to prepare such reports as marketing situation analyses, audience trend studies, and "competitives" (detailed summaries of when and where a competitive product or brand was advertised and approximately how much was spent on that brand in each month, quarter, or year). Information on effective reach and frequency levels is also critical to the media planner. Many times introduction test market experiments are called for to determine effective reach and frequency levels before bringing out a national product. Some very large agencies have research specialists within their media departments, and in a few cases separate media research departments exist.

Creative department.

Much investigation and analysis is conducted prior to the creation of the advertising message. It is essential that creative personnel understand the brand's history, market situation, problems and opportunities, positioning statement, target market definition, and competitive picture before going about accomplishing objectives set for the brand. As such, "creatives" are end-users of market research activities of the client company and the agency.

The other major functions of the creative team are concept testing and copy testing. It is here that research can reduce the uncertainty surrounding the creative risk-taking process. Rough, semi-finished, or finished versions of print ads and commercials can be tested using a variety of methods, settings, and audiences. The information gathered can suggest strengths, weaknesses, and overall effectiveness of competitors' ads.

In the process of developing the advertisements, creatives often call on agency information centers or reference librarians to provide background or to locate little-known facts or specific details about a character, product, or situation they plan to invoke.

Suppliers, academics, and consultants.

Agencies and clients purchase a variety of services from outside firms and individuals in the course of the marketing effort. In the research area, vendors can supply completed marketing and advertising information, as well as conduct primary research activities such as interviewee recruitment, field interviewing and data collection, and data tabulation and analysis. Academics and business consultants can also provide expertise on a project basis or on a retainer basis. Unlike industry consultants who produce proprietary work for use by a specific client, many academics regularly produce detailed results of research projects in the form of books, journal articles, and other widely disseminated media available to anyone who wishes to use it.

Agency and Client Roles in the Research Process

Because there are so many potential participants in the research process, and because there are so many possible research "points of entry" in the advertising process, a well-coordinated research effort is essential. Regular lines of communication between the agency and client research and account teams is the answer. After the research responsibilities of all parties have been spelled out, a direct relationship should be forged between client and agency teams.

First, it is important to establish team reviews between client and agency personnel. These frequent meetings should be a part of the annual planning process for the brand and should be used in developing the business analysis. After the planning period they should be held semiannually or quarterly. The presence of all end-users of research makes possible a broad sharing of learning related to brand activities, strategic opportunities, and, most important, consumer characteristics.

Second, establish research planning reviews between client and agency research departments. The focus of these meetings should be on such topics as advertising effectiveness, spending programs, strategic research or management information systems, and a summary of findings related to the client's product category. These reviews encourage involvement of client and agency research management and enable early feedback on proposed research activities. They also foster mutual respect and represent an opportunity to better know colleagues and to plan joint research activities.

How Should Suppliers Be Chosen?

With the proliferation of services available from independent research firms and consultants, it is essential that the research dollar be allocated to the proper outside supplier. One marketing research manager has suggested that proper identification of advertising research needs and objectives can set the criteria for supplier selection. A supplier's advertising research specialties should match research needs of the client or agency.

A scheme of advertising measurement objectives is used to define supplier relations as follows:

Advertising Measurement Objectives to Define Supplier Relations

If the Measurement Objective Is . . .	Then Use Suppliers Offering Services Which Measure . . .
• Attention	• Viewer Involvement • Personal Relevance • Message Uniqueness
• Perception	• Message Recall • Main Idea • Product Associations
• Reaction	• Level of Arousal • Emotions Evoked • Brand Affect

Source: D. William Jolley, "Advertising Research: Optimizing Its Effectiveness in the Firm," *ARF Key Issues Workshop,* Advertising Research Foundation, 1982.

How Can Research Help Creative People?

The stereotyping of agency personnel such as "creatives" and "research number-crunchers" often overstates the differences between the two, exaggerates antagonism between them, and blurs the common purpose they have been hired to serve. One could easily envision the relationship as a tug-of-war between the intuitive and analytical wills of either side.

Despite their similarities and common goals, it is often the differences between the groups that are stressed. The fact is that both researchers and creatives have much in common in pursuit of their work. They gather information when confronted with a problem, come up with a hypothesis about how to solve the problem, and test their work on peers, colleagues, and consumers as their ideas finally take shape.

Two factors are critical in the successful side-by-side functioning of research and creative personnel. First, researchers must gain the confidence of the creative department by contributing to the creative development of advertisements. Second, researchers must actively seek the participation of creatives in their research process. The need for cooperation has prompted one research director to recommend a code of conduct for creative and research personnel:[8]

1. **Development**

   Creatives should insist upon a maximum amount, and quality, of consumer input to nurture inspiration before making ads.

   Researchers should help creatives internalize known facts and facilitate experiences with consumers in qualitative, dynamic ways.

2. **Understanding**

   Creatives should state what would convince them an ad is working as intended and insist that it be studied realistically with consumers.

   Researchers should be method-flexible and open-minded to avoid narrow interpretations of numerical results.

3. **Evaluation**

   Creatives should accept that at the moment of marketing truth, when a message, attitude, or sale is supposed to have happened, copy tests and tracking studies are the only practical measures available.

   Researchers should examine the available tests and the numerous design assumptions, recommend the most appropriate in each case, and avoid being dogmatic or doctrinaire in analysis.

The three phases in which research is most beneficial to creative personnel are development of copy strategy, pre-testing of concepts and executions, and campaign evaluation.

Development of copy strategy.

The creation of a copy strategy requires a variety of highly complex tasks. Of all the possible ways to approach the creative assignment, the agency team will decide on only one, and only after much deliberation. In "Everything an Account Representative Should Know about Creative Research," Daniel Lissance pinpoints the two functions creative research serves at the copy strategy development stage:[9]

- The gathering of a wide range of intelligence about motivations and needs associated with the product.
- The sifting, winnowing, and evaluation of all possible strategy alternatives to select the one that is most likely to provide consumers with a powerful, competitive reason to buy a product.

One key area of contribution from a research department to the creative department is information for the creative brief. A creative brief serves as a creative "master plan" for the advertising effort. At its best, it combines elements of brand and category analysis, target market description, consumer insights, and creative focus. Figure 3–10 includes the types of questions and topics usually addressed in the creative brief. Secondary and primary research can supply a succinct description of the target audience using demographics and psychographics. Information from consumer surveys, focus groups, and one-on-one interviews can supply the "consumer insights," which focus the creative message on key areas of consumer interest and importance. In some agencies, the creative brief is co-authored by creatives and researchers, especially in agencies that practice account planning.

Figure 3–10
Research Contributions to the Creative Brief

To whom are we directing this advertising message?
A concise description of the target market. At the very least, it includes demographics but preferably contains psychographic or lifestyle information.

What is the consumer's relationship with the category?
What does the product mean to the consumer (physically, psychologically, etc.)? Are products in this category purchased to reflect a consumer's self-image, or are they purchased as impulse buys? How do consumers use it?

What is the consumer's relationship with our brand?
What are the "accepted consumer beliefs" about our brand? Do they view it as something they shouldn't buy for themselves but would like to? Is it something they perceive should be used only on special occasions? These types of consumer insights can really give creatives something to work with. If advertising for Brand X is currently running, information on the consumer's relationship with it can be of help here as well.

What do we wish the advertising to accomplish?
The goal of the advertising is key to the creative brief. Is the purpose of the advertising to encourage consumers to try our brand? To remind them to buy more? To overcome a specific misconception they might have about the product?

What is the key proposition?
In view of whom we are directing the message to, how they feel about the product category and our brand, and what we feel the advertising should accomplish, what is the *single most important message we would like the target audience to remember?* This statement is usually brief, such as "Brand X is the only brand with all the essential ingredients I need," or "Brand X is like an old friend; it's always there when I need it," or "Brand X is the best brand and I deserve it." The challenge to the creative team is then to make the key proposition come alive through the advertising. Research often serves as the basis for generating the key proposition. Focus group statements, personal interviews, competitive advertising claims, and conversations with those who design or test the product all can provide clues to the advertising proposition.

How will the key proposition be supported?
In addition to many other sources of support, such as testimonials, demonstration, and endorsements, results of consumer research can serve as substantiation for the advertising claims. "Four out of five dentist recommended . . . is quite a bit stronger than "Brand X is the brand professionals use."

What do we want consumers to feel about our brand as the results of advertising?
The tone and "feel" of the advertising contributes to the overall image of a brand, and the creative brief should state what type of brand image the advertising is intended to create. After being exposed to the advertising, should the consumer feel that our brand is friendly, warm, caring, superior, sophisticated, entertaining, "hip"?

It is useful for the creative team to become familiar with strategies and executions that have previously been used by competitors. This can be accomplished by reviewing old advertisements and studying their content. With respect to consumer research, the results of in-depth interviews and focus groups can be used to gain insight into consumer motivations, beliefs, fears, and attitudes toward the product.

In analyzing data, the researcher may come up with a number of hypotheses, or unproven hunches, about consumer motivation. The account and creative teams would then formulate several possible creative strategy statements. These would be narrowed down by agency personnel working together and using criteria established by the agency for all campaigns (such as emotional involvement, information content, etc.) or specific criteria for the product in question.

Pretesting executions.

Typically, once the desired strategy has been decided on, several executions of ideas are formulated by the creative team. At this point, the researcher can offer the creative team an evaluation of how effectively the individual execution met the agreed-on objectives. A variety of methods from *portfolio tests* to *animatics* to *simulated media tests* is available to the researcher, and a range of criteria—from memorability to liking to purchase intent—can be the basis of measurement and analysis.

It is here, as we will discuss in later chapters, that a considerable amount of controversy has surrounded the creative research function. Issues in the discussion of whether copy-testing procedures are the best measures of predicting advertising effectiveness include those of internal and external validity, memory, duration of exposure, and statistical levels used for acceptance or rejection. Anyone developing advertising, whether an account representative, creative person, or researcher, should be aware of the advantages and disadvantages of copy-testing procedures. One factor is critical to their effective use—decisions concerning which criteria will be used for decision making must be made *before* the testing ever takes place. (More will be discussed about copy-testing procedures in Chapter 12.)

Campaign evaluation.

Another way research can help creative people is by studying the effectiveness of a given campaign over time. Such longitudinal consumer attitude measurements are sometimes called "tracking" studies, because they follow the campaign to determine whether it met its objectives in the field. This form of feedback usually involves survey methodology to generate data, which is sometimes used to correct a campaign in midstream or to terminate an ineffective campaign effort. Campaign evaluation results not only give a reading on the current advertising program, but also can be used for comparison with past efforts and as a basis for decision making in future strategic planning.

In summary, the researcher can assist the creative team in many ways throughout the campaign process to produce the best advertising possible for the agency. A variety of methods can be used in seeking creative solutions, and often these will vary from one campaign assignment to another. At every stage in the agency's work, the researcher should attempt to reduce the uncertainty surrounding the campaign planning process. In so doing, the researcher is contributing to the formulation of the agency's best work. In advising account representatives on how to get the best out of their creative team, John Noble emphasized the need for information:[10]

> Number one: Feed them facts. Bore them with facts. Make sure they know not only your client's product and problems, but also the competition's product and problems. Never assume that any fact you find inconsequential is inconsequential. "Oh yes, it works great in hot weather, too," just may be the smartest thing you can say. And one of the sweetest things they ever heard. It's their job to sift. It's your job to supply plenty of sand.

Should an Agency Practice Account Planning?

Lack of integration with the day-to-day agency planning activities is cited consistently as one of the principal shortcomings of the traditional agency research department. Critics charge that agency research departments are reactive rather than proactive when it comes to participating in agency business. An example would be a situation wherein the agency research department was involved only in the copy-testing for an advertising campaign, rather than having a hand in the *development* of the message.

Furthermore, critics say, most agency researchers spend more time buying research from outside suppliers and passing it along to the rest of the agency and the client than they spend talking to real live consumers and finding out what they're thinking. That fact, the British concluded in the 1960s and 1970s, results in agency personnel at all levels who are out of touch with what is going on in the minds of the client's customers.

The British solution to an underutilized and poorly integrated agency research department is to revamp agency management structure and replace the research department with account planners. The system of account planning exists today in only a few U.S. agencies, some of which hired British planners for their expertise and experience. Though most of the agencies practicing account planning seem to be convinced that the switch was for the better, it is believed that large U.S. agencies will exhibit continued reluctance to implement such a drastic reorganization, because their old structure is well-entrenched.

The mission of the account planner is to gain a greater understanding of consumers in an effort to:

- Establish how advertising can help a brand. (What is the role of advertising?)
- Help determine what the advertising should communicate. (What should the message be? How should consumers feel after seeing it?)
- Help provide input on how the message can be communicated.

The account planner has been likened to a cross between a creative, a researcher, and an account manager. The important point in that comparison is the scope of the account planner's involvement—ideally the account planner is involved at every step in the campaign planning process.

Basically, account planners differ from the "traditional" researcher in that they (1) act as the voice of the consumer, (2) attend most agency and client meetings, (3) make their ongoing research and recommendations available to the appropriate agency departments (usually in the form of "briefs"), and (4) conduct most of their research themselves.

This translates into a career of seeking out and listening to consumers on a daily basis. Account planners often conduct their own focus groups and in-depth interviews, as well as work on sample surveys of the target market. Planners have been described as the "voice of a thousand consumers," because they respond to potential advertising executions and marketing strategies as if they were the consumers themselves. Account planning relies heavily on results of qualitative research, a fact which emphasizes its existence as an alternative to traditional quantitative data and analysis.

Account planning has not been without its headaches in the United States. Some contend that a "jack of all trades is the master of none," in reference to the planner's roles of account manager, creative, and researcher. Still others contend that most U.S. agencies find themselves attempting work intended to please the client, not the consumer. Furthermore, agency work must be produced within a very short time, a situation which does not lend itself well to lengthy processes of investigation. As mentioned earlier, though many agencies embrace the concept of account planning as an attractive method, the difficulty of implementing such a system has stymied its development in most cases. It is possible that in the coming years the concept of account planning will be more fully developed in mid-size or small agency settings where increased organizational flexibility might better facilitate such a change. Sources for additional reading on account planning are listed at the end of this chapter.

What Types of Research Should Be the Focus of a Research Plan?

After interviewing 170 executives and researchers from key agencies, client companies, and research consulting firms, Zaltman and Moorman reported that research conducted for advertising purposes is carried out to find three types of basic information:[11]

1. What is the right thing to do? (Developmental research, e.g., concept development and positioning research)

2. How do you go about doing it right? (Developmental and confirmatory research, e.g., copy development and testing research)

3. Have you done it right? (Evaluative research, e.g., brand recognition studies and persuasion scores)

The authors concluded that agency and client research alike tends to favor evaluative research, even though the major thrust of an agency's responsibility is to generate creative solutions, which would seem to call for developmental and confirmatory research. This emphasis on after-the-fact investigation has been likened to a surgeon who spent 85 percent of training learning how to evaluate the success or failure of a particular operation and only 15 percent of training learning how to perform the task itself.

Zaltman and Moorman recommended that client management should take primary responsibility for the execution and use of both developmental and evaluative research. This responsibility, they argue, will increase the likelihood that advertising research activities and the advertising program subsequently created will be integrated into the company's total marketing mix.

Also recommended was increased focus on developmental research, which can significantly increase the likelihood of capturing a set of good advertising options and selecting the best one. Good developmental research should have the following objectives as its focus:

1. Find ways of expressing the basic and distinctive concept behind a product.

2. Find ways of relating that concept to important customer needs.

3. Identify special barriers to buying that can be addressed by advertising.

Review

In this chapter we saw that:

- To be of value, research must fit within the advertiser's or agency's advertising and marketing strategies.
- The FCB Grid uses perceptual mapping to measure consumer involvement with particular products or services.
- *Designing Advertising Goals for Measured Advertising Results* (DAGMAR) was constructed by Russell Colley to help advertisers plan the advertising campaign by specifying its objectives and providing the criteria by which to judge it.
- It is vital to establish a meaningful, durable, and profitable positioning strategy to influence consumer perception of the advertiser's and competitors' brands by the following steps:
  1. Identify the competitors.
  2. Determine how the competitors' products or services are perceived and evaluated.
  3. Determine the competitors' positions.
  4. Analyze the customers.
  5. Select a position.
  6. Monitor the position.
- Aaker's six approaches to positioning strategy are by attribute, by price/quality, by use or application, by product user, by product class, and by competition.
- The many participants in the advertising research process whose efforts must be coordinated include client firms' marketing departments, agency research departments, suppliers, consultants, and academics.
- The British-originated concept of account planning is slowly taking hold in U.S. agencies, with mixed results.

Endnotes

1. Russell Colley, *Defining Advertising Goals for Measured Advertising Results* (New York: Association of National Advertisers, Inc., 1961).
2. Al Ries and Jack Trout, *Positioning: The Battle for Your Mind,* Rev. ed. (New York: McGraw-Hill, 1986).
3. David Aaker, "Positioning Your Product," *Business Horizons,* May–June 1982, pp. 56–62.
4. Ibid.

5. William Wells and Douglas Tigert, "Activities, Interests and Opinions," reprinted in "Advertising Research Classics," *Journal of Advertising Research,* September 1982, pp. 30–38.

6. Jack Lesser, "How to Conduct an $80,000 Market Study for Pocket Change," *Management Review* 77, no. 6, June 1988, pp. 36–43.

7. Alfred S. Boote, "Market Segmentation by Personal Values and Salient Product Attributes," *Journal of Advertising Research* 21, no. 1, February 1981, pp. 29–35.

8. Richard L. Vaughn, "Point of View: Creatives Versus Researchers: Must They Be Adversaries?" *Journal of Advertising Research* 22, no. 6, December 1982/January 1983, pp. 44–50.

9. Daniel Lissance and Leland Ott, "What Every Account Representative Should Know about Creative Research," American Association of Advertising Agencies, 1978.

10. Carl Hixon and John Noble, "What Every Account Representative Should Know about the Creative Function," American Association of Advertising Agencies, 1979.

11. Gerald Zaltman and Christine Moorman, "The Management and Use of Advertising Research," *Journal of Advertising Research* 28, no. 9, December 1988/January 1989, pp. 11–18.

Sources for Additional Reading on Account Planning _____

Barry, Thomas, Ron Peterson, and W. Bradford Todd. "The Role of Account Planning in the Future of Advertising Agency Research," *Journal of Advertising Research* 27, no. 1, February/March 1987, pp. 15–21.

Meyers, Bruce. "To Plan or Not to Plan." *Journal of Advertising Research* 26, no. 5, 1986, pp. 25–26.

Mitchell, Arnold. *The Nine American Lifestyles: Who We Are and Where We Are Going* (New York: Macmillan Publishing Co., Inc., 1983).

Sharkey, Betsy. "Do British-Style Account Planners Have a Future in the U.S.?" *ADWEEK,* Eastern Edition, August 10, 1987.

Stewart, Jennifer. "The Role and Evolution of the Agency Planner." *Journal of Advertising Research* 26, no. 5, 1986, pp. 22–24.

Part 2 Secondary and Primary Advertising Research Methods

Chapter 4   Secondary Research

Introduction

Secondary research uncovers information that is available in published form, whether in printed documents such as books and periodicals or in one of many on-line computer databases. The process of searching for and gaining access to such published information is called *secondary research*. This is one of the crucial first steps in planning a primary research project.

Why Conduct Secondary Research?

In spite of the widely held notion that information is "outdated before it is published," there are still very important and practical reasons for conducting secondary research. Secondary research can provide the following benefits:

- **Answer specific questions definitively.** If the answer to a research question lies in published documents and must simply be ferreted out, then secondary research is an end in itself. If the researcher is looking for demographics of populations in certain key marketing areas, for example, he or she need only consult the appropriate published sources, such as U.S. Census Bureau statistics.

- **Refine the research questions.** The impetus for conducting a primary research study often stems from a very general question. Secondary research can help in the formulation of specific objectives to narrow the area of inquiry.

- **Help build detailed files of previous findings and keep current with major developments.** Advertising researchers all too often "reinvent the wheel." Whatever questions a new research study aims to answer, there's always a possibility that previous studies have conducted the same research and published the results. It's just a matter of finding the published report. Although it's rare that the exact same study has already been carried out, often a sufficiently similar study has. Assuming the results can be applied to the project under consideration, secondary research can save the agency and client both time and money.

- **Suggest appropriate research methods.** When developing research ideas and setting objectives, the researcher needs to know what methods will achieve the desired results. A perusal of previous research in the area will offer insight into the sample procedures, data-gathering methods, and analytical techniques other investigators have employed. Their own evaluation of methodology and their suggestions for future research, both of which typically appear at the end of research journal articles, also prove valuable. Furthermore, the appendices of reports often include copies of the questionnaires or other tools used in the studies. These can provide an excellent starting point for developing your own research tools.

- **Help position the current study.** Just as a product or brand occupies a certain position among others in the same category, so researchers can position their projects among existing studies on similar issues.

  In the literature review section of a research journal report, authors discuss their research effort in the context of earlier studies, usually concluding with a positioning statement that differentiates the project, on the basis that no previous study addressed or answered the question at hand.

Using Information Sources in Advertising Research

The field of advertising is interdisciplinary by nature—incorporating material from business, psychology, sociology, anthropology, and other diverse sources. To complete a study, researchers may need, for example, industry overviews, product information, market share data, information on competitive products and strategies, and a broad range of information on consumer life-styles and attitudes. No one source is likely to provide all of this data. The successful researcher must become an expert not only on where to look for each type of information, but also on how to use each source correctly.

Both marketing and advertising information is necessary for the day-to-day activities of advertising agencies and advertising departments. An agency's new business team, for example, relies on a wide variety of marketing and advertising sources in its search for new clients and new business opportunities. In the course of its work, the new business team will use sources containing information on the business climate in a particular industry, major competitors of the target company, product histories, marketing strategies, past advertising expenditures, and campaign themes. A sample company/brand analysis checklist is shown in Figure 4-1. Much of this type of information can be found in directories, periodical indexes, and computer databases. How well the team collects and integrates information from such sources and applies it to specific advertising problems affects the success of new business.

Figure 4-1
Company/Brand Analysis Checklist

I. Company
- location
- organization and major activities; subsidiaries
- history
- financial data
- annual report
- key personnel/managers
- recent news from database sources, newspapers, etc.

II. Category
- category definition
- size of category in units, dollars, etc.
- category history and growth
- category growth projections
- distribution channels/methods of distribution
- major manufacturers/players
- seasonal factors
- regional factors
- other factors relevant to category
- legal considerations
- major trade publications/trade organizations in category

III. Products within category
- share of category by product form
- product form description (size, flavor, model, etc.)
- new product introductions
- benefits and appeals of new products
- new packages, innovations, etc.
- recent news about/affecting category

Brand Analysis
- top brands by dollar or unit sales
- growth trends of top brands
- category share nationally and by region
- pricing trends
- recent news about/affecting brand

Consumer Profile
- demographics of users
- frequency of purchase/usage
- place of purchase
- heavy user profile
- awareness and attitudes toward brand
- decision-maker v. purchaser
- normal purchase cycle
- brand loyalty/switching

Advertising

Messages
- creative strategies of top brands
- specific promises, appeals, claims, special effects
- examples of past and current executions

Media
- category and brand spending
- seasonality (by quarter)
- regionality (spot buying)
- major media employed by top brands
- spending patterns—flighting, continuous, etc.
- spending compared with market share

Promotion
- promotions used in category
- major brand promotion types and examples
- success rates of promotions

Other pertinent information
- personal interviews
- other information sources

Advertising agency and client company libraries have had to keep pace with the burgeoning volume of marketing information available from an increasing number of sources. The agency library, or information center, typically becomes the repository for such documents, and major agencies employ full-time librarians to manage information. Media departments also typically collect demographic, marketing, and media information. Agencies or advertising departments without library facilities generally begin their secondary research in local public libraries or university libraries, or with companies that provide research information to subscribers for a fee.

The rest of this chapter describes frequently used advertising research sources and explains how to use them effectively.

Professional Organizations

Several advertising and media organizations commission research studies, have research councils, publish journals, and hold research conferences and workshops. The American Association of Advertising Agencies and the Association of National Advertisers commission research studies and also act as information sources for their member companies around the country. The Direct Marketing Association and Marketing Science Institute publish research reports, journals, and proceedings of their conferences. Media industry organizations such as the Newspaper Research Bureau, Cabletelevision Advertising Bureau, Magazine Publishers of America and Radio Advertising Bureau also commission research studies and maintain libraries for their members.

Advertising Research Foundation (ARF)

Formed in 1936 under joint sponsorship of the Association of National Advertisers and the American Association of Advertising Agencies, the Advertising Research Foundation (ARF) is the most visible of professional sources of advertising information.

The early years at ARF were dominated by media research studies, but after reorganization in 1951, the priorities of the organization were more broad-based, reflecting the diversity of the industry and its research needs. In those days, ARF endorsement of a study greatly increased the rate of its acceptance by the industry.

The current membership of the ARF ranges from associations, advertisers, agencies, research corporations, media companies, and research firms. Associate members include universities and overseas firms. Its objectives include the following:

- To conduct state-of-the-art research projects ranging from assessing validity of a research measure to pinpointing the contribution of advertising in a specific situation.

- To ensure integrity of research information by auditing syndicated research services for honesty, accuracy, and thoroughness.
- To develop and distribute new guidelines, criteria, position papers, and other publications of value to the industry.
- To maintain an active and continuing program of conferences and workshops which bring current developments in key areas directly to practitioners at all levels.

A major activity of the ARF is its key issues workshops. The proceedings and reports from these meetings are an excellent source of research information on specialized advertising issues. The ARF publishes a range of periodicals for the advertising industry, most importantly the *Journal of Advertising Research* and a quarterly newsletter to members. ARF also maintains committees to investigate and report on key issues. These have included, for example, video electronic media and research quality.

Published Sources

Research Journals and Scholarly Publications

Various academic societies and professional organizations publish research journals featuring original reports of industry or academic research. In most cases, submissions are chosen by a process known as "blind review," in which two or more members of an editorial review board evaluate the manuscript without knowing the identity of the author. Journal articles typically begin with detailed analyses of existing literature on a particular subject and then offer specific information about research methodology employed in the current study, followed by data analysis, major findings, and conclusions.

The Journal of Advertising Research, published by the Advertising Research Foundation, and the *Journal of Advertising,* published by the American Academy of Advertising, are the two leading journals in the field. They account for a large percentage of the advertising research articles published in a given year. Other publications containing significant research in advertising as part of their content include:

- *Journal of Marketing* (American Marketing Association)
- *Journal of Marketing Research* (American Marketing Association)
- *Journal of Consumer Research* (Journal of Consumer Research, Inc.)
- *Journal of Consumer Affairs* (Council on Consumer Information)
- *Journalism Quarterly* (University of South Carolina Association for Education in Journalism and Mass Communications)
- *Journal of Consumer Marketing* (Grayson Associates)
- *Journal of Direct Marketing* (Direct Marketing Educational Foundation, Inc.)

While most major journals are published quarterly, a few other industry and scholarly publications of importance to advertising researchers appear less frequently. Examples of these include *Current Issues in Research in Advertising,* an annual publication containing original articles and reviews of pertinent research topics, conference proceedings such as those of the American Academy of Advertising and the American Marketing Association.

Trade Publications

Trade magazines, newsletters, and other industry publications are excellent sources of timely developments in advertising, though they offer less depth in coverage of research issues. Nonetheless, these publications cover industry trends, new methods and services, account movement, legal issues, and other topics of importance to practitioners. Some of the major trade publications in advertising include:

- *Advertising Age* (Crain Communications)
- *ADWEEK* (A/S/M Communications)
- *Media Week* (A/S/M Communications)
- *Marketing News* (American Marketing Association)
- *Broadcasting* (Broadcasting Publications)
- *Editor and Publisher* (Editor and Publisher Co.)

General Directories, Industry and Company Overviews, and Periodical Indexes

When an agency is contemplating taking on a new client or when a researcher is conducting a study on behalf of a client, there are many unknowns about both the company and the industry. Before any detailed research is possible, researchers need information such as the following:

- The type of business the prospective client company is in.
- Who its owners, shareholders, and directors are.
- Where its offices are located.
- Who its major competitors are.
- How successful the company is and what volume of business it does.
- The climate of the industry in which it operates.
- What the experts are saying about the future of this industry and this company.

General Directories

Business directories and indexes are an excellent source for general information. Here are some of the directories most commonly used by advertising researchers.

America's Corporate Families (Dun's Marketing Services).

Also called the *Billion Dollar Directory,* this book covers 500 "ultimate parent companies"—those with $1 billion or more in annual sales. Parent companies are listed alphabetically, and a useful cross-reference guide is available to trace the parent company from a subsidiary or division name. Geographic and industry classification sections also are included. The information given includes state of incorporation, address, import/export, annual sales, number of employees, principal bank and accounting firm, SIC codes, officers, and directors.

Million Dollar Directory (Dun's Marketing Services).

This is a directory of 160,000 public and private U.S. businesses with a net worth of more than $500,000. More than two-thirds of the listings are for privately owned businesses. Volumes are indexed alphabetically, geographically, and by industry. Information in each listing includes address and telephone number of headquarters, industry classification, sales volume, employment size, company officers, and directors.

Standard & Poor's Register of Corporations, Directors and Executives (Standard & Poor's Corporation).

The first of three volumes gives an alphabetical list of corporations with names of top management, accountant and primary bank, employment size, and brief descriptions of products provided. The second volume includes listings of officers, directors, trustees, partners, etc., with business and residence addresses, and college attended. The third volume is a series of indexes arranged by SIC code, alphabetically, by geographic location, and by corporate family.

Ward's Directory of 51,000 Largest U.S. Corporations (B. H. Ward Publications).

This is considered one of the most comprehensive sources of information on manufacturing and nonmanufacturing companies, ranked by SIC code. Zip code and alphabetical indexing are also used. *Ward's Directory of 49,000 Private U.S. Companies* is also available.

Directory of Corporate Affiliations (National Register Publishing Co.).

Subtitled *Who Owns Whom,* this annual publication details the corporate structure of more than 4,000 major U.S. companies and their 40,000 divisions, subsidiaries, and affiliates. Includes information on parent companies as well as summaries of mergers, acquisitions, and name changes. A supplement called *Corporate Action* updates the directory five times a year.

Industry Overviews

Standard & Poor's Industry Surveys (Standard & Poor's Corporation).

This source offers information on major domestic industries in the form of a basic industry analysis and a current analysis. Trends, problems, and recent developments in each industry are given, accompanied by market, industry, and company statistics. Financial appraisals and earnings information are also provided.

U.S. Industrial Outlook (U.S. Department of Commerce).

This book contains economic data and analysis of specific industries. Dollar forecasts, statistical tables, historical data, and industry forecasts are included. The advertising industry is among those areas analyzed each year.

Company Overviews

Moody's Industrial Manual (Moody's Investors Service, Inc.).

This is a seven-volume financial manual, providing straight factual information from published sources on U.S. companies. Titles include *Bank and Finance Manual, Industrial Manual, International Manual, OTC Industrial Manual, Public Utilities Manual, Transportation Manual, Complete Corporate Index,* and *OTC Unlisted Manual.* Semiweekly or weekly *News Reports* updates are also available.

Standard & Poor's Corporation Records (Standard & Poor's Corporation).

This multivolume set covers various publicly held corporations. Information provided includes corporate assets, corporate backgrounds, and stock information. A biweekly supplement entitled *Daily News* is distributed to subscribers as an update.

Periodical Indexes

Business Periodicals Index.

BPI is a cumulative index to English-language periodicals in many specific businesses, industries, and trades. Among the publications indexed are those specifically related to advertising, such as *Advertising Age, ADWEEK, Marketing & Media Decisions, Marketing News,* as well as journals such as *Journal of Advertising, Journal of Advertising Research,* and others.

Predicast's F&S Index United States.

This is an index of business, industrial, and financial periodicals containing information on U.S. companies, products, and industries.

Market and Demographic Information Sources

For anything more than a general review of an industry or company, specialized research sources are needed. For example, if the research problem involves finding out more about a specific product or brand, you might need to research the following:

- Who uses this product/service and where they live.
- What the demographic characteristics of users are.
- If a new brand, in which areas of the country prime prospects live.
- Which brands are the leaders in this product category and what share of market they command.
- What the marketing environment is for this product/service.

The sources below are available in most public or university libraries.

Special Reports

Survey of Buying Power (Bill Publications).

This special issue of *Sales and Marketing Management,* published each July, is the source of the much-discussed Buying Power Index (BPI). Survey features and highlights include current trend data such as the metropolitan areas with the highest median age, leading African-American metropolitan areas, etc. Next are U.S., regional, and state summaries, followed by metropolitan market rankings, then county and city data by states. Instructions for calculating "custom BPIs" are explained.

Editor & Publisher Market Guide.

This annual publication contains facts and figures about all U.S. and Canadian daily newspaper markets, including a ranking of markets by population, disposable income, income per household, and total retail sales. Individual market surveys cover number of passenger autos, average temperatures, major retail stores, shopping centers, transportation, etc. It also includes population, income and retail sales estimates by state, county, and metro area.

Indexes

American Statistics Index: A Comprehensive Guide to the Statistical Publications of the U.S. Government (Congressional Information Service).

ASI has taken on the task of attempting to serve as master guide and index for most publications of the largest compiler of statistics in the world—the U.S. government. Included are federal publications containing primary and secondary research data, as well as special studies and analyses of a wide variety of topics, industries, social concerns, etc. Congressional hearings on advertising are among the items covered.

Statistical Reference Index (Congressional Information Service).

The two-volume SRI set contains printed abstracts and indexes of business, financial, and social statistical data issued by a variety of private concerns, universities, and state governments. The first volume contains the index, arranged by subject, category, title, and issuing source. Abstracts, contained in the second volume, include citations, overviews, contents summaries, and descriptions of statistical data.

Statistical Abstracts of the United States (Department of Commerce, Bureau of the Census).

Published since 1878, *Statistical Abstracts* contains selected data from a variety of statistical publications both governmental and private. Most of the data are national, though some are broken down by state or region. Major sections reflect specific industries or topics, such as education, business enterprise, population, communications, domestic trade and services, etc. Sources are given for all information cited, and supplements to the main volume are recommended for additional information.

Syndicated and Commercial Research Sources

Simmons Market Research Bureau Study of Media and Markets.

Based on a sample of approximately 20,000 adults, the results of this annual survey are projectable to the U.S. adult population. Simmons collects and tabulates data in the areas of media usage, product usage, and demographics. Each of dozens of volumes contains information on specific topics from women's travel habits to hair care and shaving product use. This versatile resource can provide detailed information that can help advertisers in defining target markets, matching appropriate media to target markets, and comparing media vehicle audiences.

Mediamark Research Inc.

A major competitor of SMRB, MRI also provides media and market data based on a national sample of adults.

A. C. Nielsen Co.

Nielsen provides estimates of share-of-market data for food and drug products based on a national sampling of retail stores. Retail and wholesale prices, dealer support, and inventory estimates also are available.

News about Business and Advertising

One of the most effective means of researching the potential of new products or business categories is to find out about the competition. The types of questions asked focus on how competing products have been marketed and advertised in the media and any relevant business developments. Here is a selection of common sources of competitive marketing information.

Public Affairs Information Service Bulletin.

PAIS identifies and indexes public affairs information in the areas of public policy, economics, political science, public administration, international law and relations, sociology and demography, professional issues and public affairs commentary. Periodical articles, books, government documents, and special reports are included. This is a very broad index and encompasses a variety of public affairs topics of potential interest to the advertiser.

New York Times Index.

This index contains descriptive phrases about significant news, editorial matter, and special features published in the daily and Sunday *New York Times*. Classifications are under subject, geographic, organization, and personal name headings.

The Wall Street Journal Index/Barron's Index (Dow Jones & Co., Inc.).

WSJ Index is divided into sections entitled "Corporate News" and "General News." *Barron's Index* combines the two. Each entry is accompanied by a brief description and citation.

Art Index (H. W. Wilson Co.).

Domestic and foreign publications in the areas of film, graphic arts, photography, and other related fields are indexed by subject and author. Several publications covering advertising communications are included.

Advertising Media Sources

Numerous sources are available for the various media rates, coverage, etc. Following are a few of the major titles.

Standard Rate & Data Service, Inc.

SRDS publishes detailed information media vehicles in the following areas: consumer magazines and agri-media, business publication display and classified advertising, newspaper, spot television, and spot radio advertising. Detailed market information for media markets also is provided.

Broadcasting/Cablecasting Yearbook (Broadcasting Publications, Inc.).

This source contains sections on history of broadcasting, directories of radio and TV stations, information on U.S. and Canadian cable systems, satellites, programming, an advertising and marketing section, and listings of professional services including research firms.

Leading National Advertisers.

These quarterly publications detail advertising expenditures by company, product, and brand in the following media: network television, spot television, cable, network radio, national spot radio, outdoor, syndicated television, magazines, and newspaper supplements. Figures are based on sampling procedures from which monthly estimates and year-to-date totals are calculated. LNA is a major source of competitive media spending data. See Figure 4–2 for example.

Sources for Information on Agencies and Advertising

The following sources profile major advertising agencies, advertising companies, annual billings, client profiles, specializations, and personnel.

Figure 4-2
LNA/ARBITRON Multi-Media Service

AD $ SUMMARY
COMPANY RANKINGS

LNA/ARBITRON MULTI-MEDIA SERVICE
January - March 1991

TOP 1000 COMPANIES RANKED BY 10 MEDIA DOLLARS (000)

RANK	COMPANY	10-MEDIA TOTAL	MAGAZINES	SUNDAY MAGAZINES	NEWSPAPERS	OUTDOOR	NETWORK TELEVISION	SPOT TELEVISION	SYNDICATED TELEVISION	CABLE TV NETWORKS	NETWORK RADIO	NATIONAL SPOT RADIO
1	PROCTER & GAMBLE CO	280,375.0	33,715.0	--	966.3	375.1	122,125.1	66,148.6	34,755.7	16,455.1	4,245.7	1,577.8
2	PHILIP MORRIS COMPANIES INC	277,173.8	49,080.9	3,102.4	1,653.7	16,720.9	98,575.8	57,575.9	34,838.8	6,482.5	1,090.2	7,267.7
3	GENERAL MOTORS CORP	272,193.9	67,444.9	641.8	11,906.3	1,315.5	142,525.4	22,495.6	11,464.5	8,051.1	3,661.5	2,677.3
4	PEPSICO INC	140,552.9	1,228.8	--	758.3	546.1	61,634.4	61,557.1	6,776.6	3,086.1	1,702.9	3,292.6
5	FORD MOTOR CO	118,772.4	31,194.6	982.4	4,678.7	155.9	55,566.1	16,268.2	4,738.2	4,921.2	0.2	256.9
6	GENERAL MILLS INC	103,510.1	5,001.9	--	98.7	208.1	36,056.8	49,074.0	3,852.7	7,035.0	1,310.7	72.2
7	UNILEVER NV	99,724.4	21,930.2	--	166.4	270.5	47,729.2	15,710.6	11,550.9	1,555.1	--	811.5
8	CHRYSLER CORP	99,461.0	27,825.1	405.5	1,906.3	75.4	44,572.0	13,179.3	1,782.4	2,005.0	5,519.4	2,186.0
9	MARS CORP LTD	98,705.8	3,588.7	421.9	67,112.1	1.2	13,275.0	5,850.5	2,148.5	1,201.1	513.6	4,483.2
10	SEARS ROEBUCK & CO	97,659.5	2,643.2	102.1	18,598.0	154.1	39,237.0	8,183.5	7,360.4	4,948.1	15,276.7	1,149.4
	TOP 10 TOTAL	1,588,128.8	244,419.3	5,616.1	107,846.0	19,862.8	661,316.8	316,087.3	119,219.7	56,565.3	33,320.9	23,874.6
11	MCDONALDS CORP	94,959.4	924.0	--	97.4	1,369.3	43,330.1	36,166.5	7,425.4	4,082.5	--	850.2
12	TOYOTA MOTOR CORP	90,502.3	22,502.1	301.5	3,389.7	408.1	29,631.3	27,126.3	4,312.1	1,562.0	632.8	34.4
13	TIME WARNER INC	89,543.2	18,748.2	2,339.8	9,145.9	100.8	13,051.6	19,820.9	11,990.8	12,710.9	511.0	365.3
14	RJR NABISCO INC	88,252.4	20,948.0	3,087.8	2,796.2	14,313.4	33,151.9	2,728.4	5,915.4	5,151.6	207.7	48.0
15	GRAND METROPOLITAN PLC	87,621.9	17,488.2	630.5	320.1	2,278.7	31,224.9	16,227.6	13,614.8	3,901.7	--	1,935.4
16	NESTLE SA	87,417.0	29,457.6	645.5	225.5	80.1	35,252.9	17,865.6	9,028.1	3,144.6	--	715.1
17	KELLOGG CO	84,121.0	933.2	--	--	--	48,443.0	16,256.3	15,878.3	2,610.2	--	--
18	AMERICAN HOME PRODUCTS CORP	77,993.5	5,915.4	--	--	--	46,677.8	18,272.8	1,236.7	5,183.7	--	757.1
19	JOHNSON & JOHNSON	76,535.8	8,498.0	236.7	26.7	--	52,202.4	5,170.7	7,822.6	2,308.6	--	170.1
20	AMERICAN TELEPHONE & TELEGRAPH CO	67,291.5	2,170.2	1,144.3	4,039.2	219.3	38,086.5	7,940.3	4,833.7	3,208.0	5,120.7	1,028.7
21	VALASSIS INSERTS	66,959.3	--	--	66,959.3	--	--	--	--	--	--	--
22	HONDA MOTOR CO LTD	65,771.6	19,536.1	653.1	2,689.5	253.1	31,663.4	6,046.8	995.6	1,738.8	--	1,295.1
23	ANHEUSER-BUSCH COS INC	65,278.9	4,622.1	40.3	528.9	1,247.9	32,498.8	13,671.6	3,381.3	5,814.6	172.0	3,300.8
24	NISSAN MOTOR CO LTD	60,044.8	7,147.9	140.3	2,540.7	324.6	16,184.8	28,643.9	3,546.0	893.2	--	615.4
25	WARNER-LAMBERT CO	59,385.0	836.1	--	--	--	26,261.2	16,509.5	18,379.5	1,138.2	2,154.1	106.3
	TOP 25 TOTAL	2,750,406.4	395,146.4	14,537.1	260,614.1	40,458.1	1,139,728.4	544,656.5	227,556.0	118,614.1	42,119.2	35,196.5
26	COCA-COLA CO	58,587.9	2,507.5	141.5	460.4	475.5	30,889.6	13,059.7	6,403.7	2,160.9	550.0	1,869.1
27	WALT DISNEY CO	56,500.6	8,862.0	546.0	5,485.0	178.9	19,296.6	13,959.4	6,031.4	1,485.0	331.6	332.7
28	BRISTOL-MYERS SQUIBB CO	52,991.7	5,200.8	--	57.1	--	31,002.6	3,072.3	8,709.9	1,641.7	2,527.4	779.9
29	SONY CORP	52,813.5	15,563.3	14,604.8	7,549.3	68.1	7,152.6	4,532.8	1,691.1	1,140.2	190.2	321.1

Standard Directory of Advertisers (National Register Publishing Co.).

This directory gives listings of advertising companies by state and principal city. Information provided includes company/organization name, address, telephone, type of business, key management, advertising agency, advertising account executive, and amount spent on advertising. It is published annually but updated with biweekly bulletins. The classified section contains listings of companies in 51 product classes. Classifications are also noted by the SIC given at the beginning of each product classification. A trademark list of more than 50,000 names enables the subscriber to locate an advertiser's name when only the tradename is known.

Standard Directory of Advertising Agencies (National Register Publishing Co.).

The *Agency Red Book* is issued three times per year in February, June, and October. Among information included is number of employees, year founded, annual billings, breakdown of billings by media, agency specialization, branch offices, key personnel, major accounts, affiliation with associations, address, and telephone. Nine times per year the *Agency News Bulletin* is published as an update to the Red Book. Geographic and alphabetical listings are included.

Sources of Information on Advertising Effectiveness

Sources include academic or scholarly publications—reports on investigations into the effects that advertising influences on individuals and on society as a whole. It is here that in-depth discussions of the results of historical, longitudinal, experimental, and survey research programs can be found.

Some of the periodical sources mentioned previously, including BPI, also index material relating to scientific investigation of advertising effectiveness.

Psychological Abstracts (American Psychological Association, Inc.).

This source, which summarizes the "world's literature in psychology and related disciplines," is contained in two companion volumes, the abstract volume and an annual index volume. Index volumes for each year list subjects using psychological index terms, a short statement of the concepts contained in the original document, the type of document, a descriptive phrase, and an abstract number. The abstract can be found in the appropriate monthly issues of *Psychological Abstracts*. A "Thesaurus of Psychological Indexing Terms" is included.

Sociological Abstracts (Sociological Abstracts, Inc.).

Publications is sociology, anthropology, economics, education, philosophy, statistics, political science, and other areas are indexed by subject and author and abstracted in this source. It should be used in conjunction with the "Thesaurus of Sociological Indexing Terms."

Social Sciences Index (H. W. Wilson Co.).

SSI covers entries in more than 300 English-language periodicals in the fields of anthropology, economics, minority studies, political science, psychiatry, psychology, social work, sociology, urban studies, and others. Indexing is done by subject and author.

Other Sources

It should be noted that other, less obvious sources of information often are available to the researcher. Associations often compile information on their members and make the information available to nonmembers. Some large daily newspapers commission extensive local market surveys in an effort to provide potential advertisers with information about an area. Chambers of Commerce often publish compiled statistics on the local population and industries. In addition, the business news section of the local newspaper will provide coverage that national sources do not.

Using Data from Published Sources

Many times secondary research will turn up information in the form of numerical estimates, tables, or other presentations of quantitative information. As you might imagine, not all data from published sources is useful to the researcher. Below are some basic questions that should be asked to determine the value of published data.

1. Is it pertinent to the subject?
   Does the information located address the subject explicitly, or is it somehow peripheral to the main subject? Many times, especially in a database search where key words result in a number of articles off the mark, the data obtained does not fit the objectives of the study or contribute to answering the research question. Upon locating a number of articles, you should arrange them in order of how well they will contribute to your efforts to answer a research question.

2. Are the data in useable form?
   If you need numerical treatment of a subject, and the information you obtain is qualitative—such as depth interview transcripts—then it will be of limited value. Often an abstract or other description will include "tables" or "graphs" which might give a clue as to what an article or report contains. If raw data are available, you might want to use them in a statistical program to suit your special needs. Even in situations

---

where numerical data from several sources are located, difficulty inevitably arises in trying to directly compare data from studies with different samples done at different times and using different instruments of measurement.

3. Are the data reliable/objective?
   Accepting at face value the findings of a study for which you have no methodological information is a big leap of faith, and definitely not an advisable one. Is detailed information included as to how the sample was chosen, which data gathering methods were used, and what was the response rate? It is possible that the study is not generalizable to any larger group, especially if a convenience sample was used, and therefore caution should be used in extrapolating the results any further than the original study.

4. Are the data complete?
   Typically a published research study "hits the high points" of the findings and does not include a complete reporting of every aspect of the project. For instance, a report of advertising expenditures by category of product might not provide the same information by individual brand, in which case you must consult other sources.

5. Are the data current enough to be useful?
   Much published information is several years old, and its utility might be limited in view of current marketplace conditions such as new brand introductions, new media vehicles, and so forth. When quoting from a published study you should always be sure to say when the data were collected in the first place. Some reports are published regularly, such as the annual Advertising Age Leading National Advertisers special edition and Adweek's annual salary survey. Many of the syndicated research companies publish sales volume information on a quarterly basis.

6. Are the data available from the original source?
   Much published data appears in articles written by those other than the original researchers. In these cases, if the information is not reported in sufficient detail, it might be possible to obtain the research report from the original source, such as an industry organization, company, independent research firm, or university professor.

7. Does the report suggest other sources to consult?
   Many research reports or articles themselves contain a bibliography or other mention of related materials. The "paper trail" that results from locating sources listed in the bibliography of one report might well provide the type of data you require for your study. This is particularly true of academic research journal articles that often contain exhaustive reviews of related literature and bibliographies on a subject. Using this information can be a real time-saver.

Using Databases

Advances in computer technology have enabled huge volumes of text to be stored on mainframe computers. The contents of these files are made available to subscribers via telephone transmission. The expanded research avenues that this on-line database searching affords can appear mind-boggling, but as we will see, they are somewhat limited.

An on-line database is simply an accumulation of information from various sources, stored in increments called *records,* which can be searched and/or copies by a subscriber or user. Most database companies, or vendors, require that the user have only a terminal to display or print out the information generated from a search. Normally there is a charge incurred by users according to the number of minutes they are on-line, or in communication with the mainframe computer. Results of a search can either be printed out on-site by the user, which results in additional connect charges, or they can be mailed from the vendor in a few days. University libraries, public libraries, research firms, and some agencies and corporations can perform database searches. Users pay for the cost of the search and might incur a separate fee from the institution.

A handful of vendors dominate the market, among them System Development Corporation (SDC), Bibliographic Retrieval Services (BRS), and Dialog Information Services, the largest database vendor, with more than 200 databases.

Executing a Database Search

Using Dialog as an example, a researcher would first express the topic or question as briefly as possible, preferably in a single sentence. Usually the librarian will have a database search strategy sheet (see Figure 4–3), on which all the components of the search plan can be assembled. It is strongly suggested that the persons ordering the searches do a bit of manual searching beforehand to familiarize themselves with the range of relevant indexing terms for the topic and to crystallize the topic itself. In the example shown, the topic is "advertising by medical doctors."

Next, the idea must be reduced to key words or key concepts. Most research ideas involve the combination of two or more issues, areas, populations, etc. These components of the research topic must be identified separately, and then synonyms or spelling variations must be given. It is at this point that the searcher must try to anticipate the range of terms under which the current topic might appear. For our example, the terms *doctor, physician,* and *medical* were used as alternatives for the first search concept, and *advertising, promotion,* and *marketing* for the second. The identification of proper search terms and their various spellings is probably the most critical phase of the search planning process. Forgetting, ignoring, or misspelling an operant term could result in either generating a number of inappropriate references or missing a number of appropriate sources.

Figure 4-3
Doctors/advertising Search Sheet

Search Worksheet

DIALOG
INFORMATION SERVICES, INC.

Topic: Advertising by Doctors
Databases: ABI/INFORM

CONCEPT 1   CONCEPT 2   CONCEPT 3

doctors   advertising
physicians   promotion

AND   AND

OR

Sample TYPE commands:
Set number
Format number
Range of records

?t 3/6/1-4
?t 9/5/all

Format Number Guidelines:

Format 5   for FULL RECORD
Format 6 or 8   for BROWSING

DIALOG Bluesheets must be consulted for database-specific format descriptions.

9/85

Search Request Form

DIALOG
INFORMATION SERVICES, INC.

TO BE FILLED OUT BY REQUESTOR

Requestor Name: _____
Address: _____   Date: _____
Telephone: _____
Search Title: Advertising by doctors
Narrative Description of Topic: How many doctors use advertising to attract patients? What types of ads do they use? What do doctors/consumers think about the subject?

Date Required: _____
Known Authors or Articles: --

Types of Materials of Interest: All x   If not "All", specify as follows:
Articles _____   Reports _____   Patents _____   Conference Papers _____
Books _____   Dissertations _____   Other _____
Year to be Covered (only if such a limit is necessary) 1988 to present
Languages of Interest All   English
If not "All", specify those of interest: _____
How many relevant items do you think might be found?: _?_
Maximum amount to be spent: $20.00

TO BE FILLED OUT BY SEARCHER

Formats to be used: _____
Results to be done: TYPEd _____   PRINTed _____
Preliminary databases to consider: _____
Appointment scheduled for: (time) _____
Searcher Name: _____   Date _____

There are two basic methods of searching for information using key terms: "controlled vocabulary-based" and "free text-based." When an indexer for a database makes use of a predetermined list of terms (controlled vocabulary) to describe contents of documents, those terms are usually referred to as "descriptors." In free text searching, any key words, whether from controlled vocabularies or not, can be used to search a title, descriptor field, or depending on the database, the full text of an article. Theoretically, the use of descriptors helps the searcher hone in on the *most relevant* articles, since the descriptor presumably would reflect a major focus of the document. Free text searching, on the other hand, sometimes results in less relevant articles and documents, as *any* mention of the key word in the search field (title, descriptors, full text) would mean that article would be selected.

Choosing appropriate databases to be searched is the next step. A number of databases index primarily business-related information, and some index publications cover advertising and promotion. A good source to consult at this point is the *Directory of Online Databases,* published quarterly, for a complete listing of databases from the various vendors. Here are a few examples of databases that could be used in a business information search:

ABI/Inform (1971–present).

Provides coverage of more than 660 business and management periodicals. Aspects of business covered include new product development, competitive intelligence, marketing, advertising, and sales management.

PTS Promt (1972–present).

Covers articles on companies, industries, products, and marketing in over 1,100 magazines, trade journals, and newspapers.

PTS Mars (1984–present).

Marketing and Advertising Reference Service covers the subjects of advertising by media, agencies, campaigns, and regulations/ethics. Information is abstracted from 70 key publications.

Donnelley Demographics.

Data from the 1980 census and estimates and projections by Donnelley include information on age, sex, race, industry, occupation, marital status, households, income, and selected market data from Arbitron and A. C. Nielsen.

Findex (1977–present).

Indexes industry and market research reports, studies, and surveys commercially available from U.S. and international publishers.

National Newspaper Index.

Indexes the *New York Times* (1979–present), *The Wall Street Journal* (1979–present), the *Washington Post* (September 1982–present), the *Christian Science Monitor* (1979–present), and others.

Magazine Index.

Covers articles in more than 435 popular magazines for the period 1959–1970 and 1973 to the present.

Other databases not directly related to advertising and marketing cover a broad range of topics, from engineering to medicine to literature.

Next, the combination of sets, or concepts, must be specified so that the computer can put the search into motion. A procedure is used based on "Boolean logic," named after a British scientist who applied algebraic principles to the operations of logic.

The last command involves the output desired, whether the format should be bibliographic citation only, citation and abstract, etc. A decision must also be made about whether all relevant citations netted in the search are desired, or only a specified quantity, such as the first dozen. An example of output from a database search is shown is Figure 4–4.

Advantages of Database Searching

Broader search capabilities.

Database searching goes beyond mere subject headings. In most cases, the searcher can search a document by words in titles, descriptors, and sometimes by words in an abstract or even the full text. This enables the searcher to locate items that might not focus exclusively on the desired topic but that contain pertinent information. In some cases document types such as research studies, reviews, etc., can be specified.

Whereas in a typical manual search of indexes the searcher must separately pursue each concept associated with a topic, such as "doctors," then "advertising" (although indexes generally do have a certain number of pre-linked terms such as "advertising by doctors"), the computer search enables two or more concepts to be searched simultaneously. If the terms are being "and-ed" together, the output would look like this:

doctors	621	records
advertising	1,242	records
doctors AND advertising	37	records

Of course, only those items containing material on both doctors and advertising are of interest.

Figure 4-4
Output from a Database Search—Citation and Abstract

15/3,AB/17
88034722
    Price Hikes Loom for TV's Hot :15s; Magazines Plan Big Hikes
    Gay, Verne; Reilly, Patrick
    Advertising Age v59n36 PP: 1,3,62,64 Aug 29, 1988
    AVAILABILITY: ABI/INFORM

    A large demand for the limited amount of 15-second commercials on the 3
major television networks raises the probability of advertising price
increases. The popular 15-second format currently is priced at half the
cost of a 30-second commercial. ABC will be the first network to test the
market's reaction to a price increase by charging premiums for 15-second
commercials on selected fall 1988 telecasts. If the networks choose to
increase the supply of 15-second commercials available in a pod, ad clutter
and product protection will become major issues. Consumer magazine
publishers are planning advertising rate hikes of 6%-10% for 1989 due to
postage and paper cost increases. Rate increases at the higher levels will
add to pressure on magazines to give rate-card discounts. Increases of
8%-10% will be protested by ad agencies as more than paper cost increases.
Graphs.

Source: ABI/Inform.

Updating capabilities.

On-line databases often provide indexing to articles only weeks after publication and, in some cases, before a periodical is circulated. Most paper indexes take six weeks or more before providing coverage for the same time period.

Time savings/efficiency.

Depending on the nature and scope of the search, the computer can save the searcher a considerable amount of time. A manual search for information over a period of years requires that the searcher duplicate the search strategy with each volume of each index used. The computer can simultaneously search over a period of years, for a combination of concepts, and in some cases over more than one database.

Disadvantages of Database Searching

Systematic exclusion of certain materials.

All information sources have boundaries, and the computerized database is no exception. Most computerized databases index material no earlier than the late 1960s and 1970s, which does not enable the searcher to obtain relevant material before that time. Though most advertising searches probably would be of relatively recent information, often an original or "key" article is desired, and it will have to be found elsewhere.

Another systematic exclusion has to do with the types of documents available on-line. Most databases in the business area primarily contain research reports and journal articles. Books, though they are sometimes indexed, are not done so in any predictable fashion, so the searcher has no way of knowing if all applicable titles are included.

Inconsistency in indexing terms.

Not all databases are arranged using the same descriptors, and the use of an improper term could result in entire areas of relevant information being overlooked. As with paper indexes, the searcher should be aware of the idiosyncrasies of usage of various terms between databases. This is particularly important in the case of advertising and marketing topics, which because of their interdisciplinary nature often require a multi-database search. Often it is difficult to generate an exhaustive list of all appropriate terms under which the information could be indexed.

Cost.

On-line searching can range from $15 per hour to more than $300 per hour. Although the computer is highly efficient in terms of speed, a very simple search might require only a few minutes of manual searching. It all depends on the situation. If the search is being billed to an advertising agency client, the searcher should be able to justify the cost of the on-line connect time compared with other alternatives.

Lack of serendipity.

Anyone who has had the experience of being unable to find a word in the dictionary, only to spot it on the opposite page because he or she had an incorrect spelling, can attest to the role of serendipitous discovery. A computer is programmed to take instructions to the letter (this is intended both literally and figuratively), and it will never generate citations that were not requested properly. With computer output, we only see what was netted during the search; we never have the benefit of seeing what was nearby but not chosen. The lesson to be learned here is to be aware of inherent limitations in the database holdings and to recognize the precision with which the search must be conducted. In advertising, where many terms are used to refer to different phenomena, and where precision of definition often is lacking, extra care must be taken to choose proper key words and concepts.

Review

In this chapter we saw that:

- Secondary research is the process of searching for and gaining access to published information in books, periodicals, or one of many on-line computer databases.
- The benefits of secondary research are to answer specific questions definitively, to refine research questions, to help build detailed files of previous findings, to keep current with major developments, to suggest appropriate research methods, and to help position the current study.
- Sources of secondary research include professional organizations, such as the Advertising Research Foundation; research journals and scholarly publications such as the *Journal of Advertising Research;* trade publications, such as *Advertising Age;* general and special directories, industry and company overviews, survey reports, and indexes; and computer databases, such as DIALOG.

Chapter 5 Primary Research: An Overview

When secondary research results are not available or need to be supplemented by new data, primary research becomes necessary. As we saw in Chapter 4, whereas *secondary* research is the use of data that has previously been gathered or published by others, *primary* research is the gathering of new or original data to solve an advertising problem.

Almost everyone will recognize the names of the most common advertising research methods: market survey, opinion poll, homemaker panel, sweep, TV ratings and shares, focus group, life-style description, attitude change, tracking study, market experiment, the Nielsen TV meter and people-meter, Starch magazine readership, day-after TV recall, copy testing, "straw poll," Universal Product Code scanner, and so on.

You may even know about other less familiar types and methods—laboratory copy experiment, galvanic skin response (GSR), eye-movement camera, psychographics, electroencephalograph (EEG), content analysis, participant observation, segmentation study, program analyzer, split-cable experiment, electronic test marketing, random digit dialing, mall intercept, heavy-up weight testing, perceptual mapping, and Cloze procedure—perhaps even "garbology." The list seems formidable, but these can all be understood as variations on a few basic research designs, using the research notational system, or "alphabet," to be described in this chapter. We will explain what the common advertising research designs are, how they work, and how they can be used to simplify the research process.

The Research Design Alphabet: P, M, S, T

As a means of categorizing the many different types of research methods available, we have developed a notational or "alphabet" system. We think of it as a research method for people who hate research, as it avoids the use of highly statistical or technical jargon. Instead, the notational system describes research in terms of just four basic ingredients. Though simple, it is used by experienced researchers to plan even the most complicated research projects.

Just as the 26-symbol English alphabet can be used to communicate almost any message, the four-symbol research design alphabet—P, M, S, T—can be applied as a means of understanding or creating almost any research study.

P = One or more *populations* or groups of people (or things) under study

M = One or more *measurements* or observations of the population under study

S = Any stimulus presented to the population members or to which they're exposed

T = The timing or sequence in which measurement and stimulus occur

You can understand—and even plan—almost any research study by simply specifying the population(s), the measurement(s), the stimulus(s), and the time(s) when these events occurred. You can also analyze and critique published research or in advertising media and "selling" studies, so that you will know whether to believe in and use the data, rather than simply accept (or blindly reject) every "scientific study" you read.

How the Notational System Works

Researchers can use the notational system to create a diagram or model that gives an immediate visual overview of the basic ingredients of a particular research study. The population group or groups investigated are plotted on a vertical axis, and the horizontal axis becomes—from left to right—a timeline. The different measurements and stimuli are inserted as appropriate to indicate at what times and on which population groups they are used. For example, look at this *group comparison* design:

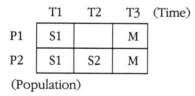

	T1	T2	T3	(Time)
P1	S1		M	
P2	S1	S2	M	

(Population)

This diagram shows that two groups (P1 and P2) were exposed to a stimulus (S1) at one point in time (T1). Later, group P2 was given a further stimulus (S2). Later still, the reactions of the two groups to the stimuli were measured (M) at time T3. As we work through the rest of this chapter, the purpose and applications of models like this will become clear to you.

To help you understand how any research study can be modeled into a design diagram of this type, let's review the most common types or genres of research studies and devise design diagrams for each.

Generic Research Design

A generic design may be regarded as an outline sketch of a research project. It serves the same purpose as an architect's first plan of a building, before all the detailed specifications are inserted. This helps the advertising professional analyze existing research, find its strengths and weaknesses, and evaluate the truth or falsehood of its conclusions. It also helps the professional plan original research studies. Just as an outline of a term paper serves as an aid to thinking and writing, the generic design of a planned research project can bring more reliable results. The precise notational system used here was invented by the author, Jack Haskins.[1]

The seven most common generic research designs and diagrams are listed below. They are explained in detail in this chapter.

1. One-shot design:

2. After-only or posttest-only design:

3. Panel-change design:

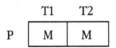

4. Group-comparison design:

5. Longitudinal-panel design:

T1   T2   T3   T4   T5

P | M | — | M | — | M |

6. Longitudinal-cohort design:

	T1	T2	T3
Pa	M	—	—
Pb	—	M	—
Pc	—	—	M

7. Before-and-after (pretest-posttest) design:

	T1	T2	T3
P	M	S	M

Why You Need to Know Research Design

Even if you are not a research specialist, you need to know research design simply because it can save you from the most horrible fate in advertising—the creation of a highly successful campaign which, because of the wrong research, either goes unnoticed or even appears to have had negative or boomerang effects. The wrong research design can make a winning campaign look like a losing campaign. This has happened uncounted times in the advertising business—the good guys have been fired and the bad guys have been promoted. For example, let's say the respected Juste-DeWitt Agency has mounted a special one-month advertising campaign for an established brand of men's underwear in the top 100 markets of the United States. Let's call them Condominimums, designed for short men who live in apartment houses. You have done all the necessary developmental and formative research, have spent a big advertising budget in the correct media with the best creative people creating the right messages at the right time. In short, let's assume you have done everything in this campaign just right.

For the sake of this example, let's imagine there is a big infra-red laser scanner in an orbiting satellite which can determine the true effectiveness of any advertising campaign, and let's assume that it has monitored sales of all products and has established that this campaign has been highly successful—incremental sales and incremental profits are in fact 25% higher because of this campaign. But let us also assume that, unfortunately, the Supreme Advertising Being has decided that no one can have access to this information—not you, not the agency, not the sponsor. Only after five years will it be possible to obtain and interpret the true advertising effectiveness data on your Condominimum campaign—a truly successful campaign by any standards. In the meantime you will have to use conventional research methods and research designs. And you'll be evaluated for promotion, raises, and professional competence on the basis of present-day research methods.

So, Juste-DeWitt Agency selects the most common but erroneous research design used to measure the sales effectiveness of advertising—the one that has sent a lot of good advertising people into door-to-door sales or worse. It's the before-and-after or pre- and-post-campaign design. Here's how the agency researched the effectiveness of the Condominimum campaign.

- Condominimum sales were measured during August 1991, the month before the campaign, at 4,000,000 sales.
- The massive new Condominimum campaign was run during September.
- Sales were measured in the month immediately after the campaign, October 1991, showing 3,000,000 sales.
- The apparent results of the campaign: a drop of one million sales, or a 25% decline in sales.

The research design notation looks like this:

	T1	T2	T3
P1	M1	S1	M1

P1 = The top 100 markets

M1 = All Condominimum unit-sales

S1 = New advertising campaign

T1 = August, 1991

T2 = September, 1991

T3 = October, 1991

The sales results look like this:

Before campaign: 4,000,000 units
After campaign: 3,000,000 units
Change after campaign: minus 1,000,000 units

The campaign apparently not only failed, it seemed to have had *negative* effects—the boomerang effect resulting in fewer sales than without the campaign.

The client was furious. Why were Condominimum sales down? Right away, of course, the agency started looking for loopholes, ways to dress up the data, looking for flaws in the research.

Many possible explanations were thought of, explored, and found fruitless. In the end, by all the possible measures of advertising effectiveness—sales, attitudes, share-of-market, seasonally corrected data, total profits, profit per dollar invested, everything—the Condominimum campaign had apparently failed miserably. Condominimum, naturally, moved its account—to the flashy but unscrupulous Magic Ad Aid Agency. The brilliant Juste-DeWitt account executive and the award-winning creative chief were demoted with a cut in salary. The copywriter resigned in despair.

Five years later, the true results of the campaign proved that the creative and media teams were not at fault. It was the incompetence of the research people at the agency and the client company that was to blame—the campaign had, in fact, been very successful—*but the before-and-after-campaign research design could not detect it*. All the rest of the research had been done correctly—sampling, measurement, data analysis, interpretation. Only the research *design* was wrong—and that was fatal.

The correct research design—a controlled field experiment, probably in the form of a randomized markets experiment—would have detected the true effects of the campaign. Despite the fact that DuPont, Ford, and many other sophisticated advertisers have been accurately measuring campaign effects with the field experiment design for more than three decades, many companies and agencies still don't do any campaign effectiveness research or use poor research methods, or the wrong research design.

Here's how the Juste-DeWitt agency could have used the correct randomized markets field experiment design:

- Two hundred markets would have been randomly divided into two equivalent groups of 100 each, designated as P1a and P1b (samples *a* and *b* of the 200-market population, P1).

- P1a markets would receive the *usual* Condominimum campaign; the P1b group would receive the *new* campaign, in September.

- All other market conditions and research methods would remain the same, resulting in the following design:

	T1	T2	T3
P1a	M1	S1	M1
P1b	M1	S2	M1

P1a, P1b = 2 equivalent groups of 100 cities each

T1, T2, T3 = August, September, October

M1 = Total unit sales

S1 = Usual campaign (treatment stimulus 1)

S2 = New campaign (treatment stimulus 2)

This design would have shown the following results:

- In the usual campaign (S1), 4,000,000 sales the month before the campaign, 2,000,000 sales afterwards: net, minus 2,000,000 sales.

- In the new campaign (S2), 4,000,000 before, 3,000,000 the month after: net, minus 1,000,000 sales.

- *True* campaign effects: net, plus 1,000,000 sales. The true effect of the new campaign is 1,000,000 incremental sales—one million more than the usual campaign produced.

Thus though the new campaign was more successful than the old one, the agency was fired because researchers used the wrong research design while the product market was declining.

Common Types of Advertising Research

Let's continue our discussion of the notational systems by looking at diagrams for the simplest types of advertising research. These are:

1. The market survey
2. The day-after-advertising recall study
3. The attitude change study
4. The market comparison study
5. The homemaker panel
6. The tracking study
7. The before-and-after advertising study.

1. The Market Survey (a one-shot design)

The purpose is to get some descriptive information from a specified group of people about something. For example, market surveys can collect information on shopping habits, media use, advertising exposure, product attitudes, and more through mail, telephone, or personal interview questionnaires.

Example.

Imagine you are the marketing manager for the Plymouth minivan, and you wish to assess owner satisfaction both with the minivan and with dealer service when purchases were made. You decide to send a short questionnaire to all Plymouth minivan owners as of August 1991 in Longwood, Florida, on which you ask three simple questions.

1. Are you satisfied with your purchase?
2. Where did you make your purchase?
3. Are you satisfied with dealer service?

The research design diagram would look like this:

T1

P1 | M1—M3

P1 = 2,473 car owners described above

T1 = August 1991

M1, M2, M3 (or M1—M3) = Answers to questions 1–3

Generic design type: One-shot
Data-gathering method: Mail survey

Discussion.

You will note that the *generic* one-shot design does not use specific numbers with P and M, i.e.

T

P | M

However, *specific* studies must use number designations.

Any study in which one simply goes out and measures something on one occasion, for purely descriptive purposes, has the generic label of a *one-shot* design. The market survey is simply one of many possible variants on that design. Note that there can be several measures in any study. In fact, most surveys have dozens of questions/measures, including some standard demographic and classification questions. However, in the notational diagram we only note those of direct relevance to the study at hand. Notice that no stimulus (S) is mentioned in the research diagram, even though a mail questionnaire and a question are necessary in order to elicit (stimulate) the answer (measurement or M). Two rules need to be used here: First, in surveys, both the question-asked and the data-gathering-method (mail survey, in this case) are considered to be part of the measurement process and not a separate stimulus. Second, since we are in fact constantly in the midst of all kinds of stimuli all the time, it would be impossible to record them all in the research diagram. Consequently only those stimuli that are directly relevant to the research study are recorded in the diagram, as you will see in the next example.

Besides the market survey, other examples of a one-shot design might be:

- A focus group discussion on "irritating" commercials
- A content analysis of newspaper ads for use of color
- A mall intercept study of women's favorite TV programs

2. The Day-after-Advertising Recall Study (an after-only or posttest design)

The purpose is to determine whether a group of people can remember an advertising message and correctly associate it with the sponsor. They are questioned by telephone the day after an ad has appeared on television or in newspapers or in some other medium.

Example.

Sea World wants to find out if its advertising agency is doing a good job in terms of media selection and message effectiveness. The company engages a local research firm to conduct a telephone survey of Orlando metropolitan households. The goal is to determine the extent of exposure to and recall of a Sea World TV commercial that was broadcast over several local stations on the evening of August 28, 1991. (The company is aware, of course, of all the research that demonstrates that recall of an advertisement is not related to actual sales. Some very sales-effective advertisements have low recall, while many high-recall advertisements have little demonstrable effect on increasing sales.) The telephone survey is carried out the day after a Sea World commercial is aired.

The research design diagram looks like this:

	T1	T2
P1	S1	M1, M2

P1 = TV households in the Orlando metropolitan area (several counties) that subscribe to a telephone service

S1 = Sea World commercial

T1 = August 28 at 9:58 p.m. EST (the time when the commercial aired)

T2 = August 29 (the date of the telephone survey)

M1 = Question on TV viewing the previous evening

M2 = Question on recall of Sea World commercial

Generic design type: After-only or posttest only
Data-gathering method: Telephone survey

Discussion.

Note the use of numbers with P, M, and S, as distinguished from the generic design. Any study in which measurement of a group takes place after the group has been exposed to some stimulus is called an after-only or posttest design. The day-after-advertising exposure recall study is just a frequently used variant on the generic design.

Further examples of after-only research designs include:

- Starch ad readership studies
- Diary records of TV programs viewed

3. The Attitude-Change Study (a panel-change design)

The purpose is to determine whether attitudes toward a product or advertiser have improved or declined over some period of time. To do this, one simply measures an attitude at two different points in time.

Example.

The Ford Motor Company wants to know if attitudes of owners of a particular popular model, the Taurus, are becoming more favorable or less favorable toward the entire Ford Motor Company during the first year after they buy the Taurus. (This study starts from the hypothesis that the well-designed Taurus might improve their attitudes toward the whole company.) From the national registry of new car buyers, the Ford advertising research manager gets the names of 20,197 people who bought the new 1990 Taurus and then mails to them in February a one-page questionnaire that includes an attitude-toward-Ford scale (along with several other questions which don't concern us here). Then, in February 1991, the research manager administers again the same question to the same people. Here's the research design diagram:

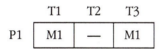

P1 = Buyers of new 1990 Taurus

M1 = Attitude toward Ford Motor Co.

T1 = February 1990

T2 = March 1990 to January 1991

T3 = February 1991

Generic design type: Panel-change design
Data-gathering method: Mail survey

Discussion.

Any study in which the same population or group is measured on two or more occasions is called a *panel design*. If the same measure is taken on two occasions, it is a *panel-change design*. The attitude change study is just one variation on the generic type. In this example, the same measure (M1) was administered twice,

---

a year apart. This made it possible to measure improvement or decline in consumers' general attitude toward Ford during that period. Other examples of the panel-change design include:

- 1985–1990 awareness of advertisements for office products (survey)
- 1989–1990 usage of male and female actors on TV programs (content analysis)

4. The Market Comparison Study (a group-comparison design)

The purpose is to compare two or more groups of people or geographic regions to determine if and how they differ on some measure such as brand purchasing, product purchasing, market share, media habits, demographic characteristics, or any other measurable quality. It might be as simple as comparing men and women on their favorite TV shows, or as complex as comparing 40 different zip-code-consumer-types on psychographic characteristics. Both of these cases can be reduced to the same basic study type—the market comparison study—and the same basic group-comparison design.

Example.

Chevrolet wants to compare the Midwest with New England, the Southeast, and the Pacific Coast on two different measures: Chevrolet purchases during 1991 and "free publicity"—the number of times Chevrolet is mentioned in major city newspaper stories. The research design diagram for market comparison of four geographic regions looks like this:

	T1
P1	M1, M2
P2	M1, M2
P3	M1, M2
P4	M1, M2

P1 = New England

P2 = Southeast

P3 = Midwest

P4 = Pacific Coast

M1 = Number of Chevrolet sales in 1991 (obtained from automotive industry sales registration data)

M2 = Free publicity (content analysis; number of mentions of Chevrolet in major city newspapers in 1991)

T1 = A 12-month period from January to December 1991

Generic design type: Group comparison

Two data-gathering methods: Sales audit (analysis of sales records) and content analysis (of newspapers)

Discussion.

Any study in which two or more populations or groups of objects are compared is a *generic group comparison* design, and the market comparison is just one variation. In this example, we use not the ubiquitous question-and-answer survey but two other data-gathering methods: sales figures taken from audit records and instances of free publicity taken from content analysis of newspapers. Look at the diagram and ask yourself this question: If the actual data gathering and measurement took place in 1992, why does the diagram show M1 and M2 occurring in 1991? The answer is that because our purpose is to show what happened in 1991, the diagram should show when the actions or behavior, the stimuli, and/ or measurements actually occurred, not when the research was conducted. Even if we waited until 1995 to analyze what happened in 1991, the diagram should reflect what we really want to know—what happened in 1991. Further examples of group comparison designs would be the following:

- Content analysis to determine the use of color in advertisements from *several different magazines*
- Audit of station records to discover the level of competitive advertising on radio stations in *cities of different sizes*

5. The Homemaker-Panel Study (a longitudinal-panel design)

The usual purpose is to measure the attitudes, purchases, and behaviors of the same group of homemakers at intervals over a long period of time. By recruiting a continuing "panel" of househusbands and housewives, instead of a different group for each study, the results are more comparable and the data-gathering is simpler. This is merely one application of the generic longitudinal-panel design.

Example.

The makers of Howdy Doody Chocolate Laxative for Kids are not convinced that data gathered from a question-and-answer survey are accurate indicators of what people actually buy. Therefore, they decide to do a "validation" study to determine whether survey information is a valid predictor of actual behavior. Thus, a homemaker panel group is measured at four different times using both telephone survey and the "garbology" method (the group's garbage is examined to see what people have actually bought and used).

Here's the research design diagram:

	T1	T2	T3	T4	T5	T6	T7
P1 (I)	M1, M2	—	M1, M2	—	M1, M2	—	M1, M2

P1 = 13,452 homemakers in the national panel maintained by a commercial research firm. (The firm sells the list in whole or in part on a one-time or frequent-use basis to a number of different clients.)

P1(I) = A subgroup of P1 made up of 511 homemakers with children under age 12 in the Orlando area. Note: This is not a random sample.

T1 = 15 January 1991 to 22 January 1991

T3 = One month after T1

T5 = Two months after T1

T7 = Six months after T1

T2, T4, T6 = Time between measurements

M1 = Telephone survey questions, such as "How much, and what brands, of children's laxative have you bought in the last month?"

M2 = "Garbology" study (inspection of discarded packages in homemakers' garbage) to determine number and brands of laxatives used in households.

Generic design type: Longitudinal panel
Two data-gathering methods: Telephone survey and observation (of discarded garbage)

Any study in which the same group is measured on several different occasions is a *longitudinal panel* design, and the homemaker panel is just one of many variations on that generic design. Note the use of the designation P1(I) to indicate that a large population group is broken down into smaller, selective subgroups for testing, not a random sample P1a. Further examples of a longitudinal-panel design include:

- Quarterly count of amount of direct-mail advertising received in homes (physical traces)
- Annual count of customer complaints (records)

6. The Tracking Study (a longitudinal-cohort design)

Whereas the longitudinal-panel design examines the *exact same* group of people over time, the longitudinal-cohort design uses different samples from the same population group. The purpose of this design is to determine changes in the same population over several periods of time by using a different representative sample of the population each time.

The term *cohort* means an exactly equivalent, but different, sample of the same population. While the purpose is the same as that of the longitudinal-panel design, the use of different samples prevents an earlier measurement from influencing later ones. And sometimes different samples are easier to get than searching out the original sample. Another name for the tracking study is the *continuing attitude study*.

Example.

In a continuing attitude study of automobile buyers, Ford keeps track of the attitudes of the nation's "principal drivers" (a broad definition of Ford's target market) at three-month intervals. Attitudes include, among other things: brand awareness, advertising awareness, car "image," car attitude, and six-month buying intentions. Attitudes toward all immediately competitive makes or cars as well as the Ford brand are studied. Here is the design diagram:

	T1	T2	T3	T4
P1a	M1–M5	—	—	—
P1b	—	M1–M5	—	—
P1c	—	—	M1–M5	—
P1d	—	—	—	M1–M5

P1 = All "principal drivers" in the United States

P1a = A random sample from P1, N = 800

P1b = A different but equivalent random sample

P1c = A different but equivalent random sample

P1d = A different but equivalent random sample

M1 = The "brand awareness" question: "When you think of low-priced cars, which brand comes to mind first?" (Answers to this question are a very good predictor of actual sales.)

M2 = The "advertising awareness" question: "When you think of automobile advertising, which car's advertising comes to mind first?"

M3 = Several car "image" questions, such as "Thinking of just Ford, Chevrolet, and Plymouth, which one has the most comfortable ride?" (most attractive styling, fewest squeaks and rattles, fewest repair problems, best value for the money, etc.)

M4 = An attitude question, such as "Which of the cars named do you like best?"

M5 = A buying intention question, such as "If you were going to buy a car in the next six months, which one would you most likely buy?"

T1, T2, T3, T4 = Feb., May, Aug., Nov. 1991

Generic research design: Longitudinal-cohort
Data-gathering method: Personal-interview survey

Discussion.

Any study in which we follow a group's attitude and/or behavior over a period of time is a longitudinal design. In this case we used the *longitudinal-cohort* design, instead of the longitudinal-panel design. (There is another type, the *longitudinal-trend* design.) Each has its advantages and limitations, and reasons for picking one over the other will be discussed later. The tracking or continuing attitude study is just one variant of the longitudinal-cohort generic design. In this case, measurement occurred on four occasions; therefore, four equivalent groups, random samples from the same population, were needed.

Note the difference between P1a, the first group in this study, with P1(I) in the previous example. The former designates a random sample from P1. The latter is a deliberately chosen subgroup that is not representative of the total P1. This is an important distinction, as will be seen.

Examples of other longitudinal cohort designs are as follows:

- Public opinion surveys of the U.S. population at five-year intervals
- Syndicated media usage studies (such as those published by Simmons) of U.S. adults every other year

7. The Before-and-After Advertising Study (a pre- and post-design)

The usual purpose of the before-and-after-advertising study, or pre-post advertising study, is to get a very rough indication of an advertising campaign's effects. A common method is to measure both sales and attitudes before a campaign begins, then measure the same group after the campaign ends. This is the design used in the "horrible fate" example earlier in this chapter.

Example.

Plymouth is about to launch an advertising campaign in the middle of a model year to appeal to a very specific target market: the affluent 55-and-over age group. The advertised product is the Silver Panther minivan, customized with special features for the senior traveler. Plymouth decides to conduct a before-and-after-advertising study to get a rough indication of the campaign's effectiveness. (The researcher did not realize, as many marketing people don't, that a much more accurate measure of campaign effects could have been obtained with a split-run or split-cable experiment at very little extra cost and effort). In its simplest form, the research design diagram would look like this:

	T1	T2	T3
P1	M1	S1	M1

You simply take a group of people from the target market, measure their car purchases (M1) during the first month, then you stage the campaign (S1) during the next month, then measure sales again (M1) in the third month.

However, now that you have learned the research notational system, let's use a more realistic, and slightly more detailed, example from the real world—and learn a little about advertising into the bargain.

	T1	T2	T3	T4	T5	T6	T7
P1a	M1	S1	S2	S3	M1	—	M1

P1 = All subscribers to *Modern Maturity* magazine (N = 20,000,000)

P1a = A representative random sample of P1 drawn from *Modern Maturity*'s mailing list (N = 1 million)

T1 = January 1991 (before campaign)

T2, T3, T4 = February, March, April (campaign period)

T5 = May 1991 (just after campaign)

T6 = June to August 1991 ("gestation" period)

T7 = September 1991 (five months after the campaign)

M1 = New Silver Panther sales

S1 = Silver Panther Ad 1: 4-page spread

S2 = Ad 2: 2-page spread

S3 = Ad 3: 1-page ad

Generic design type: Before-and-after or pretest-posttest design
Data-gathering method: Sales audit

Discussion.

Any study in which a population is measured before a stimulus is presented and again afterward is a generic before-and-after or pretest-posttest design. In this case, there were several stimuli and several measurement occasions.

The campaign consisted of three advertisements. If sales had been measured all through the campaign, perhaps to detect monthly sales changes, the design might be called a before-during-and-after study as a minor variation. Though only one measure is designated above, there could be several more sales measures, such as:

M1 = Number of Silver Panther minivans purchased

M2 = "Regular" Plymouth minivans purchased

M3 = All Plymouth models purchased

M4 = Dodge minivans purchased

M5 = Competitive makes of minivans purchased

M6 = All makes and models of new cars purchased

This would enable Plymouth to measure Silver Panther sales and also whether there had been any "rub-off" advertising effects on other Plymouth minivans, on other Plymouth models, and even on Dodge and Chrysler sales. These additional measures also determine changes in "share of market" (SOM), the Silver Panther's share of the Plymouth minivan market, of the total minivan market, and of the total car market. SOM, a measure derived form sales figures, is often more useful than absolute sales figures in determining market position or advertising effects. The additional measures above would show whether sales of Silver Panthers represent

1. Additional sales that would not otherwise have occurred,
2. Simply "borrowed" sales from other Plymouth, Chrysler, or Dodge purchases, or
3. Stolen sales from competitors.

By measuring sales five months (or longer) after the campaign, we can also determine the following:

1. Whether there is a time lag between advertising and sales. If so, the just-after measurement alone would not have detected total purchases.
2. Were these additional (i.e., incremental) sales or merely accelerated buying (i.e., simply speeding up purchases that would have been made anyway)?

As we have seen, this design is not always a good indicator of advertising's sales effects. Too many outside influences can affect results. More will be said later about improving designs to determine cause and effect and find out the degree to which advertising influences sales or attitudes.

Other examples of before-and-after designs might be:

- Grocery store sales volume before and after installing commercials in in-store music programs

- Numbers of people looking directly at a billboard before and after a three-dimensional image of Madonna is installed

Review

In this chapter we saw that:

- Most primary research studies, both simple and complex, are variations on a few basic research designs, symbolized with the letters P (population), M (measurement), S (stimulus), and T (timing).
- Seven common generic research designs are the following:
    1. One-shot design
    2. After-only or posttest-only design
    3. Panel-change design
    4. Group comparison design
    5. Longitudinal-panel design
    6. Longitudinal-cohort design
    7. Before-and-after or pretest-posttest design

    A specific advertising study for each of these designs has been exemplified.
- The research design notation can be used to help the researcher analyze existing research, find its strengths and weaknesses, and evaluate the truth or falsehood of its conclusions, as well as to help plan original research studies.

Endnote

1. A more detailed description of the P, M, S, T notational system may be found in "A Precise Notational System for Research Planning and Analysis," Jack B. Haskins, *Evaluation Review,* 1981.

6 Qualitative Research: An Overview

One way to categorize research methods is by their analysis orientation. *Quantitative research* involves the collection and translation of information into statistical data (hard numbers). Some typical techniques are TV viewer counts, the use of scanners in supermarkets to record purchases, market experimentation tied into sales results, and simple question-and-answer surveys. Quantitative research is covered in detail in Chapters 7–10; this chapter discusses qualitative research.

Qualitative research is exploratory in nature and elicits in-depth, often subjective responses that are not measurable in hard numbers. Researchers seek qualitative data to form an *impression* rather than a *definition* of a market or population group. Open-ended questions, in-depth interviews, and focus groups are all common qualitative methods.

The Advertising Research Foundation defines qualitative research as follows:

> The intent of qualitative research is to gain insights concerning consumer attitudes, beliefs, motivations and behaviors. When creatively and perceptively analyzed and reported, qualitative research offers insights which go beyond the surface. The qualitative research approach provides "feel," "texture," a sense of intensity, and a degree of nuance. Qualitative research is usually reported discursively, often in respondents' own words. Qualitative research typically uses a relatively small sample and relies on non-directive, semi-structured interviews.[1]

Quantitative and qualitative research, used separately or in conjunction, make unique contributions to collecting and evaluating information on particular topics.

Reasons for Using Qualitative Research

- *As an idea generation tool:* To observe consumer interaction with products; to study reactions to advertising, brand names, or packaging; or for creative brainstorming.

- *To aid in development of a quantitative study:* To develop research hypotheses; to identify target consumers, such as purchase decision makers, for quantitative studies; to identify issues associated with a product or with advertising; or to select and refine materials to be used in quantitative studies, namely questions for questionnaires.
- *As follow-up to a quantitative study:* To explore reasons for findings in a quantitative study or to describe factors contributing to attitude change.
- *As and end in itself:* In some cases that do no lend themselves to quantitative analysis, qualitative methods are the techniques of choice. Some advertising agencies rely almost exclusively on qualitative research for their consumer input and for copy testing.

Qualitative Research Methods

The most frequently used qualitative methods are projective techniques, depth interviews, dyadic interviews, and focus group interviews. Let's look at each in detail.

Projective Techniques

John Pigram, senior account planner at Livingston & Company, a Seattle advertising agency, considers projective techniques "enabling techniques," because they allow consumers to talk about their emotions rather than discuss topics on a rational basis. Projective techniques enable people to inject their feelings into otherwise ambiguous stimuli, as we will see with the examples below.

The possibilities for the use of projective techniques in focus groups or other settings are many. Researchers often use projective techniques toward the end of focus group sessions, after a group has "warmed up" enough to offer their emotional input. In some cases, a single technique is used, while in other situations a variety of techniques or combinations of techniques are introduced. Following are a few common projective techniques used in interviewing consumers.

Word association.

This exercise calls for participants to list any words that come to mind when a brand name, category, product, or person is mentioned. It is argued by those who employ word association exercises that much can be learned from such responses that might not come to light in a more "rational" conversation. As with all projective techniques, it is important for the interviewer or moderator to facilitate an un-inhibited volunteering of ideas—in this case, words. An example of a word association question is "When I say Lotsafizz soda, what words come to mind?"

The moderator and other group members should not discourage participants from declaring their candid responses.

In the example of Figure 6–1, pleasure travelers over the age of 60 were asked to name potential titles or words that came to mind when a magazine targeted to their travel needs were described. The sessions with the mature travelers were held in part to generate possible titles for a new magazine directed to senior citizens who travel frequently. With the exception of the proposed title *Extravaganza,* most of the responses emphasized longer, well-planned vacations that were educational and enriching, as opposed to "getaway" travel, which is the focus of many travel articles. Indeed, older travelers have different needs and expectations of their travel experiences than younger travelers.

Figure 6–1
Word Association with Senior Citizen Focus Group

"Which words come to mind when you think of the mature travel magazine just described?"

Extravaganza	*Exploration*
Around the World	*Adventure Travel*
Travel Time	*Travel Wise*
Destinations	*Travel Adventure*
Travel Companion	*Travel Digest*

Analogies.

An analogy is a relation of likeness between two things or of one thing with another. When talking with consumers, it is often quite instructive to learn what they think a product or brand is "like," or if it has similarities to other objects, people, places, and so forth. The interviewer's job is to encourage a respondent to make a meaningful connection between the product or brand in question and some other referent. A typical question here might be: "If Car X were an animal, what would it be?"

In this case, the "code set," or entity to which a connection is to be made, is animals. Some researchers prefer to suggest that respondents employ code sets closer to their personal situations, such as likening a brand to one of their friends or a family member. These comparisons, they contend, are more likely to be emotional, because they refer to personalities and personal relationships. Whatever the code set, results of a session in which analogies are elicited can reveal quite a bit about consumer perception of a brand. If, for instance, a company or store is likened to "my penny-pinching uncle who always tried to shortchange me," a major rethinking of the establishment's relationship with its customer might be needed.

Projections.

One way to elicit emotional responses to brand or product stimuli is to ask a respondent to describe "what your mother (or others) would think of you" in certain product-usage or brand-choice situations. Projections are often elicited by way of sentence completion exercises in which a sentence is begun by the interviewer and completed by the respondent, for example, "If I purchased a BMW, my friends would say . . . . Proponents of this technique claim that it is often easier for people to express feelings when they can attribute them to someone else, such as a relative or friend. And because reference groups play such an important part in consumer behavior, it is useful to note how an individual consumer believes a member of a reference group might react.

Bubble drawings.

"Bubble" drawings are so named because of the dialog balloon placed above a person or object in a rough illustration involving a product or brand under study. Respondents are asked to supply dialog or thoughts for the person. Like other projective techniques, bubble drawings allow respondents to "speak through someone else" about their own attitudes or convictions. In some cases, a person in the illustration is pictured performing an action, and a second person's dialog balloon is available to comment on the action. In other cases, a respondent can provide words for one product to talk about another product. Some illustrations show the back of a person's head. The purpose for this is to encourage the respondent to "see through his or her eyes" and predict what he or she would say.

The example in Figure 6–2 is the classic use of a dialog balloon. The illustration shows people having a conversation to which the respondent is asked to contribute. In this particular case, a mail survey was commissioned by a newspaper publisher seeking input from people who had placed personal classified ads—a way of meeting people that many singles prefer to dating services—to determine whether they would recommend that course of action to a friend. The same illustration was sent to nonusers of the personal classifieds to measure any differences of opinion between those who had and had not used them. The bubble drawing technique constituted one page of a six-page questionnaire, which was mailed to a random sample of readers who did or did not use the service.

Photosorts.

A number of techniques involve a series of photographs from which respondents are asked to select an image for a particular brand. A wide selection of photos of different people, the same person with different expressions, zany drawings, animals, or other subjects is usually provided.

One application of the photosort technique is used in the Foote, Cone & Belding Visual Image Profiles (VIP) procedure. One hundred photos of 50 men and 50 women have been evaluated for personality and life-style characteristics by a sample of American consumers. The photos are used in consumer research to profile brand users, identify brand personalities, and personalize communication messages. Respondents are handed a set of photos and asked to "read" the faces by choosing the ones they feel are related to the brand or the brand user. The belief behind the VIP is that the human face can convey feelings through its expressiveness and that vivid profiles of a brand can result from the sorting of visual cues such as photographs.

In another variation of the photosort method, pictures of celebrities are provided, and respondents must choose which celebrities are suited to which brand, after which they are asked their rationale for doing so. Again, the suggestion here is that often consumers find it easier to associate a product or brand with a personality, mood, or celebrity image than to enumerate the reasons why they like or dislike the product. Researchers must be careful in choosing celebrity photos or names that are known to all respondents—a difficult matter to deal with sometimes—to obtain the best results. Otherwise, the nonfamiliarity of subjects with celebrities might affect responses.

Figure 6–2
Example of a Dialog Balloon

Source: Reprinted with permission of the *Dallas Observer.*

Brand obituaries.

"If Lotsafizz soda 'died' tomorrow, how would it be remembered?" This sort of question would allow respondents to write a product "epitaph," which provides an opportunity for them to project their own feelings on an otherwise neutral object—the tombstone. An epitaph for a person is intended to capture his or her personality, spirit, or image; the brand obituary or epitaph exercise is designed to elicit "bottom line" feelings about a brand. In this case, the consumer has the "last word" about the brand, and an unflattering response could give clues to the root of an image problem.

Storytelling

Storytelling, in which participants begin or finish a story involving a brand, product, or situation, can result in valuable qualitative information on brand image, product performance, and target markets. Storytelling can be particularly effective in copy development, as individual respondents are shown rough or finished advertisements and asked to tell a story about the characters, the scenario, or the product. A major by-product of storytelling is knowledge of the consumer "vocabulary" for a product category, an important tool in copy development. Proponents of the storytelling technique claim that advertising pictures are "worth a thousand words," and that consumers, if given a chance to tell a story about what they see, will offer a wealth of information different from that elicited through more traditional and less flexible survey procedures.

Little if any methodological research is available on the use of projective techniques in marketing and advertising. Yet it is clear that much can be learned about the subtleties of consumer evaluation from their use.

Depth Interviews

One-to-one, semi-structured interviews with consumers can tell a great deal about individual consumer behavior or about feelings and attitudes toward brands or products. If it is felt that the group interview scenario could suppress participation by certain nonusers of a product, for instance, then the less-threatening, single-subject depth interview may be preferred. And in cases where group interviews allow little time for individual participants to offer enough information on a given question, or when the time allocated expires before the entire agenda has been covered, depth interviews are an excellent means of filling in the gaps.

One drawback of the depth interview is the lack of group interchange and group dynamics. The interviewee cannot respond to alternative points of view, and ideas cannot be triggered by the remarks of another. Cognizant of this fact, the interviewer must compensate for the lack of group exchange by taking an active role in drawing out the participant and touching on all relevant points.

Dyadic Interviews

Interviewing two people simultaneously can offer a variety of interesting combinations that might prove fruitful in terms of depth and quality of responses. For instance, the twosome to be interviewed, depending on the nature of the information sought, could both be users or nonusers of the product, or one could be a user and one a nonuser, one male and one female, etc. Caution must be exercised to prevent awkward and nonproductive pairings, and, as with any extended interview, the interviewer must be highly skilled in eliciting the most accurate and detailed information possible.

Focus Group Interviews

The focus group is by far the most widely used of the qualitative research methods. It is an in-depth discussion of a specific topic by a group of eight to ten carefully selected participants. Focus groups require detailed planning of both recruiting participants and deciding content for discussion.

Using a carefully constructed agenda or interview guide, a trained moderator leads the session, which can be observed, usually behind a one-way mirror, by sponsors of the research. Typically, the interview is videotaped and/or audiotaped for later reference and analysis.

Agenda.

A detailed, structured agenda is essential for a successful focus group meeting. It will act as a guide during the session and will reflect the objectives of the research project and of each research question. When more than one focus group is conducted by the same or different moderators as part of the same project, a strong agenda is indispensable. It will keep each group on track and ensure that the same ground is covered. The moderator uses the agenda primarily as an organizational tool, so that a basic structure can be followed during the discussions. Generally speaking, the agenda begins with fairly general questions and progresses to more complex or specific items. Within each area of questioning, broad questions are posed and then followed up with more evocative, or *probe,* questions. The agenda indicates when stimulus materials are to be shown.

Moderator/interviewer.

The moderator is responsible for guiding participants through the agenda and balancing the small-group dynamics to ensure contributions from all interviewees. While there is no single profile of an effective moderator's credentials, previous experience with group interviewing and good recommendations are desirable. Academic training in the social sciences can be good preparation, but good focus group interviewers come from diverse backgrounds.

Not all experts agree on the most effective style of communication for a moderator to adopt. Some moderators are quite successful in playing a low-key, passive role, while others are more active, sometimes playing the "devil's advocate." It is essential that moderators maintain an air of objectivity and distance from the research sponsor, lest they compromise their rapport with participants. The choice of a male or female moderator generally is not an issue, unless the material to be discussed is gender-specific or unusually sensitive.

Participants.

Following the directives of the research client, the focus group recruiter seeks to locate and enlist the participation of people who fit the designated demographic, geographic, and product-usage profile. This is usually accomplished through a questionnaire containing screening questions, or *screeners,* the answers to which serve to qualify or disqualify potential participants. Respondents usually are compensated with cash or gifts for their time. Payments range from $20 to $100, depending on the nature of the respondent and the difficulty of recruiting.

Several issue associated with the choice of participants must be dealt with on a project-by-project basis. One issue is whether to have *homogeneous* or *heterogeneous* groups; for instance, should men and women be recruited for the same discussion groups, or should users and nonusers be grouped together? The researcher's overriding concern should not be whether the groups are alike or different in some way, but whether such sameness or difference will enhance or inhibit the end product—honest, meaningful discussion.

Another issue is that of familiarity among group discussion participants. While it might seem that people who know each other socially might be likely to discuss matters more openly together than in the company of strangers, in fact the opposite has been found. In one recent study it was found that a greater volume of ideas was generated in nonfamiliar groups than in groups whose members were acquainted. Many people feel somewhat inhibited when being interviewed alongside their social or professional peers, which results in less information and possibly less accurate information than results from nonfamiliar groups. Thus, the practice of recruiting from social organizations, parent-teacher groups, or other available groups is not necessarily a sound one.

The problem with the prospect of "no-shows" at focus group sessions can best be handled by taking extra steps to remind participants of their discussion time and place and by over-recruiting. A general rule of thumb is to recruit 25 to 50 percent more consumers than are actually needed. Just prior to the discussion, participants should be re-screened to ensure accuracy of group composition and to prevent embarrassing discoveries once in session. If more than ten qualified subjects are present, an appropriate number can be sent home after they are paid for their cooperation.

Setting.

A comfortable, convenient location is ideal for a focus group session. Beyond these simple requirements, it is desirable for the facility to have a single table that seats the entire group. If research sponsors wish to observe the meeting, consider using a one-way mirror.

The interview.

Typical focus group interviews last about two hours. The moderator follows the agenda for the most part, but allows the discussion to take its natural course as long as interchange is relevant. An example of a focus group agenda is provided in Figure 6–3. Participants who are reluctant to speak are encouraged to do so, and those who would dominate the conversation are kept in check with reminders that all should have a chance to contribute.

Figure 6–3
Focus Group Agenda: Excepts from Focus Group Studies of Chicago-Area Zoogoers

---

Cognitive Domain

    I'd like to ask some general questions about the Milwaukee Zoo:

        location

        cost of admission

        hours of operation

        off-season attractions

        special effects

        animal exhibits

    How is the Milwaukee County Zoo supported? Taxes? Admissions? Vending?

    Generally speaking, what would you think is the largest amount in a zoo's annual operating budget?

        animal food?

        salary and wages?

        animal purchases?

        physical plants?

Affective Domain

    What do you *like most* about zoos?

        about the Milwaukee County Zoo?

    What do you *dislike* most about zoos?

        the Milwaukee County Zoo?

    What are your favorite zoo attractions? Why?

    What are your favorite animals? Why?

How could zoos be improved?
>   rest rooms
>   directions, maps, street signs
>   parking
>   animal settings and cages
>   food, cafeterias
>   signs at animal displays; what should the signs say?
>   are zoos clean? is there litter?
>   picnic areas?
>   scenery?
>   souvenirs; souvenir shops

Do you like the way animals are housed? Cared for? Why? Why not?
>   ask about specific animals

Would you pay to have a guided tour? How much would you pay?

What do you feel about the cost of admission to zoos? Milwaukee County Zoo?

How would you compare:
>   Milwaukee County Zoo
>   Lincoln Park Zoo
>   Brookfield Zoo
>   (probe about physical facilities, animals, services, etc.)

Are zoo personnel, in general, friendly and knowledgeable?

Do you find zoos educational and informative? Do you children?

Do you find zoos amusing? Entertaining?

Do you go to the zoo because it is amusing or because it is educational?

Are zoos too crowded?

Are zoo crowds friendly and unthreatening?

If you had to choose among various leisure activities, how would you rank the following?
>   zoo
>   baseball game
>   circus
>   theatre—movie
>   museum
>   aquarium

Do you feel closer to nature at the zoo?

Do you feel better about things while at the zoo?

Do you think zoos are too crowded?

Why don't you attend zoos more often?

What would inspire you to attend the zoo more often?

Source: Reprinted with permission of Milwaukee County Zoo.

Generally speaking, focus group observers should not be visible during the discussion. Their presence can inhibit both the interviewer and the participants. Observers can sit behind the one-way mirror, a position giving them a firsthand, yet undetected perspective. If observers wish to communicate with the moderator, written messages can be delivered with a minimum of distraction, or the interviewer may step out during the course of the discussion for a brief conference.

Since the moderator is too preoccupied to take extensive notes on points made during the discussion, and because the word-for-word comment and tonal emphasis are so valuable to the analysis of results, most focus groups are tape-recorded, video-recorded, or both. Two tape recorders are suggested as a precaution against equipment failure.

Analysis.

Reports of focus group discussions can take many forms. In most cases the moderators will write reports for their own groups, and overall results are compiled for the client by another researcher. Components of the report can include the following:

- Executive summary
- Description of research objectives, methodology, and procedures
- Discussion of major findings, including illustrative quotations
- Summary of limitations of the research

An example of results from a series of focus groups on the topic of specialty advertising is shown in Figure 6–4. Typically a transcript or audiotape or both are made available to the client, or a videotape if available.

Figure 6–4
Excerpt from Focus Group Sessions for Consumer and Business Recipients
of Specialty Advertising Items

Consumer Groups

The eight specialty advertising items ranged from an unusual, fat ballpoint pen worth less than one dollar to a plush beach towel worth more than $25 wholesale. Included were a keychain/light, an outdoor thermometer, a photo album, a large calculator/note pad combination, a waterproof jacket and a windbreaker. All of these items were deemed to be non-specific, non-business-oriented.

Ballpoint Pen—Because of its appearance, some women thought it was a combination ballpoint/ink pen. Most women did not like it because it was too big and bulky. Advertising imprint did not bother the men; if the pen was good quality, they would use it. If the pen was not of good quality, they would "trash it." Both groups seemed to agree that a good pen was always useful, but a pen that was inappropriate or inferior would have a short lifespan with them.

Keychain/Light—The idea of a battery-operated light in the car appealed to both men and women, but neither group wanted to use it as a keychain. Both groups perceived it as potentially unreliable and said that when it quit working, they would throw it away. Several said they would give it to a young child. Both groups pointed to bulkiness as a problem.

Outdoor Thermometer—men unanimously saw the thermometer as unreliable, an item they would not display, except in a garage or workshop area. It might go over in a colder climate, they said. Women were, on the other hand, unanimous in their endorsement of the thermometer. Some suggested the patio as an appropriate place to display it.

Photo Album—There was agreement among both groups that the photo album had a utilitarian use. Most would use it to store photos, but not for displaying them—photos taken for records, i.e., insurance. Most would not display it with an advertiser's imprint on the cover; a tastefully done imprint on the inside cover might make a difference. Some suggested they would keep business cards in the album. Most agreed it was a quality item.

Calculator with Notepad—There was enthusiastic approval for the calculator/notepad. Both groups liked the big keys, the notepad, the fact that it was solar powered. They thought it was a quality item and almost all agreed that an imprint, tastefully done, would not lessen their acceptance. A broad range of uses was suggested.

Waterproof Jacket—Hardly anyone objected to imprinting the jacket, but few said they would use it. Suggestions were that it be stored in a car trunk, golf bag, camper, car glove box or camera case. Most objected to it because they perceived it to be of poor quality.

Lined Windbreaker Jacket—The windbreaker received mixed reviews from both groups. Both saw it as having good quality but confessed that they would not use it much. An advertiser's imprint would reduce its appeal, they said. Some suggested that a windbreaker is a personal thing and this would not replace what they already have.

Beach Towel—Every person viewed the beach towel as a quality, useful item. It would not matter to them if it was imprinted, in fact imprinting might serve to recall a special occasion. They definitely would have good feelings toward the giver, they said.

Business Groups

Focus group sessions were conducted on the next evening following for business women and men. Different specialty items were selected for the business groups; specifically, items chosen were deemed appropriate for one's desk or office environment. The eight items included a plastic cup, a highlighter pen, letter holder, folder with pad, desk organizer, large calculator, scissors and letter opener with case, and a battery-operated desk clock.

Men and women in the business groups were more frequent recipients of specialty gifts; in fact, were themselves sometimes purchasers of specialty items that they distributed to their customers. Mentioned most often as gifts they received were pens, cups, caps, and calendars. Recipients were largely favorable toward specialty gifts and several mentioned a favorite gift they treasured. Their opinions concerning specialty items paralleled opinions held by consumer groups, the primary difference being a great intimacy with the industry.

Plastic Cup—Several business women expressed their dislike for plastic cups, as did some men. Both saw plastic cups as a utility item, something to keep around for guests to drink out of, in the office coffee room, for example, or "for the yard man," as one woman pointed out.

Highlighter Pen with Two Colors—Women recipients were much more enthusiastic in their acceptance of the pen. They enumerated ways in which they might use it. Men were not negative toward the pen, just lukewarm in their response to it.

Letter Holder—Both men and women saw the letter holder as a useless item for the desk. Women saw it more appropriately placed in the home, near the telephone. With logo imprinted, it lessened in value for both groups.

Folder with Pad—There was general agreement that notepads are great utilitarian items to have, and in various situations, the pad would always be used. Exceptions would be when the logo would be displayed to an inappropriate person, i.e., someone who might be in competition with the business displayed on the pad. A logo tastefully imprinted on the inside cover would cause the pad to be more widely accepted by both groups.

Desk Organizer—Women were more impressed with the desk organizer than men. They saw it as a prestige item that would go on their desk and be useful. Some men saw it as an item they would keep if it were personalized. Some from both groups said they would more likely take it home and use it there.

Large Calculator—There was only one man who could find a use for the large calculator on his desk. Several women liked the calculator. Those who did not— men and women—said they had their own special calculator. None objected to the idea of an imprint on the calculator.

Scissors and Letter Opener—The majority in both groups liked the scissors. They did not like the case and were not enthusiastic about the letter opener. The imprint didn't seem to matter, although it was pointed out that it peeled very easily.

Battery-Operated Clock—Women generally like the idea of the clock on the desk. They saw it as a quality item that had a definite use. The men were somewhat ambivalent about the clock; they perceived it as just another item for the desk that would require space.

Both men and women business persons regard their desks as their own personal space, and they are very particular about what goes on it. To gain a position on a business person's desk, the specialty would need to be of good quality; the imprint would have to be tastefully done, and not too blatant; but most importantly, the item would have to compete with numerous other items that had already been preselected.

Conclusions

Generally speaking, one might draw the following conclusions from remarks made by the group participants:

- Imprinting a useful item does not significantly lessen acceptance.
- Imprinting an expensive item, if tastefully done, does not lessen its value.
- A personal item, blatantly imprinted, will not be displayed (the photo album).
- Pens are used, imprinted or not, if they are good pens.
- Inexpensive items with batteries are perceived to be short-lived throwaways.
- Recipients ascribe good or bad qualities to the giver, in direct relationship to the quality of the gift.
- An appropriate gift—toothbrush from dentist—takes on an added value and makes a lasting impression, imprinted or not.

Source: Reprinted with permission from Specialty Advertising Association International.

Industry Guidelines on Qualitative Research

The Qualitative Research Council of the Advertising Research Foundation has compiled a checklist for qualitative projects; it is summarized below.

Planning the Project

- It is important to obtain written confirmation of study objectives from the client. Telephone conversations may be misleading, and unclear objectives can jeopardize a project.

- Discuss with the client how much time should be spent on each section of the discussion guide. This will avoid the risk of too much time being spent on what the client may consider unimportant issues.

- When transporting important materials for qualitative interviews, carry them personally, rather than depending on airline baggage handling or mail delivery.

- While most major metropolitan areas have competent and experienced field services to arrange focus groups, often the field services in isolated areas may be quite inexperienced and naive about setting up focus groups. It is important to make sure directions are detailed and explicit and to check and double-check all arrangements.

- Recruiters should receive written screening instructions and questionnaires to ensure proper screening.

- When preparing a screening questionnaire for recruiters, and it is desirable that respondents *not* know the topic for discussion, one should make sure the screener is carefully disguised so respondents cannot determine what the real topic is.

- Necessary audio and video equipment should be requested well ahead of time. Many facilities do not own equipment and must arrange to rent it. Equipment should be checked out well in advance of interview time to make sure it is operational and that a technician is not needed. If using film projectors or slide projectors, it is advisable to request extra bulbs and extension cords.

Before Interviews

- Before inviting respondents into the interviewing room, all respondents should be rescreened to verify that they are qualified.

- In the event that several respondents do not show up for an interview, generally it is a good idea to interview those who come, even though they may not represent a full group session. Even with three or four respondents, some information will be gained.

- When arranging interviewing set-up and showing props to respondents, it is important to be considerate of viewers who are observing the interviews, either through a one-way mirror or by closed-circuit television. If possible, stimulus materials should be shown to respondents in a way that makes them visible to viewers, also.

- If interviewing in a facility with a one-way mirror, viewers should be reminded that they must not talk or laugh loudly during the interview because respondents may hear them.

- Whatever means of observation and recording are used, respondents should be informed of the situation before the interview. It is also prudent to have all respondents sign a release form indicating that they have been informed that they are being observed or recorded and granting the researcher the right to use their comments in any way.

During Interviews

- If taking notes during an interview, a moderator should not let note-taking disrupt attention to the flow of the interview. The tape recording provides a record of the conversation; copious notes are unnecessary.
- Occasionally, despite careful screening and rescreening, an unqualified respondent is discovered after a group session has begun. If the interviewer believes the participation of this unqualified respondent will in some way jeopardize the group session, the interviewer must be prepared to tactfully ask that respondent to leave.

After Interviews

- If verbatim quotes are used in a report, they should be identified according to the particular interview and by key demographics.
- When analyzing qualitative data, it is important to avoid overloading the report with responses from verbose or particularly inarticulate respondents.
- When transporting audiotapes or videotapes of interviews from an out-of-town interviewing site, it is a good idea to carry one set to assure its safe and timely arrival.

Release Form

The ARF advises that participants sign a legal release form before the focus group discussion. (See Figure 6–5.) The form states, among other things, that the researchers and/or their clients retain sole rights to materials or ideas generated during the course of the discussion. Sometimes focus group conversations or comments are used in subsequent advertising campaigns.

Figure 6–5
Sample Legal Release Form

RESEARCH CONSENT, RELEASE AND ASSIGNMENT

For valuable Consideration, receipt of which is hereby acknowledged, I give full permission irrevocably and in perpetuity to _____ and/or its clients, subsidiaries, affiliates, agents and assigns, hereinafter called Grantees, to make or reproduce throughout the world, either alone or in conjunction with other material, any photographs, audio recordings, films and videotapes made in connection with the Research Group Meeting identified below hereafter called the Meeting, incorporating my name, photo likeness and/or voice, either in whole or in part, in material prepared for purposes of advertising, research and client presentation.

I understand that there may be observers at the meeting as well as those involved in recording and conducting the proceedings.

I grant to _____ all rights, including the right to copyright, in any ideas, slogans, plans, suggestions, sketches, artwork or other material that I may produce during or in connection with the Meeting.

It is further understood that Grantees may use said material with or without my name and that Grantees may make reasonable changes in testimonial copy, if any, provided the spirit and content of my remarks are not distorted.

I further waive any right of approval with respect to use of said materials and hereby release and discharge Grantees from any claim or liability, including without limitation invasion of privacy or defamation of character based upon such use.

I hereby assign the Consideration to which I am entitled to _____ . (Fill in only if applicable.)

_____   Signature: _____
Meeting Identification   Address: _____
                           Date: _____

If the above is a Minor, the following statement must be signed:

I, the undersigned, am the _____ father _____ mother _____ guardian of the below-named Minor and as such am fully authorized to enter into this agreement on his/her behalf. I agree that the Consideration, receipt of which is acknowledged, is sufficient and agree to hold harmless Grantees against any loss from any claim, action or demand brought at any time by any party.

I hereby assign the Consideration to _____ (Fill in only if applicable.)

Child's name: _____
Parent's signature: _____
Address: _____
Date: _____

Source: Advertising Research Foundation.

Review

In this chapter we saw that:

- Qualitative research is exploratory in nature and elicits in-depth, often subjective responses that are not measurable in hard numbers.
- Qualitative research can be applied in the following ways: as an idea generation tool; to aid in development of a quantitative study; as follow-up to a quantitative study; and as an end in itself.
- Common qualitative methods are projective techniques, in-depth interviews, dyadic interviews, and focus groups.

Endnote

1. *Marketing Insights through Qualitative Research: Proceedings of the ARF Qualitative Research Workshop* (New York: Advertising Research Foundation, 1987).

7 Surveys: Random vs. Non-random Samples

If you ask the average non-businessperson, "What is marketing research?" a naive reply might be, "Surveys, right?" Well, that's not really wrong, but it's far from being complete. It is undoubtedly true that the survey is a ubiquitous, frequently used, and well-known advertising/marketing research method. But this does not mean it's necessarily the best nor the most appropriate. And, frequently, it's the most expensive method there is.

Too often in advertising and marketing, when information is needed, a common knee-jerk response is, "I've got it—let's do a survey!" This attitude overlooks the fact that the most valuable aspect of research—thinking the problem through before deciding which kind of research is needed—is virtually free. Commercial research firms, which routinely charge $100 or more for each personal interview, understandably do little to discourage this temptation. One can't solve advertising problems just by throwing money at them.

There are many different varieties of surveys, and some can be safely and validly used for many different purposes. However, surveys are far too often conducted for the wrong purposes or are so poorly done that pure subjective judgment would give more accurate answers—and save a lot of money. As any true professional will confirm, no research is better than wrong research. We hasten to add: The right kind of research is better still.

What Is a Survey?

A survey is the use of questions and answers to gather information from any group of two or more subjects. The group can be a whole population (census survey); a scientifically chosen representative sample of a population (random sample survey), or a nonrepresentative portion of a population (nonrandom sample survey). Many survey elements must be handled correctly for results to be accurate. Among these are population definition, question development and sequencing, interviewing and data collection, statistical analysis, and interpretation of findings. In this chapter we focus on the importance of correct sampling methods.

Surveys come in a variety of sizes, shapes, and qualities. Among the most common are telephone surveys, mail surveys, personal interview surveys, group surveys, phone-in surveys, newspaper or magazine printed questionnaires, drop-off surveys, mall intercepts, man-in-the-street polls, straw polls, in-depth surveys, and motivation surveys. Although they are not strictly considered surveys, we can even include focus groups and use diaries in the basic definition, because they use questions and answers to elicit generalizable information from a group. Let's take a closer look at some of the terms used in our basic definition of *survey* above.

A *sample* is any fraction or portion of some larger body or population. We sample a pot of soup to see if it's done properly. One taste is a sample size of N = 1. Or a blood sample is drawn from the arm: N = 1 is the sample size. In homogeneous populations such as soup or blood, a sample N = 1 is adequate. But in heterogenous populations of people or cities, larger samples (i.e., greater numbers of sampling units) are required. The purpose of testing a sample is to use the results to form generalizations about the population as a whole.

A *random* or *probability sample* is scientifically drawn to ensure that it is representative of an entire population. In a random sample, each member of the population has an *equal opportunity* of being selected. The sample should, therefore, reflect accurately the true characteristics of the population. This means that generalizations about the population as a whole can reasonably be made from the research results.

A *nonrandom* or *nonprobability* sample is chosen unsystematically or unscientifically. In a nonrandom sample, members of the population do *not* have an equal chance of being selected. One cannot, therefore, safely generalize to the parent population.

A *census survey* is the gathering of question-and-answer data from every single member of a whole group or population with no intention of generalizing to some larger group. There is no sampling error, therefore no statistical probability statement is necessary.

A *sample survey* is the gathering of question-and-answer data from either a random sample or a nonrandom sample. *One should not assume a sample is random unless so stated, with evidence.* Before we go any further, let's take a closer look at the differences between random and nonrandom sample surveys. A random sample is the ideal for which a surveyor strives.

Random vs. Nonrandom Sampling

If you are presented with a list of percentages that were "from a survey," should you believe the numbers are accurate? Not without knowing a great deal more. What if the figures are from a "scientific" survey? Not yet. From a telephone survey done by Scientific Survey Corporation, "one of the biggest survey companies in the country"? From a sample with "300,000 respondents"? No. What you need to know is, "Was it a true random sample survey?" We obviously need to be able to distinguish between random sample surveys and nonrandom sample surveys.

Let's be precise about the meaning of a *random sample.* As we have seen, a random sample is a rigorously selected fraction taken from some larger population. It is intended to be representative of the entire population. By testing the random sample, researchers can make generalizations about the entire population without having to test all of its members.

Suppose, for example, you select a true random sample of 1,100 people (N = 1,100) from the entire U.S. population of 250 million. If 50 percent of your sample agree with the statement "I hate TV commercial clutter," you can be quite sure (95 percent sure, in fact) that, had you surveyed the whole population, the true figure would be between 47 and 53 percent. The 50 percent from the sample is an *unbiased estimate* of the true population figure. By *unbiased* we mean it can be off by the *same* known amount in either direction; by *estimate* we mean it is not exactly correct. From the results of the random survey, we can confidently assume, therefore, that between 47 and 53 percent of the U.S. population dislikes TV commercial clutter. In Chapter 8, you will learn how these percentages (the margin of error) are derived.

Now let's suppose that the survey used a nonrandom instead of a random sample of the population. If 50 percent of these respondents claim to dislike clutter, this estimate would be *biased* to some unknown amount; that is, there would be an *unequal and unknown* amount of error on either side if the results are generalized to the entire population. In a nonrandom sample survey, no probability statement is possible about the true situation in a larger population, and the sampling error is not computable. The bottom line is: one can believe with confidence in the results from a random sample, but not from a nonrandom sample.

There are many different kinds of nonrandom samples. An *intentional* sample is a deliberately chosen, nonrandom sample from a population (e.g., selecting men only or left-handed, red-headed heavy drinkers for some particular purpose.) A *haphazard* sample is simply a nonscientifically drawn sample. Haphazard samples are usually used out of ignorance of the correct method and with the erroneous assumption that they are representative. A *convenience* sample is usually a quick-and-dirty selection of units from the population. Convenience samples are used not so much out of ignorance as from impatience, carelessness, and nonprofessionalism. A *cross-section* sample, or a *quota* sample, is a subgroup intentionally (nonrandomly) drawn to have certain superficial characteristics of the larger population (e.g., 50 percent men, 50 percent women; or one-third each of low-income, middle-income, and high-income persons). The aim is to ensure a reasonable spread of certain kinds of people in the sample. This is a doubly deceptive kind of nonrandom sample, because on the surface it appears to be typical of the population in certain visible characteristics, but it is usually atypical on certain intangible characteristics such as attitudes, opinions, beliefs, personality characteristics, and so on. The fallacies of these and other nonrandom sample surveys used in marketing and advertising are discussed in detail further on.

The various kinds of nonrandom samples are almost never representative of any population except themselves. The people selected are atypical in terms of demographics (sex, age, education, etc.), behavior (buying habits, shopping habits, spending patterns, etc.), product usage (brands purchased, frequency of purchase, etc.), media behavior (usage and attention, choices of newspapers, television, radio, magazines, etc.), personality characteristics, advertising reactions, attitudes, opinions, and beliefs. In short, nonrandom samples are biased samples and cannot be safely believed.

Figures projected to a larger population from nonrandom samples can range from almost accurate to completely misleading. They can be deceptive, however, and surveyors almost always present the nonrandom sample survey results as generalizations, although not always with the deliberate intention to deceive. Sometimes shoddy survey results will include weak or illogical disclaimers to the effect that "while not a representative sample, the results may be useful." (How's that again? The results are inaccurate but useful?) The naive believer of results is the sufferer, regardless, and that is why advertising professionals should be able to discriminate between nonrandom and random sample data.

It's worth repeating that advertising decisions made from sound judgment and available (valid) evidence are undoubtedly better than those made from inaccurate research.

The Ideal Random Sample

A pet peeve of the professional researcher is the shoddy survey conducted by well-meaning amateurs or by untrained commercial researchers. This is aided and abetted by journalists and broadcasters, who routinely and indiscriminately transmit both accurate and inaccurate survey data to the public without bothering to verify information. There is some excuse for the general public's being unable to discriminate between valid and invalid survey information; they assume media professionals will screen out the blatantly erroneous. However, there is no excuse for the advertising and marketing professional to accept flaky survey data; it goes with the professional's territory to know good from bad evidence.

How, then, can we tell whether survey information is likely to be accurate? An ideal random sample survey has the following characteristics:

1. **The target population has been rigorously and painstakingly defined.** The researcher, for example, might specify not just "the total U.S. population," but "all persons aged 18–65 living in telephone-owning households, listed and unlisted, in the 48 contiguous states."

2. **The sample size is large enough to give the desired level of precision in the results.** For example, if a sampling "error" (variation) of plus or minus 6 percent has been decided in advance to be precise enough for decision-making purposes, the sample size can then be decided. "Decided precision" means not too large, not too small. A good

and expensive reason for not making unreasonably precise demands on survey data is that sample size must be quadrupled to reduce sampling errors by one-half.

3. **Every household or person in the defined population must have an equal probability of being selected into the drawn sample.** Otherwise, the drawn sample will be biased in some, usually unknown way.

4. **A high proportion of the drawn sample—ideally at least 60 percent—must be reached and their responses obtained.** A high completion rate on a drawn sample is an absolute necessity. Both the drawn sample *and the completed sample* must be random and representative of the parent population.

Completion of 100 percent is, of course, almost never achieved. The most expensive and rigorously conducted sample surveys sometimes reach a 90 to 95 percent completion rate. Completion of 70 percent on a perfectly drawn sample is accepted in advertising and marketing research circles as an excellent sample; even so, the 30 percent who are nonrespondents, who could be systematically quite different from the respondents, introduce considerable bias into the results.

As of 1989, 60 percent completion of a perfectly drawn sample is the minimum acceptable by the Advertising Research Foundation. Unfortunately, much lower completion rates are cited in many published survey results, often as low as 40, 30, and even 20 percent. The prestigious, scientifically oriented American Psychological Society, for example, recently published in its official periodical the results of a member survey with only a 52 percent completion rate. It appears that even scientists, once a survey is complete, are reluctant to throw out low-response marginal data. Many studies with a low completion rate will add a stock phrase, ". . . and this is considered usually good for studies of this kind." Not so. A low survey completion rate can produce biased results, and researchers should try to achieve as high a response rate as possible to ensure accuracy.

The problem of nonresponse.

Some surveys do not report completion rates, for the obvious reason, and report misleading completion rates. A major women's magazine of 3,000,000 circulation recently printed a "sex survey questionnaire" to which about 100,000 readers responded, a true completion rate of about 3 percent. But the survey report, expensively produced and widely publicized, stated that "10,000 randomly selected replies were analyzed for this report." A random sample of a nonrandom sample is not a representative sample of the population. The magazine report also projected the results to the whole U.S. female population, another distortion, because no magazine's readers are typical of the general public.

To highlight the importance of high completion rates and the nonresponse problem, Bernard Guggenheim, senior vice president of a major advertising agency, conducted a *validation study,* which was reported in the *Journal of Advertising*

Research.[1] His firm compared the results from a known-to-be-accurate study with those from a low-response-rate study to determine how random and nonrandom surveys differ. As expected, the low-response-rate survey was very biased, leaving out the mobile and active people who are more difficult for a survey to "catch." These hard-to-catch missing persons were the very sort that most marketers are more interested in—young, affluent, well-educated professionals and business owners. They read considerably more magazines and newspapers, listen to more radio, and view more cable television but are lighter TV viewers in general. Just as important, the nonrespondents' choices for attention within those media were different from the less mobile and active respondents. Guggenheim's study is a clear indication that *data gathered in low-completion surveys is so biased that it can lead to costly advertising decision errors.*

The problem of weighted results.

Watch out, too, for surveys that report "weighted results." After conducting a nonrandom survey, researchers use a technique whereby some respondents are given more "weight" when the results are tabulated. The purpose is to approximate more closely the true population. For example, if the U.S. adult population is 60 percent female, and a survey produces 80 percent female respondents, one could either (a) eliminate enough female responses to bring the female proportion into line, or (b) multiply or replicate enough male responses. Samples can be "adjusted" in this way for as many variables (sex, age, geographic origin, etc.) as the researcher wishes. This is done to make the sample look superficially like a true random sample. It is not.

Sampling Method versus Sample Size

What is the relative importance of sampling method versus sample size? To put it as forcefully as possible: to predict the behavior of the entire U.S. population of approximately 250 million persons, we would unhesitatingly choose a true random sample of only 100 persons (N = 100) over a nonrandom sample of ten thousand or even one million. With the random sample of 100, we could safely bet 19-to-1 (i.e., $95 to $5) that any percentage obtained in the survey would be accurate within plus or minus ten (i.e., a *sampling error* of 10 percent). Conversely, with the large nonrandom sample, it is impossible to compute sampling error; such a biased sample may be 20 percent too high or 2 percent too low, or off the mark in either direction to an unknown degree. A sample of ten thousand, or one million, certainly seems better than a sample of 100. So does one million apples sound better than one hundred, until you learn that the million are rotten while the hundred are healthy.

The lesson should be clear: Don't be deceived by a large sample size. Look at the sampling method, specifically for a random, or probability, method, where every unit in the population has an equal chance of being selected. To put it even more strongly: Always be skeptical about sampling method.

Some Common Types of Nonrandom Surveys

Despite their unreliability, nonrandom surveys are frequently conducted in advertising and marketing. The reason is understandable: They're cheaper than random sample surveys, and they take less knowledge, time, thought, and study to accomplish. They appear so frequently, even experts may mistakenly assume they're acceptable.

If conducted under strict conditions, however, some nonrandom surveys are worthwhile. If the investigator is interested in the results from the specific group surveyed *only* and does not intend either consciously or unconsciously to generalize the results to some larger group, nonrandom surveys can be effective. Focus groups, for example, are often justified on these grounds, and as such can be useful. Nonrandom methods are also worthwhile when results have been validated, that is, results from the nonrandom method have been directly compared with those from a properly executed random sample, or with the results from a census survey of the entire population, and shown incontrovertibly to be equivalent.

Validation studies are expensive, but if they can demonstrate that a less rigorous and less expensive form of sampling can produce valid (equivalent) results, they can be useful in the long run. (The reason random sampling has been accepted as a good sampling method is only that early validation studies showed incontestably that the results were valid representations of the population.) Though it's wise to be skeptical of all nonrandom surveys, their results can be useful to researchers who are aware of all the possible flaws and who can make the proper allowances for them. The best safeguard is to learn how to spot the imperfections in any research results you use.

Nonrandom survey methods include the following:

- Focus groups
- Mall intercept surveys
- Motivation or "in-depth" surveys
- Magazine audience surveys
- Questionnaire-in-magazine surveys
- Phone-in polls
- Fixed-location opinion polling machines
- Magic Town, Splitsville, and Magic Markets surveys
- Pay-to-participate polls

Focus Groups

As we saw in Chapter 6, a focus group is basically a discussion group convened for a specific marketing or advertising purpose. At the relatively reasonable cost of around $2,500 per session, researchers can get immediate feedback or ideas directly from the consumer, uncontaminated by tables of statistics, researchers' interpretations, or the well-meaning opinions of advertising experts. As a means of gathering qualitative (not quantitative) information, the focus group almost completely bypasses a great many sources of possible research error. The results from a skillfully conducted meeting can provide the advertising professional with very useful insights into real consumers: their reactions to creative ideas; their perceptions of products; their own ideas and motives; their understanding, or misunderstanding, of advertisements and questionnaires; and so on.

Because the information gathered is qualitative, it cannot be quantified or projected to any larger population than the group itself. Focus group samples, therefore, are generally either intentional samples of a narrow specialized segment of the population, or cross-sectional (i.e., quota samples deliberately chosen to represent a wide range of views).

As an example, take an intentional sample of blue-collar men aged 25–34 who drink one or more beers per week. In a focus group they can give valuable feedback on specific beer advertisement ideas, they can tell the copywriter how they feel when they drink beer, and why they choose one particular beer over another. No other research method can obtain the same type of information. Let's say the group is composed of 16 men, all from the same city, who agree to come to a central location at a particular time. They're in an unfamiliar setting, with a group of guys they've never seen before (including the obtrusive discussion leader). They're also conscious of their role as consumer "experts for a day" and are perhaps eager to say something memorable and intelligent.

They are "typical beer-drinkers" perhaps, but they are not representative of either the national 25–34-year-old blue-collar beer drinker or even the local counterpart. Even if the 16 are a true random sample (which focus groups never are), the sampling error would be too excessive to generalize to a larger population. For example, if 11 of the 16, or 69 percent, prefer the "more fun" theme over the "good taste" theme for an upcoming beer campaign, the sampling error of almost 26 percent really means that 69 percent plus or minus 26 percent prefer the "more fun" ad. This means the true population figure (i.e., parameter) is really between 43 and 95 percent, and, therefore, the real preference could be for the "good taste" ad. And this error could really lead to some wrong advertising decisions.

The *American Newspaper Publishers Association* Bureau of Advertising recently commissioned a number of focus groups around the United States to find out what newspaper readers thought about certain aspects of editorial and advertising matter, with the laudable purpose of improving the newspaper editorial product. Many new insights came out of each of the two dozen or so cities studied, one focus group from each. But then, with understandably good intentions to get some extra mileage from the studies, the researchers combined the results from all of the focus groups into one set of summary statistics that were presented, with some qualifying remarks, as valid for the U.S. newspaper reader population. Consider the following: The cities were not typical of all U.S. cities and neither were their newspapers; focus group discussants were not typical of their own city populations; and questioning techniques varied somewhat from city to city (as they should in "discussant-centered" focus groups). Does this result in a representative and accurate picture of the United States as a whole? Of course not.

In summary, focus group studies are very valuable and legitimate for certain purposes, but they are nonrandom surveys and should not be quantitatively projected to any larger population beyond themselves.

Mall Intercept Surveys

In a mall intercept survey, interviewers are stationed in shopping malls to intercept passersby and ask them questions. Unfortunately, this research method frequently produces wrong data and can lead to wrong advertising decisions, which lead in turn to millions of wasted advertising dollars and even product failure.

The reason for conducting mall intercept surveys, as with other nonrandom sample surveys, is all too often that they are quick, cheap, and seem on the surface to produce high-quality data. To illustrate by comparison, a well-conducted random-digit-dialing telephone survey can produce about two completed ten-minute interviews per interviewer-hour, a generalizable random sample, and quality data. A mall intercept interviewer can produce five ten-minute interviews per hour. On average, total interviewing costs for the mall intercept method are less than half that for telephone interviewing. One problem, however, is that mall intercept data cannot be projected to any larger group than the very people interviewed. At best, the mall intercept method has produced dubious data at a lower cost; at worst, wrong marketing and advertising decisions based on this data can cost millions of dollars if projected to any larger population.

Why dubious data? Because mall intercept samples are not representative of any larger group in terms of demographics, media and buying behavior, attitudes, opinions, advertising preferences, or anything else. Evidence from validation studies has already been accumulated to verify this. Simple logic will lead us to the same conclusion. Let's take, for example, a fictitious mall intercept survey conducted in any big city—say Lenox Square Mall in Atlanta. Wait a minute, you say, Atlanta is not a "typical" city and Lenox Square is an atypical, up-scale mall. Exactly; there is *no* typical mall and *no* typical city anywhere. And those are just two of the problems with mall intercept surveys.

But let's say we take any city you choose and pick any mall you consider to be typical *of that city*. Let's analyze the results of a survey conducted in Prototype Mall in Prototype City during any three-day period in any month of the year: Tuesday, Wednesday, and Thursday, during the interviewers' normal working hours of 10 a.m. to 4 p.m., in the second week of May 1991. Highly skilled interviewers (not always true, but let's assume it here) collect 1,000 ten-minute interviews using an absolutely perfect objective questionnaire. Five interviewers are stationed at the five busiest spots scattered "strategically," approximately equidistant around the mall.

Their interviewing procedure is as follows: Mall interviewers are given a quota by age and sex, say "women only, aged 18–34," or "two-thirds women and one-third men, in each sex one-half aged 18–34 and the rest aged 35–64." Watching the interviewer at work, one notices some people deliberately giving the interviewer a wide berth, others curious to see what she's doing, others waiting around eager to be interviewed. The interviewer naturally approaches only neat, friendly looking, receptive people who are making eye contact, not the sour-faced scowlers, the worriers, or the badly dressed. Even so, some of the people approached refuse to be interviewed, and the interviewer without debate simply passes on to the next receptive mall stroller. At the end of the day, the interviewer goes home with the satisfaction of a job well done (from her point of view). She has completed interviews with 20 women and 10 men, 15 aged 18–34 and 15 aged approximately 35–64. Over a period of three days, Monday through Wednesday between the hours of ten and four, the five mall interviewers will collect about 450 interviews in this manner, on the surface a "good cross-section," as the reports say, of adult shoppers in the community.

There are several glaring reasons why the results of this 450-interview sample cannot be projected to the whole community, nor to all mall shoppers in the community, nor even to all shoppers in this particular mall. Remember, for a sample's information to be representative of any population, every individual in the population must have an equal chance of being included in the sample. If not, the sample selection is biased, and the information will be biased. Here are some of the kinds of people systematically *excluded* from the mall intercept procedure above. These same people can be extremely important to advertisers and marketers.

- People who infrequently or never visit malls
- People who live in another part of town, shop in different malls, or have transportation problems to this mall
- People who do their mall shopping after 4 p.m. (e.g., most working people; those with heavy daytime responsibilities)
- People who do their mall shopping on Thursday, Friday, and weekends
- People who are out of town on business or vacation during this particular week (e.g., people with jobs that involve travel; people with money to travel; and people on vacation)
- People in the mall who are in a hurry, have a lot of purchases to make, or simply don't want to be bothered (e.g., busy, active, mobile people)

Those are just a few obvious "missing persons" in the usual mall intercept sample. The upshot is that too few of the very kinds of people that marketers and advertisers want to hear from are interviewed—people who are busy, working, high-income, well-educated, highly mobile, and heavy consumers of certain products. The missing people also differ from the willing, receptive mall interviewees in terms of personality, attitudes, behavior, and many other product-use characteristics.

To summarize, the problem with mall intercept samples can be reduced to two kinds of selection bias:

1. The self-selection bias of people who choose to go to malls
2. The respondent-selection bias of interviewers choosing easy-to-interview mall shoppers

Using quota samples, or "weighting" the results cannot change a nontypical sample of people into a random representative sample of any other population.

Motivation or In-Depth Surveys

Motivation studies were very big in the 1950s, largely through the efforts of a German psychologist, Dr. Ernest Dichter. From his imposing medieval aerie at Hastings-on-the-Hudson, Dr. Dichter converted advertisers into true believers that "depth interviews" would uncover secrets of the human psyche not revealed in ordinary survey research. There are major differences between motivation studies and other surveys:

- Interviews are much longer.
- There is less emphasis on fixed questions.
- There is more emphasis on "why" (i.e., motivation-inquiry) questions.
- Projective techniques (e.g., word association, inkblot interpretation, etc.) are used.
- Highly trained psychologists are needed as interviewers.
- There is more emphasis on qualitative than quantitative analysis.
- Interpretations of results are highly subjective and psychoanalytically based.
- The cost per interview is higher.
- The samples used are usually relatively small samples and usually are not randomly chosen.

"In-depth" interviews are based on the same rationale as psychoanalytic theory. If you can bypass the conscious mind, with its deliberate or accidental distortions of "true motivation" and dig deep enough into one person's unconscious, or perhaps just semi-deep into a few people, you will encounter the bedrock of universal human motivations. (And the whole world can be revealed in a grain of sand—theoretically.) Unfortunately for marketers and advertisers, psychology, psychiatry, and psychoanalysis do not as yet have the knowledge or tools to verify that laudable theory. This is not to disparage the legitimate qualitative use of motivation surveys to supplement random (projectible) survey data, just a caution to recognize its limitations.

The term *in-depth interviews* is now sometimes loosely and erroneously used to describe amateurishly conducted studies with poorly written questionnaires that allow respondents to ramble on at length. In its original form, however, the in-depth, clinical-approximation survey interview provides some needed supplemental information to the highly structured survey interview. It can give researchers at least a peek at some unconscious motivations not revealed by typical, simplistic questions such as "Why do you like that one?" At its best, the motivation survey provides some wholistic analysis of results that allows an overview of the marketing forest instead of just the individual trees. At its worst, it provides loose, sloppy data.

The savvy advertiser has no quarrel with the motivation survey when it is used legitimately as qualitative data. But look out for research reports that project the findings of motivational studies to a larger population. The results will not be valid for two simple reasons: They usually are based on nonrandom samples and on samples that are too small to be representative of a larger group. Random samples for motivation surveys are hard to obtain. Many refusals occur because subjects are reluctant to spend the necessary two or three hours—one kind of nonresponse bias. To eliminate that reluctance, subjects are sometimes paid to participate; this introduces two more kinds of sampling and response bias. Geographical dispersion is hard to achieve: With a national sample of, say, N = 200, one or two interviews per city would require 100–200 psychologically trained interviewers, or a great deal of travel cost and time spent by a few clinicians. True motivation interviews are very expensive—perhaps three to six times as expensive per interview as an ordinary personal interview. Therefore, samples must be kept small to keep costs in line. And the smaller the sample, the larger the sampling error.

Even if it were possible to find a sufficiently large, true random sample, you should still watch out for phony motivation surveys. These purport to measure motivation by simply asking a few free-response *why* questions. For example, let's assume a respondent claims that the last brand of vodka she bought was Stolichnaya. An easy follow-up question would be "Why did you buy that brand?" Since taste test have shown little detectable difference between moderate and expensive vodkas, the most frequent answer, "It tastes better," is likely to be a rationalization. Few would volunteer a more likely motivation, "To impress my friends," even if they were conscious of it. A whole chapter could be written on the meaninglessness of the question *why*. Here, we simply say that "why" does not a motivation survey make.

In summary, like the focus group, a good motivation survey can provide useful preliminary and/or supplementary qualitative data. But if results are to be projected quantitatively to some larger population, look carefully for adequate sample size and scientifically chosen random samples.

Magazine Audience Surveys

A survey by mail, telephone, or personal interview of magazine readers is called a *magazine audience* survey. As long as the data from a true random sample of a publication's readers are projected only to the reader population, then one can have no quarrel with the results, and they can be very useful in understanding that particular publication. But when the results of a magazine survey, even assuming it is a rigorously conducted random sample survey, are projected to a larger population, such as the general public, then they lose their validity.

First of all, the population of people who read a particular magazine is different from nonreaders and thus is not representative of the total population. The same goes for newspaper readers. Second, the readers of any specific magazine are different from readers of any other magazine, even magazines of the same general type; for example, *Newsweek* readers are different in many respects from *Time* readers, *Playboy* readers are different from *Penthouse* readers, *Redbook* readers are different from *Cosmopolitan* readers. After all, reader differences are the stock in trade for a publications's advertising sales. Third, even general large-circulation magazine readers are different from the general public and different from each other.

It's tempting, because of their large variegated reading audiences, to consider *Reader's Digest* or *TV Guide* readers as "a cross-section of America" or as "the voice of the public." The truth is, however, that all magazines and newspapers, to one degree or another, are "specialized audience" publications. The opinions, behaviors, and consumer habits of *Reader's Digest* readers cannot be projected to the general public. Neither can the sex habits of *Redbook* readers be considered typical of U.S. women. Nor can the buying habits of readers of the *Orlando Sentinel* be considered typical of Orlando consumers.

Nevertheless, advertisers and the general public are regularly presented with news stories or promotional material claiming that the attitudes, behavior, life-styles, and media habits of some publication's audience are true of some larger public group. This is invalid, even if based on random samples, which they rarely are.

Questionnaire-in-Magazine Surveys

A questionnaire printed on the pages or inserted into the binding is becoming increasingly common in magazines and newspapers. What a nice cheap way to get consumer information to help us sell space, says the magazine advertising manager! Ditto the editor, under the delusion the survey will reveal reader-interest information to help in selecting articles that will build readership, audiences, and subscriptions.

And they're right; in-magazine questionnaires are a great way to get a lot of cheap data. But it's useless information at best, and harmful at worst if any internal decisions are made as a result. It's said that free advice is worth just what it costs. In this case, the free survey is worth less than it costs, since it can actually lose money for the periodical. As we shall see, data from questionnaires like this can distort our picture of a magazine's audience make-up and can thus result in the loss of advertising revenue. They can also deceive editors into printing editorial material aimed at a false image of the audience, resulting in loss of the readers' interest and, thus, the loss of subscriptions.

Why do in-magazine questionnaires always produce a distorted picture of a publication's audience? Simply put, people who take the time to fill out in-magazine questionnaires and mail them back in are people with time to spare or with greater-than-usual interest in the publication. This small fraction always results in a very low response rate. The resulting large body of "missing persons" may be quite different in their reading interests from those who do respond. As a rule, nonrespondents are usually "higher quality" consumers than those who do respond. They're usually more active, better educated, make higher incomes, have more expensive tastes, and are generally more knowledgeable and demanding as consumers. As with other nonrandom surveys, nonrespondents differ from respondents in terms of media habits, life-styles, buying and shopping habits, attitudes, beliefs, and general behaviors. In-magazine surveys, then, almost always attract responses from only a fraction of the readership, and the image they project is of a "low-quality" audience. If editors or advertising managers trust the data that is collected, the magazine suffers.

While knowledgeable advertisers now insist on the research standards stipulated by the Advertising Research Foundation (i.e., 60 percent minimum completion rate from a scientifically rigorous random sample), many media buyers do not know how to spot inaccurate in-magazine questionnaire surveys. And because they cost so little, magazines are tempted to keep using them. Imagine, bound into your magazine you can put your questionnaires in the hands of thousands—even millions—of readers and get a response rate of 2, 5, or 10 percent, adding up to thousands of replies. All this at insignificant out-of-pocket cost. Why should you spend, say, $100,000 on a professional mail survey of 2,500 respondents, when (as a recent *Redbook* survey showed) you can get 30,000 replies almost free from an in-magazine questionnaire?

As an advertising professional, look out for the tell-tale signs of seductive in-magazine surveys: The large number of questionnaires produced; the mistaken assumption that a well-known magazine or publisher or newspaper couldn't possibly be ignorant about research quality or deceptive with their data; and the slick, expensively produced, four-color hardcover reports of survey results. The rule in evaluating this kind of survey data is simple: Results are only true of a small number of self-selected respondents.

Phone-in Polls

Every TV viewer has been exposed to a phone-in poll of one kind or another: A question is printed on the screen or spoken by an announcer and viewers are invited to call in with their answers or opinions. A common feature is to have a different phone number for each possible response, usually *Yes-No* or *Agree-Disagree*. Sometimes a free 800 number is provided; sometimes there's a long-distance toll charge; sometimes a 900 number with a fee is given; and sometimes a local number for a local poll is given.

The results of phone-in polls are usually announced over the air or reported in the news and are occasionally quoted in newspapers as being "the opinions of the viewing audience" and even sometimes as "public opinion." The truth is that the TV (or radio) phone-in poll is absolutely useless for depicting the opinions

Chapter 7 Surveys: Random vs. Non-random Samples

133

of any larger group than simply those people who called in. The results are nongeneralizable, nonprojectible, and nontypical of any definable population.

First, how does the TV phone-in poll stack up as representative of "the viewing audience"? It is well-known that the viewers of one particular station make up only a small fraction of all stations' viewers. Similarly, viewers at a particular time of day are only a fraction of a single station's total viewing audience over a whole day or week or month. Beyond those obvious biases, however, phone-in respondents are simply different from all other viewers of that specific station at that particular time. Results cannot even be projected to all same-station, same-time viewers. Consider the following:

1. People who voluntarily respond to surveys, or who volunteer for any kind of research, are quite different from those who do not. That's why well-run surveys provide for several call-backs to every respondent, because few people will volunteer or are attainable on the first try.

2. If several people are watching in a household, the one (usually) who decides to respond has different opinions from the rest.

3. Many callers are systematically and nonrandomly excluded because lines are busy; therefore, only the most persistent will get through.

4. A long-distance toll charge will systematically exclude people who are concerned about cost; a 900 number charge will exclude even more.

5. Busy people and casual viewers will not even be tempted to call in. Callers are likely to be avid TV viewers with time and money on their hands.

Those are only a few of the reasons why TV phone-in polls tell us nothing about the general public, the TV population, or even the same-station, same-time TV viewers. As an advertising professional, ignore TV poll results. As a viewer, treat them as entertainment. Write-in or phone-in responses to questions printed in a newspaper have the same basic flaws as the TV phone-in poll.

Fixed-Location Opinion Polling Machines

Opinion-polling machines are found in amusement parks, transportation centers, shopping malls, and anywhere with high-density foot-traffic and pedestrians with the time to respond. The Epcot Survey at Disney World in Florida is typical. These polls are an interesting game to participate in, can gather thousands of responses in a single day, and are a completely harmless amusement—unless you take the results seriously.

Opinion-polling machine surveys produce a great deal of entertaining but misleading information. Typically, a video display showing one or more public opinion questions is installed in a high-traffic public walking area, along with response buttons permitting *yes-no, true-false, agree-disagree,* or multiple-choice answers. The questions can range from the serious ("Should marijuana be legalized?") to the trivial ("Do you think there is intelligent life in outer space?"), from demographic prompts ("What is your age and sex?") to marketing-related ones ("Where did you first hear about this place: from newspapers, radio, outdoor advertising, television, or some other source?").

Results of opinion-machine surveys are absolutely worthless when considered as projectible information. The nonrandom, self-selected sample of respondents is not typical of any other group; it's not even representative of all persons in that public facility at that time, nor of all those passing by the machine, nor of those who respond the next day. And it's certainly not a representative sample of any larger group, such as the American public, or vacationers to Florida, or shoppers.

Obviously, no one would take such figures seriously—or would they? Results from the Epcot Poll have been distributed to and printed by newspaper editors all over the country, sometimes on the front page because of the titillating nature of the questions. These editors either believe the results are valid or don't care about the validity of material they distribute to their readers. The danger is that disclaimers like "while not a scientific survey, the results are indicative of the views of a significant segment of the population" lead naive readers to mistakenly assume that the results are valid. Business readers might even make decisions based on the results, thereby deceiving themselves and their clients into wasting money.

To illustrate, imagine a poll machine is set up at the turnstiles of a popular amusement park. On July 19, 1990, let's say, 30,451 people visit the park, almost all of them vacationers from widely scattered spots around the United States and the world. They are mostly families with children and have enough disposable income for the trip and the hefty admission fees. They visit the park mostly in groups of at least two or more. Of these 30,451 paying visitors, let's say 5,000 answer a number of questions on the poll machine. The compiled answers to two of the questions could be of interest to marketers and advertisers:

1. *A question that collects usage data:* The sources from which respondents say they received information about the park, certain brands, products, or whatever

2. *A question that collects information on purchase dates or frequency of buying various high-ticket brands and products:* Scotch, luxury cars, shipboard cruises, etc.

The media-usage data could influence some advertisers in making future advertising media decisions. The high-ticket product-purchase data might persuade marketers of luxury brands to consider advertising at the amusement park.

In both cases, the data would be misleading because of the following reasons:

• The population visiting the park is not representative of any definable larger group—the general public, theme-park visitors, or vacationers. And therefore neither are their attitudes, media habits, life-styles, demographic characteristics, product usage, and so on.

- The population visiting the park on any one day, week, or month is not typical of visitors over any longer period. Results cannot be billed as "Park visitors have the opinion that . . ."
- Users of the poll machine are not typical of all visitors to the park for that day and certainly are not representative for any longer period. Some people seek out poll machines, some don't notice them, some deliberately avoid them, some—especially children—operate them several times. Responders epitomize the self-selected and therefore nonrandom, nonrepresentative sample.

Remember, it is impossible for machine polls like this to produce verifiable results. Don't trust them.

Magic Town, Splitsville, and Magic Markets Surveys

Magic Town surveys.

In an old movie called *Magic Town,* a reporter looks for, and finds, a town with the same voting pattern in national elections as the whole country. By finding out in advance how this little Magic Town votes, he shrewdly figures out he can predict what will happen in an upcoming national election. Some market researchers and pollsters are still looking for Magic Town, a single market area or city that is a perfectly matched microcosm of the nation or of a particular market segment (e.g., "typical America," "senior citizens," "typical housewives," or "the Southeastern region.")

So where's the catch? What's wrong with Magic Town surveys? Let's assume a single Magic Town has been located that is almost perfectly representative of national buying patterns, attitudes, demographic and psychographic characteristics, media habits, and many other relevant consumer variables. This could, and probably does, happen. There are several hundred sizable cities in the United States, and by chance alone, at any one time, one or a few will be highly similar to national characteristics, a few will be at the opposite end of the scale (highly dissimilar), and the others will be distributed along the similar-dissimilar scale in a normal, or bell-shaped, curve.

If Magic Town is perfectly similar to the national picture at one particular time, what's wrong with using it as a regular area for prediction? The primary problem is that towns change over time. The nation changes, and the typical community this month or year is not typical next time. A second problem is that no city, small or large, can be representative of all the various markets and people currently involved in target marketing, market segmentation, media proliferation, and audience fragmentation. The results of a Magic Town survey, therefore, cannot reliably be projected beyond the town itself during the period in which the survey is conducted. Remember the political proverb, "As Maine goes, so goes the nation!" They said that for a while, but not any more.

Splitsville surveys.

One variation on the Magic Town survey is the Splitsville survey. A Splitsville is a Magic Town that is set up as a more or less permanent field laboratory for pilot testing advertisements. For testing TV commercials, every other home can be wired to two different cables. In the same block, Cable A and Cable B are wired alternately to successive homes, ABABAB and so on. With this "split-cable" arrangement, two different commercials for the same product can be aired simultaneously throughout the town. Or A-homes can be exposed to twice as many commercials as B-homes. Or 15-second commercials can be contrasted with 30-second commercials. Many other experimental variations can be tested. For testing newspaper ads, alternate homes or blocks or carrier routes within a single city can simultaneously carry several experimental ads for a comparison of their effects.

Results from Splitsville experiments are more useful to advertisers than results from Magic Town surveys. True, the usual Splitsville in the United States is selected for being typical in much the same way as a Magic Town, with some additional criteria thrown in. But unlike a Magic Town survey, the purpose is not to make assumptions about the population as a whole; instead, it is to make a comparative analysis—i.e., to determine whether advertisement treatment A is better than, worse than, or the same as treatment B. It serves an experimental purpose, to determine cause-and-effect or relative effects. In the results, one will be projecting only the A versus B difference, not the absolute results. For example, if 3 percent of advertisement-A viewers buy the advertised brand, versus 6 percent of advertisement-B viewers, the conclusion is that B is better than A, perhaps (but not certainly) twice as good. The advertising researcher would *not* conclude that advertisement B would produce 6 percent sales, or any other absolute number, in other markets or nationally. By contrast, in a Magic Town descriptive study, the purpose is to project absolute numbers. In short, projecting comparative-treatment experimental results from Splitsville is much more likely to be accurate than projecting absolute descriptive numerical results.

Magic Markets surveys.

Magic Markets surveys use several Magic Towns at a time to test new products or new advertising campaigns. This type of survey is typically used by marketers to pilot-test new products or advertising before going national.

In a Magic Markets survey, test market cities are chosen that correspond as closely as possible to certain typical demographic and product-use characteristics. Since many mass-marketers and advertisers are looking for the same kinds of markets, though for different products, they tend to pick the same test market cities. Thus, there has emerged a particular group of two or three dozen communities, from small to large, that are used as test markets time and time again. These Magic Markets are exposed to a steady barrage of pilot tests of new products and new advertising campaigns, only a fraction of which are subsequently used nationwide. Even though the demographic profile of the Magic Markets is unchanged by all this special marketing attention, the resulting sophistication of the consumer population—their "test wiseness"—could potentially make them no longer typical in terms of their attention to advertising or their reaction to and use of consumer products.

However, when an experimental design is used, the results of test marketing or advertising pilot-testing to the consumers in these Magic Markets can be projected nationally. This kind of experimentation has a two-fold purpose:

1. To produce advertising comparative-treatment results as in Splitsville experiments.

2. To produce realistic, descriptive figures within the ballpark of what might be expected nationally

Test marketing in Magic Markets does an excellent job on the first purpose and can do a fairly good job on the second, depending on the representativeness of the experimental markets.

Summary.

No Magic Town is a random probability sample of a larger universe, and therefore provide somewhat risky information for marketers to a larger or different population. Splitsville communities can produce reasonably valid comparative results of different advertising treatments, as long as no projection of absolute numbers is made. Test marketing in Magic Markets combines the virtues of both Splitsville and a random sample survey: It produces very valid comparative results of different advertising treatments and ballpark-projectible descriptive results.

In Chapter 9, there will be more details on the various levels of advertising experiments: laboratory experiments, split-household (Splitsville) experiments, split-market experiments (test marketing, Magic Markets), and the ultimate type, nationwide controlled field experiments.

Pay-to-Participate Polls

The pay-to-participate poll has not caught on as a market survey tool, but it may be just a matter of time. People are already laying out cash to give their opinions on entertainers, sports, politics, and other matters.

Two major types have surfaced so far. Most visible is the TV phone poll in which you dial one of several different 900 numbers and are charged on your phone bill to vote for A or B, for or against, or as many numbers as there are choices. Another is the donor-member survey, in which one pays up to several hundred dollars a year to become a member of an organization, usually a political interest group. A major function of the organization, other than cashing the checks of the members, is to survey them periodically and "bring the results to the attention of Congress" and other decision makers. For as long as people feel the need to have their opinions heard, there will undoubtedly be other variations of the pay-to-play survey. And there will always be entrepreneurs ready to collect the cash.

Like all other nonrandom surveys discussed, the results of the pay-to-play polls are not projectible to any population or group other than the respondents themselves. The major reason should be obvious—the self-selected sample bias. If the legislators do get the results of the donor-member surveys, they would be wise not to think they are "the voice of the public." A little reflection tells us such respondents are not typical. Their unusual concern with the issues under question, their willingness to part with their money, and their demographic, psychographic, and consumer characteristics are quite distinctive.

In short, the pay-to-participate polls may provide harmless, if costly, amusement and catharsis for the respondents and profits for the survey-taker. But they do not provide valid projectible information for advertisers, marketers, or any other decision makers.

Other Nonrandom Survey Types

Variations on the nonrandom, nonprojectable survey are virtually endless. Some of the more common types include the "person on the street" polls, often connected by news media as a sidebar to a controversial news story; voter exit polls, conducted among nonrandom samples of people who have just cast their vote (a group who is neither representative of all voters nor necessarily truthful about their voting behavior); and write-in polls such as those conducted by Ann Landers and other columnists. Again, the danger with these surveys is their lack of representativeness of any larger population. Results should be presented as representative only of the self-selected, nonrandom sample who participated.

Review

In this chapter we saw that:

- A survey is the use of questions and answers to gather information from any group of two or more subjects.
- Many varieties of surveys can be used validly for many different purposes, but surveys are often conducted for the wrong purposes or are so poorly done that pure subjective judgment would give more accurate answers.
- Types of surveys include census (entire population), random sample (scientifically drawn and representative of the entire population), and nonrandom sample (nonscientifically drawn and not generalizable to the entire population).
- The ideal random sample has the following characteristics: (1) the target population has been rigorously and painstakingly defined; (2) the sample size is large enough to give the desired level of precision in the results;

(3) every individual in the defined population has an equal probability of being selected into the drawn sample; and (4) A high proportion of the drawn sample—at least 60 percent—must be reached and their responses obtained.

- Some common types of nonrandom surveys are focus groups: mall intercept surveys; motivation or "in-depth" surveys; magazine audience surveys; questionnaire-in-magazine surveys; TV phone-in polls; fixed-location opinion polling machines; Magic Town, Splitsville, and Magic Markets surveys; and pay-to-participate polls.
- When randomized group experiments are used, as in Splitsville and Magic Markets, comparisons of treatments can be valid, even though absolute numbers may not.

Endnote

1. Bernard Guggenheim, "All Research Is Not Created Equal," *Journal of Advertising Research,* February/March 1989, RC7–11.

8 Conducting a Random Sample Survey

In Chapter 7 we examined a number of popular survey research practices which, for a variety of reasons—especially biased sampling procedures—are flawed and of very limited use to the advertiser. Here we turn our attention to the steps to be taken in conducting a random sample survey from which results can be properly projected to a larger population.

A random sample survey is a means of gathering self-reported or observed information from respondents. This is the only type of survey in which the responses are indeed representative of the larger population from which the survey sample was drawn.

In advertising, the random sample survey is commonly used to collect feedback from a variety of populations—businesspeople, senior citizens, automobile owners, magazine readers, etc.—on a variety of subjects, such as product knowledge, attitudes, brand image, demographics, product usage, and so forth. There are four key steps in the proper execution of a sample survey: (1) drawing a random sample, (2) constructing the questionnaire, (3) setting the research environment, and (4) setting criteria for evaluating surveys. These four steps will be discussed in detail in the rest of this chapter.

Drawing a Random Sample

Political polls and public opinion surveys, when properly done, are examples of true sample surveys. By employing a random selection procedure, researchers are able to measure the voting preferences or opinions of a small fraction of the entire population and then draw conclusions with a substantial amount of certainty about the votes and/or opinions of the population from which the same was drawn. Without going into the statistical rationale behind random sampling selection, suffice it to say that decades of highly accurate presidential political polling by Gallup and other survey research organizations attest to both the efficiency and accuracy, within accepted error tolerances, of sample survey methodology. It is fortunate that sampling is available as an option to the researcher, because constraints of time and money would prohibit most efforts to conduct census surveys (interviewing of entire populations of subjects).

Before you draw a random sample, there are three important decisions to be made: (1) selecting a sampling method, (2) determining the desired sample size, and (3) determining acceptable levels of sample error and confidence.

Selecting a Sampling Method

A key characteristic of random, or probability, sampling is that each member of the population under study must have an equal probability of being included in the sample. This is the only way you can ensure that random samples are representative of the populations from which they are drawn. There are four basic probability sampling methods, each appropriate to different research tasks. They are called simple random, stratified random, systematic random, and area random sampling. Let's look at each in detail.

Simple random method.

The purest and most defensible of the probability sampling methods is simple random sampling. The easiest way to think of simple random selection is to picture the hopper of numbered ping-ping balls at a bingo parlor. Each time a ball is selected, every other ball had an equal chance of being chosen. In advertising research, populations are often available in list form, and the task of sampling involves choosing names or addresses from the list. One could select a simple random sample from a list in similar fashion to the bingo game by cutting out each name or address and drawing the individual items from a container. Again, each member has an equal chance of selection each time an item is drawn. (It should be noted that most lists are imperfect approximations of the actual or true population in question, but often a list is the only option available.)

A more traditional way to choose a simple random sample from a list is to number each item and transfer the numbers into table form. Then simply begin at a random point on the table and progress in some regular fashion, vertically, horizontally, or otherwise, through the table until the desired sample size is reached. If a number selected from the table corresponds to a number of the list, that member is chosen for inclusion in the sample. Numbers not corresponding to members of the list are ignored. An example of a table of random numbers is included in Figure 8–1. Simple random sampling techniques can be time-consuming, and so researchers often opt for faster, systematic random sampling methods.

Stratified random method.

The term *stratification* suggests division, and stratified random sampling involves dividing the population list according to some relevant characteristic or variable.

Figure 8–1
Table of Random Digits

```
52762 66073   23158 48218   02789 48863   29791 31397   46772 52034
35542 01928   70603 84190   25960 43181   75565 17498   04143 57865
67200 39553   82800 04016   42894 04013   66915 99982   26232 19268
73559 31451   32998 02675   57844 57102   77871 52187   01384 51308
10866 24011   70241 12694   03950 37364   99593 24162   85870 01154

50732 51992   27237 96222   78821 39937   81900 07784   17713 01815
98529 31871   03617 83693   67431 12329   71209 02371   01465 35838
00449 96753   73075 71100   65130 97884   60922 63892   07276 61578
55495 22756   42163 10257   85531 56295   10022 12755   82794 93137
93058 96911   25066 30906   47551 31082   57240 39079   95911 64014

74908 18202   50410 05263   85069 84824   51203 12026   86614 16307
22514 20209   56792 50334   56349 83722   60337 42485   37967 47066
09478 27994   07531 14221   35428 04684   32072 24988   42445 68438
56197 64337   90247 98510   80235 54564   77043 18653   38219 37187
23782 07290   53850 38222   68506 10059   73152 22690   13960 63211

41014 99879   53415 38691   26930 25072   35216 07897   16578 03495
36822 45937   66307 42423   30528 84660   82748 97257   71454 60601
66243 37845   58806 57164   52953 95369   72626 71024   30550 08546
81632 21052   21317 76746   49596 02668   00503 69094   10805 21870
60542 45834   72139 37245   94306 34435   24919 12757   12981 36491

22172 88227   54203 63416   24086 94307   81243 55246   78558 55146
59363 71962   30413 97322   13034 43062   74644 38885   29261 56155
97294 28105   47594 21460   49496 24370   45734 57770   74668 04268
92276 98706   51824 02512   75559 31046   56365 53563   73785 48207
69291 45853   90030 66679   52305 50666   59992 14675   93186 97980

49960 03809   88034 03601   32757 16165   94632 09661   56206 17715
80174 89838   06960 67940   91806 32282   78185 20048   73154 56539
58138 75269   84977 30557   76483 66233   41088 21418   53542 38481
70380 14522   42437 44504   66043 22846   12744 29136   80167 27288
64972 36642   18491 61544   66893 64637   34687 73441   51268 81308

44917 46723   70700 65605   04373 48630   41031 82567   23976 71678
80153 26936   42164 79658   97611 37114   54971 66765   91937 33813
27162 73899   46308 37829   27193 43308   97331 22064   55452 50924
11619 07862   44240 22786   01632 84613   13773 73334   54115 33531
35528 21979   38014 19755   20221 04746   23888 75529   56469 86316

25436 49830   10580 73347   63178 36756   33342 11560   28409 52134
86069 32798   64506 72364   38908 70009   89080 24925   94093 06037
35066 47833   35876 75654   50113 55670   47619 22710   36496 98730
00014 01953   18582 33946   73090 05701   22104 18711   39691 47150
24613 79087   11607 76318   91862 86520   66606 63290   07789 44091

69409 24160   88836 67751   15779 53424   58188 61522   41618 72632
96768 11625   49555 33326   86621 61117   20296 62077   03026 77503
37005 07752   22792 80023   07035 74543   72406 79308   18981 54042
95041 54633   17845 93010   12919 60767   62665 94558   37430 95209
74808 84851   33761 83211   08985 34390   81893 60819   91122 54890

27250 61275   13369 77513   18907 62245   82105 78013   83112 51204
53788 01463   69691 86699   12063 45301   74008 61963   67372 53797
80284 55000   76969 87310   34713 20276   29836 77516   45321 18376
85587 51060   08201 84871   66599 88508   48405 30343   20287 97332
36055 48368   13450 34015   95279 43980   57686 37275   41616 87840
```

Source: *A Million Random Digits*, The Rand Corporation, 1955.

Figure 8–1 (continued)
Table of Random Digits

```
61055 19392   95601 05134   18046 41780   64121 93550   39649 33440
60083 63789   90211 45898   82541 81508   40606 59318   45772 72930
41270 56184   10155 98837   22742 43211   51521 37401   48405 90061
35304 20811   84872 64215   13990 68726   58713 63220   70508 68032
44396 67803   02874 75098   34373 95812   22576 12725   59859 13371

34916 52029   11401 85583   83645 81751   16868 31536   09987 68722
93036 78065   18937 86687   74076 89317   09757 64711   46683 09876
25434 35776   97060 11204   74403 57422   45725 51088   22203 85570
79208 76636   58954 96841   27180 09644   64053 47642   26335 08783
15081 95371   05623 48156   55084 03440   25307 64497   84675 52612

08757 17635   31688 57856   73401 05251   12412 22926   54124 25266
07815 99845   12505 76385   15821 89560   07213 72199   82704 03431
67400 15167   92450 30436   91284 71474   07319 59811   54467 92567
97476 48344   49665 34800   82696 82291   10244 29821   00031 23567
63030 82195   49452 07037   03792 12562   58638 27133   94889 12372

94350 85989   51844 33801   11816 02663   68008 02883   94027 26394
64118 25484   90015 12945   68039 67110   37833 04542   06136 70344
76229 45749   28589 90287   75976 01676   72153 12585   82403 71043
79378 11934   72136 27507   98146 58896   54624 30386   98667 90016
32912 65278   11023 47545   47951 13411   48233 32799   60395 47383

77548 07273   89956 17488   70738 63990   28461 01303   78785 45222
93777 73240   73668 39353   33011 38333   87541 37552   33467 65245
81895 43691   96938 00724   56356 17257   82394 01103   77312 73088
17333 51756   35901 08608   71551 98335   57443 66045   01170 95216
75578 40499   96692 29183   26439 14270   96884 74260   74574 56516

16295 07137   40349 77523   03855 32436   74834 73273   86439 10320
79184 08083   42323 17978   41346 24633   32571 39487   17751 17431
30872 53665   24217 38904   22479 96079   27256 44947   28350 42300
12814 19353   98187 95392   97575 75803   65002 25052   39324 07507
78618 69938   55813 69077   72005 08206   67849 98574   45854 98822

94267 92158   02377 94677   37946 15240   93618 78506   58548 19846
08925 21577   63013 99028   41524 56018   14442 63606   83649 73110
69171 38625   04619 14563   42181 68863   80121 31294   05679 10391
24446 26696   87113 89227   84813 17508   08895 14220   11682 77046
63750 54601   21686 24373   33100 29039   49456 37504   82249 57252

26572 17339   64805 10579   16136 58305   73264 89988   30841 42318
98108 99447   14133 22402   33969 83233   83719 34379   03128 86872
50861 64413   83292 36025   20098 88603   44523 27205   54285 52264
50843 12994   63844 49487   08136 16682   25951 30401   90741 45528
98743 06068   66632 64101   52378 71232   09629 18732   36568 27904

09632 28848   11055 50443   49486 01388   19730 32161   15167 41926
28516 97385   27275 94299   38571 11238   34219 19949   76664 59880
47252 00624   80635 73592   49631 49945   94378 87716   89944 52491
83095 36850   73787 22163   13226 31233   40905 18738   73609 62624
52763 88253   32168 12097   01578 95421   43522 47895   52620 22791

94520 82996   26493 54232   15162 20562   28570 25919   03136 56601
33428 81309   16910 74161   10050 89018   76604 30681   73618 45262
26843 48344   58005 50447   51427 49247   95442 53365   15717 16078
37035 92880   93900 61357   84552 29436   94784 23916   80554 64522
37521 11597   77500 57284   53226 37389   39783 82583   87850 75927
```

Source: *A Million Random Digits,* The Rand Corporation, 1955.

Simple random sampling procedures are then used until the desired population subgroup size is reached. As an example, recent research reveals that women are key influencers in automobile purchase decisions, even though purchases are frequently recorded under men's names. This means that although a simple random sample of purchasers of new trucks would certainly be representative of a population list, it would probably include more males than females. In fact, there might be so few females that if they were then further divided based on geographic area, their numbers might be so small as to be unusable. The simple random method, therefore, cannot effectively select male and female purchasers equally; the stratified random method can. Male and female purchasers are sampled in equal proportions, and their responses are compared. If the researcher does not wish to distort results for the sample as a whole, the male and female responses can be weighted differently to reflect their incidence in the true population. Remember that there must be a compelling reason for using a stratified random sample; there must be some relevant characteristic on which to divide the original population and a need to overrepresent that characteristic in the sample to be drawn.

Systematic random method.

Systematic random sampling imposes a "system" or prescribed "short cut" in the selection process. It saves time and effort in drawing a representative sample of a population. Three types of systematic random sampling techniques are commonly used. The first, known as *interval sampling,* requires that a researcher begin at a random point on a given population list and then choose every "*n*th" member— the member that falls at the predetermined interval. To arrive at the appropriate interval, one that will enable a researcher to traverse the entire list, one must simply divide the population size by the desired sample size, as follows:

Population of new car buyers = 9000

Desired sample size = 300

9000 ÷ 300 = 30

Interval = 30

In this example, every 30th member of the population list is chosen.

It is important to note that when conducting any kind of random sampling, the first member selected from the population also should be randomly chosen. That is, the researcher must *begin* at a random point in the list. A common mistake is to begin at the first name on a given list and then randomly select subsequent items. If the first name on the list is chosen arbitrarily, or because it is the first name, or for whatever reason, then it technically does not fit out definition of random selection—when the first name was chosen, every member of the population did not have an equal chance of being selected.

The second type of systematic random sampling is commonly called *cluster sampling.* The researcher follows interval sampling procedures, except that fewer intervals are used and more population members are selected for the sample at

---

each of those intervals. The researcher chooses the number of intervals as well as the size of the cluster; when multiplied, they produce the desired sample size. Using the previous example of new car buyers, here are some possible options:

Population = 9000
Desired sample size = 300

Number of Intervals	Cluster Size	Sample Size
30	10	300
20	15	300
10	30	300

The researcher selects the first cluster of samples at a random point and then additional clusters at prescribed intervals.

Area random method.

Area sampling is used when population lists are unavailable or otherwise impractical. It involves selecting geographic areas, such as census tracts, church congregations in various cities, and so forth. These "areas" are chosen randomly, usually after being assigned a number. Once selected, a census can be taken of members, or random sampling procedures can be used within each area.

Sample Bias

The possibility of sample bias is the primary threat to the representativeness of a sample. As we saw in Chapter 7, nonrandom samples are typically biased because they are selected unscientifically. Theoretically, proper execution of true random sampling procedures should overcome sample bias. However, there is one major exception, known as *periodicity*. Periodicity is the bias introduced to the sample (even though it was randomly selected) by virtue of the arrangement of the population or population list. Periodicity is the result of the coincidence of two arrangements—that of the population list and that of the sampling. For example, imagine working with a university undergraduate population list that happens to be arranged in the following manner: freshman, sophomore, junior, senior, freshman, sophomore, junior, etc. Imagine also that the interval chosen for the sample is a multiple of four, say, 8, 20, or 40. The result of the interaction of the arrangement of the list and the sampling interval will be overrepresentation of members of one college classification, because the interval will by design result in selection of students in the same year of study. When considering the use of interval or cluster sampling, remember to determine whether a systematic arrangement scheme was used in preparing the list and, if it was used, to determine whether the chosen sampling interval will result in systematic bias.

Determining the Desired Sample Size

An important decision in choosing a sample is determining how many members it should contain. Obviously, from a time and money standpoint, a researcher desires as small a sample as will provide accurate or representative results. In an ideal sample a minimum amount of interviewing would be required and the projectability of the data would be high. While there is not sufficient space here to fully explain the derivation of suggested sample sizes, suffice it to say that appropriate sample sizes are determined by considering the size of the total population, the type of question being asked, and the level of accuracy desired.

The novice researcher might be surprised to find that in many cases a random sample of only several hundred is sufficient size to represent a metropolitan area or the entire country. Generally speaking, sample sizes smaller than 50 are believed to be too small to compute the sample error. A formula for determining sample size and sample error is discussed below.

Determining Acceptable Levels of Sample Error and Confidence

One important characteristic that distinguishes probability samples from nonprobability samples is the ability to calculate within a certain range of confidence the error introduced in the sampling process.

Sample error refers to the level of inaccuracy that occurs when the results of a sample survey are used to estimate a characteristic in the entire population from which the sample is taken. It is the deviation between the observed characteristics of a sample and the characteristics of the larger population. Inaccuracy is inevitable. The question, then, is how can we estimate the extent to which our projections are off? Also, how sure are we that our estimates are right? Expression of sample error addresses both of these issues. Statisticians have developed formulas to calculate sampling error, but for the purposes of our discussion it is not important to examine them in detail. It is important, however, to understand how researchers apply them. Using actual results (the statistic) from a sample survey, the researcher sets a *confidence interval:* a range of expected error expressed in plus and minus percentage points above and below the statistic. When the statistic is projected to a larger population, the confidence interval represents the area into which the actual population parameter is likely to fall.

For example, if the sample figure (or statistic) is 40 percent *yes* to the question "Have you seen a commercial for Lotsafizz soda on television in the past week?" then the number of people likely to respond *yes* in the entire population would be 40 percent ±5 percent. That is, the actual result is expected to be between 35 and 45 percent. The confidence level is simply the degree to which the researcher is certain that the population parameter is accurate. In the example, a 95 percent confidence level would mean that the researcher was 95 percent certain that the number of people in the entire population like to answer *yes* lies between 35 and 45 percent. All of these figures are based on what is known about sample distributions and inferential statistics. For the purpose of advertising research, it is important to be aware of the phenomenon of sampling error and to take it into account in our analysis of results.

A quick and easy formula can be used to compute the sample error of a percentage estimate in a sample study.[1] In this formula, the 95 percent confidence level is used. The formula is as follows:

$$\pm 1.96 \sqrt{\frac{pq}{n}}$$

where: p = proportion of answers falling into a certain category (for instance, 40 percent)

q = 100 − p

n = sample size

The value of p and q are related to the proportion of scores that fall into a certain category, such as 40 percent. A very conservative way of approaching this formula is to assume the maximum variation of "split" among scores—50 percent (.5) at the 95 percent confidence level. In that case, to compute the sample error for a sample of 500, the formula would be:

$$\pm 1.96 \sqrt{\frac{pq}{n}}$$

$$\text{or} \pm 1.96 \sqrt{\frac{.25}{500}}$$

$$\text{or} \pm 1.96 \sqrt{.0005}$$

$$\pm 1.96 \times .0224$$

$$= \pm 4.38$$

So, if our sample statistic was 42 percent, our confidence interval would be between 37.6 percent and 46.4 percent, or 42 percent plus or minus 4.4 percent.

Constructing the Questionnaire

The questionnaire is what the survey is all about. The questions it contains represent the areas where uncertainty exists, and the purpose of the survey is to gather information from a specific group to reduce that uncertainty. Four aspects of the questionnaire will be discussed here: (1) substance of questions, (2) structure of questions, (3) wording of questions, and (4) sequencing of questions. All four of these factors contribute to the overall effectiveness of the questionnaire as a tool of measurement.

Substance of Questions

The content of a questionnaire depends on the kind of information the researcher is seeking from the respondent. It is advisable at the outset of planning for a particular study that a researcher write down specific questionnaire objectives that address question subject matter. For instance, a specific questionnaire objective might be to measure respondent awareness of a current advertising campaign theme. Another specific questionnaire objective might be to measure the amount of a particular product a respondent uses in a given month. The choice of questions is built around these objectives. Typically in advertising research, the objectives are to gain information on demographic facts, product awareness, knowledge, attitudes, opinions, convictions, and reported past behavior.

Demographic facts.

These questions are designed to capture any number of objective pieces of information, such as variables of age, gender, income, and so on.

Example:

Check the income category that includes your total annual household income.

____ $10,000 or less	____ $20,001 to 25,000
____ $10,001 to 15,000	____ $25,001 to 30,000
____ $15,001 to 20,000	____ $30,001 to 35,000
	____ More than $35,000

Awareness/recall.

Items designed to measure awareness ask respondents whether they recall seeing or hearing a message. If no prompting is used and the respondent simply draws on recent memory, the question is *unaided*.

Example:

Please list the news magazines you have seen over the past month.

_____

_____

_____

Aided recall questions use prompts, or lists of potential answers to help the respondent.

Example:

Which of the following news magazines have you seen over the past month?

_____ *Time*   _____ *U.S. News & World Report*

_____ *Newsweek*   _____ Other: _____

Another type of awareness question measures *recognition,* which is the respondent's ability to recognize slogans, characters, commercials, or other message elements to which they have been exposed.

Example:

Which of the following covers of news magazines do you remember having seen over the past month? [Show covers]

Knowledge.

These items ask respondents what information they have about certain products or product advertising.

Example:

Lee Iacocca is a spokesperson for which brand of automobiles?

____ Chrysler   ____ Ford   ____ Mercedes Benz   ____ BMW

Attitude/opinion.

A variety of scaling techniques and other methods are used to measure attitude and opinion. Advertising researchers commonly use a 5-point scale.

Example:

Please put a check in the space that best describes how much you like or dislike Lotsafizz soda:

Like _____ _____ _____ _____ _____ Dislike

Brand image.

A brand image question aims to identify the beliefs a consumer holds about a brand.

Example:

Place a check in the appropriate space for each characteristic you believe each brand of tennis balls to possess:

	Durable	**Tough**	**Consistent**	**Inexpensive**
Dunlop	_____	_____	_____	_____
Penn	_____	_____	_____	_____
Wilson	_____	_____	_____	_____

Conviction.

A question about consumer conviction is concerned with a prediction by the respondent that he or she plans to take some action in the future.

Example:

In the next 30 days, which of the following items do you plan to purchase at least once?

_____ Corn chips   _____ Potato chips

_____ Pretzels   _____ Popcorn

_____ Cheese puffs

Reported past behavior.

A common type of question in consumer research is reported past behavior. Respondents typically are asked about their purchase behavior over a specified period of time. These are often used as screening questions to select appropriate individuals for an upcoming study.

Example:

Which of the following types of milk have you consumed at least one 8-ounce glass of in the past week? (Check all that apply)

_____ Whole milk	_____ ½-percent milk
_____ 2-percent milk	_____ Buttermilk
_____ 1½-percent milk	_____ Sweet acidophilous milk
_____ 1-percent milk	_____ Other: _____

Structure of Questions

A few basic question structures predominate in most questionnaires. All fall into one of two major types: open-ended and closed-ended.

Closed-ended questions.

In closed-ended questions, several answers are provided from which the respondent chooses. All of the examples in the preceding section are closed-ended questions. There are several forms, including the following.

Dichotomous. Sometimes called "yes-no" questions, they often are just that.

Examples:

Do you own a car?

_____ Yes   _____ No

What is your attitude toward the commercial you just viewed?

_____ Like   _____ Dislike

Multiple response. A multiple response or "multiple choice" question includes several options from which the respondent can choose.

Example:

Which slogan do you prefer for Lotsafizz soda? (Choose one)

_____ Lotsafizz. The name says it all.

_____ More bubbles for your buck.

_____ It'll tickle your nose.

In cases were a researcher is uncertain whether all possible response options have been provided, respondents can be asked to specify their "other" response.

Checklist. A checklist allows respondents to indicate which items they like or dislike.

Example:

Place a check beside the brands of soda you like. Check as many as you like.

_____	Coca-Cola	_____	7-UP
_____	Pepsi	_____	Dr Pepper
_____	Lotsafizz		

Rating scale. Verbal rating scales of attitude or image use any number of degrees of response along a continuum or scale. Some have an odd number of responses, which affords a mid-point or "point of neutrality." Others, by offering an even number of options, force the respondents to choose among the available positions, either positive or negative.

Example:

Please indicate how much you like or dislike each brand of soda by placing a check in the appropriate space:

	Strongly Like	Like	Neither Like nor Dislike	Dislike	Strongly Dislike
Coca-Cola	____	____	____	____	____
Lotsafizz	____	____	____	____	____
Pepsi	____	____	____	____	____
Dr Pepper	____	____	____	____	____
7-UP	____	____	____	____	____

Ranking. One method of allowing respondents to indicate a preference for response options is to have them rank or order the items according to some specified criterion. Ranking criteria might be to order items from most to least expensive, from most liked to most disliked, from best-tasting to worst-tasting, etc.

Example:

Please rank the following brands of sugar-free colas. Which do you like best? Which is your second choice? Third choice? And so on.

Brand A	_____	Brand D	_____
Brand B	_____	Brand E	_____
Brand C	_____		

A variation of the above method is to offer the respondent a limited number of "points" to be allocated among the items to be evaluated. This allows respondents to indicate the magnitude of difference between the objects.

Example:

You have a total of 100 points to be divided among the brands of sugar-free colas below. You may give as many or as few of your total 100 points to each as you wish.

Brand A _____ points   Brand C _____ points

Brand B _____ points   Brand D _____ points

Semantic differential.   A very popular technique in consumer questionnaires, the semantic differential involves presenting opposite response choices with seven intervals in between to allow a respondent to indicate intensity of feeling. Sometimes called an "expanded dichotomy," semantic differential scales follow a particular format.

Good	__	__	__	__	__	__	__	Bad
Fresh	__	__	__	__	__	__	__	Stale
Like	__	__	__	__	__	__	__	Dislike
Attractive	__	__	__	__	__	__	__	Unattractive

Likert scaling.   While the semantic differential uses as its evaluation referent a brand or object, the Likert scale is employed to measure respondent agreement or disagreement with a particular statement. In the true Likert format, five degrees of response are available.

Example:

Please indicate your level of agreement with the following statement by checking the appropriate space.

I consider myself loyal to one brand of toothpaste.

_____	_____	_____	_____	_____
Strongly Agree	Agree	Neither Agree nor Disagree	Disagree	Strongly Disagree

Open-ended questions.

In open-ended questions, the respondents provide the answers. Open-ended questions are usually used to give the respondents the opportunity to answer in their own words. Ideally, this lends some insight into their level of knowledge, attitudes, opinions, and so on. Open-ended questions are also used so that the researcher can avoid having to predict all of the possible responses a respondent might give. By asking the question in open-ended fashion, the researcher does not lead respondents into a set of predetermined answers, but instead allows them to express their responses in their own way.

Examples:

Which commercials for soft drinks can you recall having seen in the past month?

Describe the type of person who drives a Cadillac automobile.

What do you like best about Lotsafizz soda? What do you like least about Lotsafizz?

One advantage of using open-ended items in a questionnaire is the opportunity to receive verbatim feedback from consumers in a completely unstructured manner. This important advantage, however, could be offset by the difficulty often encountered when trying to interpret, tabulate, and report the results. Responses must be read and somehow categorized or grouped in a meaningful way. Nonetheless, open-ended items offer valuable information to the researcher and are often used to explore the motivations behind consumer actions. Open-ended items can be used in conjunction with closed-ended items in the same questionnaire.

Wording of Questions

It's been said many times that the way a question is asked will determine to a great extent the answer that will be given. When constructing questionnaires, researchers must be aware that verbal nuances, ambiguities, and a variety of other communication pitfalls can seriously jeopardize the accuracy of their results. The true test of any question is whether it will elicit the desired information from the respondent, so pretesting individual items or entire questionnaires is highly advisable. Draft the questions and test them on small groups of respondents before proceeding with a study. It is almost unheard of to arrive at a perfect draft of a questionnaire on the first try. More than likely, a number of revisions will have to be made, often up to five or six, before the questionnaire items are honed adequately. Even after taking these precautions, it is not unusual for one or more items to be thrown out after the survey is conducted because they were found to be confusing.

Following are a few general guidelines for question working. In each case it is important to consider the viewpoint of the respondent and how he or she might interpret or misinterpret what the interviewer is trying to communicate.

Keep it simple.

Questions should be written using the simplest, most direct language possible for a given audience. Beyond the types of words chosen, which will be discussed below, the instrument itself should be simple in design, and only those questions necessary to the completion of the study should be included. This means that a questionnaire should be free of superfluous verbiage, which only serves to confuse, bore, or even anger respondents who have other things to do with their time than fill out questionnaires. In every way possible, the researcher should attempt both to gather the needed information from respondents and to minimize their time and effort commitment.

Avoid difficult or technical language.

Difficult or unnecessary technical language can distract or confuse the respondent and place the validity of the findings in jeopardy. Don't give in to the temptation to use advertising jargon in formulating questions instead of finding commonly understood terms. Imagine asking the following question of a grocery store customer as he or she exits the store: "Did you notice the new merchandising techniques in the store this week?" The average grocery store patron probably has little or no understanding of the term *merchandising techniques*. Respondents may react in many different ways to a question like this. Some may ask for a definition of the term before answering yes or no. Other will attempt an answer so as not to appear ignorant of the term. After all, it's just a yes-no question. This, of course, poses serious validity problems for the question. In either case, unfamiliar language will confuse and often annoy respondents and must be avoided.

Don't make assumptions about respondent knowledge or expertise.

Make sure you are aware of the respondents' degree of understanding of a subject or experience with a product. One cannot assume, for example, that registered voters are necessarily aware of the candidates running for a particular office, that purchasers of a bonnet-type hair dryer bought it for themselves, or that TV viewers are aware of the average length of a commercial. In fact, some studies have suggested that consumers perceive commercials to be longer than they actually are. Because consumer knowledge and experience can be measured, not to do so can pose problems with interpretation of results. Appropriate screening questions can help alleviate interviewer uncertainty about the level of respondent knowledge or experience.

Example:

I am calling about the bonnet-type hair dryer you purchased in December. Did you buy it for yourself or for someone else?

_____ Bought for self   _____ Not for self

Avoid double negatives.

A common error in questionnaires is the use of double negatives that confuse the respondent. These should be avoided if possible. For instance, the question "Which of the following is *not* a brand of dishwashing soap that does *not* wash away grease?" can be rephrased simply as "Which of the following brands of dishwashing soap is effective against grease?"

Beware of ambiguity.

A common mistake in question working is that the question or the response options have multiple meanings and hence require separate answers.

Example:

Do you consider ACME products and services to be:

_____	_____	_____	_____	_____
Excellent	Very Good	Average	Below Average	Poor

In this case, the respondent might have separate evaluations of ACME products and ACME services, making it difficult to choose only one answer on the scale.

Avoid loaded questions.

If the interviewer poses a question in a way that suggests a preferred answer or implies certain information about the respondent, the question is said to be *loaded.*

Example:

"Have you used your fax machine today?   _____Yes   _____No

This question suggests that the respondent has a fax machine, when in fact he or she may not. Even if those who do not own faxes answer "no," the results are still unclear.

Example:

Please check the space next to the range that includes your annual household income:

_____ $200,000 or more	_____ $75,000–99,999
_____ $150,000–199,999	_____ $50,000–74,999
_____ $100,000–149,999	_____ Less than $50,000

These response options are loaded toward the high end of the income scale. (The average income of U.S. households is, in fact, much lower than $50,000.) A respondent with an above-average income of, say, $40,000 would have to select the last option, which implies that he or she is somehow below the "norm." Some respondents might be tempted to choose a higher category than their actual income, just so they don't appear to be on the low end of the scale.

Make response options exhaustive.

Few things can alienate a respondent as much as the inability to find an appropriate response option to describe his or her situation. As question writers, researchers must ensure that every response possibility has been accommodated in each questionnaire item. To the extent that all answers cannot be anticipated, the researcher may choose to make the response options exhaustive by using the "other" response.

In a study of Dallas college students' media habits, the question below was created to measure readership of various daily newspapers in the area.

Which newspapers do you read? (check all that apply)	How often? (per week)	How long do you spend reading this paper each day?			
		(1) 1–15 min.	(2) 16–30 min.	(3) 31–60 min.	(4) 1 hr.+
____ The Daily Campus	1 2 3 4	____	____	____	____
____ USA Today	1 2 3 4 5 6 7	____	____	____	____
____ Wall Street Journal	1 2 3 4 5 6 7	____	____	____	____
____ Dallas Morning News	1 2 3 4 5 6 7	____	____	____	____
____ Dallas Times Herald	1 2 3 4 5 6 7	____	____	____	____
____ Ft. Worth Star Telegram	1 2 3 4 5 6 7	____	____	____	____
____ New York Times	1 2 3 4 5 6 7	____	____	____	____
____ Other (please specify)	1 2 3 4 5 6 7	____	____	____	____

The "other" response was included to allow for responses not listed, such as out-of-town papers a student might receive in the mail each day. The "please specify" instructions allowed researchers to determine whether certain daily newspapers not generally available in the Dallas area were extensively read by students.

Provide mutually exclusive answers.

If at all possible, responses to questionnaire items should be conceptually discrete or separate. Consider the following item:

Please check the category that includes your age:

_____ Younger than 20

_____ 20–25

_____ 25–30

_____ 31–35

_____ 36 or older

This particular set of responses is perplexing for the 25-year-old, who is torn between two options that both include the correct answer. Obviously this was a careless error, but other instances of non-mutually exclusive responses can be more subtle. A question writer must consider whether it is possible to fashion mutually exclusive responses in every case. If it is not, instructions might be changed to allow respondents to choose more than one answer.

Sequencing of Questions

When arranging the various elements to be included in a questionnaire, care should be taken to consider whether the ordering of items will facilitate completion by the respondent. One way to get the respondent into the flow of the questionnaire is to include a brief instruction message at the top. If possible, questions should then be arranged from easiest to most difficult. This prevents a respondent from becoming discouraged at the complexity of difficult questions at the outset. A certain amount of response momentum is possible if questions are arranged according to their level of difficulty. This can give confidence to a respondent, who is then encouraged to finish the questionnaire.

Sensitive questions or those that might cause a respondent to terminate early in the questioning should be saved for last. Again, this allows respondents to answer questions they are comfortable with before encountering potential "terminators." An example of a terminator is the income question. A considerable percentage of respondents regularly refuse to answer a question about their income. If the income question were to appear early in the question sequence, some might terminate. Placing the income question or other very difficult or sensitive questions at the end should minimize such behavior, though it is by no means assurance that respondents will be cooperative with the same question in another position.

Setting the Research Environment

The research environment for a survey relates to the method of data collection chosen, whether it be the personal interview, mailed questionnaire, or telephone interview. These options are representative of two major avenues of questionnaire administration: interviewing, which involves an interviewer who reads the questions and records the responses; and self-administered questionnaires, where the interviewees fill out the questions themselves. Each method of data collection has its strengths and weaknesses, and it is up to the research planner to determine which type of interviewing scenario is appropriate, as well as affordable, for the project at hand.

Personal Interview

Also called the *face-to-face* or *in-person interview,* the personal interview requires that interviewer and respondent meet for the purpose of data collection. The setting can be the respondent's residence or place of business, a shopping mall or other public place, or an agreed-on "neutral" site.

Advantages.

- *Feedback and clarification:* In the event of respondent uncertainty or confusion, the interviewer can offer additional information about or an explanation of a particular question.

- *Fewer unanswered questions:* Because an interviewer can offer clarification and explanation about the survey, the intent of a question, or the language used, it is less likely that a respondent will leave questions blank as a result of misunderstanding.

- *High response rate:* Compared with the mail questionnaire, the personal interview can produce a much higher completion rate. In many cases the respondent is phoned ahead of time to set up the interview, then reminded of the interview date as it approaches. These extra precautions contribute to a high completion percentage.

- *Interviewer observation:* As well as recording answers to specific questions, the interviewer can observe and record the respondent's situation and surroundings. Information of interest might be the type of dwelling, type of neighborhood, respondent dress and mannerisms, etc.

Disadvantages.

- *Implementation costs:* The personal interview is usually the most expensive of the three basic data-gathering options. Interviewers must be recruited and trained, an expense which does not factor into planning for a mail survey. If the interview is to take place at a site other than the research workplace, additional costs of travel are incurred.

- *Accuracy of sensitive information:* Because the personal interview involves two human beings, their reactions to each other might come into play in the course of the questioning. This phenomenon has especially serious implications for sensitive or personal questions, where truthful answers might cause embarrassment or discomfort to the respondent. Rather than express privately held opinions on such topics as sexual practices, illegal behavior, or generally unaccepted moral beliefs, interviewees may be tempted to "go with the crowd." Even though interviewers guarantee anonymity, self-administered questionnaires get better results in such circumstances.

- *Interviewer-respondent interaction:* Just as in social situations certain people tend to "hit it off" better than others, the interaction between interviewer and respondent can affect the outcome of a personal interview. Respondents react differently to different interviewers. The best solution to this problem is careful training of interviewers so that an emphasis is placed on uniformity of collection procedures. Interviewers should not respond in ways that suggest approval or disapproval of answers, and questionnaire items must be read verbatim so that bias is not injected by the interviewer.

Telephone Interview

Because nearly 97 percent of American households have telephones, telephone interviews are a popular data-gathering method and are easy to conduct. Samples drawn from telephone lists yield a fairly representative picture of the population, although it has been estimated that nearly one in five households with less than $15,000 annual income does not have a telephone.

Advantages.

- *Convenience:* The telephone survey requires no travel time or expense on the part of the interviewer or the respondent. Calls can be made from a central office or phone bank at whatever time of the day is appropriate for the interview. Random digit dialing (RDD), a system that gives access to both listed and unlisted phone numbers, eliminates potential bias in selecting sample households.
- *Turnaround time:* Telephone data are captured immediately and can be analyzed as soon as the interview is completed, if desired. Telephone interviewing has become even more efficient with the introduction of computer-assisted telephone interviewing (CATI). A computer program dials random phone numbers and then prompts the interviewer with scripted questions. Answers are entered directly into the computer terminal by the interviewer, who is then prompted with the next appropriate question. Ongoing analysis of data is made possible because the information can be instantly machine-read and tabulated.
- *Feedback:* Though limited to verbal messages, interaction is possible with telephone interviews. Respondents can ask for clarification from telephone interviewers, and interviewers can ask respondents to explain or expand on their answers.

Disadvantages.

- *Noncooperation rate:* Completion rates can be low for telephone interviews. As prospects often mistake research interviewers for telemarketing sales callers, it's important at the beginning of the call to emphasize that this is a research study. Otherwise, prospects may terminate the call.

- *Sampling frame:* Although most households have telephones, in some geographic areas the number of nonsubscribing households is high. A larger problem is that inaccurate or outdated phone lists mean that time is lost in the sample selection process. In local telephone directories, for example, up to 20 percent of the names, phones numbers, and addresses change from one year to the next. Researchers should always try to obtain as accurate a telephone list as possible and usually should allow for a degree of unavoidable inaccuracy with every telephone survey.

- *Sensitive questions:* As with face-to-face interviews, there is potential for problems with sensitive or embarrassing questions in telephone surveys. Again, interviewers must do their best to create as uninhibited an exchange as possible so that respondents are encouraged to be open and honest in their answers.

Mailed Questionnaires

In many business-to-business research programs, as well as some consumer studies, the mail questionnaire is the method of choice.

Advantages.

- *Lower cost:* The mail survey is usually less expensive than either personal or telephone interviews, especially if research is conducted on a national sample. Costs for the mail survey are limited to printing to the questionnaire and outbound and return postage (a self-addressed, stamped envelope should be provided).

- *Flexibility of completion:* The mail survey allows the respondent to choose when and where he or she participates. Upon receiving the questionnaire, the respondent may choose to fill it out right away, fill out a part of it and return to it later, or save the entire task for a later time. While some questionnaires are kept indefinitely or thrown away, many are completed at various times after being received.

- *Sensitive questions:* Because mail questionnaires are self-administered, the respondent is not subject to the interaction factor that, as we have seen, can result in exaggerated or untrue answers.

Disadvantages.

- *Time frame:* Obviously, it takes a certain amount of time for a mail questionnaire to reach its destination and be completed and returned. A researcher must wait about two weeks before most questionnaires that will be returned actually come back. If a second mailing or "wave" is scheduled to increase response rate, that time would be at least doubled.

- *Sample frame:* An accurate mailing list, preferably complete with names of respondents, is necessary for a successful mail survey. Questionnaires addressed to "the occupant," "the manager," or other generic title might receive less attention or may not be forwarded promptly to the appropriate recipient. Using the correct name of the target respondent gives an added degree of control.

- *Potentially low return rate:* Unsolicited mail of any kind runs the risk of being ignored by the recipient. Even if it is received and read, the questionnaire may not be filled out properly and on time and returned. Generally speaking, a 50 percent response rate is considered minimally acceptable, with a 70 percent rate more desirable. Sometimes researchers must initiate multiple follow-up mailings or waves to attain acceptable overall response rates.

Setting Criteria for Evaluating Surveys

The Advertising Research Foundation offers a series of questions concerning the reporting of survey research results in a document entitled *ARF Criteria for Marketing and Advertising Research.* Figure 8–2 contains the ARF guidelines.

Figure 8–2
Presentation of Survey Findings

Key questions concerning the presentation of findings in a research report are as follows:

A. Are the results fairly presented? Do the data support the interpretations and conclusions? Are the actual findings clearly differentiated from the interpretation of the findings?

B. How is the response rate presented?

C. Are the complete findings presented?

D. Is there a distinction made between association and causation?

• • •

A. Are the results fairly presented? Do the data support the interpretations and conclusions? Are the actual findings clearly differentiated from the interpretation of the findings?

It is important that the reporting of study findings and the conclusions drawn from them be clearly distinguished. Reporting of the research data should be expressed in language which clearly represents the findings and from which all readers may obtain the same understanding of what is presented.

Interpretations or conclusions based on findings may be subject to differing points of view, and are acceptable as long as the findings logically support that point of view.

B. How is the response rate presented?

As previously defined, the response rate is the proportion of sampling units originally designated for the sample that actually provide information for the research. In other words, the response rate is the percent of the pre-designated units that are in the tabulated sample. Since the base is pre-designated units, substitutes cannot be counted in the computation of response rates.

The computation of response rates is sometimes difficult, particularly when a unit must be contacted before it can be determined that it is to be designated for the sample. For example, for a study of the teen-age population, it may not be possible to determine whether there are qualified respondents (teen-agers) in those households that refuse access or where no one is at home. When random digit dialing is used for a telephone study of the household population, it may be difficult to determine whether no answers and busy signals represent businesses, households, or phantom numbers. To meet such difficulties, working assumptions are sometimes made to adjust calculations on the basis of data compiled from contacted units.

The report of the response rate should describe the method along with the numbers entering the computation. For multi-stage and stratified samples, it may be of interest that response rates be reported by stage and stratum. It is desirable when there are key sub-groups for analysis, that response rates be given for each key sub-group for which data are available to make the computation. Sometimes only partial information is obtained from a sampling unit. Report of response rate should show the number and percentages that supplied complete information; that provided sufficient information for most analyses; that were rejected because of non-verification, incompleteness, or illegibility; and that were not reached at all or refused.

C. Are the complete findings presented?

Although it is not necessary for a research report to contain a written statement of every item of data gathered during the study, all relevant items which are specifically related to the study's objectives should be analyzed and shown. This is true even if one or more of the items is inconsistent with the overall conclusions drawn from the research. Findings not included in the report should be available to the report user upon request.

D. Is there a distinction made between association and causation?

Association and causation mean different things and therefore should not be used interchangeably.

In most research studies conducted, association is the proper terminology when doing a statistical analysis. For example, when analyzing differences in demographic sub-group levels of brand usage, associations are being examined. There are occasions, however, when causality is a proper term to use or infer during interpretation of the results. In controlled experiments where assignments of treatments are made at random, such as in advertising weight tests, causality can be attributed in the interpretation of data.

If the research objectives require a conclusion about causality as distinct from association only, the study procedure must be designed accordingly.

Source: Advertising Research Foundation, *ARF Criteria for Marketing and Advertising Research*, pp. 28–29.

Review

In this chapter we saw that:

- A random sample survey is a means of gathering self-reported or observed information from respondents that are representative of the larger population from which the sample was drawn.
- To be random, each member of the population under study must have an equal probability of being included in the sample.
- The four methods of basic probability sampling are simple random, stratified random, systematic random, and area random sampling.
- Periodicity is the result of the coincidence of two arrangements, that of the population list and that of the sampling, resulting in overrepresentation of members of one classification.
- The confidence level is the degree to which the researcher is certain that the population parameter is accurate, expressed as plus or minus some percentage of error.
- The four aspects of the questionnaire to be considered are the substance of questions, the structure of questions, the wording of questions, and the sequencing of questions.
- Each method of data collection has its strengths and weaknesses: personal interviews, telephone interviews, and mailed questionnaires.

Endnote

1. This discussion is based on Guido Stempel and Bruce Westley, *Research Methods in Mass Communication*, Prentice Hall, 1981, 56–61.

Chapter 9 Controlled Experiments

Controlled experiments serve an entirely different purpose than surveys, which we examined in Chapter 8. Surveys, focus groups, and other so-called *descriptive* research methods are mostly used to describe people (populations, audiences, etc.), their demographic characteristics, habits, media usage, consuming and buying behaviors, attitudes, motivations, psychographics, and so on.

The purpose of controlled experiments, on the other hand, is to determine *cause-and-effect,* or causal relationships between advertising and behavior, advertising and attitudes, or advertising and knowledge.

A controlled experiment is the most precise and scientific way to determine, for example:

- Which advertising medium, newspapers, radio, or television, will (or did) produce the most profit from a one million dollar budget?
- Which year-long campaign theme, A or B, will (or did) produce more incremental sales?
- Which commercial, A or B or C, will (or did) create the most favorable brand image and attitude?
- How much the advertising budget should be next year—normal (i.e., like this year), one-half of normal, one-half more than normal, double normal, or five times normal?

Descriptive market research—one-shot surveys, etc.—can only tell you what is. But *successful* advertising research—the kind we advocate—is knowing, not just what happened, but why it happened or what *caused* it to happen.

Let's distinguish clearly here between *experiment* and *controlled experiment*. In everyday language, when we experiment with something, we simply mean trial-and-error: "Let's try something different and see what happens." It's the age-old common-sense, but not very precise, method for determining a causal relationship. However, conducting a *controlled experiment* is a more scientific and accurate way of determining the effect of that "something different."

Components of a Controlled Experiment

A controlled experiment, or more accurately a *randomized-groups experiment,* whether conducted in a laboratory or in the field, requires the following ingredients:

1. *Randomized groups:* Two or more equivalent random-sample groups of people from the population being studied—one group for each of the treatments to be tested, plus one *control* (placebo or "no-treatment") group.

2. *Equivalent conditions for all groups:* All groups must be treated in exactly the same way—only the experimental treatment (independent variable) will differ. There must be exact equivalence, for example, on non-treatment stimuli, the measures (dependent variables), the environmental situation, the researchers, and the timing—everything except the treatment.

3. *Measurement after treatment:* Either after-only or before-and-after quantitative measurement of one or more dependent variables (e.g., sales, attitudes, knowledge, etc.).

Under these controlled conditions, the randomized groups are considered identical (within statistical limits), and therefore:

- If the groups are identical to start with; and
- If different treatments are administered to the groups; and
- If all other conditions are identical among groups; and
- If differences in the groups appear only after treatment;
- *Then the measured differences are effects that could only have been caused by the experimental treatments.*

That is the impeccable logic of the controlled experiment as used in all the true sciences. The logic is the same in the laboratory and in the field, for advertising as well as psychology and the hard sciences.

Next, we'll take a closer look at each of the two major types of controlled experiments—laboratory experiments and field experiments—as used in advertising.

The Laboratory Experiment

The laboratory experiment takes place in a controlled and somewhat unnatural environment. In advertising, this often means an auditorium, a viewing room, a simulated grocery store, or some other facility that enables the researcher to control the research setting. Twin theaters are ideal, permitting random assignment of people and test advertising. The laboratory setting allows people to be studied under highly controlled conditions. Pretesting and posttesting are possible using observation techniques, mechanical laboratory apparatus, interviews, and many other kinds of measures.

As an example, a laboratory experiment might be used to measure the effectiveness of a new commercial about the dangers of alcohol. Subjects are assigned to either a control or experimental group. A pretest in the form of a paper-and-pencil questionnaire measuring subjects' beliefs about the dangers of alcohol is administered to both groups. Then, while the control views either a non-related commercial (placebo) or no commercial embedded in a program, the experimental group is exposed to the experimental stimulus: the commercial emphasizing alcoholism as a disease, embedded in the same place in the same program. Next, a posttest of both groups is conducted. The results of the pretest from the two groups are compared to determine the initial degree of group similarity on the dependent variable, which is beliefs about the dangers of alcohol. Then, results of the posttest are compared with pretest scores in both groups to determine whether the test group has changed more than the control group.

Examples of Common Laboratory Experimental Designs

Here are some variations of the use of laboratory experiments in advertising. We will use the P, M, S, T notation system (see Chapter 5) for precise and simple description. Visualize these as television commercials being tested in twin theaters. P1a and P1b represent two randomly assigned samples from group P1.

The effectiveness of one test ad (S1).

Treatment group vs. control group laboratory experiment—posttest only: Comparison of two randomized groups with forced exposure to treatment and treatment withheld, respectively. Repeated for additional treatments:

	T1	T2	T3
P1a	—	S1	M1
P1b	—	—	M1

Treatment group vs. control group "classical experiment"—pre-post test: As above, with pretest added to both groups:

	T1	T2	T3
P1a	M1	S1	M1
P1b	M1	M	M1

The relative effectiveness of two test ads (S1 and S2).

Comparative treatments experiment: Comparison of two randomized groups, with forced exposure to two treatments (ads S1, S2): posttest only shown; pretest may be added.

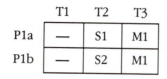

	T1	T2	T3
P1a	—	S1	M1
P1b	—	S2	M1

In all three examples, additional test ads (S3, S4, etc.) might be evaluated for effects by adding additional randomized groups (P1c, P1d, etc.). Also, a placebo ad, designated as Sp, might be used as a comparison or control treatment.

The principal advantage of any experiment is its ability to establish cause-and-effect relationships between treatment variables and subject response. The laboratory experiment, compared to the field experiment, offers a higher degree of researcher control over assignment of the treatment variables, the research environment, and the groups under study. Another advantage is the ability to measure and evaluate results immediately. An additional advantage of the laboratory experiment is the usability of mechanical methods of advertising effects. Mechanical devices such as the eye-movement camera, the eye pupil camera, the psychogalvanometer and the tachistoscope are often superior to conscious, verbal question–answer methods. Used in various forms of psychological testing, these devices can yield highly objective information on the subject's physiological response to a message. Mechanical methods are described in more detail in Chapter 17 where we discuss copytesting.

A primary disadvantage of the laboratory experiment is that it is conducted in an artificial research environment. In this environment, for instance, a respondent may focus a higher degree of attention on the advertising stimulus than he or she would at home. Just the fact of being observed can make subjects react differently than they would in more natural situations. Volunteer or paid subjects don't react in the same way as unpaid subjects or non-volunteers. A related problem has to do with the limited extent to which the findings from any one experiment can be applied. We've said that the nature of the laboratory is to isolate the effect of treatments under highly controlled conditions. In the actual marketplace, advertising is received in a much more unpredictable fashion and may interact with each other to produce a highly different effect than that witnessed in the laboratory. Using the earlier example of the alcohol commercial, if a viewer was in the company of a companion who disagreed convincingly about the dangers of alcohol, the viewer might respond differently than in the laboratory setting where no discussion was allowed.

A second disadvantage is that the samples used in laboratory experiments are usually not representative of a larger population. This is a matter of *external validity,* to be discussed in more detail later.

Despite its shortcomings, the laboratory experiment has produced much of the existing evidence of the effects of modern advertising. Examples of advertising experiments are listed at the end of this chapter.

The Field Experiment

The controlled field experiment is the most sophisticated design used by advertising researchers. It combines the advantages of the laboratory experiment while avoiding its major disadvantages. DuPont, Ford, Curtis Publishing, and others pioneered in the use of this design in the 1950s and 1960s.

Field experiments differ from laboratory experiments by virtue of greater external validity—i.e., generalizability—resulting from, for example, the use of "normal" subjects, times, and settings, unobtrusive treatment, unobtrusive measurement, and "opportunity for exposure" to advertising, rather than forced exposure.

Field experiments may utilize any or all of the designs employed in laboratory experiments—experiment vs. control, treatment vs. placebo, comparative treatments, factorial designs, etc.—and numerous actual examples are described in references at the end of this chapter. Two simple designs are shown below, along with a "blackout" experimental design, unique to field experimentation. In addition, Chapter 19 discusses some other uses in research on "money."

Examples of General Designs of Field Experiments

Sales effects of additional advertising.

Treatment group vs. control group field experiment: posttest only. Comparison of two randomized groups, with opportunity for exposure to treatment and treatment withheld, respectively; naturalistic conditions and unobtrusive measurement:

	T1	T2	T3
P1a	—	S1	M1
P1b	—	S2	M1

S1 = "normal" advertising

S2 = normal, plus additional campaign or media

M1 = sales

Treatment group vs. control group field experiment: pre-post test. Same as above, with added pretest:

	T1	T2	T3
P1a	M1	S1	M1
P1b	M1	S2	M1

Evaluation of ongoing campaign effectiveness.

"Blackout" field experiment. Stimulus not under investigator's control presented as opportunity for exposure to one group, but withheld from random sample of the same group. The (S1) means the ongoing campaign was withheld.

	T1	T2	T3
P1a	—	S1	M1
P1b	—	(S1)	M1

Detailed Example: A "Super" Copy Test

For this example, let's take the testing of two new advertising themes for Lotsafizz soda in several U.S. cities. A relatively new product, Lotsafizz, has been judged in taste tests to rate above other sodas on the market in both taste and "fizziness," or degree of carbonation. Campaign T emphasizes taste and campaign F emphasizes fizziness.

Fifteen U.S. cities, all highly similar in terms of population size, demographics, media availability, income levels, and soda sales are selected. Each is randomly assigned to one of three groups:

Campaign T (taste) is run in markets 4, 9 10, 1, 14

Campaign F (fizziness) is run in markets 13, 2, 12, 3, 7

No campaign is run in markets 5, 6, 8 15, 11

Levels of soda sales are obtained for each market for the month before the introduction of the two campaigns.

Media for the campaigns is limited to black-and-white newspaper advertisements. The executions for groups T and F run in equal numbers and sizes and on the same days in the test markets.

After the campaigns have run for one month, soda sales levels are again obtained and compared with figures from the previous month. The research design looks like this:

	T1	T2	T3
P1a	M1	ST	M1
P1b	M1	SF	M1
P1c	M1	SC	M1

P1a, P1b, P1c = Three randomized groups of five cities each

ST = Taste campaign

SF = Fizz campaign

SC = Control, or no campaign

M1 = Cases sold

T1 = July

T2 = August

T3 = September

The table of results would look like this:

Test group	July sales	August: Number of ads	September sales	Change in sales	Effect: Net change due to advertising*
T	9,000 cases	8	15,000 cases	+6,000	+5,500
F	10,000 cases	8	14,000 cases	+4,000	+3,500
C	9,500 cases	0	10,000 cases	+500	—

*Campaign sales minus change in control group sales = net change in sales, indicating effect of campaign on sales:

Taste: 6,000 − 500 = 5,500 = sales effect of campaign

Fizz: 4,000 − 500 = 3,500 = sales effect of campaign

5,500 − 3,500 = 2,000 = Superiority of taste campaign over fizz campaign

It should be noted that although soda sales was the only dependent variable measured in this example, researchers had several measures from which to choose, including awareness of the ads, knowledge of the advertising claims, or attitude toward Lotsafizz. Since sales figures are readily available, there was no additional expense in obtaining them. Sales is the most valid (true) measure of advertising effects.

Note that in the pretreatment July sales column, sales were similar but not identical in the groups of markets tested. Slight variations like this are to be expected with random assignments of several markets. And note that sales increased in all three groups, even Group C, where the product was not promoted. This could occur due to a number of phenomena in the marketplace: carry-over effects, loyalty, habits, impulse buying, word-of-mouth influence, etc. The natural sales change in the control group must be taken into consideration when calculating the net effect of advertising on the experimental groups. This is accomplished by subtracting the control group change from the change in experimental groups. This results in the net change, i.e., the effect of the campaign.

The beauty of the field experiment is that it can determine the effect of advertising under the natural conditions of the marketplace. Although the field experiment does not allow the researcher to control or eliminate all of the nonadvertising influences on sales such as competitive promotions, word-of-mouth, etc., it does allow such factors to be held constant for all treatments and their effects accounted for. This is done through random assignment of subjects to treatment conditions and the use of a control group. Thus, the incremental effects of the advertising alone can be determined.

Another major advantage is that the field experiment can measure sales behavior, which—unlike verbal response—is the true goal of advertising.

Problems and Issues Associated with Experiments

To make experiments successful and valid, there are several ground rules for conducting and interpreting their results. Researchers must anticipate potential *confounds*—factors that limit our ability to determine true results—before an experiment takes place. This is the only way to eliminate experimental uncertainties.

Two principal criteria for judging an experiment are its *validity* and *reliability*.

Validity

Experimental validity means, quite simply, whether results of an experiment are true. *Internal validity* is the extent to which the experiment has measured true cause and effect, and not just correlation. Results are internally valid only if you can show that it was the experimental stimulus (independent variable) that *caused* any change observed in the measure of effects (dependent variable). *External validity* concerns the extent to which the results of a given experiment can be generalized (externalized) to the real world. Would we achieve the same effect in the real world of advertising?

In a classic work published in 1963, Donald Campbell and Julian Stanley identified and analyzed the major threats to internal and external validity and then detailed the specific experimental designs that could control for each of these negative factors. The threats to internal validity are the following:[1]

1. *History:* Change-producing events other than the experimental stimulus which occur between the first and second measurements in the experiment.

2. *Maturation:* Biological or psychological processes within respondents that are affected by the passage of time, such as hunger, fatigue, boredom, and age.

3. *Testing:* The effect that taking a test can have on taking another test at a later date.

4. *Instrumentation:* Changes in measurement due to changes in observers or scorers or to changes in the measuring instrument itself. This is one basis of the reliability of the experiment.

5. *Statistical regression:* When groups are selected because of their extreme scores, their tendency to subsequently gravitate toward the norm may account for a difference in measurement.

6. *Selection:* The effects of using different recruitment criteria for selecting experimental groups, especially if groups have been allowed to "self-select" or request to be exposed to the experimental stimulus.

7. *Experimental mortality:* The differential loss or drop-out rate of respondents from the comparison groups renders the groups unequal.

8. *Selection-maturation interaction:* The combined effects of selection and maturation being mistaken for the effect of the experimental variable.

External validity is generalizability, or the extent to which the findings can be extrapolated to other groups and other settings. Four variables were identified by Campbell and Stanley as jeopardizing the external validity or representativeness of an experiment:

1. *Interaction effect of testing:* The sensitizing effect of a pretest on a subject's subsequent performance.

2. *Selection:* The effects of selection biases and method of sampling.

3. *Multiple-treatment interference:* The inability to "erase" the effects of prior treatments on subjects.

4. *Reactive effects of experimental arrangements:* The generalizability of effects to those persons not in an experimental setting are precluded.

Ideally, researchers employ designs that are strong in both internal and external validity, because both qualities bear heavily on the interpretability of the research.

Non-Experimental and Quasi-Experimental Designs

As we have seen, a true experiment must have two or more test groups, assigned randomly to treatment and control situations. For a variety of reasons, such as lack of time or money, the research environment, or inability to manipulate subjects or treatments, true experiments are not always possible. This is when researchers fall back on *non-experimental* and *quasi-experimental* designs. Some examples of these were described in Chapter 5.

Quasi-experiments attempt to approximate true controlled experiments and are somewhat more elaborate in their attempt to compensate for potential confounds.

Examples of Quasi-Experimental Designs

As we have noted, it is a reality of research practice that not every investigation lends itself to the use of a true experiment. In cases where one or more criteria for experimentation cannot be met, the resulting design can only approximate. Thus the term quasi-experiment is used to describe designs that fall short of true experimentation and hence do not precisely identify causes and effects. Some examples are shown, without elaboration, below. Quasi-experiments are better than non-experiments at determining advertising effects, but they are not nearly as valuable as true controlled experiments.

Time series experiment.

In the time series experiment, periodic measurements are taken using a single group, and at some point(s) a treatment stimulus is introduced, after which periodic measurements resume. An example might look like the following:

	T1	T2	T3	T4	T5	T6	T7
P1	M1	M1	M1	S1	M1	M1	M1

Equivalent time series design.

This design requires that the stimulus and measurement conditions be alternated, using a single group for the duration of the measurement period. An equivalent times series design might look like this:

	T1	T2	T3	T4	T5	T6	T7	T8
P1	M1	S1	M1	S1	M1	S1	M1	M1

Non-equivalent control group design.

The non-equivalent control group design uses a pretest and posttest of two different groups (P1 and P2) that have not been randomly assigned. As a result, any change could be due either to the nature of the group or to the treatment. No clear causal conclusion is possible. The design could be depicted as follows:

	T1	T2	T3
P1	M1	S	M1
P2	M1	—	M1

Other Experimental and Almost Experimental Designs

As you probably can imagine by now, an almost endless number of variations on a few basic experimental and near-experimental designs is possible. A list of sources at the end of the chapter provides more detailed discussion of additional designs.

Review

In this chapter we saw that:

- A controlled experiment is a scientific investigation controlled by the researcher in which one or more test groups is given some kind of stimulus, and a control group is not. The components of a controlled experiment are: two or more randomized groups; equivalent conditions for all groups except for the treatment; measurement of the groups after (and possibly before) treatment.

- A laboratory experiment takes place in a controlled environment that the researcher can manipulate, but which has the disadvantage of being artificial. It has internal but not external validity.

- A controlled field experiment is the most sophisticated design used in advertising research. Because it is controlled and is conducted in the field under natural conditions, it provides more generalizable results than the laboratory experiment. It has both internal and external validity.

- Non-experimental designs use test groups that have not been randomly assigned. As a result, no causal conclusion is possible.

- Quasi-experimental designs attempt to approximate true controlled methods, but they have less internal validity.

Sources

Jack B. Haskins, *How to Evaluate Mass Communications: The Controlled Field Experiment.* New York: Advertising Research Foundation, 1968.

Jack B. Haskins, "A Precise Notational System for Planning and Analysis," *Evaluation Review,* 1981 (Sage Publications).

Endnote

1. Donald T. Campbell and Julian C. Stanley, *Experimental and Quasi-Experimental Designs for Research.* Chicago: Rand McNally, 1963.

Chapter 10 Analysis of Quantitative Data

Once research has been conducted, the data must be arranged in a meaningful way for the end user. As we will see in this chapter, there are many methods of arranging sets of data. The researcher must choose those formats most appropriate for the nature of the information gathered and the makeup of the audience who will receive it.

A distinction can be made between the terms *data analysis* and *data interpretation*. Data analysis involves the *arrangement* of information; data interpretation is the process through which *meanings* are extrapolated from information. In practice, data analysis and interpretation usually are integrated activities carried out by the researcher, or sometimes by an outside firm specializing in data tabulation and presentation.

The following discussion is only an introduction to data preparation and analysis. A wide variety of statistical tests, ranging from elementary to complex, can be found in research reports and academic journals. Space does not permit a comprehensive discussion of those techniques, nor is such necessarily appropriate for the beginning student of research. Many introductory statistics textbooks further explain statistical techniques. Of particular relevance to the advertising researcher are books with examples from marketing or the social sciences. Some of these are listed at the end of this chapter.

The first part of this chapter will introduce some common forms of data arrangement and analysis used in advertising research. The second part of the chapter will explain content analysis procedure, a special type of data analysis used to describe advertising and its many components.

Statistical Methods of Data Analysis

Data analysis begins at the start of the research process, even before the data are collected. For example, in designing questionnaires, researchers plan for the analysis stage by predicting the *type* of usable data the questionnaire responses will generate and precoding questions accordingly. Some researchers go so far as to set up examples of tables or figures that will be generated from the questionnaire responses. The more organized one can be at the questionnaire construction stage, the easier the later tasks of data analysis, interpretation, and writing the research report will become.

Before conducting a research study, then, the researcher should determine the procedures appropriate for analyzing the data that will be collected.

Descriptive Statistics

The first step in making sense of a series of numbers resulting from the collection of data in a research project is to *describe* them. Once the data have been organized, for example, from low to high, we can describe them by identifying the "average" or "typical" respondent or response, or the *measure of central tendency*. We can also compute simple *frequencies* of the occurrence of each response and—even more meaningful—we can derive *percentages* for each response. If two variables are computed, the data can be arranged in *contingency tables* so that subsegments of the population can be compared. Finally, an *index* can be computed so that, for example, the response or performance of one individual or group can be compared with the average response of a larger group. Let's take a closer look at each of these and some other common ways of describing data using statistics.

Levels of Measurement

Not all methods of data analysis are appropriate for all types of data. An important way to categorize variables is by their level of measurement: nominal, ordinal, interval, or ratio.

Nominal variables include those with categories that are mutually exclusive (they don't overlap) but that have no relation to each other. Variables such as gender (male or female), country of origin (Sweden, Yugoslavia) and college major (history, biology, political science) are at the nominal level. All of the response options in these cases are separate, or discrete, with no relationship to each other. Other levels of measurement have relationships among categories.

Ordinal-level variables have a rank-order relationship among categories. Examples of ordinal variables are social class (lower, middle, upper) and any other variable that involves a ranking (favorite commercials, product attributes). Data from questions like the following, which ask respondents to order items according to specified criteria, are ordinal.

Example: Please rank the brands of dog food on the right from highest quality to lowest quality by placing a "1" next to the highest quality brand, a "2" next to the second-highest quality brand, etc.

__2__	Poochie Plate
__5__	Doggie Dinner
__1__	Canine Cuisine
__4__	Fido Feast
__3__	Puppy Plan

Interval data come from categories with real differences between them. The classic example of interval data is the Fahrenheit temperature scale, where the difference between 30 and 40 degrees is the same as the difference between 40 and 50 degrees. Purchase data can be interval as well; the difference between a frequency of five and six purchases is the same as that between eight and nine purchases.

It is interesting to note that not all researchers agree whether "scaled" items such as Likert scales are truly interval data. Conservative statisticians contend that a scaled item like the following is merely ordinal, with answers greater or lesser than each other but without equal intervals.

Example: Please rank the ideal family restaurant.

Traditional	___	___	___	___	___	___	___	Modern
Fun	___	___	___	___	___	___	___	Serious
Relaxed	___	___	___	___	___	___	___	Formal
Bright light	___	___	___	___	___	___	___	Low light

It is common practice, however, to use interval-level statistical tests on scaled items, and the research journals abound with examples of that trend. The argument made is that the intervals between response options, while not truly "equal," are at least "equal appearing."

Ratio data have all the qualities of interval and also have a real zero point. The classic example is age in years; 20 is twice as old as 10, and there is a real zero point. Purchase data can be expressed in similar fashion: four purchases per month is twice two purchases. Other examples are length of residence in years or some other time period, amount of TV programming watched, etc.

When performing data analysis, it is important that the statistical technique chosen is appropriate for the level of measurement the data possess. Again, depending on the question format chosen, different statistical tests will be called for. Assumptions about the level of measurement required for specific statistical tests are clearly detailed in basic statistics manuals.

Measures of central tendency.

The three measures of central tendency for a series of data are the *mean,* the *median,* and the *mode.*

Mean. The mean is the actual numeric average of the individual responses counted. The mean is calculated by dividing the sum of the answers by the number of answers. We can compute an authentic mean only for data that are at the interval level (where there is equal spacing between intervals) or at the ratio level (interval level with absolute zero point).

If 11 college students are asked how many cans of soda they drink in an average day, the array of responses might be as follows:

$$1\ 1\ 2\ 2\ 2\ 2\ 2\ 2\ 3\ 4\ 6$$

Dividing the sum of responses (27) by the number of responses (11), we arrive at the mean response: 27 ÷ 11 = 2.45. Another descriptive statistic, the range, can be given using the lowest and highest scores. In this case, the range would be 1–6.

Median. The median is the score that appears in the middle of the distribution. Using the same example, the median for the distribution is 2. It is the sixth score out of 11, or the score that splits the distribution in half. While the mean required that data attain the interval or ratio levels of measurement, the median can also be computed for ordinal data (whose responses may be rank-ordered or graduated).

Mode. The least frequently used measure of central tendency is the mode, which is appropriately used with data at the nominal level (where scores have no numeric relationship to each other). The mode is the most frequently occurring score in the distribution. In our example, the mode is 2, because it occurs six times, more than any other value in the distribution. It is possible for more than one mode to occur in a given distribution, assuming that the values each occur an equal number of times. Some researchers report up to three modes; others will report that no mode exists in the case of multiple modes.

Frequencies and percentages.

Frequency is a method of organizing data by counting the number of times each value occurs in a distribution. The scores can then be arranged in a table. It is then a simple procedure to determine percentages for each score, or its size relative to the entire distribution.

Frequencies can be tabulated by hand or by computer. If you are dealing with a fairly small number of responses, you might hand-tabulate frequencies by tallying each score on a blank or master copy of the test instrument, as shown in Figure 10–1. The percentages are computed by simply dividing the frequency of a given score by the total number of scores. This total is sometimes called the *n*. In this case, rounding is used at the one-tenth of a percentage point. In some cases, the act of rounding will cause the total of the percentage column to fall just short of or exceed 100 percent.

One value of using the percentage as a descriptive statistic is the opportunity to *compare scores from population samples of varying sizes.* The use of the percentage distribution brings the otherwise difficult-to-compare scores of the two groups into perspective (see Figure 10–2).

Figure 10–1
Tally Sheet for Hand-Tabulation of Data

10. During the past three months, have you noticed any advertisements for American Express, Discover, MasterCard, or Visa?

‖‖ ‖
‖‖ ‖‖ ‖‖ ‖‖ ‖‖ ‖‖ yes

‖‖ no (If no, please go to #13.)

Please specify the media in which you have noticed an advertisement for the following credit cards.

	American Express	Discover	MasterCard	Visa
TV	‖‖ ‖‖ ‖‖ ‖‖ ‖‖‖‖	‖‖ ‖‖ ‖‖	‖‖ ‖‖ ‖‖	‖‖ ‖‖ ‖‖ ‖‖ ‖‖ ‖
Radio	‖‖	‖‖	‖‖	‖‖ ‖‖
Magazines	‖‖ ‖‖ ‖‖‖‖	‖‖‖‖	‖‖	‖‖ ‖‖ ‖‖‖‖
Newspapers	‖‖‖	‖‖	‖‖	‖‖
Billboards	‖‖‖	‖	‖‖‖	‖‖‖
Direct mail	‖‖ ‖‖ ‖‖ ‖‖‖‖	‖‖ ‖‖ ‖‖	‖‖ ‖‖ ‖‖ ‖	‖‖ ‖‖ ‖‖‖‖
Other (Specify: _____)	‖	‖	‖	‖
	(display)	*(display)*	*(display)*	*(display)*
	n=69	*n=40*	*n=47*	*n=67*

Figure 10–2
Raw Scores Converted to Percentages

10. During the past three months, have you noticed any advertisements for American Express, Discover, MasterCard, or Visa?

37 (86.0%) yes

6 (14.0%) no (If no, please go to #13.)

n = 43

Please specify the media in which you have noticed an advertisement for the following credit cards.

	American Express	Discover	MasterCard	Visa
TV	*24 (39.7%)*	*15 (31.5%)*	*15 (31.9%)*	*26 (38.8%)*
Radio	*5 (17.2%)*	*5 (12.5%)*	*5 (10.6%)*	*7 (10.4%)*
Magazines	*14 (20.2%)*	*4 (10.0%)*	*5 (10.6%)*	*9 (13.4%)*
Newspapers	*3 (4.3%)*	*2 (5.0%)*	*2 (4.2%)*	*2 (2.9%)*
Billboards	*3 (4.3%)*	*1 (2.5%)*	*3 (6.3%)*	*3 (4.4%)*
Direct mail	*19 (27.5%)*	*12 (30.0%)*	*16 (34.0%)*	*19 (28.3%)*
Other (Specify: *in-store display*)	*1 (1.4%)*	*1 (2.5%)*	*1 (2.1%)*	*1 (1.4%)*
	(display)	*(display)*	*(display)*	*(display)*
	n=69	*n=40*	*n=47*	*n=67*

In a 1983 study, Harmon, Razzouk, and Stern examined the informational nature of comparative and noncomparative magazine advertisements.[1] All full-page advertisements in *Newsweek, Ladies Home Journal, Esquire,* and *Reader's Digest* during a one-year period were coded for a variety of informational variables. The researchers' first step in presenting the data was to show how many advertisements used each type of comparison. Table 10–1 shows their results, which were reported using frequencies and percentages. The use of percentages makes possible a quick comparison of the proportionate occurrence of each type of comparative advertisement in each magazine as well as in the total of all advertisements combined.

Table 10–1
Comparative Nature of Advertisements by Magazine

Nature of Comparison	Ladies Home Journal (%)		Newsweek (%)		Esquire (%)		Reader's Digest (%)		Total (%)	
Strict comparison	38	(5.0)[a]	42	(7.8)	15	(4.2)	38	(5.1)	133	(5.6)
Implied comparison	197	(26.1)	169	(31.2)	123	(34.7)	153	(20.5)	642	(26.8)
Non-comparative	520	(68.9)	330	(61.0)	216	(61.1)	554	(74.4)	1620	(67.6)
Total observations	755	(31.5)[b]	541	(22.6)	354	(14.7)	745	(31.2)	2395	(100.0)

[a]Column percent.
[b]Row percent.

Source: Robert Harman, Nabil Razzouk, and Bruce Stern, "The Information Content of Comparative Magazine Advertisements," *Journal of Advertising* 12, no. 4, 1983, pp. 10-19.

Contingency tables and cross-tabulations.

Once we have arranged the data for each variable according to frequencies and percentages, we may wish to examine the scores for two variables simultaneously to note trends in the data. In the example used in Table 10–1, a contingency table is used for cross-tabulation—for looking at the same population on the basis of two variables. As we will see later in this discussion, contingency tables are used for tests of significant differences and other statistical procedures. In the example given, we can examine the frequencies and percentages of scores in each resulting cell.

Standard deviation.

A measure of central tendency by itself is not always the best way to describe a group of responses, because it tries to typify—rather than to differentiate—responses. Measures of variability, on the other hand, give us additional information on the values within the data set. They are used in conjunction with measures of central tendency.

Standard deviation is a measure of variability or dispersion, which is the extent to which scores deviate or vary from the mean. It can only be applied if data are at the interval level of measurement. The standard deviation is actually the square root of the variance. The variance is computed using the following four steps:

1. Determine the deviations of each score from the mean.

2. Square the deviations.

3. Sum the squares.

4. Divide by the number of scores.

Using our earlier example, the equation for figuring the standard deviation for soda-drinkers' scores is as follows:

$$S = \sqrt{S^2} = \sqrt{\frac{\Sigma x^2}{N}}$$

where:

S = Standard deviation

Σx^2 = Sum of the squared deviation scores

N = Sample size

A shortcut is often advisable in computing the standard deviation. The key value in the equation above is Σx^2; the following equation for computing Σx^2 prevents the lengthy procedure of squaring the deviation score of each individual score and then summing them.

$$\Sigma x^2 = \Sigma X_i^2 - \frac{\left(\Sigma X_i^2\right)}{N}$$

where:

ΣX_i^2 = Sum of the squared raw scores

ΣX_i = Sum of the raw scores

N = Number of scores

Table 10–2 shows the distribution of soda consumption, the sum of the raw scores, the sum of the squared raw scores, and the computation of the standard deviation.

Table 10–2
Computing Standard Deviation

Raw Score	Square of Raw Score
1	1
1	1
2	4
2	4
2	4
2	4
2	4
2	4
3	9
4	16
6	36
$\Sigma X_i = 27$	$\Sigma X_i^2 = 87$

$$\Sigma X^2 = 87 - \frac{(27)^2}{11}$$

Now, back to the original formula:

$$= 87 - \frac{729}{11}$$

$$= 87 - 66.3$$

$$= 20.7$$

$$\sqrt{20.7} = 4.5$$

$$S = \sqrt{\frac{\Sigma x^2}{N}}$$

$$= \sqrt{\frac{4.5}{11}}$$

$$= \sqrt{.41}$$

$$S = .64$$

The standard deviation is .64

Pearson correlation.

Pearson correlation is one of several measures of association between two variables. We may use such measures when we wish to determine whether two continuous variables fluctuate together. For instance, we may believe that advertising agency pay for comparable jobs increases as agency size increases. In other words, we hypothesize that the two variables of pay and agency size are associated, or correlated, or related. (Note that although these terms often are used as synonyms, *associated* is the weakest of the terms, and *related* suggests a stronger, causal relationship.)

Swartz wished to study the relationship between two communication source variables: source expertise and source similarity.[2] She hypothesized that an inverse, or negative, relationship existed between the two variables. In other words, if sources were considered to be experts, they would likely not be considered similar to most consumers. Likewise, if they were considered to be similar to the consumer, they would most likely not be considered to have expertise.

Three sets of four print advertisements each were evaluated by female respondents. The advertisements were for cosmetics, a TV set, and a macaroni-and-cheese mix. One advertisement in each pair featured a source model with one of the following expert/similarity characteristics:

- High expertise/high similarity
- High expertise/low similarity
- Low expertise/high similarity
- Low expertise/low similarity

Each advertisement was evaluated using the variables of similarity and expertise measured on a seven-point scale.

Results of the Pearson Product Moment Correlations for the variables of expertise and similarity are shown in Table 10–3. The correlation procedure yields coefficients of correlation, which can range from +1 (a perfect positive correlation) to –1 (a perfect negative correlation).

Table 10–3
Pearson Correlation Scores for Expertise and Similarity Measures

Source Characteristics	All	Cosmetics	Television	Macaroni and Cheese
High expertise/high similarity	.32[a]	.46[a]	.31	.31
High expertise/low similarity	.02	.26	–.25	.11
Low expertise/high similarity	.14	.01	.52[a]	.07
Low expertise/low similarity	.53[b]	.67[b]	.35	.36
Overall within product group		.15	.08	.18

[a]Significant at $p < .05$
[b]Significant at $p < .01$
Note: $n = 15$ for each treatment group, except macaroni and cheese low expertise/high similarity where $n = 14$.

Source: Teresa Swartz, "Relationship between Source Expertise and Source Similarity in an Advertising Context," *Journal of Advertising* 13, no. 2, 1984, pp. 49–55.

Though in a few instances the correlations were found to be significant (in this case, significantly different from zero, or no correlation), the evidence failed to show the hypothesized negative correlation. Swartz concluded that since the negative correlation did not exist between the variables of expertise and similarity, advertisers should be advised to consider those two dimensions of source credibility separately.

Chi-square.

The chi-square is an example of a "goodness-of-fit" test, a test of whether a given distribution of data differs significantly from a hypothesized or expected distribution. The chi-square test is appropriate for data at the nominal level of measurement. Also, it is best used with sample sizes of 25 or more.

Bush, Hair, and Bush studied the various levels of animation in network advertising.[3] They recorded the animation characteristics of 2,454 commercials on three major networks and three cable networks, placing each commercial into one of the following categories: total animated, mixed, or no animation. Some of their results are shown in Table 10–4. As we can see, the chi-square procedure indicated that significant differences existed between networks in their use of mixed animated commercials.

Table 10–4
Advertisements with Animation by Network

Network	Total		Mixed[a]		No Animation		Total Ads
ABC	16	(3.1%)	101	(19.7%)	396	(77.2%)	513
CBS	19	(3.7%)	114	(22.0%)	381	(74.3%)	514
NBC	13	(2.0%)	68	(10.5%)	565	(87.5%)	646
WTBS	9	(3.5%)	32	(12.5%)	212	(84.0%)	253
CNN	7	(2.3%)	41	(13.6%)	254	(84.1%)	302
ESPN	5	(2.2%)	54	(23.9%)	167	(73.9%)	226
Total Ads							2454

[a]Chi-square indicates difference between networks significantly differ at the .0001 level.

Source: Alan Bush, Joseph Hair, and Robert Bush, "A Content Analysis of Animation in Television Advertising," *Journal of Advertising* 12, no. 4, 1983, 20–26.

Indexes.

Generally speaking, for market research purposes, an index is a number that results from dividing one percentage by another. It can also be arrived at by employing some other formula that incorporates several variables for different populations. Indexes can be used to compare population statistics over time, or to compare statistics of one population segment or market against another.

Mediamark Research, Inc. (MRI) gathers and cross-tabulates data in three areas: product usage, media usage, and demographics. A portion of a typical page of MRI report is featured in Figure 10–3. Notice that column D for All Users of packaged dry dog food contains indexes, and that the index for All Female Homemakers, or the entire population under study, is 100. For interpreting this type of index, a 100 score is considered the population average. The index under the section titled "heavy users" means that 10.1 percent of all female homemakers are heavy users of packaged dry dog food. This average percentage then becomes the base for figuring how all other subgroups of the female homemaker population compare with the average. So, for instance, if we wanted to determine whether specific demographic subgroups are likely to be heavy users, we could compute and evaluate their heavy user indexes.

From a computational and analysis standpoint, one of the primary benefits of using the index is that it overcomes problems with different sample sizes that yield raw numbers (such as trying to compare two numbers from column A in Figure 10–3), which are difficult to interpret by mere inspection.

Looking in column C for female homemakers in County Size A, we see that 7.9 percent of that group are heavy users. If we compute 7.9 ÷ 10.1, we get .79. This figure is multiplied by 100. Thus the index is expressed as a whole number, or 79. For County Size D, 15.4 ÷ 10.1 equals 1.52, which multiplied by 100 gives an index of 152. These figures suggest that those who live in smaller counties (size D) are 52 percent more likely than average to be heavy users of packaged dry dog food than average. County Size A households are 21 percent below average in terms of heavy users.

BDI.

A Brand Development Index (BDI) refers to sales potential for a brand. One could assume that, all things being equal, 1 percent of the population would consume 1 percent of Brand X. Of course, all things are not equal, and some areas of the country consume more of certain brands. How much more? One way of computing the BDI is to divide an individual market brand consumption figure by the percentage of the U.S. population that market segment represents. So, for example, if Dallas represents 1.1 percent of the U.S. population, and Dallasites consume 1.5 percent of all Green Giant whole kernel corn sold in the United States, then the Dallas BDI for that brand would be 1.5 ÷ 1.1 = 1.36 percent. This number is then multiplied by 100, and the index is expressed as a whole number, or 136. As with the MRI example, with 100 as an average index, Dallas is consuming 36 percent more than average. (See Table 10–6.)

Figure 10–3
MRI Table with Frequencies, Percentages, and Indexes

144 PACKAGED DRY DOG FOOD

BASE: FEMALE HOMEMAKERS	TOTAL U.S. '000	ALL A '000	B DOWN %	C ACROSS %	D INDEX	HEAVY MORE THAN 24 A '000	B DOWN %	C ACROSS %	D INDEX	MEDIUM 10-24 A '000	B DOWN %	C ACROSS %	D INDEX	LIGHT LESS THAN 10 A '000	B DOWN %	C ACROSS %	D INDEX
ALL FEMALE HOMEMAKERS	79236	22778	100.0	28.7	100	8022	100.0	10.1	100	7530	100.0	9.5	100	7226	100.0	9.1	100
WOMEN	79236	22778	100.0	28.7	100	8022	100.0	10.1	100	7530	100.0	9.5	100	7226	100.0	9.1	100
HOUSEHOLD HEADS	27114	5661	24.4	20.5	71	1700	21.3	6.3	62	1807	24.0	6.7	70	2045	26.3	7.5	83
HOMEMAKERS	79234	22778	100.0	28.7	100	8022	100.0	10.1	100	7530	100.0	9.5	100	7226	100.0	9.1	100
GRADUATED COLLEGE	12005	3057	16.1	30.5	106	1250	15.7	10.5	104	1286	17.1	10.7	113	1112	15.4	9.3	102
ATTENDED COLLEGE	13697	3086	17.5	29.1	101	1584	19.7	11.6	114	1296	17.1	9.4	99	1116	15.4	8.1	89
GRADUATED HIGH SCHOOL	33217	9005	43.9	30.1	105	3563	44.3	10.7	106	3350	44.5	10.1	106	3092	42.8	9.3	102
DID NOT GRADUATE HIGH SCHOOL	20318	5141	22.6	25.3	88	1626	20.3	8.0	79	1607	21.3	7.9	83	1907	26.4	9.4	103
18-24	7140	1711	7.5	24.0	83	*665	8.3	9.3	92	*473	6.3	6.6	70	*674	7.9	8.0	88
25-34	19497	6183	27.2	31.8	110	2430	30.4	12.5	124	2128	28.3	10.9	115	1625	22.5	8.3	91
35-44	15715	5004	26.3	38.1	133	2282	28.2	14.4	142	2001	26.6	12.7	134	1730	23.9	11.0	121
45-54	11324	3736	16.4	33.0	115	1212	15.1	10.7	106	1477	19.6	13.0	137	1046	14.5	9.2	101
55-64	11154	2905	13.1	26.8	93	1081	13.5	9.7	96	721	9.6	6.5	68	1183	16.4	10.6	116
65 OR OVER	14406	2158	9.5	15.0	52	303	4.5	2.5	25	738	9.7	5.1	53	1057	14.8	7.4	81
18-34	26637	7904	34.7	29.7	103	3104	38.7	11.7	115	2601	34.5	9.8	103	2198	30.4	8.3	91
18-49	48167	15794	69.3	32.8	114	5914	73.7	12.3	121	5444	72.3	11.3	119	4436	61.4	9.2	101
25-54	46536	15021	69.9	34.2	119	5913	73.7	12.7	126	5606	74.4	12.0	127	4401	60.9	9.5	104
EMPLOYED FULL TIME	34842	10833	47.6	31.1	108	4006	49.9	11.5	114	3575	47.5	10.3	108	3252	45.0	9.3	102
PART-TIME	7143	2158	9.5	30.2	105	877	10.9	12.3	121	570	7.6	8.0	84	708	9.8	9.9	109
NOT EMPLOYED	37251	9788	43.0	26.3	91	3130	39.1	8.4	83	3384	44.9	9.1	96	3264	45.2	8.8	96
PROFESSIONAL	6473	2012	8.8	31.1	108	722	9.0	11.2	110	863	8.8	10.2	108	628	8.7	9.7	106
EXECUTIVE/ADMIN/MANAGERIAL	4555	1460	6.4	32.1	111	681	8.5	15.0	148	414	5.5	9.1	96	*385	5.1	8.0	88
CLERICAL/SALES/TECHNICAL	18435	5710	25.1	31.0	108	2084	25.7	11.2	111	2012	26.7	10.9	115	1634	22.6	8.9	97
PRECISION/CRAFTS/REPAIR	1000	*377	1.7	37.7	131	*144	1.8	14.4	142	*115	1.5	11.5	121	*119	1.6	11.9	130
OTHER EMPLOYED	11522	3430	15.1	29.8	104	1272	15.9	11.0	109	942	12.5	8.2	86	1215	16.8	10.5	116
H/D INCOME $50,000 OR MORE	14304	4958	21.8	34.7	121	1785	22.3	12.5	123	1792	23.8	12.5	132	1381	19.1	9.7	106
$40,000 - 49,999	9821	3435	15.1	35.0	122	1203	15.0	12.2	121	1305	17.3	13.3	140	926	12.8	9.4	103
$35,000 - 39,999	6500	1988	8.7	30.6	106	721	9.0	11.1	110	873	11.6	13.4	141	*394	5.5	6.1	66
$25,000 - 34,999	13806	4382	19.3	31.8	111	1680	20.7	12.0	119	1402	18.6	10.2	107	1330	18.4	9.6	106
$15,000 - 24,999	15616	4163	18.3	26.7	93	1300	17.3	8.9	88	1134	15.1	7.3	76	1630	22.7	10.5	115
LESS THAN $15,000	19190	3842	16.9	20.0	70	1283	15.7	6.6	65	1023	13.6	5.3	56	1536	21.5	8.1	89
CENSUS REGION: NORTH EAST	16966	4030	17.7	23.8	83	1303	16.2	7.7	76	1446	19.2	8.5	90	1282	17.7	7.6	83
NORTH CENTRAL	19582	6460	28.4	33.0	115	2395	29.9	12.2	121	2142	28.4	10.9	115	1923	26.6	9.8	108
SOUTH	27346	7788	34.2	28.5	99	2450	30.5	9.0	88	2580	34.4	9.5	100	2748	38.0	10.1	110
WEST	15342	4500	19.8	29.3	102	1874	23.4	12.2	121	1353	18.0	8.8	93	1273	17.6	8.3	91
MARKETING REG.: NEW ENGLAND	4656	1135	5.0	24.4	85	*332	4.1	7.1	70	388	5.1	8.3	87	417	5.8	9.0	98
MIDDLE ATLANTIC	13652	3288	14.4	23.9	83	1110	13.8	8.1	80	1194	15.9	8.7	92	968	13.4	7.1	78
EAST CENTRAL	11204	3620	15.5	31.4	109	1258	15.7	11.2	111	1143	15.2	10.2	107	1119	15.5	10.0	110
WEST CENTRAL	12679	4258	19.1	34.4	120	1758	21.9	13.8	137	1401	18.6	11.0	116	1180	16.6	9.5	104
SOUTH EAST	14499	3847	16.9	26.5	92	1008	12.6	7.0	69	1484	19.7	10.2	108	1354	18.7	9.3	102
SOUTH WEST	9788	2904	12.7	31.3	109	1086	13.3	11.5	111	782	10.4	8.4	89	1056	14.6	11.4	125
PACIFIC	13258	3748	16.4	28.3	98	1481	18.6	11.2	111	1140	15.1	8.6	90	1115	15.4	8.4	92
COUNTY SIZE A	32384	7985	35.1	24.7	86	2574	32.1	7.9	79	2840	37.8	8.8	93	2542	35.5	7.9	87
COUNTY SIZE B	23508	6942	30.5	29.5	103	2150	26.9	9.2	91	2617	34.8	11.1	117	2166	30.0	9.2	101
COUNTY SIZE C	12456	3037	17.3	31.6	110	1800	20.1	12.9	128	903	13.2	8.0	84	1335	18.5	10.7	118
COUNTY SIZE D	10888	3813	17.2	35.9	125	1870	20.9	15.4	152	1071	14.2	9.8	104	1182	16.1	10.7	117
MSA CENTRAL CITY	28361	6880	30.6	24.6	85	2283	28.5	8.0	79	2474	32.9	8.7	92	2211	30.6	7.8	85
MSA SUBURBAN	32254	9431	41.4	29.2	102	3184	39.7	9.9	98	3325	44.2	10.3	108	2922	40.4	9.1	99
NON-MSA	18601	6378	28.0	34.3	119	2586	31.8	13.7	136	1731	23.0	9.3	98	2093	29.0	11.3	123
SINGLE	8850	1333	5.9	15.1	52	*485	6.0	5.5	54	*448	5.9	5.1	53	*400	5.5	4.5	50
MARRIED	50063	17172	75.4	34.3	119	6313	78.7	12.6	125	5713	75.9	11.4	120	5146	71.2	10.3	113
OTHER	20323	4272	18.8	21.0	73	1225	15.3	6.0	60	1360	18.1	6.7	71	1678	23.2	8.3	91
PARENTS	31882	11680	51.3	36.6	127	4440	55.5	14.0	138	3778	50.2	11.8	125	3453	47.8	10.8	119
WORKING PARENTS	19985	7280	32.0	36.4	127	2840	35.4	14.2	140	2187	29.0	10.9	115	2252	31.2	11.3	124
HOUSEHOLD SIZE: 1 PERSON	13148	1622	7.1	12.3	43	390	4.9	3.0	29	461	6.1	3.5	37	772	10.7	5.9	64
2 PERSONS	23406	6220	27.3	26.6	92	1999	24.9	8.5	84	2187	29.0	9.3	98	2034	28.1	8.7	95
3 OR MORE	42682	14935	65.6	35.0	122	5633	70.2	13.2	130	4882	64.8	11.4	120	4420	61.2	10.4	114
ANY CHILD IN HOUSEHOLD	34747	12683	54.7	35.9	125	4758	59.3	13.7	135	4042	53.7	11.6	122	3883	50.7	10.5	116
UNDER 2 YEARS	5971	1580	7.0	26.6	93	784	9.8	13.1	130	*424	5.6	7.1	75	*382	5.3	6.4	70
2-5 YEARS	13551	4337	19.0	32.0	111	1583	19.7	11.7	115	1522	20.2	11.2	118	1232	17.0	9.1	100
6-11 YEARS	16228	5860	25.7	36.0	125	2227	29.0	14.3	142	1838	24.4	11.3	119	1606	23.3	10.4	114
12-17 YEARS	15479	6317	27.7	40.8	142	2448	30.5	15.8	156	2050	27.3	13.3	140	1811	25.1	11.7	128
WHITE	68615	21355	93.8	31.1	108	7555	94.2	11.0	109	7115	94.5	10.4	109	6685	92.5	9.7	107
BLACK	8816	1085	4.7	12.1	42	*352	4.4	4.0	39	*296	3.9	3.4	35	*417	5.8	4.7	52
HOME OWNED	54889	17911	78.6	32.6	114	6337	79.0	11.5	114	5955	79.1	10.8	114	5419	77.8	10.2	112
DAILY NEWSPAPERS: READ ANY	46387	13736	60.3	29.6	103	5105	63.6	11.0	109	4408	58.5	9.5	100	4223	58.4	9.1	100
READ ONE DAILY	37130	10879	48.2	29.3	102	4081	50.9	11.0	109	3535	46.9	9.5	100	3363	46.5	9.1	99
READ TWO OR MORE DAILIES	9258	2857	12.1	29.8	104	1024	12.8	11.1	109	873	11.6	9.4	99	859	11.9	9.3	102
SUNDAY NEWSPAPERS: READ ANY	49444	14545	63.9	29.4	102	5300	66.2	10.7	106	5030	66.8	10.2	107	4206	58.2	8.5	93
READ ONE SUNDAY	43413	12661	55.6	29.2	101	4495	56.0	10.4	102	4477	59.5	10.3	109	3889	51.1	8.5	93
READ TWO OR MORE SUNDAYS	6031	1884	8.3	31.2	109	814	10.1	13.5	133	583	7.3	9.2	96	518	7.2	8.6	94
HEAVY MAGAZINES - HEAVY TV	20671	8292	27.6	30.4	106	2314	28.8	11.2	111	2147	28.5	10.4	109	1830	25.3	8.9	97
HEAVY MAGAZINES - LIGHT TV	18757	5060	26.2	31.8	111	2372	29.6	12.6	125	2046	27.2	10.9	115	1542	21.3	8.2	90
LIGHT MAGAZINES - HEAVY TV	20250	5318	23.3	26.3	91	1852	19.8	7.9	78	1709	22.7	8.4	89	2018	27.9	10.0	109
LIGHT MAGAZINES - LIGHT TV	19558	5207	22.9	26.6	93	1745	21.8	8.9	88	1627	21.6	8.3	88	1835	25.4	9.4	103
QUINTILE I - OUTDOOR	15906	5697	26.2	37.5	130	2259	28.2	14.2	140	1836	24.4	11.5	121	1862	25.8	11.7	128
QUINTILE II	16049	5015	22.0	31.2	109	1857	23.1	11.6	114	1604	21.3	10.0	105	1553	21.5	9.7	106
QUINTILE III	15880	4626	20.3	29.1	101	1500	18.8	9.5	94	1697	22.5	10.7	112	1420	19.7	8.9	98
QUINTILE IV	15866	4328	19.0	27.2	95	1440	18.0	9.1	90	1581	21.1	10.0	105	1297	17.9	8.2	90
QUINTILE V	15515	2851	12.5	18.4	64	867	11.9	6.2	52	811	10.6	5.2	54	1093	15.1	7.0	77
QUINTILE I - MAGAZINES	15649	5284	23.2	33.8	117	2082	25.7	13.3	132	1016	25.4	12.2	129	1306	18.1	8.3	92
QUINTILE II	15680	4544	19.9	29.0	101	1838	22.9	11.7	116	1174	21.6	8.5	89	1380	19.1	8.8	97
QUINTILE III	16383	4011	21.5	29.9	104	1652	20.6	10.1	100	1789	23.8	10.9	115	1480	20.2	9.0	99
QUINTILE IV	15915	4388	19.3	27.6	96	1374	17.1	8.6	85	1371	18.2	8.6	91	1643	22.7	10.3	113
QUINTILE V	15608	3861	16.1	23.5	82	1007	13.7	7.0	69	1127	15.0	7.2	76	1437	19.9	9.2	101

This work is comprised of confidential and copyrighted material and is the property of Mediamark Research Inc., on loan to its subscribers for their exclusive and confidential use pursuant to a written agreement with Mediamark Research Inc.

Spring 1988

144   PACKAGED DRY DOG FOOD

BASE: FEMALE HOMEMAKERS

Columns per group: A = '000, B = DOWN %, C = ACROSS %, D = INDEX. Groups: ALL; POUNDS/LAST 30 DAYS — HEAVY (MORE THAN 24); MEDIUM (10–24); LIGHT (LESS THAN 10).

	TOTAL U.S. '000	ALL A '000	B DOWN	C ACROSS	D INDEX	HEAVY A '000	B DOWN	C ACROSS	D INDEX	MEDIUM A '000	B DOWN	C ACROSS	D INDEX	LIGHT A '000	B DOWN	C ACROSS	D INDEX
ALL FEMALE HOMEMAKERS	79236	22778	100.0	28.7	100	8022	100.0	10.1	100	7530	100.0	9.5	100	7226	100.0	9.1	100
WOMEN	79236	22778	100.0	28.7	100	8022	100.0	10.1	100	7530	100.0	9.5	100	7226	100.0	9.1	100
HOUSEHOLD HEADS	27114	5561	24.4	70.5	71	1709	21.3	6.3	62	1807	24.0	6.7	70	2045	28.3	7.5	83
HOMEMAKERS	79236	22778	100.0	28.7	100	8022	100.0	10.1	100	7530	100.0	9.5	100	7226	100.0	9.1	100
GRADUATED COLLEGE	12005	3657	16.1	30.5	106	1250	15.7	10.5	104	1286	17.1	10.7	113	1112	15.4	9.3	102
ATTENDED COLLEGE	13697	3846	17.5	29.1	101	1584	19.7	11.6	114	1286	17.1	9.4	99	1115	15.4	8.1	89
GRADUATED HIGH SCHOOL	33217	8095	43.9	30.1	105	3653	44.3	10.7	106	3250	44.5	10.1	106	3092	42.8	9.3	102
DID NOT GRADUATE HIGH SCHOOL	20318	5141	22.6	25.3	88	1636	20.3	8.0	79	1807	21.3	7.9	83	1907	26.4	9.4	103
18-24	7140	1711	7.5	24.0	83	*605	8.5	9.3	92	*473	6.3	6.6	70	*574	7.9	8.0	88
25-34	19497	6183	27.2	31.8	110	2438	30.4	12.5	124	2128	28.3	10.9	115	1625	22.5	8.3	91
35-44	15715	5694	26.3	36.1	133	2282	28.2	14.4	142	2001	26.6	12.7	134	1730	23.9	11.0	121
45-54	11324	3735	16.4	33.0	115	1212	15.1	10.7	106	1477	19.6	13.0	137	1046	14.5	9.2	101
55-64	11154	2985	13.1	26.8	93	1081	13.5	9.7	96	721	9.6	6.5	68	1183	16.4	10.6	116
65 OR OVER	14406	2150	9.5	15.0	52	363	4.5	2.5	25	730	9.7	5.1	53	1067	14.8	7.4	81
18-34	26637	7894	34.7	29.7	103	3104	38.7	11.7	115	2801	34.5	9.8	103	2199	30.4	8.3	91
18-49	48167	15794	69.3	32.8	114	5014	73.7	12.3	121	5444	72.3	11.3	119	4436	61.4	9.2	101
25-54	46536	15921	69.9	34.2	119	5013	73.7	12.7	126	5406	74.4	12.0	127	4401	60.9	9.5	104
EMPLOYED FULL TIME	34842	10433	47.6	31.1	108	4006	49.9	11.5	114	3675	47.5	10.3	108	3252	45.0	9.3	102
PART-TIME	7143	2150	9.3	30.2	105	877	10.9	12.3	121	570	7.6	8.0	84	700	9.8	9.9	109
NOT EMPLOYED	37251	9788	43.0	26.3	91	3130	39.1	8.4	83	3384	44.9	9.1	96	3264	45.2	8.8	96
PROFESSIONAL	6473	2012	8.8	31.1	108	722	9.0	11.2	110	663	8.8	10.2	108	628	8.7	9.7	106
EXECUTIVE/ADMIN./MANAGERIAL	4555	1480	6.4	32.1	111	681	8.5	15.0	148	414	5.5	9.1	96	*385	5.1	8.0	88
CLERICAL/SALES/TECHNICAL	18435	5790	25.1	31.0	108	2084	25.7	11.2	111	2012	26.7	10.9	115	1634	22.6	8.9	97
PRECISION/CRAFTS/REPAIR	1000	*377	1.7	37.7	131	*144	1.8	14.4	142	*115	1.5	11.5	121	*110	1.6	11.9	130
OTHER EMPLOYED	11522	3430	15.1	29.8	104	1272	15.9	11.0	109	942	12.5	8.2	86	1215	16.8	10.5	116
H/D INCOME $50,000 OR MORE	14304	4958	21.8	34.7	121	1705	22.3	12.5	123	1792	23.8	12.5	132	1361	19.1	9.7	106
$40,000 - 49,999	9821	3435	15.1	35.0	122	1203	15.0	12.2	121	1306	17.3	13.3	140	926	12.8	9.4	103
$35,000 - 39,999	6500	1988	8.7	30.6	106	721	9.0	11.1	110	873	11.6	13.4	141	*394	5.5	6.1	66
$25,000 - 34,999	13806	4302	18.9	31.8	111	1800	20.7	12.0	119	1402	18.6	10.2	107	1330	18.4	9.6	106
$15,000 - 24,999	15616	4163	18.3	26.7	93	1300	17.3	8.9	88	1134	15.1	7.3	76	1639	22.7	10.5	115
LESS THAN $15,000	19190	3242	16.9	20.0	70	1263	15.7	6.6	65	1023	13.6	5.3	56	1566	21.5	8.1	89
CENSUS REGION: NORTH EAST	16966	4030	17.7	23.8	83	1303	16.2	7.7	76	1446	19.2	8.5	90	1282	17.7	7.6	83
NORTH CENTRAL	19582	6480	28.4	33.0	115	2305	29.9	12.2	121	2142	28.4	10.9	115	2033	26.6	9.8	108
SOUTH	27346	7780	34.2	28.5	99	2450	30.5	9.0	88	2580	34.4	9.5	100	2749	38.0	10.1	110
WEST	15342	4500	19.8	29.3	102	1874	23.4	12.2	121	1353	18.0	8.8	93	1273	17.6	8.3	91
MARKETING REG.: NEW ENGLAND	4656	1135	5.0	24.4	85	*332	4.1	7.1	70	386	5.1	8.3	87	417	5.8	9.0	98
MIDDLE ATLANTIC	13652	3280	14.4	23.9	83	1110	13.8	8.1	80	1194	15.9	8.7	92	966	13.4	7.1	78
EAST CENTRAL	11204	3528	15.5	31.4	109	1568	15.7	13.8	111	1143	15.2	10.2	107	1119	15.5	10.0	110
WEST CENTRAL	12679	4354	19.1	34.4	120	1756	21.9	13.8	137	1401	18.6	11.0	116	1190	16.6	9.5	104
SOUTH EAST	14499	3847	16.9	26.5	92	1008	12.6	7.0	69	1494	19.7	10.2	108	1354	18.7	9.3	102
SOUTH WEST	9288	2604	12.7	31.3	109	1066	13.3	11.5	113	782	10.4	8.4	89	1056	14.6	11.4	125
PACIFIC	13258	3740	16.4	28.3		1401	18.6	11.2	111	1140	15.1	8.6	90	1115	15.4	8.4	92
COUNTY SIZE A	32384	7905	35.1	24.7	86	2574	32.1	7.9	79	2849	37.8	8.8	93	2542	35.5	7.9	87
COUNTY SIZE B	23508	8042	30.5	29.5	103	2159	26.9	9.2	91	2617	34.8	11.1	117	2166	30.0	9.2	101
COUNTY SIZE C	12456	3837	17.3	31.6	110	1608	20.1	12.9	128	993	13.2	8.0	84	1335	18.5	10.7	118
COUNTY SIZE D	10888	3913	17.2	35.9	125	1679	20.9	15.4	152	1071	14.2	9.8	104	1162	16.1	10.7	117
MSA CENTRAL CITY	28381	6988	30.6	24.6	85	2283	28.5	8.0	79	2474	32.9	8.7	92	2211	30.6	7.8	85
MSA SUBURBAN	32254	9431	41.4	29.2	102	3184	39.7	9.9	98	3325	44.2	10.3	108	2922	40.4	9.1	99
NON-MSA	18601	6378	28.0	34.3	119	2565	31.8	13.7	136	1731	23.0	9.3	98	2093	29.0	11.3	123
SINGLE	8850	1333	5.9	15.1	52	*485	6.0	5.5	54	*448	5.9	5.1	53	*400	5.5	4.5	50
MARRIED	50063	17173	75.4	34.3	119	6313	78.7	12.6	125	5713	75.9	11.4	120	5148	71.2	10.3	113
OTHER	20323	4272	18.8	21.0	73	1225	15.3	6.0	60	1368	18.2	6.7	71	1678	23.2	8.3	91
PARENTS	31882	11600	51.3	36.6	127	4448	55.5	14.0	138	3778	50.2	11.8	125	3453	47.8	10.8	119
WORKING PARENTS	19985	7280	32.0	36.4	127	2840	35.4	14.2	140	2187	29.0	10.9	115	2252	31.2	11.3	124
HOUSEHOLD SIZE: 1 PERSON	13148	1622	7.1	12.3	43	380	4.9	3.0	29	461	6.1	3.5	37	772	10.7	5.9	64
2 PERSONS	23406	8220	27.3	26.6	92	1999	24.9	8.5	84	2187	29.0	9.3	98	2034	28.1	8.7	95
3 OR MORE	42682	14936	65.4	35.0	122	5633	70.2	13.2	130	4882	64.8	11.4	120	4420	61.2	10.4	114
ANY CHILD IN HOUSEHOLD	34747	12463	54.7	35.9	125	4758	59.3	13.7	135	4042	53.7	11.6	122	3663	50.7	10.5	116
UNDER 2 YEARS	5971	1590	7.0	26.6	93	784	9.8	13.1	130	*424	5.6	7.1	75	*382	5.3	6.4	70
2-5 YEARS	13551	4237	19.0	32.0	111	1983	19.7	11.7	115	1522	20.2	11.2	118	1232	17.0	9.1	100
6-11 YEARS	16728	5450	25.7	36.0	125	2327	29.0	14.3	142	1838	24.4	11.3	119	1686	23.3	10.4	114
12-17 YEARS	15479	6317	27.7	40.8	142	2448	30.5	15.8	156	2059	27.3	13.3	140	1811	25.1	11.7	128
WHITE	68615	21366	93.8	31.1	108	7555	94.2	11.0	109	7115	94.5	10.4	109	6685	92.5	9.7	107
BLACK	8814	1006	4.7	12.1	42	*353	4.4	4.0	39	*296	3.9	3.4	35	*417	5.8	4.7	52
HOME OWNED	54889	17911	78.6	32.6	114	6337	79.0	11.5	114	5955	79.1	10.8	114	5619	77.8	10.2	112
DAILY NEWSPAPERS: READ ANY	46367	13736	60.3	29.6	103	5106	63.6	11.0	109	4408	58.5	9.5	100	4223	58.4	9.1	100
READ ONE DAILY	37130	10979	48.2	29.6	103	4081	50.9	11.0	109	3535	46.9	9.5	100	3363	46.5	9.1	99
READ TWO OR MORE DAILIES	9258	2757	12.1	29.8	104	1024	12.8	11.1	109	873	11.6	9.4	99	850	11.9	9.3	102
SUNDAY NEWSPAPERS: READ ANY	49444	14545	63.9	29.4	102	5309	66.2	10.7	106	5030	66.8	10.2	107	4206	58.2	8.5	93
READ ONE SUNDAY	43413	12081	55.6	29.2	101	4495	56.0	10.4	102	4477	59.5	10.3	109	553	7.2	8.6	94
READ TWO OR MORE SUNDAYS	6031	1884	8.3	31.2	109	814	10.1	13.5	133	553	7.3	9.2	96	518	7.2	8.6	94
HEAVY MAGAZINES - HEAVY TV	20671	6282	27.6	30.4	106	2314	28.8	11.2	111	2147	28.5	10.4	109	1820	25.3	8.9	97
HEAVY MAGAZINES - LIGHT TV	18757	5980	26.2	31.8	111	2372	29.6	12.6	125	2046	27.2	10.9	115	1562	21.3	8.2	90
LIGHT MAGAZINES - HEAVY TV	20250	5318	23.3	26.3	91	1591	19.8	7.9	78	1709	22.7	8.4	89	2018	27.9	10.0	109
LIGHT MAGAZINES - LIGHT TV	19558	5207	22.9	26.6	93	1745	21.8	8.9	88	1627	21.6	8.3	88	1836	25.4	9.4	103
QUINTILE I - OUTDOOR	15406	5087	26.2	37.5	130	2250	28.2	14.2	140	1836	24.4	11.5	121	1862	25.8	11.7	128
QUINTILE II	16049	5015	22.0	31.2	109	1857	23.1	11.6	114	1604	21.3	10.0	105	1553	21.5	9.7	106
QUINTILE III	15880	4620	20.3	29.1	101	1500	18.4	9.5	94	1607	22.5	10.7	112	1420	19.7	8.9	98
QUINTILE IV	15856	4228	19.0	27.2	95	1440	18.0	9.1	90	1581	21.1	10.0	105	1297	17.9	8.2	90
QUINTILE V	15515	2851	12.5	18.4	64	857	11.9	6.2	61	801	10.6	5.2	54	1003	15.1	7.0	77
QUINTILE I - MAGAZINES	15649	5284	23.2	33.8	117	2082	25.7	13.2	130	1918	25.4	12.2	129	1306	18.1	8.3	92
QUINTILE II	15680	4654	19.9	29.0	101	1838	22.9	11.7	116	1326	17.6	8.7	89	1380	19.1	8.8	97
QUINTILE III	16383	4801	21.3	29.9	104	1652	20.6	10.1	100	1700	23.8	10.9	115	1460	20.2	8.9	98
QUINTILE IV	15915	4388	19.3	27.6	96	1374	17.1	8.6	85	1371	18.2	8.6	91	1643	22.7	10.3	113
QUINTILE V	15608	3061	16.1	23.5	82	1087	13.7	7.0	69	1127	15.0	7.2	76	1437	19.9	9.2	101

Spring 1988

Table 10–5

Figuring a Brand Development Index for a Hypothetical Metro Area

Metro Area	Percentage of U.S. Pop.	Percentage of U.S. Sales of Brand X	Brand Index
A	.33	.37	.37/.33 x 100 = 112
B	.42	.53	.53/.42 x 100 = 126
C	1.10	.92	.92/1.10 x 100 = 84

CDI.

The Category Development Index (CDI) indicates the sales potential of a class or category of products, such as canned corn. Continuing with the Dallas example, if Dallasites account for only 0.9 percent of the country's canned corn purchases, we can figure the CDI as follows: 0.9 ÷ 1.1 = .82. Multiplied by 100, this yields an index of 82, which is 18 percent below the average index. (See Table 10-7.)

Table 10–6

Figuring a Category Development Index for a Hypothetical Metro Area

Metro Area	Percentage of U.S. Pop.	Percentage of U.S. Sales of Product Category	Category Index
A	.33	.45	.45/.33 x 100 = 136
B	.42	.27	.27/.42 x 100 = 64
C	1.10	.99	.99/1.10 x 100 = 90

Computers in Data Analysis

Most quantitative research done in advertising can be greatly facilitated by the use of a computer. Though most data analysis tasks can be completed by hand, the computer's ability to rapidly perform series of calculations makes it a valued tool in the process. Most of the computers available to the advertising researcher fall into one of three categories:

The microcomputer, or personal computer, is the smallest, but it might well be sufficient for the needs of an advertising researcher. This is especially true now that a variety of spreadsheet programs and data analysis packages such as SPSSx (Statistical Program for the Social Sciences) are available for use on the personal computer.

Minicomputers are larger and have more memory and processing capability. A minicomputer can be used in a network capacity for a small business or research department where several microcomputers or terminals are linked.

Mainframe computers, such as the IBM mainframe, are found at many large corporations, research firms, and universities. These have greatly expanded capabilities and typically would house a number of analytical programs such as SPSSx or SAS, both packages widely used in the social sciences and marketing.

Typically, data are keyed into a computer file in an order specified in a spreadsheet program if on a personal computer or by way of a command file on a mainframe computer statistical package. Although the computer is capable of performing the types of calculations necessary in statistical tests very quickly, the output generated from computerized data analysis is only as good as the instructions, or input, given by the human user. A thorough understanding of the appropriate statistical tests is still necessary even though the computer is performing them. Some very good discussions of statistical methods can be found in the user's manual for various statistical packages. (See, for example, *SPSSx Primer, SPSSx User's Guide, SPSSx Tables,* and *SPSS Advanced Statistics Guide,* published by McGraw-Hill.)

Content Analysis

Content analysis is the systematic study of a body of content. Whether we realize it or not, every day we make assumptions based on our encounters with various types of content. It might be a decision not to read the rest of a magazine because the part you have already read wasn't particularly interesting, or a quick glance at patrons of a local nightclub to see if you "belong," or a careful study of your clothes closet to determine what item should be added to your wardrobe next. In communications, the body of content can be news articles, public speeches, topics on the evening news, advertising themes, or other visual and verbal messages. Data from content analysis can indicate trends in communication content over time, suggest priorities of communicators in various media, compare one body of content with another using the same measurement criteria, and profile "typical" communication elements in a given data set. The process of content analysis involves much more than a simple inspection of the communication data set. As we will see, it requires a rigorous methodology including procedures for sampling, categorizing, coding, and analysis.

Using Content Analysis

The decision to employ content analysis should be made after it is determined that a systematic, thorough quantification of elements of a given body of content

---

is the best method to answer a particular research question or problem. If a cursory inspection of the population will suffice, then it is unnecessary to conduct a formal—and time-consuming—content analysis.

Formulating research questions.

Like any other systematic research study, the research plan for a content analysis flows from a specific research question, problem, or hypothesis. These questions can be very practical, such as "What market share does Brand X currently hold?" or they may be more theoretical, such as "How are minorities depicted in consumer advertising?" In either case, the qualities to be investigated must be measurable, that is to say, quantifiable. The following are examples of research questions that were the basis for content analysis in advertising research studies.

- To what extent are animation techniques used by advertisers for commercials during children's and nonchildren's programming?[4]
- How does the information content of American magazine advertising compare to that of equivalent Japanese publications?[5]
- What have been the trends in magazine layout and design over the past 50 years?[6]
- How do award-winning TV commercials compare with "proven effective" commercials with respect to their information content, advertising appeals, use of visuals, themes, etc?[7]
- What sex roles are children being exposed to in children's advertising?[8]

Notice that in each of these cases, the research question itself suggests in general terms the elements to be investigated.

Determining a unit of analysis.

Once the research question has been formulated, the researcher must decide on a specific *unit of analysis,* or exactly what is to be analyzed. Will it be the entire commercial, or only its visual elements? Will it be only magazine advertising that features female models? By choosing the unit of analysis, the researcher begins to place parameters, or limits, on what is to be analyzed, paving the way for decisions about categories for data collection.

Category construction.

Categories are used to classify media content and are at the heart of any content analysis scheme. Once the units of analysis have been determined, the next step is to construct classifications for the content that will describe it accurately and thoroughly, to answer the questions the study is designed to address. According to Kerlinger, the following are some general principles of category construction.[9]

- Reflect the purposes of the research.
- Be exhaustive, in that all relevant items must be able to fit into an appropriate category. (Sometimes this is accomplished by running a small pilot test of the instrument with a portion of the data set, to ensure that representative elements all have corresponding categories.)
- Be mutually exclusive, which requires that two categories cannot have the same meaning.

In the study of information content of advertisements in U.S. and Japanese magazines, Madden et al. used a categorization scheme developed by Stern and Resnik, which included 14 advertising informational cues.[10] Table 10–7 lists and defines those informational categories.

Table 10–7
Stern & Resnik Informational Categories

---

(1) *Price-value*
- What does the product cost? What is its value-retention capability?
- What is the need-satisfaction capability/dollars?

(2) *Quality*
- What are the product's characteristics that distinguish it from competing products based on an objective evaluation of workmanship, engineering, durability, excellence of materials, structural superiority, superiority of personnel, attention to detail, or special services?

(3) *Performance*
- What does the product do, and how well does it do what it is designed to do in comparison to alternative purchases?

(4) *Components or contents*
- What is the product composed of? What ingredients does it contain?
- What ancillary items are included with the product?

(5) *Availability*
- Where can the product be purchased?
- When will the product be available for purchase?

(6) *Special offers*
- What limited-time nonprice deals are available with a particular purchase?

(7) *Taste*
- Is evidence presented that the taste of a particular product is perceived as superior in taste by a sample of potential customers? (The opinion of the advertiser is inadequate.)

(8) *Nutrition*
- Are specific data given concerning the nutritional content of a

---

particular product, or is a direct specific comparison made with other products?

(9) *Packaging or shape*
- What package is the product available in which makes it more desirable than alternatives? What special shapes is the product available in?

(10) *Guarantees and warranties*
- What postpurchase assurances accompany the product?

(11) *Safety*
- What safety features are available on a particular product compared to alternative choices?

(12) *Independent research*
- Are results of research gathered by an "independent" research firm presented?

(13) *Company research*
- Are data gathered by a company to compare its product with a competitor's presented?

(14) *New ideas*
- Is a totally new concept introduced during the commercial?
- Are its advantages presented?

Source: Bruce Stern, Dean Krugman, and Alan Resnik, "Magazine Advertising: An Analysis of Its Information Content," *Journal of Advertising Research*, April 1981, vol. 21, no. 2, pp. 39–44.

Sampling.

As with other procedures in conducting a content analysis, sampling procedures should reflect the specific research questions to be answered. If the population under study is small and easily identifiable, sampling may not be necessary; a census survey might be feasible. In many instances, however, the body of content under consideration is enormous. It might be, for example, all commercials aired by the major networks on Saturday-morning children's programming over a five-year period. In addition to the size of the population, a major determinant of whether to employ sampling is the nature of the information sought. For instance, if the purpose is to identify and describe in detail each magazine advertisement for a particular brand over a certain time period, it might be advisable to conduct a census, or an analysis of all of the magazine advertising in question, rather than a sample. A sample might miss specific and vital pieces of information.

For the same reasons that the researcher employs sampling procedures in a sample survey—time and money—the content analyst must consider coding only a portion of the content under study. There are few hard-and-fast rules in the area of sampling as it relates to content analysis, and the researcher is probably best advised to avoid some of the same sources of systematic error facing the survey researcher. Among these are overrepresentation, underrepresentation, periodicity, and others (see Chapter 8 on survey methods). The process of choosing the sample involves:

- Defining the relevant universe of content, e.g., print advertisements
- Choosing specific communication sources, e.g., individual newspapers or magazines in certain geographic areas, during certain time periods
- Sampling the documents in the sources chosen, e.g., every tenth issue of the *New York Times*

Madden et al. explained their choice of magazine content as follows:

> Six categories of magazines (general, sports, entertainment, women's, men's, and professional) were used, chosen to represent the major magazine genres present in both the United States and Japan. . . . Specific American magazines [were] chosen along with their Japanese equivalents, taken from May/June 1984 publications of each magazine. The broad range of types of magazines also provided a cross section of advertisements from each country. All advertisements in each magazine were included except classifieds, a total of 1,440 advertisements with 832 from the American magazines and 608 from the Japanese magazines.[11]

Table 10–8 illustrates their choice of specific media vehicles for study, in both the United States and Japan.

Table 10–8
U.S. and Japanese Magazines

U.S.	Japanese
General:	*General:*
Time	Shukan Shincho
Reader's Digest	Reader's Digest
Sports:	*Sports:*
Sports Illustrated	Shukan Baseball
Golf Digest	Asahi Golf
Entertainment:	*Entertainment:*
People	Shukan Mayoujou
T.V. Guide	T.V. Guide
Women's:	*Women's:*
Family Circle	Shufu no Tomo
Glamour	Non-no
Teen	Seventeen
Men's:	*Men's:*
Playboy	Shukan Playboy
Professional:	*Professional:*
Business Week	Economist

Source: Madden, Charles et al. "Analysis of Information Content in U.S. and Japanese Magazine Advertising," *Journal of Advertising* 15, no. 3, 1986, p. 41.

Training of coders/determining intercoder reliability.

Once all of the sampling and coding decisions have been made, and the documents to be studied have been located, the process of coding can begin. In an effort to establish reliability or consistency of coding, the researcher usually selects two, three, or more coders to gather the data. Typically coders meet for at least one formal training session, in which the researcher details the project procedures with an emphasis on coding activities. It is critical that coders remain objective about the outcome of the study. For instance, researchers should not share with coders their hypotheses about what the study might find. Nor should they discuss what previous studies of a similar nature have concluded. Again, this is done in an effort to ensure that coders do not inject bias into their judgments.

One method of establishing the consistency of coding decisions is to use a formula for intercoder agreement, or intercoder reliability. Several different methods are available for computing intercoder reliability, but all yield a number, or coefficient, which represents the percentage of common judgments among coders. One simple method of computing this score is the ratio of coding agreements to the total number of coding decisions:

$$\text{Coefficient of reliability} = \frac{2M}{N1 + N2}$$

where M is the number of coding decisions in which the judges are in agreement, and N1 and N2 are the number of coding decisions made by judges 1 and 2.[12]

Although there is much discussion among researchers about the acceptable level of intercoder agreement, generally speaking, 60 percent or above is considered acceptable, with 80 percent or more considered desirable.

An Application of Content Analysis Techniques

Stewart and Furse conducted a large-sample study of TV commercials in order to determine which commercial techniques or content resulted in greater commercial effectiveness.[13] To obtain data for the study, two major data-gathering projects were begun. First, a content analysis of 1,059 commercials were undertaken. Second, effectiveness scores using awareness, comprehension, and persuasion measures were obtained from consumer test groups in a series of laboratory studies. Ultimately, the researchers planned to combine the two sets of data to determine which commercial elements were the most effective.

Critical to the success of the project was an exhaustive list of executional variables to be applied to the commercials. Using what has been hailed as the most comprehensive content analysis instrument to date for television, the researchers analyzed commercials that had been copytested by Research Systems Corporation. The coding guide contained 141 dichotomous, or yes-no, variables, representing the major categories of information content; congruence of commercial elements; promises, appeals, and propositions; commercial structure; commercial format; timing and counting variables; and commercial finish. In addition, 14 "counting" variables were recorded, such as the length of time a product was on camera. Coders for the massive content analysis recorded whether each of the dichotomous variables was present or absent in each of the 1059 commercials. A copy of the Stewart and Furse code book, or explanation of variables, is contained in Appendix A at the end of the book.

Review

In this chapter we saw that:

- The researcher must choose among several formats for arranging data the most appropriate for the nature of the information gathered and the makeup of the audience who will receive it.
- Data analysis involves the arrangement of information; data interpretation is the process through which meanings are extrapolated from information. In practice, they are usually integrated activities.
- The three measures of central tendency for a series of data are the mean, the median, and mode.
- Variables can be categorized by their level of measurement: nominal, ordinal, interval, and ratio.
- Standard deviation is a measure of variability or dispersion, calculated by determining the deviations of each score from the mean, squaring the deviation, summing the squares, and dividing by the number of scores.
- Content analysis is the systematic study of a body of content, including rigorous methodology for sampling, categorizing, coding, and analysis.

Suggestions for Further Reading: Basic Statistics Books

Champion, Dean. *Basic Statistics for Social Research*. New York: Macmillan, 1981.

Hamilton, Lawrence. *Modern Data Analysis: A First Course in Applied Statistics*. Pacific Grove, Calif.: Brooks/Cole, 1990.

Johnson, Robert. *Elementary Statistics,* 5th ed. Boston: PWS-Kent, 1988.

Ott, Lyman. *An Introduction to Statistical Methods and Data Analysis,* 3d ed. Boston: PWS-Kent, 1988.

Endnotes

1. Robert Harmon, Nabil Razzouk, and Bruce Stern, "The Information Content of Comparative Magazine Advertisements," *Journal of Advertising* 12, no. 4, 1983, pp. 10–19.

2. Teresa Swartz, "Relationship between Source Expertise and Source Similarity in an Advertising Context," *Journal of Advertising* 13, no. 2, 1984, pp. 49–55.

3. Alan J. Bush, Joseph H. Hair, and Robert P. Bush, "A Content Analysis of Animation in Television Advertising," *Journal of Advertising* 12, no. 4, 1983, pp. 20–26.

4. *Ibid.*

5. Charles Madden, Marjorie Caballero, and Shinya Matsukubo, "Analysis of Information Content in U.S. and Japanese Magazine Advertising," *Journal of Advertising* 15, no. 3, 1986, pp. 38–45.

6. Florence Feasley and Elnora Stuart, "Magazine Advertising Layout and Design: 1932–1982," *Journal of Advertising* 16, no. 2, 1987, pp. 20–25.

7. Alice Gagnard and Jim Morris, "Clio Commercials from 1975–1985: An Analysis of 151 Executional Variables," *Journalism Quarterly,* Winter 1988, pp. 859–868.

8. M. Carole Macklin and Richard Kolbe, "Sex Role Stereotyping in Children's Advertising," *Journal of Advertising* 13, no. 2, 1984, pp. 34–42.

9. F. N. Kerlinger, *Foundations of Behavioral Research: Educational and Psychological Inquiry* (New York: Holt, Rinehart and Winston, 1964).

10. Charles Madden, Marjorie Caballero, and Shinya Matsukubo, "Analysis of Information Content in U.S. and Japanese Magazine Advertising," *Journal of Advertising* 15, no. 3, 1986, pp. 38–45.

11. *Ibid.,* pp. 39–40.

12. Ole Holsti, *Content Analysis for the Social Sciences and Humanities* (Reading, Mass.: Addison-Wesley Publishing Co., 1969).

13. David Stewart and David Furse, *Effective Television Advertising* (Lexington, Mass: Lexington Books, 1986).

Chapter **11** Writing the Research Report

Reporting the results of a research project can be accomplished in the form of a written document, an oral presentation, or both. This chapter outlines the major components of an effective written research report and provides suggestions for effective written discussion and graphic presentation of research information.

Importance of the Research Report

Some of the researcher's most important work is done after the research project is completed. No matter how well a research project is conducted or how important its findings to the problem at hand, if it is not communicated properly to its audience or end users it cannot be used effectively.

It is essential to keep the end user in mind when preparing a research report. A mistake many researchers make is writing reports that are intelligible only to other highly trained research personnel. The fact is, however, that most end users of research—advertising managers, media planners, and creative directors—do not have formal research training and are often unfamiliar with highly technical research language. Therefore, the research report should be written in a style that is easily understood by the nonresearcher. If it is too technical to comprehend, then its writing is at odds with the purpose of conducting the research in the first place: to reduce uncertainty surrounding the advertising planning process.

Beyond the immediate necessity of communicating the research findings to appropriate end-users to they can make advertising decisions, the research report also serves as a document to be added to the body of knowledge about advertising. Each report should, therefore, be a complete, self-contained document. Even if the research is one of a series of research assignments to be completed over a period of time, the report should be written in such a way that the findings can stand alone, detailing the specifics of one particular phase of the research. In fact, one of the criteria used to measure the precision of a research report is that it should include sufficient detail so that another investigator at a later date could conduct a study in the same way.

Just like the advertising campaign itself, the quality of the research report reflects on the organization and individuals who generate it. An agency-generated report typically bears the agency's name and logo on the cover and the name of a contact person responsible for answering readers' questions inside. A well-organized, well-written document reflects positively on the preparedness and professionalism of the organization. A poorly written, confusing report could leave a lasting negative impression of its authors.

Components of the Research Report

Whether they appear in trade or academic research journals or are published separately by an agency, client, or outside research company, most formal research reports are organized into the following sections:

1. Letter of transmittal
2. Title page and cover
3. Table of contents
4. Executive summary
5. Introduction
6. Methodology
7. Findings/results
8. Conclusions/limitations
9. Recommendations
10. Appendix

Title Page and Cover

Reports can begin with a title page, cover, or both. The cover may bear the company logo and possibly the title of the project. A title page includes the company name and address, the title, the sponsor of the research, the date, and sometimes the name of the principal investigator. If the report is to be presented at a conference or other meeting, it is common for the name of that organization and the date, place, and time of the presentation to be included.

The title of a research report plays a major role in positioning it for the reader as well as giving an indication of content. Hence it is important that the title be as descriptive and accurate as possible. While it may be tempting to fashion a clever or entertaining headline to brighten up the subject matter, this should be avoided; it could mean that the report is misunderstood or poorly cataloged. It also detracts from the professionalism of the document.

Table of Contents

A table of contents at the front of the research report lists the major divisions of the document, as well as the subdivisions if the length of the report warrants such. Sometimes a separate list of figures and tables is appropriate. In these cases, both the figure number and the title of the figure should be provided. An example would be "Figure 2: Television Advertising Expenditures by U.S. Automotive Manufacturers in 1988."

Executive Summary

A well-written, concise, 1–3 page summary of major findings should be a part of every formal research report. This section serves as a brief synopsis of the information contained in the report, and sometimes it is circulated by itself to those who do not need or want access to the entire report. Often this secondary audience is not interested in the precise details of the project, but they can benefit from a distilled version of the study's findings and implications. Thus, the executive summary may have a life of its own. Because it summarizes parts of the larger research report, the executive summary is written after the rest of the document is complete. Figure 11–1 shows part of an executive summary for an experiment to determine how young adults responded to different public service announcements.

Figure 11–1
Executive Summary

The purposes of this study were to examine message evaluation of selected public service advertisements by a young adult population and to test whether local and non-local source attribution would influence those evaluations. A secondary objective of the study was to determine to what extent audience characteristics such as fatalism and social responsibility predict responses to PSAs.

The issues selected for this study elicited a wide range of message evaluation from the young adult audience. The Alcoholism PSA was the most highly rated message in the series, and the American Economic System PSA was the lowest-rated item. A rank-order of PSA issues used in this study seems to suggest a hierarchy of response patterns which indicates the subjects' ability to discriminate among the various issues.

Overall in this particular study, the hypothesis that a local source attribution would produce significantly higher message evaluations could not be confirmed. However, one exception—the Child Abuse ad—did show a significant difference in message evaluation, which would indicate that in certain instances the inclusion of a local source could enhance evaluation by a young audience.

The regression analysis showed the independent variables as accounting for considerably more variance in the local-source than in the non-local-source situation. However, social responsibility emerged as the most predictive variable in both treatment situations. Fatalism, which emerged as a significant negative predictor of message evaluation, was prominent only in the local-source situation.

Often a very brief summary called an *abstract* accompanies research reports that are published in academic journals. These 50- to 250-word summaries announce the purpose of the study and include only selected major findings.

Introduction

The introduction sets the stage for the report. It includes background information to explain the decision to undertake the research study. For example, in a report focusing on the performance of a particular brand, included might be the recent history of the brand and its advertising, problems facing the brand, previous relevant research findings, research objectives or research questions, and an indication of how the results of the study will be used.

One important method of positioning an individual research study is to compare it with previous studies on the same or similar topics. In academic research reports appearing in journals, this discussion is called the "Review of Literature" and often warrants a separate major section of the report (see Chapter 4 for a discussion of sources of published information). In the case of industry reports, references can be made to both published and unpublished research reports. A brief review of the major findings of such studies traces the history of investigation and points to areas in need of further examination.

Special emphasis should be placed on the objectives of the research study. These research goals or questions not only provide the structure for the rest of the report but also indicate the limits of the study's intended investigation. Just like the objectives for the advertising campaign, the objectives for the advertising research study should be articulated clearly and agreed to by those parties undertaking the research (see Chapter 3).

The Richards Group conducted a study for Motel 6 to determine the recognition of colors used in the Motel 6 logo and property. Though much of the survey did not ask questions specifically geared toward advertising, the intent was to determine to what extent the various colors contributed to the image and brand signature value of the Motel 6 properties and messages (see Figure 11–2).

Figure 11–2
Background for a Survey Research Project

Introduction

Background

- As in many drive-by businesses, Motel 6 uses a prominent colored logo, easily visible from the road, to announce its presence.

- In addition to the logo, Motel 6 has traditionally painted its guest room doors orange.

- In an attempt to cut the operational cost of frequently repainting the orange doors, which tend to fade rapidly, and hopefully improve aesthetics, Motel 6 management would like to change the door color to beige. Consumer issues that would influence the decision are of concern to management.

— How strong is the consumer association between the orange doors and Motel 6? Will there be a loss of identity, signature or logo value in changing the color?

— To what extent do the orange doors act as aid to Motel 6 recognition, especially in California, where many motels are located beside busy freeways, amidst visually confusing backgrounds?

— What is the consumer's aesthetic preference between orange and beige?

- Two recent surveys concerning these issues have been completed. The first, limited to the Riviera Beach, Florida, Motel 6, revealed no significant brand link between Motel 6 and the color orange. However, in the subsequent survey, conducted at the Arlington, Texas, Motel 6, the majority (55%) of respondents (through aided color questioning) said they associate the color orange with Motel 6. Seven in ten said the source of their orange awareness is the guest room doors.

- Few respondents from the two studies said their decision to stay at Motel 6 was influenced by the orange doors. In fact, the majority of total respondents supported, on aesthetic grounds, a switch from orange to beige—a color which the Florida survey surprisingly suggested was more strongly associated with Motel 6 already.

- In light of the Arlington finding—that the association with orange was to some extent significant—the present research is necessary in order to gauge the response from all areas of the country, especially California which traditionally has been the Motel 6 Heartland.

Methodology

This section describes in detail how the research was conducted. Among the decisions made by researchers at the planning stages of a project are decisions about sample selection criteria, data-gathering methods, instruments of measurement, the time frame for data collection, and methods of analysis. The section on methodology covers each of these.

Sample.

The population under study should be thoroughly defined. If a sample of a larger population was used, the method of choosing the sample should be revealed. Did the investigator use a random sample, a quota sample, or a convenience sample? If the sample used was not a random sample, what efforts were made by the investigator to increase the representativeness of the group under study?

How many were included in the sample? Were these decisions made to achieve maximum generalizability of the findings, to provide maximum comparability with previous studies, or for some other reason?

Data-gathering method.

This portion of the methodology section introduces the data-gathering method of choice and gives the rationale for using it. The choice of data-gathering methods is sometimes an obvious one. At other times, the best method is selected from several viable alternatives. Should we use telephone interview, personal one-to-one interview, mail survey, focus groups, observation, or some other method?

Instruments of measurement.

These can range from paper-and-pencil attitude questionnaires, to tests of knowledge, to the number of coupons redeemed. The discussion here should focus on how the instruments were chosen if existing tests were applied to the current study. If new instruments were created by the researcher, this section should address how they were derived, pretested, and validated. The types of items used (scaled questions, open-ended items) should be addressed, as should the structuring and ordering of questions. Usually the questionnaire is described in terms of its physical length (number of pages) or the number of individual items, but you may also note the duration of interviews, especially if they were relatively long.

Research time frame.

The scheduling of the various stages of the research project should be disclosed here. Particular emphasis on the timing of the treatment or spontaneous stimulus vis-à-vis the measurement period is appropriate.

Data tabulation and analysis.

This section tells the reader how the questionnaires were handled after the data collection phase and what type of analysis was conducted. Included in this discussion could be any precoding arrangements, statistical packages used, and statistical procedures employed.

The section on methodology is also the place to explain your reasons for selecting certain research methods and rejecting others. For example, in a potentially sensitive study—such as one that focuses on religious or ethical beliefs—you may have decided not to use focus groups or telephone interviews, anticipating that these methods might inhibit respondents or might solicit superficial or untrue responses. Your choices should be explained to readers. It is important that they understand the rationale for employing specific methods and techniques. Figure

11–3 includes the objectives and rationale for a focus group study to determine preferences for pizza delivery services. Figure 11–4 explains copy-testing procedures for a study by Waste Management.

Figure 11–3
Objectives and Methods for a Focus Group Study

Objectives

- To explore consumer behaviors, perceptions, and attitudes relating to the purchase of home delivery foods.
- To examine home delivery food usage patterns and the factors that influence usage.
- To develop an understanding of the perceptions and preferences of consumers relative to existing home delivery food services.
- To investigate the decision process involved in the selection of a home delivery food service.
- To evaluate the reactions of consumers to several proposed home delivery service concepts and related advertising concepts.

Methods

Four focus group discussions were conducted, as follows:

Market (User Type)	Date of Interview	Number of Respondents
1. Dallas, heavy users	02/11/86	10
2. Dallas, medium users	02/12/86	10
3. Chicago, heavy users	02/14/86	10
4. Chicago, medium users	02/15/86	10

All respondents were 18 to 39 years of age and past three-month users of home delivery food services. The "heavy users" had ordered foods for home delivery three or more times in the past three months. "Medium users" had ordered home delivery foods one or two times in the past three months. Males and females were evenly represented within each focus group (five males, five females). All participants were residents of the respective cities. No one employed in the advertising, marketing research, or food service industries was allowed to attend the group sessions. No one who had participated in a marketing research study of any type in the previous six months was allowed to attend. All four focus groups were audio and videotaped.

Focus Group Technique

Focus group discussions, or group depth interviews, give marketing and marketing research executives an opportunity to learn how consumers think and, more importantly, how consumers feel about a given product, service, or idea. The focus group, consisting of 8 to 10 discussants and a moderator, provides a facilitative atmosphere in which consumers feel comfortable and feel free to express their ideas and feelings. The discussion is unrehearsed, non-directive, and spontaneous. The typical session lasts about 1 1/2 hours and the audio is recorded on tape.

The group moderator subtly guides the discussion in a neutral, non-biasing way. He tends to introduce topics rather than ask questions. His interviewing techniques are usually non-directive. The moderator creates and maintains an open, accepting, non-threatening atmosphere. He makes sure that all participants have an opportunity to express their thoughts. The moderator's role in the discussion can vary, however, from passive to active, from non-directive to directive, if the social and personality characteristics of the group require it. The moderator makes sure that all major topics on the discussion outline are covered.

The benefits and advantages of focus groups are manifold. From the free flow of opinions and emotions often come ideas and responses unanticipated by the moderator or his client, and this is one of the bonus benefits of the technique: the revelation of unknown or unexpected attitudes and behaviors. Focus groups indicate the "why" of consumer behavior and attitude by showing the logical relationships among various ideas and feelings and perceptions.

The emotional tone and intensity of a group discussion demonstrate how strongly consumers feel about a given issue. The group discussion reveals the vocabulary of the consumer related to a given subject—a great aid in designing questionnaires or writing advertising copy. Because of its open, free-ranging nature, the focus group is a powerful creative stimulus to the researcher and adds breadth of perspective to his research attack. Despite its many advantages, the focus group technique lacks statistical precision and, hence, the ideas and understanding produced by focus groups are viewed as hypotheses, to be verified or disproved by subsequent statistical, or quantitative, research.

A Caution

The results of this study are presented as *hypotheses,* not as incontrovertible facts; the sample sizes were small and not representative in a statistical sense. The hypotheses to follow should be checked against quantitative data on the same subject and/or verified by additional quantitative research.

Source: Decision Analyst, Inc.

Figure 11–4
Methodology for a Copy-Testing Study

Commercial Pre-Testing
- Done to determine whether commercial ideas for Waste Management:
  — Would be understood and favorably received by the general public
  — Could help develop favorable attitudes toward the company
- Each commercial idea is shown, in rough form, to 100 adults in markets where Waste Management does business. Adults with little interest in environmental issues are excluded from the sample.
- After watching the commercial, respondents are questioned to determine:
  — Ideas recalled from the commercial
  — Reactions to the commercial—both positive and negative
  — Perceptions of Waste Management
- Commercial recall and reactions are obtained by asking a series of open-ended questions that allow the respondent to answer in detail and in his/her own words.
- Perceptions of Waste Management are determined by having respondents rate the company on various corporate attributes (such as trustworthiness). Respondents place the company, using a 7-point semantic differential scale, on a continuum between opposing attributes (such as trustworthy vs. untrustworthy).
- A control group of 100 respondents has rated Waste Management without seeing a commercial. These responses are compared to post-commercial ratings to determine each commercial's effect on company image.
- Research results are used by Waste Management and Ogilvy & Mather to help decide whether to produce, revise, or not pursue potential executions.
- A copy of the questionnaire follows.

Source: Waste Management, Ogilvy & Mather

Findings/Results

This is the heart of the report. The findings of the research represent the contribution the study will make to what is already known about a particular subject. If it is an example of practical research, the report also provides the basis for a managerial decision to be made by an end user.

A typical results or findings section includes information in both narrative and graphic form. It is important to note that these two arrangements can be highly complementary. Both a purely narrative treatment and a purely graphic treatment of results could be monotonous and difficult to follow. The discussion of findings interspersed with appropriate tables and figures can provide a welcome balance and structure for the reader.

The findings section usually opens with a report of the number of people interviewed and, if appropriate, the percentage of the desired sample frame they represent. If more than one wave of interviewing was necessary to increase the response rate, the response level to each such effort can be included.

Next is a description of the sample that was measured. Depending on which characteristics were measured, this could include demographic or geographic information, or the sample could be described in some other way, such as product purchase behavior, attitudes toward a product, and so on.

The rest of the results section contains a detailed account of the findings of the study. A question-and-answer format is popular and effective for this part of the report. (See Figure 11–5.) The research question is stated, followed by relevant data and interpretation of that data in answer to the question. However it is organized, the results section should be thoroughly written. It should cover every area of investigation introduced in the methodology section, and it should be easy for the end user to understand.

Figure 11–5
Question-and-Answer Format for Presentation of Findings

Table 6: Q. 5A—Stayed at Motel 6 past three years
Nineteen percent of the sample had not stayed at Motel 6 in the past 12 months, but had stayed in the past three years. (This was a minimum qualification to be counted toward the quota.)

Table 7: Q. 5B—Total number of nights stayed in Motel 6 past three years
Among the one in five respondents with Motel 6 experience only in the past three years (not the past 12 months), the mean number of nights claimed was 6.2.

Table 8: Q. 5C—When first used Motel 6
This question was an attempt to infer the impact of the Tom Bodett advertising campaign, since its inception, to attract new users. The advertising has been in place since the end of '86/start of '87, or roughly the past three years.

Almost four persons in ten—38%—declared that they had *begun* using Motel 6 only during the past three years, suggesting that the advertising may have had a considerable impact in generating trial.

The balance of the sample was split almost equally between those who said they first used the brand during the 1980s, but before '86 (32% of the base), and those whose first time goes back prior to 1980 (29%).

Table 9: Q. 5D—Use of Motel 6 between 1980 and 1986

Among the sample who had first used the brand prior to 1980, nine in ten— 90%—also used Motel 6 sometime between 1980 and 1986, implying a strong brand allegiance.

Table 10: Q. 6A—Colors associated with Holiday Inn

Consistent with the protocol from the earlier trademark colors studies (where the data were collected in person), respondents were asked to name colors, if any, they associate with given lodging brands.

Half the sample—51%—said they think of "green" when they think of Holiday Inn. 5%—the next highest observation—said they think of "yellow."

Table 11: Q. 6B—Colors associated with Red Roof

Predictably, a clear majority—71%—claimed "red" in association with Red Roof. Next most frequent in mention was "don't know": 28%.

Table 12: Q. 6C—Colors associated with Howard Johnson

Thirty-eight percent (38%) were unable to associate a color with Howard Johnson; however, a similar number—37%—volunteered "orange" and one in six associated turquoise, aqua, or light blue with Howard Johnson.

Table 13: Q. 6D—Colors associated with Days Inn

More than one in three—37%—volunteered "yellow" in association with Days Inn, though half the sample (49%) could bring no specific colors to mind.

Table 14: Q. 6E—Colors associated with Motel 6

Three in ten, in net (30%) volunteered "blue" in connection with Motel 6. Next occurred "red" (15%), then "orange" (7%).

Source: Motel 6, The Richards Group

Conclusions/Limitations

This section contains concluding statements, which should flow from the data presented in the previous section. While the results section consists of a very straightforward presentation of the data, the conclusions section requires the author to cite trends in the data, to question the reliability or validity of certain parts of the study, and to state within limits of confidence just what is known and what still remains unknown about the questions under study.

In some studies a related discussion of the limitations of the present study is included in the conclusions. In others, it is treated in a separate section. As a part of the research analysis, the investigator should provide an objective assessment of any inherent flaws or problems in the research design, any problems in the data-gathering or analysis phase, and any other factors that might have affected the outcome of the study or limited its generalizability. Often these remarks center more around what was not done than what was done. For example, in hindsight, the investigator might regret the use of certain dichotomous or yes-no questions rather than scaled responses, which would have resulted in a higher level of data and an indication of intensity of respondents' attitudes. Other limitations might involve the choice of sampling procedure, the intensity of the treatment stimulus, and so forth. These statements of limitations serve not only to describe and position the present study but also to provide suggestions for future investigation of the topic. Figure 11–6 details the conclusions of the Motel 6 survey of color preferences.

Figure 11–6
Conclusions of Motel 6 Survey

Conclusions

- Nationally, there is a weak association between the color orange and Motel 6: only one in ten total respondents volunteered an association between the color and Motel 6, and more respondents associated blue or no color at all to the brand.

- No significant pre-existing linkage with beige was observed in unaided attributions, but in *total* mentions (unaided plus aided), beige was the most frequently associated color (51%).

- The association with orange is slightly stronger in California, where one in eight respondents (unaided mentions) linked the color to Motel 6.

- If changing the color of the doors, there would be minimal risk of losing any brand signature value, especially if one compares the existing association with orange to that of the logo colors (red, blue), or even beige.

- Only one in ten guests aware of orange claimed the source for this awareness was the guest room doors. This was also the result among the California subgroup. The higher awareness of the orange guest room doors observed at the Riviera Beach and Arlington Motel 6 properties (two in ten and seven in ten, respectively) can be attributed in part to the different methodology and the visual presence of the doors.

- There is little reliance nationally on the orange guest room doors as an aid to recognition and location of Motel 6 properties. Only one in four of the 24 respondents who *liked* the orange doors claimed any identification dependency on the color. This conclusion is corroborated by the fact that only 8% of overall respondents claimed dependency to any extent on the orange doors to locate a Motel 6 properly, whether or not they like the doors.

- This proportion who claim orange dependency was slightly higher in California (13%); however it was very small compared to the eight out of ten who said they rely on property maps or the Motel 6 sign to lead them to the site.

- The majority of respondents did not hold opinions, either regarding the color of the doors or the switch to beige, unlike the previous studies where six out of ten favored the change. However, in all three studies respondents against the change have been the minority.
- The most popular reason in favor of the switch was aesthetics; respondents felt that beige was the more attractive color.
- In repainting the guest room doors, there should be minimal risk of losing a pre-existing, weak guest association with the old color. Even this weak linkage is more than offset by the strength of other colors—such as in the Motel 6 logo—as cues to a given location, and by the popularity and aesthetic appeal of switching to beige.
- Advertising has coincided with a significant proportion of Motel 6 trial usage: Four out of ten of these respondents had their first Motel 6 experience in only the past three years.

Recommendation
- Based on conclusions from all three studies which have dealt with the issue of the guest room door color, we see no downside to the proposed change from orange to beige.

Recommendations

In some reports this is a separate section; in others, it is part of the conclusions section. The recommendations should stem from the conclusions, which are themselves based on the findings. In writing the recommendations, the investigator must review the objectives of the research study, the situation analysis with respect to the object of investigation, and the findings and conclusions. Sometimes the best course is clear; at other times, it is a matter of opinion. Because they are suggestions for managerial decision making, the investigator must be very careful to present well-considered recommendations in as objective a manner as possible and including all of the known caveats and qualifications.

Appendix, Glossary, and Other Sections

Material that may be too lengthy to go in the main text of a research report can be placed in the appendix at the back. In focus group interviews sometimes a list of verbatim remarks is included in the appendix, as are blank copies of questionnaires used in survey projects. Readers can refer to the appendix for additional information or if they wish to read every detail possible. Authors often place tables depicting various data arrangements in the appendix in an effort to exhaust all of the data collected and analyzed.

If technical terms are used in a report, or if a listing of specific words and their meanings is thought to be helpful to readers, a glossary of those terms can be included in the report, again usually at the back.

Other material that is sometimes appended to the report includes a bibliography of major sources cited, examples of advertisements, pertinent letters, or other documents. In short, it is up to the researcher to include whatever explanatory materials will make the research report most useful to its readers.

Checklist for Writing the Research Report

Below are some of the important areas to be considered when writing a research report. Some have to do with the author's knowledge of the audience for whom the report is intended; others address the content. The biggest overall suggestion for writing an effective report is to establish objectives for the document and then follow them through as closely as possible in every phase of the writing.

1. Did you think clearly about what you wanted to say?

   It is virtually impossible to write something well without giving prior consideration to what you wish to communicate. One of the most important qualities of successful writing is good organization before you begin. Once the report is written, it usually needs to be rewritten at least once before it truly reflects what you were trying to say.

2. Did you consider the sophistication of your audience?

   You should assume little or no research expertise on the part of end users. Even if your language is too basic, it is better to err on the conservative side than to alienate or confuse them with something too complicated.

3. Did you omit overly technical language?

   If you must use technical terms, give a brief explanation of them on first reference, then use them when necessary thereafter without explanation. If appropriate, include a glossary of technical terms at the back of the document.

4. Did you write in a style that is your own?

   It is not necessary to mimic the style of previous research reports—many of them are poorly written and doing so will limit your creativity—and your effectiveness.

5. Did you emphasize some points and give others less emphasis?

   The major findings of a project should be recognizable from the order in which you present them, the amount of space you give them, etc. Some of the "fine print" might best be presented in the appendix so that it does not compete with the major findings.

6. Does the title reflect the contents of the report?

   Try for as descriptive a title as possible, including the major objective of the study, the client, the sample, and the method.

7. Does the content of the report accomplish the objectives set forth for the project?

   Check to make sure you are writing about what the study set out to find in the first place. This is a very basic point, but many research reports tend to stray away from their original focus at the expense of discussion of the major research questions.

8. Is the report accurate and complete, yet as brief and concise as possible?

   There is no magical length that a report must attain for it to be complete. It should accomplish the objectives set forth by the author, and that's all. A research report of 100 pages might have just as easily been contained in ten, and it would have been a lot easier for the end-users.

9. Has the report been proofread for factual as well as mechanical errors?

   It is a tedious job to go back and check all of the figures in a quantitative research report, but it's a lot less embarrassing to discover them yourself in the second draft than once the document is published and circulated. Factual errors are obviously the most damaging to the reputation of the study, but so are errors in writing. At least one other person besides the author should check the manuscript carefully for spelling, punctuation, and usage errors as these too can detract from the professionalism of the overall effort.

Illustrating the Research Report

In addition to the narrative description of the results of a study, report writers have at their disposal a variety of formats for presenting the findings graphically, usually in the form of tables or figures.

Why use graphics or tabular presentations? Rarely do simple raw-number counts provide a sufficient framework for proper analysis of data. Most data analysis goes well beyond the mere tally. And to the extent that such analysis becomes increasingly complex, so does the task of reporting it. This is where the use of tables and figures can prove extremely efficient in presenting the numbers in meaningful arrangements.

Another reason for using graphic or tabular presentations is to provide all of the numbers resulting from a particular statistical test, even though the text of the findings section might not address them. This brings up an important point about why the text, or narrative, and the graphic presentation of results are complementary. Every single statistic generated as the result of a research study need not be discussed in the body of the research report. However, it is important that a complete set of the information by available—and tables and graphs are appropriate vehicles.

Charts and Diagrams

A few commonly used charts and diagrams are described below. It should be noted that these are basic formats and that only the imagination limits the number of variations used. It should also be noted that not every graphic presentation format is appropriate for every data presentation situation. Good judgment should be used in determining whether and when to use these techniques and which is the most appropriate in a given situation.

Just as a picture attracts attention of a reader, so the use of tables and figures within the text of a report automatically draws attention to that information. Therefore the researcher must be careful to use these attention-getting elements in the proper places. Unless all of the data are displayed pictorially, only the major findings should be so treated.

Line Diagrams

Line diagrams are appropriate when depicting a situation of continuous growth or change (see example in Figure 11–7). In the example, values for each time interval are plotted, then the points representing those values are connected with a line. This brings up an important caveat about line diagrams of this type: The line is indeed continuous, but it is actually just the shortest distance between each of two measurement points. Hence it does not show, for instance, fluctuations in the value of a measure at points between those graphed.

Typically, the bottom horizontal boundary is used to display time, and the left vertical boundary contains the scale being used, such as sales in dollars, units, etc. Another suggestion in constructing a line diagram concerns the use of multiple lines or curves (as in the case of different countries measured on the same variable). It is suggested that not more than three or four separate lines be used and that each be clearly marked either on the diagram or in an accompanying legend. More than that number can be confusing to the reader.

Stratum Diagram

This variation of the line diagram uses shading between lines to represent "share" of a particular segment. The strata should be clearly marked with titles on the diagram itself (see example in Figure 11–8).

Figure 11–7
Radio's National Audience

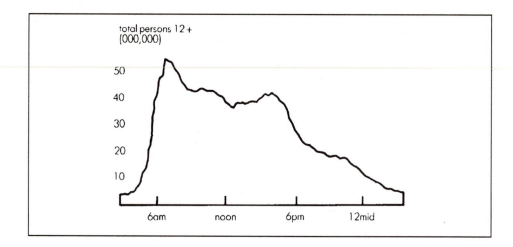

Source: RADAR; Statistical Research, Inc.

Figure 11–8
Radio Buildup over the Listening Day

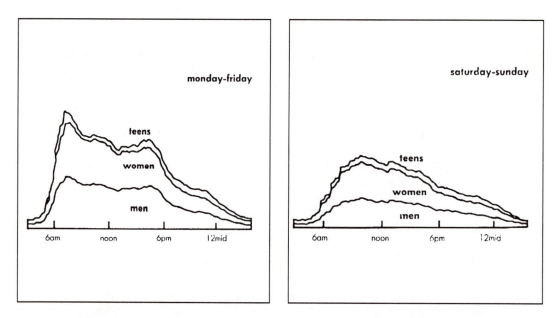

Source: RADAR; Statistical Research, Inc.

Bar Chart

This popular method of depicting measurement values at separate points has many variations and possibilities. Generally speaking, the bar chart is appropriate for situations in which a series of data is to be presented, as shown in the example. If change in individual factors is to be presented for various time periods, the factors can be grouped as shown. Figures 11–9 and 11–10 show different uses of the bar chart.

Figure 11–9
Bar Chart

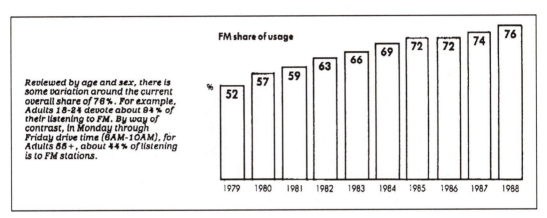

Source: RADAR; Statistical Research, Inc.

Figure 11–10
Bar Chart

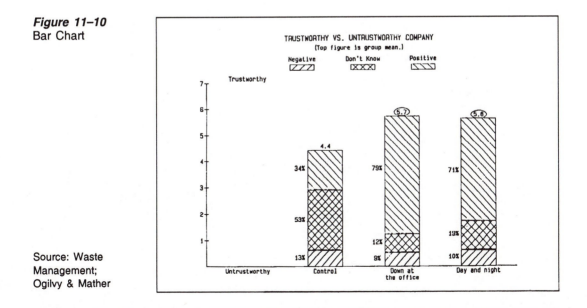

Source: Waste
Management;
Ogilvy & Mather

Chapter 11 Writing the Research Report

Pie Chart

This chart is well suited to depiction of proportions of the whole. A circle represents 100 percent of the available values, and each value is presented as a piece of the pie. Ideally, the values assigned to each slice will be included within the piece. If space does not allow, they should be written to the side. One rule of thumb to use in fashioning a pie chart is to being at the twelve o'clock position with the largest increment, then proceed with successively smaller increments in a clockwise direction. See Figure 11–11 for example.

Figure 11–11
Which of the following best describes your current employment status?

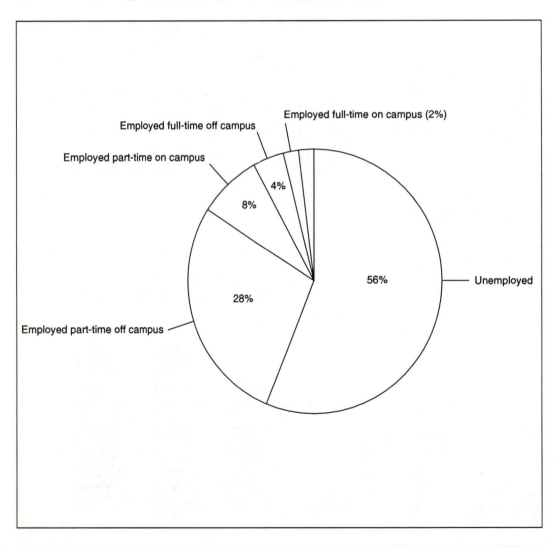

Pictograph

A variation on the bar chart, the pictograph uses figures to form the bars at a certain length. Sometimes the figures can be so small that they are difficult for the reader to follow. Pictographs are best suited for either very simple data presentation or for use as a visual aid for an oral presentation of the findings. See Figure 11–12 for example.

Figure 11–12
Pictograph

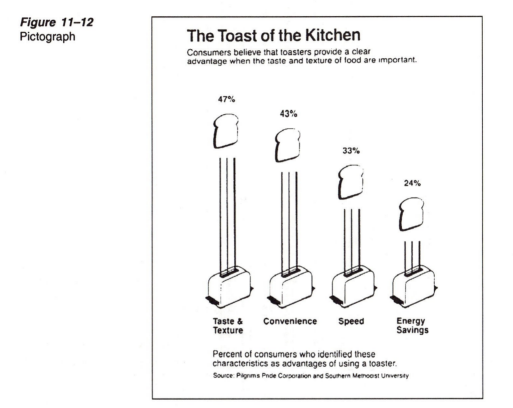

The Toast of the Kitchen

Consumers believe that toasters provide a clear advantage when the taste and texture of food are important.

47%

43%

33%

24%

Taste & Texture   Convenience   Speed   Energy Savings

Percent of consumers who identified these characteristics as advantages of using a toaster.

Source: Pilgrims Pride Corporation and Southern Methodist University

Tables

Tabular presentation of data is common in research reports primarily because of the space that it saves—often it is possible to write for several pages about the contents of a single table! Tables can be used either in the body of a research report or they can be placed in the appendix as supporting or explanatory material.

The major components of a table are its title, headings for the columns of data, headings for the rows of data, the figures themselves, and the source of information if appropriate. The results of a pilot study of advertising managers, including frequencies, percentages, and mean responses to scaled items are presented in Figure 11–13. Figure 11–14 lists percentages directly below the response frequencies.

Figure 11-13
A Table with Data from an Attitude Survey

TRADEMARK COLORS AWARENESS AND ATTITUDES RESEARCH
National Survey
Prepared for The Richards Group

Table 20

Q.8 - WHERE COLOR ORANGE IS USED AT MOTEL 6

		REGION				MOTEL 6 USERS PAST 12 MONTHS				Past 3 Years, Not Past Year	TRIP PURPOSE			AGE			INCOME		GENDER	
	Total	Calif-ornia	S.E. U.S.	S.W. U.S.	Balance of U.S.	Total	Light Users (1-2)	Medium Users (3-4)	Heavy Users (5+)		Busi-ness	Pleas-ure	Both	Under 35	35-49	50 +	Under $40K	$40K +	Male	Female
Base: Respondents who associate color orange with Motel 6 and stated where used	45 / 7.5	10 / 12.7	6 / 2.7	4 / 7.9	10 / 6.7	36 / 7.6	13 / 7.0	7 / 5.7	16 / 8.6	14 / 7.1	2.1	30 / 7.3	14 / 10.0	17 / 9.7	14 / 6.8	14 / 6.5	23 / 8.0	16 / 6.6	41 / 3.7	34 / 11.3
Sign	12 / 2.0	3 / 2.0	2.6	2.6	5 / 3.4	9 / 1.0	6 / 3.7	.8	3 / 1.1	2.4	1.9	8 / 2.9	1.6	6 / 3.4	2 / 1.9	4 / 1.0	6 / 2.2	2.5	6 / 1.0	3 / 3.0
Doors	.7 / 1.3	.2	.2		.2 / 1.3	.3 / .8	.1	.1 / .8	.3 / 1.6	.3	.3	.3	.2	.4	.2 / 1.0	.2 / 1.0	.4	.2 / .8	.2 / 1.0	3 / .7
Building exterior	.2 / .7					.2		.2	.1 / .5		.2	.1	.2	.6			.1		.1	.3
"6"	.2	.2	.1 / .7			.2	.1				.1	.2			.5	.5	.4		.1	.3
Roof	.2		.2 / .7		.2 / .7	.2	.2	.6			.2	.2			.5	.5	.3		.1	.3
Carpets/Drapes/Bedspreads	18 / 3.0	8 / 5.3	2 / 1.3	6 / 4.0	2 / 1.3	14 / 3.0	4 / 2.4	4 / 3.3	6 / 3.2	6 / 3.1	3.2	13 / 3.6	5 / 2.4	8 / 4.8	5 / 2.3	5 / 2.5	9 / 3.4	3 / 1.0	3 / 3.0	15 / 5.0
Key	.1	.1 / .7				.1	.1			.5		.1		.1	.1 / .6			.1	.1	.3
All other	.2	.2	.1 / .7			.1				.5		.1		.7	.5		.4		.1	.3
Don't know/Not sure	6 / 1.0	6 / 3.7	1 / .7	1 / .7	1 / .7	4 / .8	1 / .6	.8	2 / 1.1	1.6	2.1	5 / 1.3	3 / 1.4	5 / 2.2	3 / 1.4	2 / 1.0	4 / 1.5	2 / .8	2 / .3	4 / 1.7
Aware color used but where not mentioned	.3 / .7	.1 / .7	.1 / .7			.2 / .4						.2	.2		2 / .9		.2		.1	.3

Source: Motel 6, The Richards Group

Figure 11–14
Table with Means, Frequencies, and Percentages

Table 2

Advertising Managers' Perceptions of Advertising and Advertising Research

Evaluation Statement	Mean Response*	(n=31) Strongly Agree (%)	Somewhat Agree (%)	Neutral	Somewhat Disagree (%)	Strongly Disagree (%)
The money we spend on advertising through our agency is well spent.	4.5	20 (9.7)	8 (25.8)	3 (9.7)	—	—
Our advertising agency(ies) is expensive.	2.8	3 (9.7)	4 (12.9)	13 (41.9)	6 (19.4)	5 (16.1)
I see a direct relationship between my sales and my advertising agency's performance.	3.0	3 (9.7)	13 (41.9)	7 (22.6)	6 (19.4)	2 (6.5)
My agency(ies) is up-to-date on creative trends in advertising.	4.4	18 (58.1)	9 (29.0)	2 (6.5)	2 (6.5)	—
My agency(ies) is up-to-date on research methods.	4.1	10 (32.3)	17 (54.8)	3 (9.7)	—	1 (3.2)
I feel that I get the full value of my dollars invested in advertising research.	3.7	5 (16.1)	16 (51.6)	7 (22.6)	1 (3.2)	2 (6.5)
The general public is getting fed up with being interviewed.	3.2	6 (19.4)	6 (19.4)	9 (29.0)	7 (22.6)	3 (9.7)
Most advertising researchers are serious about improving their techniques.	4.1	12 (38.7)	11 (35.5)	6 (19.4)	2 (6.5)	—
Existing advertising research techniques are adequate in predicting how advertising will perform in a real-world situation.	3.1	—	14 (45.2)	9 (29.0)	4 (12.9)	4 (12.9)
Advertising research helps us to reduce the risk in our advertising campaigns.	4.0	9 (29.0)	15 (48.4)	5 (16.1)	1 (3.2)	1 (3.2)
Advertising research helps ensure the success of our advertising campaigns.	3.3	5 (16.1)	12 (38.7)	4 (12.9)	6 (19.4)	4 (12.9)

*Response values were as follows: strongly agree = 5; somewhat agree = 4; neutral = 3; somewhat disagree = 2; strongly disagree = 1.

Review

In this chapter we saw that:

- No matter how well a research project is conducted or how important its findings to the problem at hand, if it is not communicated properly to its audience or end users it cannot be used effectively.
- The research report should be written in a style that is easily understood by the nonresearcher; it should be a complete, self-contained document; and it should be well-organized and well-written.
- Components of the research report are the letter of transmittal, title page and cover, table of contents, executive summary, introduction, methodology, findings/results, conclusions/limitations, recommendations, and appendix.
- In addition to the text of the report, report writers should use graphic or tabular presentations to present all research results efficiently in meaningful arrangements.

Part **3** **Media
Research**

Chapter 12 Media Research: An Overview

Anyone who has worked with an advertising budget knows that the lion's share of the money spent on a campaign is typically allocated to media costs: purchase of time and space in various media to disseminate the creative message. Although the use of sponsorships, special events, and other promotional techniques has increased in the past several years—often at the expense of more traditional media expenditures—placement of advertising in media remains a critical factor in the success of an advertising effort. Literally thousands of options for media, vehicles within media, timing and distribution patterns, and frequency levels confront the media planner, and it is through media research that information is provided so that informed choices can be made. Let us review briefly the major classes of media and their relative strengths and weak points.

Strengths and Weaknesses of Major Media Types

The most common advertising media are television, radio, magazines, newspapers, outdoor/transit, and direct mail. Each has its advantages and disadvantages, the presence and effects of which—verifiable through advertising research—must be taken into account when planning a media schedule. Remember also that in many instances, a would-be strength of a particular medium, such as high *reach,* is actually a double-edged sword. For example, coverage may extend well beyond the intended target and represent "waste" circulation. The factor of *flexibility* can refer either to situations involving timing, in which flexibility refers to favorable closing dates, etc., or situations involving geographic coverage, in which scheduling a regional or local campaign or using a medium to single out markets for special emphasis is of value. Figure 12–1 lists some very general advantages and disadvantages of using various major media. Of course, exceptions to almost every factor cited could be made, but overall the following benefits and drawbacks hold true.

Figure 12–1
Strengths and Weaknesses of Major Media Types

	Strengths	*Weaknesses*
Television		
	High reach	Fleeting messages
	Ability to demonstrate	Expensive
	High-impact medium	Cluttered environment
	Prestigious	Wasted reach geographically
Radio		
	Relatively inexpensive	Fleeting messages
	Scheduling flexibility	"Background" medium—low involvement
	Audience selectivity	Clutter
	Geographic flexibility	Audience fragmentation
		Lack of research data
		Lack of visual capability
Magazines		
	Audience selectivity	Relatively expensive
	High quality of reproduction	Slow exposure build-up
	"Reference" medium	
	Upscale audiences	
	Favorable editorial environment	
	Merchandising possibilities	
Newspapers		
	"Urgent" medium	Perishability of content
	"Reference" medium	Reproduction quality poor
	Geographic flexibility	National coverage difficult
	Scheduling flexibility	Low demographic selectivity
	High market coverage	
Outdoor/Transit		
	Inexpensive	Message limitations
	Geographic selectivity	Viewer distraction
	Scheduling flexibility	Lack of reliable research data
	Creative potential	Vandalism
Direct Mail		
	Personalization	Relatively expensive
	Relatively low "clutter" factor	Reputation as "junk mail"
	No waste circulation	Potentially ignored
	Scheduling, geographic, and creative flexibility	

Evaluating Media

Let's take a look at the Advertising Research Foundation's model for evaluating media in Figure 12–2.

Figure 12–2
ARF Model for Evaluating Media

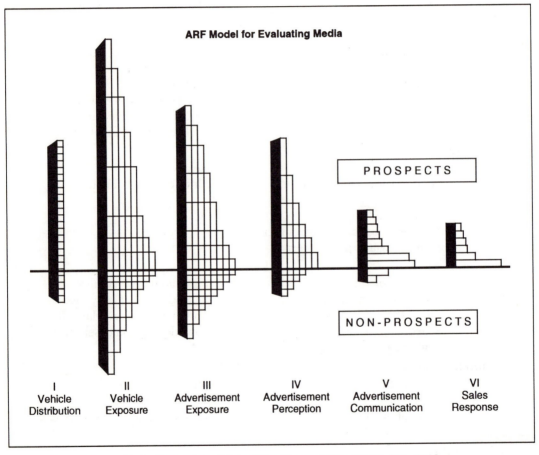

Source: "Toward Better Media Comparisons," Advertising Research Foundation, Inc., 1961.

The model includes all pertinent steps between vehicle distribution and sales response. A horizontal line serves to show the process developing as well as to divide the vehicle and advertising audience into prospects and nonprospects. Looking at the stages of the process will help reinforce our understanding of media research. They include the following:

- *Vehicle distribution:* This is a count of the *units* through which advertising is distributed. Units are not people, but rather objects, such as magazines or newspapers. The general term *circulation* is used to refer to this stage.

- *Vehicle exposure:* In this stage, the people reached and their characteristics are identified. Exposure is defined as open eyes or open ears in view of or within earshot of the vehicle.

- *Advertisement exposure:* Only a fraction of those exposed to a vehicle are also exposed to an advertisement within that vehicle. This is one of the most important distinctions in advertising terminology and practice. Technically, advertisement exposure means open eyes or ears in the presence of the advertisement itself. It does not mean that an individual saw, heard, or understood the message. It means simply that the individual was exposed to the "ad space."

The first three stages of the ARF model are related to the medium and the vehicle but not to the content of the advertisement. For example, even advertisement exposure is independent of the message and is a function of the vehicle carrying the ad. Admittedly, there is a fine line between advertisement exposure and advertisement perception, as we will see below. Keep in mind that advertisement exposure simply means eyes open facing the advertisement in the vehicle.

Message research involves measuring advertising performance, described in the three steps below.

- *Advertisement perception:* This is a count of people who see or hear an advertisement. Advertisement perception is considered to be the lowest level of advertising message effects.

- *Advertisement communication:* At this stage, changes in awareness and attitude are measured to find out how well the advertisement communicates its message.

- *Sales response:* Sales response includes the number of units purchased, the number of purchases, the number of dollars spent, etc.

The measurement of these advertising message effects will be the focus of Chapters 15 through 18.

Research Questions in Choosing Media

A consideration of what a media planner contributes to the advertising effort provides a useful framework in which to view the research questions that arise in the media planning process. Generally, a media planner works to achieve overall brand marketing goals by disseminating the creative messages in specific geographic areas to specific market segments at particular times, using selected vehicles within appropriate media. Usually a budget and at least a loosely defined target audience profile have been provided. A high premium is placed on the planner's ability to deliver the desired audience efficiently, which entails reaching the maximum number of prospects for the money, and effectively, which involves assumptions about how consumers respond to media messages. Assumptions about advertising effectiveness will be discussed in more detail later in this chapter.

In order to create the media plan, the planner requires an enormous amount of information for each part of the decision-making process. Some of the questions that must be answered to make an informed judgment include the following:

- Which media will be most effective in reaching desired goals of placement, timing, and target audience?

- Within media, which vehicles should be chosen?

- What is the optimal timing for the overall advertising effort? More specifically, should all media be used simultaneously, or should usage be alternated?

- What unit size of advertising is best? For instance, 15 seconds versus 30 seconds for television, half-page versus full-page ads for print, etc.

- How many times should target audience members be exposed to the advertising and how frequently?

Media planners receive direction as part of the market situation analysis about how the overall marketing goals require emphasis in certain geographic areas and among specific target groups. The other questions, however, constitute the various specializations, which together are referred to as *media* or *audience research*.

Common Methods Used in Media Research

Media research methods range from personal interviews to electronic measurement. Let's look at some of the major methods and the types of information each provides.

Interviews

Interviews, either at home or by telephone, are the source of much media information. Typically a random sample of a large group is drawn: readers of a specific magazine or TV households nationwide. In the case of newspapers, the interview can be just long enough to ask which papers the respondent read the previous day. With magazines, an interview could last an hour or more and involve paging through a copy of a magazine a respondent claims to have read.

Diaries

Though diaries can be used to record reading and viewing of more than one medium, the most notable use of this method has been to estimate television and radio audiences. Participants typically keep a daily log of their listening or viewing habits for a specified period, usually one or two weeks. Responses are recorded in a special booklet supplied by the research company and collected immediately upon completion. The diary, like the interview, provides researchers with media exposure information that, when coupled with demographic characteristics, yields exposure patterns.

Electronic Recording Devices

Electronic devices are used to measure which people are watching which programs on television and to estimate total audience size for programs (vehicle exposure). They do not measure advertisement exposure. Typically, participant or "metered" households, with electronic recording meters attached to TV sets, are asked to remain in a sample for a period of years, after which the sample is replaced. Existing meters are basically of two types: passive devices, which record automatically any time the television is turned on, and active people-meters, which require that individual household members indicate when they are viewing by pressing a button.

Audits

The audit of publishers' books is used to measure the level of vehicle distribution—or circulation—in print. An audit, conducted by one of a handful of companies, simply involves verifying and reporting the paid or free circulation figures claimed by a newspaper or magazine publisher.

Field Experiments

An endless number of controlled field experiments is possible in attempting to isolate the contribution made by media placement, timing, and weight. A true field experiment involves holding advertising and marketing variables constant while manipulating the experimental stimulus in order to measure its effects on one or more dependent variables (such as advertisement exposure). In addition, quasi-experimental test markets can be used for the same purpose, although the lack of adequate controls often places their results in question.

Single-Source/Combination Methods

Single-source research services combine information collected from people-meters with consumer purchase data gathered by grocery store scanners or scanner wands used in the home. The household is the unit of measurement for single-source data, which means that viewing and purchasing on the part of individual households can be directly compared. At present, single-source research focuses on the medium of television only, though vendors of such services report that they plan to measure other media exposure as well, probably with diaries. The result of single-source research is data that correlates vehicle exposure with purchase behavior.

Other Methods

Less frequently used methods of measuring exposure include the following:

- Traffic studies to estimate outdoor advertisement exposure
- Video- or still-camera recording of a person reading a print vehicle
- Mailed questionnaires to subscribers to print vehicles
- Brain wave measures to determine reader involvement

Again, the purpose of all of these methods is to estimate the audience exposure for specific vehicles and/or the advertising within them.

Issues and Problems in Media Research

As stated at the opening of this chapter, media expenditures represent such an enormous share of all dollars spent on advertising that advertisers expect to be able to account for the results of such spending. And while great strides have been made in some aspects of media research, many of the same, less-than-perfect practices are still in place, and not all of the pieces of the media research puzzle fit neatly together. A relatively small number of established syndicated companies supply the advertising industry with media research data, and the sheer expense of improving on methods or expanding sample bases has put a damper on major progress in several areas, especially in television, where measurement is very equipment-intensive. Advertisers, for their part, continue to clamor for more adequate data, but often are reluctant to pay the price for such improvements. Many advertisers conduct their own proprietary media research, often at great expense. Results of such studies usually are not made public and so are of no use to the great majority of researchers or advertisers.

This means that in the 1990s we have media measurement services supplying data for all major media, but their product, by its nature, is in almost all cases less than ideal. Below are a few of the major issues and problems associated with research in media today.

Timeliness

While the task of the media planner is to try to engineer the success of a future campaign, the data available with which to plan is at best an average of several months, possibly even years old. It is outdated before it is disseminated. Reports published annually, for instance, are in excess of a year out of date when the new volumes arrive. With some media research information, the issue of timeliness is more acute than with others.

The widespread use of computers in advertising agencies and especially in media planning has somewhat reduced the timeliness problem in some instances. Several of the syndicated research suppliers, such as SMRB and MRI, make their data available on-line to customers. People-meters and other electronic devices such as scanners allow for instantaneous availability of data on viewing behavior, purchase behavior, and demographics.

Memory

Decades of research on human learning and retention have provided us with a distinction between short-term and long-term memory and their implications for advertising researchers. Much advertising is stored in a very temporary fashion known as short-term memory—it may be remembered a few minutes, hours, or possibly days. With repetition, a message might be stored in long-term memory. Media planners often set goals for a specified number of repetitions of the advertising to the "average" viewer, reader, or listener, so that it will have a greater effect.

One problem with memory occurs in attempts to measure that all-important dimension of advertisement exposure. Respondents who claim in an interview to have watched an entire TV program the night before may be adamant that they did not see a 30-second commercial it contained. Since media researchers must rely on self-reports, which are subject to faulty memory, the factor of memory must be taken into consideration. The fact is that many people cannot remember what they've seen or read. Because of this, and because many people actively avoid watching commercials, unaided recall of commercials on television can dip as low as 10 percent. That means one in ten viewers who claim to have seen a program cannot remember having seen a particular commercial on the show. Use of aided recall techniques, which involve category or brand prompts to the respondent, can result in higher exposure estimates, but some believe that the prompts themselves act as a means of inflating scores.

Self-Reporting

Most media research data is based on people volunteering information about their past media behavior. For a variety of reasons, ranging from embarrassment to confusion, self-reports of vehicle exposure and advertisement exposure are subject to degrees of inaccuracy. A good example of this is a 1985 study in which three out of four respondents who reported to have read a magazine called *Metropolitan Home* also claimed to have the latest issues of *Metropolitan Home & Garden*. Alas, a magazine named *Metropolitan Home & Garden* did not exist. Since there are few truly passive measures of media exposure, much media research information continues to be only as accurate as respondents' self-reports.

Sample Sizes/Sample Error

The number of people measured in some media research studies results in questions being raised about sample error. Some measurement services use sample sizes as small as 150 to 300, which can result in considerable sample error, depending on the population from which they are drawn. Obviously, the practical issue here is weighing the cost of interviewing more people against available time and money resources. Even when several thousand randomly selected households are measured, as in the case of the Simmons Market Research Bureau reports on media and markets, subsample sizes resulting from cross-tabulation of data often yield figures that are considered questionable or unreliable.

Cooperation Rate

In an era when a high premium is placed on personal privacy and unsolicited contact is often unwelcome, it has become an increasing challenge for media researchers to gain the cooperation of respondents. Refusal rates for some telephone surveys are so high that attempts to identify the nonrespondent have taken on additional importance. One wonders if those who respond to a media study are similar in their media habits to their noncooperative counterparts. Historically, media measurement firms have had problems recruiting minority respondents, a fact which has improved over the past several years with the addition of minority and bilingual interviewers.

Methodological Dilemmas

The difficulty of interpreting and using media research data is made more complicated by the existence in some cases of multiple methods that yield different results. In television, the use of the new people-meter technology initially resulted in lower audience estimates than the older meters or diaries had produced. In print, controversy remains over whether a recent-reading method or the more tedious through-the-book method gives a more accurate estimate of magazine readership. Both of these methodological issues will be discussed further in the chapters on print and broadcast media research.

Industry Guidelines

Various industry groups have periodically issued guidelines and recommendations for gathering, analyzing, and reporting media research information. In addition, industry organizations have sponsored technical seminars on media measurement methods and the issues facing those who provide and use such research. These guidelines and major findings from professional research conferences will be included in the following chapters on specific media classes.

The American Association of Advertising Agencies (AAAA) provides recommended formats for reporting demographic segments for consumer media research. The guidelines are issued in an effort to standardize the way demographic information is reported in studies across all media types. (See Figure 12-3.)

The Advertising Research Foundation periodically audits the procedures of media research companies and reports its findings. The audit is a very thorough examination of the sampling, measurement, and reporting procedures used by the suppliers of audience research.

Figure 12–3

AAAA's RECOMMENDED STANDARD SEGMENTS FOR DEMOGRAPHIC CHARACTERISTICS IN SURVEYS OF CONSUMER MEDIA AUDIENCES

DATA TO BE GATHERED AND REPORTED (IF POSSIBLE, TO BE DIRECTLY ACCESSIBLE)			DATA TO BE REPORTED FOR:			
CHARACTERISTIC	MINIMUM BASIC DATA TO BE REPORTED	ADDITIONAL DATA — HIGHLY VALUED	PERSONS	HOME-MAKERS	HOUSE-HOLD HEAD	HOUSE-HOLDS
I. PERSONS CHARACTERISTICS			X	X	X	
A. HOUSEHOLD RELATIONSHIP	PRINCIPLE WAGE EARNER IN HH (DEFINES HH HEAD)					
	PRINCIPLE SHOPPER IN HH (DEFINES HOMEMAKER)					
	SPOUSE					
	CHILD					
	OTHER RELATIVE					
	PARTNER/ROOMMATE					
	OTHER NON-RELATIVE					
B. AGE	UNDER 6	2 - 5	X	X	X	
	6 - 11	6 - 8				
	12 - 15	35 - 49				
	16 - 20	25 - 49				
	18 - 20					
	16 OR OLDER					
	18 OR OLDER					
	18 - 24					
	25 - 34					
	35 - 44					
	45 - 49					
	50 - 54					
	55 - 64					
	65 - 74					
	75 OR OLDER					

— 1 —

CHARACTERISTIC	MINIMUM BASIC DATA TO BE REPORTED	ADDITIONAL DATA — HIGHLY VALUED	PERSONS	HOME-MAKERS	HOUSE-HOLD HEAD	HOUSE-HOLDS
C. SEX	MALE		x	x	x	
	FEMALE					
D. EDUCATION	LAST GRADE ATTENDED:		x	x	x	
	GRADE SCHOOL OR LESS (GRADE 1-8)					
	SOME HIGH SCHOOL					
	GRADUATED HIGH SCHOOL					
	SOME COLLEGE (AT LEAST 1 YEAR)					
	GRADUATED COLLEGE	ANY POST GRADUATE WORK				
	IF CURRENTLY ATTENDING SCHOOL	— (IF PERTINENT TO STUDY) —				
		LIVE HOME				
		LIVE AWAY				
		— LIVE IN STUDENT HOUSING				
		— LIVE OFF CAMPUS				
	FULL-TIME STUDENT					
	PART-TIME STUDENT					
E. MARITAL STATUS	MARRIED..........	SPOUSE PRESENT / SPOUSE ABSENT	x	x	x	
	WIDOWED					
	DIVORCED OR SEPARATED	SPOUSE WORKING				
	SINGLE (NEVER MARRIED)					
	PARENT	ENGAGED				
	PREGNANT					
	'LIVING TOGETHER'					

— 2 —

Figure 12-3 (continued)

CHARACTERISTIC	MINIMUM BASIC DATA TO BE REPORTED	ADDITIONAL DATA — HIGHLY VALUED	PERSONS	HOME-MAKERS	HOUSE-HOLD HEAD	HOUSE-HOLDS
F. RELIGION — POLITICAL		PROTESTANT [ACTIVE (Practicing) / INACTIVE (Non-Practicing)] CATHOLIC JEWISH OTHER NONE POLITICAL — CONSERVATIVE — LIBERAL — MODERATE	x	x	x	
G. RACE	WHITE BLACK OTHER		x	x	x	
H. PRINCIPLE LANGUAGE SPOKEN AT HOME	ENGLISH SPANISH OTHER		x	x	x	
H1. OTHER LANGUAGES SPOKEN AT HOME	ENGLISH SPANISH OTHER		x	x	x	

DATA TO BE REPORTED FOR:

– 3 –

CHARACTERISTIC	MINIMUM BASIC DATA TO BE REPORTED	ADDITIONAL DATA — HIGHLY VALUED	PERSONS	HOME-MAKERS	HOUSE-HOLD HEAD	HOUSE-HOLDS
I. INDIVIDUAL EMPLOYMENT INCOME	UNDER $10,000	$75,000 - 99,000	X	X	X	
	$10,00 - 14,999	$100,000 AND OVER				
	$15,000 - 19,999					
	$20,000 - 24,999	IEI INCOME BY QUINTILE AS DETERMINED BY THE SURVEY ZIPTILES.				
	$25,000 - 29,999					
	$30,000 - 39,999					
	$40,000 - 49,999	OTHER INCOME				
	$50,000 - 74,999					
	$75,000 AND OVER					

IEI BY QUINTILE
INCOME INTERVAL

QUINTILE	% ADULTS	LOW -	HIGH	MEDIAN INCOME
1	20	—	10,156	6,391
2	20	10,757	19,999	13,959
3	20	20,000	29,999	24,953
4	20	30,000	43,243	34,967
5	20	43,244	—	60,150

— 4 —

Figure 12-3 (continued)

CHARACTERISTIC	MINIMUM BASIC DATA TO BE REPORTED	ADDITIONAL DATA — HIGHLY VALUED	DATA TO BE REPORTED FOR:			
			PERSONS	HOME-MAKERS	HOUSE-HOLD-HEAD	HOUSE-HOLDS
J. OCCUPATION AS DEFINED BY BUREAUS OF THE CENSUS	ARMED FORCES		X	X	X	
	CIVILIAN LABOR FORCE					
	EMPLOYED	HOLD MORE THAN ONE JOB				
	— FULL TIME (35 or More Hours Per Week)					
	— PART TIME (Less than 35 Hours Per Week)					
	SELF EMPLOYED	IN HOME				
		OUT-OF-HOME				
	UNEMPLOYED — LOOKING FOR WORK					
	MAJOR OCCUPATIONAL CATEGORIES	PRIVATE COMPANY				
	— MANAGERIAL PROFESSIONAL	GOVERNMENT				
	— TECHNICAL					
	— ADMIN. SUPPORT (INCL. CLERICAL)	PREDOMINANTLY — DAY WORK				
	— SALES	— EVENING/NIGHT WORK				
	— OPERATIVE, NON-FARM LABORERS, SERVICE WORKERS, PRIVATE HOUSEHOLD WORKERS	TECHNICAL RELATED SUPPORT OCCUPATIONS				
	— FARMERS, FARM MANAGERS, FARM LABORERS					
	— CRAFTSMEN					
	— OTHER					
	INDUSTRY OF EMPLOYMENT					
	JOB TITLE					
	NOT EMPLOYED					
	RETIRED					
	STUDENT (FULL TIME)					
	HOMEMAKER (Not Employed Outside Home)					
	DISABLED					
	TEMPORARILY UNEMPLOYED					
	OTHER					

— 5 —

CHARACTERISTIC	MINIMUM BASIC DATA TO BE REPORTED	ADDITIONAL DATA — HIGHLY VALUED	PERSONS	HOME-MAKERS	HOUSE-HOLD HEAD	HOUSE-HOLDS
II. HOUSEHOLDS CHARACTERISTICS						
A. COUNTY SIZE	A COUNTY B COUNTY C COUNTY D COUNTY		X	X	X	X
B. GEOGRAPHIC AREA AS DEFINE BY BUREAU OF THE CENSUS	INSIDE METROPOLITAN STATISTICAL AREA .... — MSA CENTRAL CITY — MSA SUBURBAN — MSA OTHER OUTSIDE METROPOLITAN STATISTICAL AREA URBAN .... RURAL	METROPOLITAN STATISTICAL AREA POPULATIONS 4,000,000 AND OVER 1,000,000 — 3,999,999 500,000 — 999,999 250,000 — 499,999 100,000 — 249,999 50,000 — 99,999 URBAN: URBANIZED AREA — CENTRAL CITY — URBAN FRINGE — OTHER URBAN — PLACES OF 10,000 — 50,000 POPULATION — PLACES OF 2,500 — 9,999 POPULATION				
C. GEOGRAPHIC REGION	AS DEFINED BY BUREAU OF THE CENSUS .... — NORTHEAST — NORTH CENTRAL — SOUTH — WEST NIELSEN GEOGRAPHIC AREAS — NORTHEAST — EAST CENTRAL — WEST CENTRAL — SOUTH — PACIFIC	CENSUS GEOGRAPHIC DIVISION — NEW ENGLAND — MID ATLANTIC — EAST NORTH CENTRAL — WEST NORTH CENTRAL — SOUTH ATLANTIC — EAST SOUTH CENTRAL — WEST SOUTH CENTRAL — MOUNTAIN — PACIFIC MAJOR MARKET UNDUPLICATED TV COVERAGE AREAS	X	X	X	X
D. PRESENCE/AGE OF CHILDREN IN HOUSEHOLD	NO CHILDREN UNDER 18 YOUNGEST CHILD 6-17 YOUNGEST CHILD UNDER 6	YOUNGEST CHILD 12-17 YOUNGEST CHILD 6-11 YOUNGEST CHILD 2-5 YOUNGEST CHILD UNDER 2	X	X	X	X
E. HOUSEHOLD TYPE		FAMILY MEMBERS ONLY NON-FAMILY MEMBERS ONLY BOTH FAMILY AND NON-FAMILY MEMBERS	X	X	X	X

– 6 –

Figure 12–3 (concluded)

CHARACTERISTIC	MINIMUM BASIC DATA TO BE REPORTED	ADDITIONAL DATA — HIGHLY VALUED	PERSONS	HOME-MAKERS	HOUSE-HOLD HEAD	HOUSE-HOLDS
F. HOUSEHOLD SIZE	1 MEMBER 2 MEMBERS 3 MEMBERS 4 MEMBERS	NUMBER OF ADULTS (Persons 18 and Over) MALE/FEMALE HH FEMALE ONLY HH MALE ONLY HH	X	X	X	X
G. NUMBER OF CHILDREN UNDER 18 IN HOUSEHOLD	NONE ONE MORE THAN ONE	NUMBER OF CHILDREN 6 - 17 NUMBER OF CHILDREN UNDER 6	X	X	X	X
		NUMBER OF CHILDREN BY HOUSEHOLD SIZE		X	X	X
H. HOUSEHOLD INCOME	SEE I., INDIVIDUAL EMPLOYMENT INCOME	$ 75,000 - 99,999 $100,000 AND OVER HOUSEHOLD INCOME BY QUINTILE AS DETERMINED BY SURVEY ZIPTILES		X	X	X
I. OTHER HOUSEHOLD CHARACTERISTICS		NUMBER OF ADULTS EMPLOYED FULL TIME	X	X	X	X

J. HOME OWNERSHIP	OWN HOME
	  — PRIVATE OWNERSHIP
	  — COOPERATIVE OWNERSHIP
	  — CONDOMINIUM
	RENT HOME
		RESIDENCE FIVE YEARS PRIOR TO SURVEY
		  — LIVED IN SAME HOUSE/HOME
		  — LIVED IN DIFFERENT HOUSE/HOME
		    — IN SAME COUNTY
		    — IN DIFFERENT COUNTY
		    — IN SAME STATE
		    — IN DIFFERENT STATE
			X	X	X	X

K. TYPE HOUSING UNIT	SINGLE FAMILY HOME MULTIPLE FAMILY HOME APARTMENT MOBILE HOME OR TRAILER		X	X	X	X

DATA TO BE REPORTED FOR:

NOTE: THE RECOMMENDED MINIMUM AND ADDITIONAL DATA STANDARDS APPLY TO GENERALIZED SURVEYS. THOSE SURVEYS DONE TO MORE SPECIFIC PURPOSES—E.G. PARTICULAR GEOGRAPHIC SECTIONS OF THE COUNTRY, AFFLUENT MARKETS, PUBLICATIONS DIRECTED TOWARDS A SPECIFIC TARGET, ETC.—MAY CHOOSE TO COLLAPSE OR EXPAND CHARACTERISTIC SEGMENTS AS APPROPRIATE TO THEIR CONTEXT.

— 7 —

Review

In this chapter we saw that:

- Placement of advertising in media remains a critical factor in the success of an advertising effort; through media research, decisions can be made about media, vehicles within media, timing and distribution patterns, and frequency levels.

- The stages of the media research process include measuring vehicle distribution, vehicle exposure, and advertisement exposure.

- Message research involves measuring advertising performance in the form of advertisement perception, advertisement communication, and sales response.

- Common methods used in media research are interviews, diaries, electronic recording devices, audits, field experiments, single-source/combination methods, and others.

- Problems to be addressed in media research include timeliness, memory of respondents, the self-reporting bias, sample sizes/sample error, cooperation rate, and methodological dilemmas.

Chapter 13

Print Media Research: Magazines and Newspapers

The major print media, newspapers and magazines, are estimated to reach more than four-fifths of the U.S. adult population. Because of their ability to select audiences and the fact that they can be kept and referred to over time, print media are very attractive options for media planners. To completely evaluate the effectiveness of a specific print vehicle, such as *Time* magazine or *The Dallas Morning News,* the following pieces of information are necessary:

- *Vehicle distribution:* The number of copies in circulation. This is not a count of people, but rather of units, i.e., the number of copies of a magazine purchased or otherwise received by people.

- *Issue audience:* The total number of persons exposed to the circulated copies. It is not a duplicated figure—no matter how many times he or she picks up the magazine, each person is counted only once.

- *Issue exposure:* The total number of exposures to the circulated copies. It is a duplicated figure, allowing for multiple exposures by the same individual.

- *Advertisement audience:* The total number of persons who could be exposed to the advertisement space. This is an unduplicated figure.

- *Advertisement exposure:* The total number of times each person is exposed to the advertisement space. This is a duplicated figure, expressed in terms of the entire audience.

The foremost task of a vehicle unit (such as a specific copy of *Time* magazine) in the chain of advertising events is to achieve exposure for the advertisement among the target audience. In short, the vehicle must give the advertisement a chance to have its effect. This phenomenon of exposure is independent of and can be measured independently of message effects, such as advertisement perception and advertisement communication. These message effects can only be considered after the advertisement has been exposed to the audience.

In the following sections we will look at how researchers estimate to what extent a vehicle and its advertising are distributed and exposed. Chapter 16

---

examines the effects that print advertisements have on individuals who have been exposed to them.

Measuring Vehicle Distribution

It is a simple procedure to determine the number of copies of a vehicle distributed (its circulation). An audit of a publisher's books will determine the number of copies sold or circulated for free (controlled circulation). Most publications are distributed either through subscription or through newsstand sales. Exact figures can be obtained through a circulation audit. Rigorous procedures are followed for circulation audits, which gives advertisers assurance as to their accuracy and consistency.

Although readers are not interviewed for the purpose of vehicle distribution reports (remember that we are only interested in copies circulated at this point), certain pieces of information collected for reports such as those published by the Audit Bureau of Circulations can give indications of audience quality and loyalty. Figures indicating the percentage and number of subscriptions sold at steep discounts or for which premium items were offered can suggest that incentives played a major role in initial decisions to subscribe. Media planners pay close attention to the amount of annual audience turnover, or new subscribers won and old subscribers lost. This means that although circulation reports deal only with information about copies, inferences can be made about audience composition based on how and to whom those copies were distributed. Appendix A at the end of this book gives more details on the Audit Bureau of Circulations.

Measuring Issue Audience and Exposure

Determining the number of people exposed to an issue of a print vehicle—the issue audience—is an indication of the reach or coverage of that publication. From your own experience, you know that many more people are exposed to a publication than the number of copies printed and distributed. Every time you borrow or flip through someone else's copy of a magazine or newspaper you are proving that point. Because of this, publishers make distinctions between the three types of audiences.

1. *Primary audience:* People who purchase a publication either by subscription or from a newsstand, plus members of their immediate family or household.

2. *Secondary audience:* Individuals other than the primary audience who are exposed to the publication.

3. *Total audience:* All persons who are exposed to the publication at least once.

Issue audience is another term for total audience for a specific issue of a publication. Media planners are interested in choosing vehicles to reach the maximum number of people in their target market group. Over the years, more research of this nature has been published about magazines than about newspapers, but the methods used are quite similar. Most of our discussion here will focus on magazines. At the end of the chapter you will learn about commercial services that measure magazines and newspapers.

The concept of issue audience has three measurable dimensions: audience size, audience composition, and extent of audience exposure. A brief look at each will set the stage for a look at how each is determined.

1. *Audience size:* The number of people who are exposed to the average issue, i.e., the total issue audience.

2. *Audience composition:* Characteristics of the people in the issue audience, typically in terms of demographics, psychographics, product usage, and media usage.

3. *Extent of audience exposure:* The amount of issue exposure to individuals. This can include the number of times the vehicle is read or looked at, which items are read, and which issues are read.

Measurement of all three of the above elements is typically achieved through sample surveys, although other methods have been tested as well. Researchers have used personal interviews, telephone interviews, and mail surveys to gather the information, depending on the situation. Much consumer magazine audience research is done using the in-home interview, but in the case of busy executives and their readership of business publications, the mail survey is usually considered more appropriate.

Two aspects of the sample survey are critical to the accuracy and utility of the issue audience data. These are sample selection and question construction. The sample selection procedures and response rates ultimately determine to what extent results can be extrapolated to a larger group beyond the sample itself. And obviously, without sound, interpretable data resulting from clearly conceptualized and written questions, a media research study will result in more confusion than information.

Samples and Populations

Populations for print media research studies vary widely, and anyone who plans to use such research should pay close attention to who the crucial population is for the study and how a sample of that population was chosen. As we learned in Chapter 8, the validity of the sampling procedure weighs heavily on the validity of the entire study.

In a single-vehicle study, where a publication is available only through paid subscription, simply obtaining that list and drawing a random sample from it will produce results projectable to the primary audience. This is also the case with controlled circulation publications, which are distributed at no cost, usually to highly paid professionals or members of organizations; a random sampling of the mailing list will produce a projectable sample for an issue audience survey. (Again, this measures the primary audience, as opposed to the total audience.)

In the case of publications sold through both subscription and newsstand methods, the task is a bit stickier. One can still sample from the subscriber list, but to do so is to systematically eliminate the newsstand purchaser. The only accurate way to get both is to select a random sample of the total population in the crucial area, such as a random sample of adults in the United States for national publications, as will be described below.

Sometimes the purpose of a media research study is to assess the media habits of a particular group of people based on their purchase behavior or other actions. A study of people in the market for a new home might use a list of people who had visited a model home of a particular builder. A list of newlyweds could be obtained from an appliance distributor, or a list of new car owners from an insurance company, etc. In these cases, it is up to the researcher to determine what constitutes the crucial population and then identify methods of defining that population for the purpose of measurement.

Most major media studies conducted by commercial companies are of the multiple-vehicle variety (they measure readership of several publications) and involve the U.S. population as the crucial population. When several thousand U.S. adults are measured, as in studies by Simmons Market Research Bureau and Mediamark Research, Inc., tabulations for individual publications or advertisers are made to provide data on a specific group.

A very important point made in Chapter 7 should be reemphasized here in the context of validity of samples for media studies. Many publishers and some research companies, in an effort to minimize the time and expense of the survey sampling procedures, use a variety of self-selected or otherwise nonrandom groups whose responses are more easily obtainable than a random sample of the U.S. population. For example, imagine a readership study based on a sample of subscribers who fill out a business reply questionnaire card from a newsstand copy of a magazine. Let's assume the card asks for readership habits as well as demographic and product purchase information. Those who send in the card are a self-selected sample—they opt to fill out the card and therefore they choose to be in the measured group rather than having their inclusion left to chance. Often these "reader write-in" surveys masquerade as true sample surveys, when in fact they are nothing more than reports of a group of respondents whose actual resemblance to the crucial population will always be in question. Regardless of how large a number of nonrandom respondents it contains, a study of a nonrandom group cannot be equated with a random sample survey of the crucial population.

Operational Definitions/Questions

Equally critical in assessing the utility of a media research study is the matter of operational definitions. Which concepts did the researcher set out to measure, and how were they operationalized or formulated into questions?

Take, for example, the basic concept of a "reader" of a publication. Various studies use different operationalizations of readership in their questionnaires. The following are a handful of possible definitions of a reader of Publication A:

- A person who glanced at the magazine in a doctor's office
- A person who thumbed through the magazine on a train
- A person who looked only at the ads in the last issue
- A person who read only the lead story in the last issue
- A person who read the last issue but not the one before
- A person who has looked at three of the last six issues
- A person who can recognize the cover of the latest issue
- A person who has read Publication A once in the past six months

And so on. Beyond the agreed-on definition of a reader, a researcher must choose questions and ways of asking the questions intended to measure readership. Consider the following choices, assuming that the agreed-on definition of a reader is one who has looked into the latest monthly issue of Publication A.

- *Unaided recall:* "Could you tell me which magazines you have looked into in the past month?"
- *Aided recall (verbal):* "I'm going to read the names of several magazines. Please tell me which one(s) you have looked into in the past month."
- *Aided recall (visual):* "Here is a stack of magazine titles (logos). Please look at each one and tell me which one(s) you have looked into in the past month."
- *Recognition:* "Here is a stack of magazine covers. Please look at them and tell me which one(s) you have seen in the past month."
- *Recognition (following aided recall test):* "You said you looked into this magazine (interviewer turns to first article). Tell me, did you read this particular article? Do you remember what it was about?"

For the purpose of media planning, audience size usually means the number of people who look into the "average" issue. To determine the average issue audience size, data for several months of issues must be gathered and then averaged.

Recognition measures, as opposed to aided or unaided recall measures, are thought to yield more accurate results for publication readership. Much methodological research has been conducted on this matter, and it will no doubt continue if for no other reason than what is at stake: magazine publishers base their advertising rates, in part, on readership estimates and not just circulation. So the seemingly simple question of "Who reads Publication A?" takes on mammoth importance when considering the consequences of underestimating or overestimating the audience. Contributing to the importance of this question is the fact that most readership studies are conducted annually, so a "mistake" in audience estimation can have a temporary yet substantial effect on sales of advertising for a specific vehicle.

Which Recall/Recognition Measure Is Best?

It is generally agreed that an aided recall or recognition test is best for estimating the issue audience, but a controversy in U.S. media research circles continues concerning whether a technique known as "recent-reading" or one called "through-the-book" is more accurate. To date, there is no definitive answer, but one fact that has been established is that in the past the two measures have yielded vastly different results for certain publications.

The recent-reading technique is used by Mediamark Research, Inc. (MRI), a major supplier of media audience data. When respondents are asked by MRI interviewers about magazine readership, they are handed a stack of index cards with consumer magazine logos in black and white and asked to make a stack of those they have seen within a specified time period. For each logo card they choose, they are counted as a reader of that particular publication.

Simmons Market Research Bureau (SMRB) uses a combination of recent-reading and through-the-book techniques in the magazine readership portion of their survey. They refer to their combination method as "aided recognition." An interviewer hands a deck of cards printed with color magazine logos to the respondent, who is asked to identify which he or she has seen in the past specified time period. After the cards are sorted, the interviewer, using a copy of the magazine, shows the respondent the cover and articles inside the magazine to determine if in fact he or she has seen the issue in question. Only after determining that the respondent in fact looked into the issue in question does the interviewer count the respondent as a reader.

Generally, the recent-reading technique generates larger audience exposure estimates than does through-the-book, which is considered to be the more stringent measure. As an example, consider the 1990 figures for selected publications measured by both SMRB and MRI:

Publication	Total Adult Readership (in Millions)	
	SMRB Estimate	MRI Estimate
TV Guide	39.3	46.0
Reader's Digest	35.5	48.9
People	29.5	31.9
National Geographic	23.0	30.2

Source: SMRB, MRI.

As you can readily observe, the differences in these figures are substantial, reaching several million readers in most cases. The methods of SMRB and MRI will be discussed further later in this chapter.

Audience Composition Questions

A standard part of most audience surveys is the measurement of demographic characteristics of audiences. Often they are also measured with respect to their purchase habits. Typical demographic factors are age, gender, size of household, income, and education. Product purchase data can be rather specific, depending on the purpose of the study, such as automobile purchase habits of those who read car magazines. In the large national sample surveys, purchase information for all major product and service groups is measured so that a complete purchase/usage profile of readers of each measured publication is possible. An example of the information generated from cross-tabulation of media usage and product usage data in an MRI report is shown in Figure 13–1.

Number of Issue Exposures

Beyond ascertaining the size and composition of the print vehicle audience is the matter of issue exposure: how many times does an individual pick up the publication and look into it? Obviously, this is important information; it bodes well for the effectiveness of the content of the publication if readers look at it on more than one occasion. From a media planner's point of view, if Publication A has an average of 2.4 issue exposures and Publication B has an average of 1.3, and other aspects of both publications are similar, the greater issue exposure ratio of Publication A will warrant choosing it over its competitor. Because the concept of issue exposure has implications for advertisement exposure, it is critical to the media planner.

Unfortunately, though the concept of issue exposure is quite salient, no consistent or readily available method has been determined for measuring it. This means that only in very rare instances can we have access to reliable issue exposure data. To measure issue exposure for a particular publication, a researcher could use self-reported issue exposure measures such as: "Please tell me how many times you picked up and looked at a copy of Publication A over the past week." The problem is the potential for inaccuracies resulting from memory, desire to please the interviewer, confusion, and so forth. MRI uses a self-reported measure of page exposure to estimate the number of times the average reader has been exposed to the average page. Cahners Publishing Co. commissioned SMRB to determine the number of times a specialized business magazine reader picked up or looked into the latest issue they had finished reading. SMRB used a mail survey to 4,000 readers of specialized business magazines. More than half reported they picked up or looked into their latest issue of the magazine two to three times. Figure 13–2 contains the results of the Cahners survey.

Figure 13–1
Information from Cross-Tabulation of Media Usage and Product Usage Data

DIET COLA DRINKS 191

	TOTAL U.S. '000	ALL A '000	ALL B % DOWN	ALL C % ACROSS	ALL D INDEX	HEAVY MORE THAN 5 A '000	B % DOWN	C % ACROSS	D INDEX	MEDIUM 2-5 A '000	B % DOWN	C % ACROSS	D INDEX	LIGHT LESS THAN 2 A '000	B % DOWN	C % ACROSS	D INDEX
BASE: ADULTS																	
ALL ADULTS	183271	81081	100.0	44.2	100	37887	100.0	20.6	100	25835	100.0	14.1	100	17470	100.0	9.5	100
MONEY	8109	3942	4.9	48.6	110	2031	5.4	25.0	122	1202	4.7	14.8	105	711	4.1	8.8	92
MOTOR TREND	5483	2120	2.6	38.7	87	956	2.5	17.4	85	614	2.4	11.2	79	550	3.1	10.0	105
MUSCLE & FITNESS	5804	2212	2.7	38.1	86	864	2.3	14.7	72	752	2.9	13.0	92	604	3.5	10.4	109
NATIONAL ENQUIRER	20566	8897	11.0	43.3	98	4071	10.8	19.0	96	2939	11.4	14.3	101	1887	10.8	9.2	96
NATIONAL GEOGRAPHIC	30566	14669	18.1	48.0	109	6321	16.8	20.7	101	5075	19.6	16.6	118	3263	18.7	10.7	112
NATIONAL GEOGRAPHIC TRAVELER	2409	1166	1.4	48.4	110	462	1.2	18.8	91	396	1.5	16.4	117	*317	1.8	13.2	138
NATIONAL LAMPOON	2009	844	1.0	40.4	91	*341	.9	16.3	79	*331	1.3	15.8	112	*172	1.0	8.2	86
NATURAL HISTORY	1387	688	.8	49.6	112	*262	.7	18.9	92	*773	1.1	19.7	140	*153	.9	11.0	116
NEWSWEEK	21466	10038	12.4	46.8	106	4750	12.6	22.1	108	3135	12.1	14.6	104	2152	12.3	10.0	105
NEW WOMAN	4027	2150	2.7	53.6	121	1061	2.8	26.3	128	683	2.6	17.0	120	*415	2.4	10.3	108
NEW YORK MAGAZINE	1561	741	.9	47.5	107	408	1.1	26.0	126	*209	.8	13.4	95	*125	.7	8.0	84
NEW YORK TIMES (DAILY)	3196	1681	2.1	52.6	119	650	1.7	20.3	99	562	2.1	17.3	123	480	2.7	15.0	158
NEW YORK TIMES MAGAZINE	4257	2138	2.6	50.2	114	1050	2.8	24.7	120	491	1.9	11.5	82	597	3.4	14.0	147
THE NEW YORKER	2615	1293	1.6	49.4	112	641	1.7	24.5	119	333	1.3	12.7	90	*319	1.8	12.2	128
OMNI	3524	1392	1.7	39.5	89	686	1.8	19.4	95	448	1.7	12.7	90	*257	1.5	7.3	77
1,001 HOME IDEAS	5331	2546	3.1	47.8	108	1357	3.6	25.5	124	647	2.5	12.1	86	542	3.1	10.2	107
ORGANIC GARDENING	3773	1939	2.4	51.3	117	780	2.0	20.7	100	691	2.7	18.6	132	468	2.6	12.3	129
OUTDOOR LIFE	8631	3818	4.7	43.2	98	1634	4.3	18.5	90	1328	5.1	15.0	107	852	4.9	9.6	101
PARADE	67140	31797	39.3	47.4	107	15066	40.0	22.4	109	18012	38.8	14.9	106	6718	38.5	10.0	105
PARENTING	4416	2097	2.6	47.5	107	990	2.6	22.4	109	583	7.3	13.2	94	524	3.0	11.9	124
PARENTS' MAGAZINE	11498	5196	6.4	45.2	102	2140	5.7	18.6	90	1578	6.1	13.7	97	1479	8.5	12.9	135
PC COMPUTING	3096	1571	1.9	50.7	115	787	2.0	24.8	120	433	1.7	14.0	99	373	2.1	12.0	126
PC MAGAZINE	3184	1634	2.0	51.3	116	863	2.3	27.1	132	455	1.8	14.3	101	316	1.8	9.9	104
PC WORLD	3403	1829	2.3	53.7	122	1000	2.7	29.4	143	406	1.6	11.9	85	423	2.4	12.4	130
PENTHOUSE	5604	2102	2.6	37.5	85	863	2.3	15.4	75	736	2.8	13.1	93	502	2.9	9.0	94
PENTON EXECUTIVE NETWK (GR)	8892	4317	5.3	48.5	110	1894	5.0	21.3	104	1434	5.6	16.1	114	987	5.6	11.1	116
PEOPLE	33698	16208	20.0	48.1	109	7738	20.5	23.0	112	5209	20.2	15.5	110	3261	18.7	9.7	102
PETERSEN MAGAZINE NETWK (GR)	40275	15002	18.5	37.2	84	6816	18.1	16.9	82	4751	18.4	11.8	84	3436	19.7	8.5	89
PLAYBOY	12111	4552	5.6	37.6	85	2128	5.6	17.6	85	1427	5.5	11.8	84	997	5.7	8.2	86
POPULAR HOT RODDING	3771	1393	1.7	36.9	84	585	1.6	15.5	75	*520	2.0	13.8	98	*289	1.7	7.7	80
POPULAR MECHANICS	9834	4218	5.2	42.9	97	1885	5.0	19.2	93	1476	5.7	15.0	106	855	4.9	8.7	91
POPULAR SCIENCE	7508	3157	3.9	42.0	95	1510	4.0	20.1	96	1019	3.9	13.6	96	628	3.6	8.4	88
PRACTICAL HOMEOWNER	1656	907	1.1	54.8	124	499	1.3	30.1	146	*242	.9	14.7	104	*166	1.0	10.0	105
PRIMUSE	1481	725	.9	49.0	111	*404	1.1	27.3	133	*205	.8	13.0	98	*117	.7	7.9	83
PREVENTION	8830	4675	5.6	51.8	117	1966	5.2	22.3	108	1555	6.0	17.5	125	1055	6.0	11.9	125
READER'S DIGEST	48991	23316	28.8	47.6	108	10465	27.8	21.4	104	7984	30.9	16.3	116	4867	27.9	9.9	104
REDBOOK	13238	7243	8.9	54.7	124	3442	9.1	26.0	126	2453	9.5	18.5	131	1348	7.7	10.2	107
ROAD & TRACK	4961	1950	2.4	39.5	89	832	2.2	16.8	82	643	2.6	13.4	95	*464	2.7	9.4	98
RODALE ACTIVE SPORTS (GR)	4115	1904	2.4	46.8	106	920	2.4	22.4	109	643	1.8	11.2	80	545	3.1	13.2	139
ROLLING STONE	7644	3270	4.0	42.8	97	1524	4.0	19.9	97	1003	3.9	13.1	93	743	4.3	9.7	102
RUNNER'S WORLD	1372	664	.8	48.4	110	*284	.8	20.7	101	*148	.6	10.8	77	*233	1.3	17.0	178
SATURDAY EVENING POST	4094	1827	2.3	44.6	101	837	2.7	20.4	99	617	2.4	15.1	107	*373	2.1	9.1	96
SCIENTIFIC AMERICAN	2438	1272	1.6	52.2	118	488	1.3	20.4	99	524	2.0	21.5	152	*261	1.4	10.3	108
SELF	3287	1800	2.4	50.7	133	916	2.4	27.9	135	519	2.0	15.8	112	486	2.8	15.1	158
SESAME STREET MAGAZINE	6484	3104	3.8	47.9	108	1486	4.0	23.1	112	788	3.1	12.2	86	822	4.7	12.7	133
SEVENTEEN	5666	2922	3.6	51.6	117	1501	4.0	26.5	129	683	2.3	12.1	86	663	3.8	11.7	151
SHAPE	2290	1346	1.7	58.7	133	509	1.6	26.2	127	478	1.9	20.9	148	*347	1.5	15.7	122
SKI	2392	1120	1.4	47.2	107	472	1.3	19.7	96	334	1.3	14.0	99	*324	1.9	13.5	142
SKIING	1920	845	1.2	49.2	111	382	1.0	19.9	97	*311	1.2	16.2	115	*253	1.4	13.2	138
SMITHSONIAN	9143	4478	5.5	49.0	111	1932	5.1	21.1	103	1593	6.2	17.4	124	863	5.5	10.4	109
SOAP OPERA DIGEST	8220	3470	4.3	42.2	94	1812	4.8	22.0	107	976	3.8	11.9	84	683	3.9	8.3	87
SOUTHERN LIVING	11717	5925	7.3	50.6	114	2943	7.8	25.1	122	1781	6.9	15.2	108	1201	6.9	10.3	108
SPORT	4411	1707	2.1	38.7	88	839	2.2	19.0	92	526	2.0	11.9	85	*342	2.0	7.8	81
THE SPORTING NEWS	4181	1940	2.4	46.4	105	855	2.3	20.4	99	653	2.5	15.6	111	*432	2.5	10.3	108
SPORTS AFIELD	6021	2484	3.1	41.3	93	1282	3.4	21.3	104	744	2.9	12.4	88	*457	2.6	7.6	80
SPORTS ILLUSTRATED	21906	9220	11.4	42.1	95	4464	11.9	20.4	99	2620	10.2	12.0	85	2113	12.1	9.6	101
SIAM	10802	4565	5.6	42.0	95	2241	5.9	20.6	100	1420	5.5	13.0	93	903	5.2	8.3	87
SUNDAY MAG/NET	34696	17075	21.1	49.2	111	7747	20.6	22.3	109	5660	21.9	16.3	116	3668	21.0	10.6	111
SUNSET	4044	2234	2.8	55.3	125	966	2.6	23.9	116	636	2.5	15.7	112	636	3.6	15.7	165
TENNIS	1990	911	1.1	45.8	104	419	1.1	21.1	102	*317	1.2	15.9	113	*175	1.0	8.8	92
TEXAS MONTHLY	1497	687	.8	45.9	104	326	.9	21.8	106	*230	.9	15.4	109	*131	.7	8.8	92
TIME	24398	11178	13.8	45.8	104	5165	13.7	21.2	103	3695	14.3	15.1	107	2317	13.3	9.5	100
TOWN & COUNTRY	2809	1549	1.9	55.1	125	706	1.9	25.1	122	705	7.7	20.5	145	*264	1.5	9.5	100
TRAVEL & LEISURE	3963	1959	2.4	49.4	112	867	2.3	21.9	105	748	2.7	18.9	134	353	2.0	8.9	93
TRUE STORY	5051	2210	2.7	43.8	99	792	2.1	15.7	76	*690	2.7	13.7	97	*727	4.2	14.4	151
TV GUIDE	45321	19308	23.8	42.6	96	9374	24.9	20.7	101	5926	22.9	13.1	93	4008	22.9	8.8	93
U.S. AIR MAGAZINE	2307	1209	1.5	52.4	119	556	1.5	24.1	117	367	1.4	15.9	113	*285	1.6	12.4	130
U.S. NEWS & WORLD REPORT	13548	6149	7.6	45.4	103	2903	7.7	21.4	104	2088	8.1	15.4	109	1157	6.6	8.5	90
US	4072	2024	2.5	49.7	112	851	2.3	20.9	102	872	3.7	20.7	143	*351	2.0	8.6	90
USA TODAY	4230	2165	2.7	51.2	116	1230	3.3	29.1	141	517	2.0	12.2	87	430	2.5	10.4	109
USA WEEKEND	27470	13367	16.5	48.7	110	6567	17.5	24.0	117	4297	16.6	15.6	111	2473	14.2	9.0	94
VANITY FAIR	2791	1198	1.5	52.3	118	544	1.5	24.6	120	*367	1.6	15.7	111	*276	1.6	12.0	126
VOGUE	8108	4068	5.0	50.2	114	1770	4.7	21.8	106	1582	6.0	19.3	137	737	4.2	9.1	95
WALL STREET JOURNAL	4254	2268	2.8	53.3	121	1120	3.0	26.3	128	695	2.7	16.3	116	463	2.6	10.6	112
WEIGHT WATCHERS	4779	3008	3.7	62.9	142	1516	4.0	31.7	154	935	3.6	19.6	139	557	3.2	11.7	122
WOMAN'S DAY	22526	11556	14.3	51.3	116	5155	13.7	22.9	111	3701	14.3	16.4	117	2800	15.4	12.0	128
WOMAN'S WORLD	6277	3073	3.8	49.0	111	1333	3.5	21.2	103	1081	4.1	16.9	120	679	3.9	10.8	113
THE WORKBASKET	3563	1756	2.2	49.3	112	742	2.0	20.8	101	569	2.2	16.0	113	*444	2.5	12.5	131
WORKBENCH	3373	1484	1.8	44.0	100	651	1.7	19.3	94	540	2.1	16.0	114	*294	1.7	8.7	91
WORKING MOTHER	3202	1661	2.1	51.9	117	829	2.2	25.9	126	*358	1.4	11.7	79	*474	2.7	14.8	155
WORKING WOMAN	4093	2160	2.7	52.8	119	1918	2.7	24.9	121	733	2.8	17.9	127	*408	2.3	10.0	105
YANKEE	3244	1750	2.2	53.9	122	726	1.9	22.4	109	680	2.6	21.0	149	341	2.0	10.5	110

Spring 1991

Figure 13–2
How Many Times Is a Specialized Business Magazine Read or Looked Into?

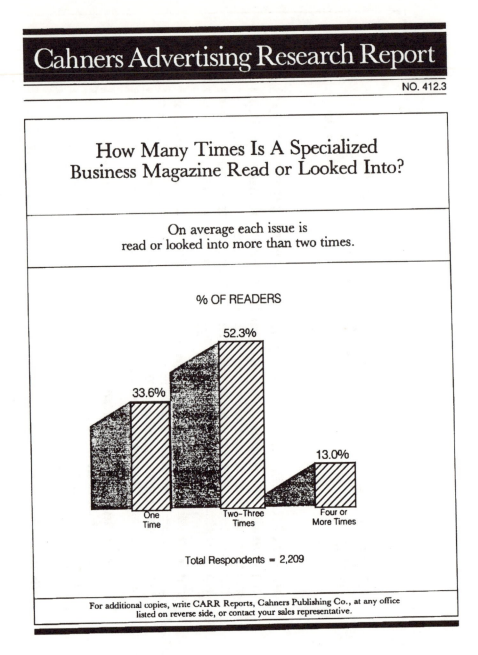

Source: Cahners Advertising Research Report, No. 412.3.

An unusual measurement approach from the early days of magazine audience measurement used "glue spots" to determine exposure to specific parts of the magazine. Glue spot research was used in a number of magazine studies to measure page exposure, advertisement exposure, and issue exposure. Tiny drops of glue form an almost imperceptible seal between pages of the publication, and after a specified period of time in the respondent's home, the publication can be analyzed to see if any of the glue spots have been broken. One of the drawbacks to the use of the glue spot technique for estimating issue exposure is the necessity of collecting the publication at regular intervals to determine if the individual has opened it. In projects conducted with consumer magazines, the researcher retrieved the publication each day and left a fresh copy behind. This in itself could affect respondent readership, because the person would suspect that he or she was being measured or observed, though it is doubtful that he or she would guess in what manner the measurement was being conducted.

Measuring Advertisement Audience and Exposure

Just because a person opens a magazine does not necessarily mean he or she is exposed to the advertising within it. If you consider your own magazine reading behavior, it's easy to deduce that vehicle exposure does not necessarily equal advertisement exposure. In fact, it rarely will, as few of us are exposed to every single page of a publication when we look into it.

It is appropriate to remind ourselves at this point of the steps in the ARF Model for Evaluating Media. Remember that advertisement exposure does not mean the same as advertisement perception, although there is a fine line between the two. Advertisement exposure means eyes open facing the advertisement. It does not necessarily mean that the individual registers having seen the advertisement. Advertisement perception, on the other hand, means that the advertisement is perceived somehow by the human senses. In short, it is noticed. As we noted in Chapter 12, it is ultimately the responsibility of the vehicle to achieve advertisement exposure. It is considered the responsibility of the advertising message, which would include copy, layout, illustration, use of color, and so forth, to create perception, communication, and behavioral response. Just for the record, you'll recall that advertisement communication occurs when a person's knowledge, attitude, or behavior is affected by the advertising message.

Research in advertisement audience and advertisement exposure is unfortunately rather thin. A practical method for measuring advertisement audience and advertisement exposure has not been found in the typical sample survey format. It has proven somewhat ineffective to query individuals about whether their eyes were open and facing certain pages, or how many times such was the case over a specific time period. The glue spot technique discussed earlier has been used to measure both advertisement audience and advertisement exposure, but this is a cumbersome and artificial procedure with inherent validity problems of its own.

Despite the lack of substantial evidence, magazine publishers and advertising media planners acknowledge that there is value in exposures beyond the first. Logic tells us that multiple exposures to an advertising space enhance the ability of the advertisement to be noticed or perceived. It also helps create brand familiarity and awareness. Without proper measurement techniques, however, it is impossible to figure the precise contribution that advertisement exposure makes to advertising effectiveness.

Vehicle Contribution to Advertisement Perception

As we have seen, there is a very fine line between advertisement exposure and advertisement perception: the media vehicle is responsible for advertisement exposure, and the message is responsible for advertisement perception and communication. The line is so fine, in fact, that it has been difficult if not impossible for researchers to tease out the precise contribution of the vehicle and the advertisement to perception. Some research has suggested that the vehicle does make some contribution to perception, but it is difficult to tell just how much.

What the vehicle has to offer in the matter of perception stems from its ability to deliver open eyes (advertisement exposure) as well as its more psychological qualities such as believability, novelty, trustworthiness, and so forth. And although these contributions cannot be measured directly, they are measured indirectly in two ways: item readership surveys and media image surveys.

Item Readership Surveys

A number of research companies conduct studies among readers of various publications to determine which editorial items or advertisements they have seen or read. Using a recognition method, researchers can record which items were noticed, read, or even acted on. The Starch Ad Readership studies described in Chapter 18 are an example of item readership studies. Using the through-the-book technique, Starch interviewers present advertisement pages from selected issues and record whether respondents have noted, associated, or read most of each advertisement. Such recognition methods for measuring the attention paid to an advertisement are actually measures of perception, not communication, because they do not indicate what a reader might have thought or felt about the message. In terms of the ARF model, these measures extend beyond vehicle exposure to advertisement perception, but in the absence of concrete data they are sometimes considered a rough measure of advertisement exposure.

One way to compare the contribution that vehicles make to advertisement perception is to place identical ads in two different magazines at the same time and then measure the perception value of each. Since the advertisements are identical and the only difference is the vehicle carrying the advertisement, any difference in perception value should be attributable to the vehicle. This technique is illustrated in Figure 13–3.

Figure 13–3
Vehicle Comparison

	Magazine A	Magazine B
Cost of one-page color advertisement	$70,000	$70,000
Circulation	3,000,000	3,000,000
Issue audience	9,000,000	8,000,000
Percentage of issue audience who noted advertisement	50%	70%
Number of issue audience who noted advertisement	4,500,000	5,600,000
CPM for readers noting advertisement	$1.56	$1.25

As we can see, though Magazine A was more efficient in delivering issue audience, Magazine B delivered more advertising perceptions, which is the reason advertisers buy vehicle space in the first place.

Media Image Surveys

Publishers often speak of the "qualitative values" that separate their vehicles from competitors'. These characteristics, which transcend objective and quantitatively verifiable statistics such as circulation and issue audience, often include such factors as believability, attractiveness, creativity, novelty, prestige, accuracy, thoroughness, innovativeness, interest value, and so forth. Many believe that these "other qualities" contribute to the publication's effectiveness and hence the effectiveness of the advertising it carries. The assumption is that the positive feelings a reader has for the publication as a whole (its image) somehow transfer to reader disposition toward and evaluation of advertising messages. This is sometimes referred to as the "halo effect": if the source is credible, so will be the message.

Qualitative characteristics of individual vehicles are usually measured by way of methods for attitude and image surveys detailed in Chapters 7 and 8. Surveys are conducted among groups of readers, and results are used to suggest "advertising climate superiority" of one vehicle over others. In Figure 13–4 is an example of a specially commissioned study to demonstrate that upper management prefers *Forbes* over two of its competitors.

Figure 13–4
Upper Management Readership of Business Magazines

Job Title	Most Prefer		
	FORBES	Fortune	Business Week
Senior Management	42%	16%	28%
(President/CEO/Chairman & Owner/Partner)			
Vice President	37	18	30
CFO	46	16	30
Director/Department Head/Other Manager	24	24	36
Total Management	43	21	36

Note: Percentages are based on individual job titles *(e.g., 42% of all Senior Managers studied prefer FORBES).*
Source: *FORBES,* based on a study by Beta Research Corporation.

Some studies have taken as their focus the comparison of media or classes within media rather than vehicles within media. Information derived from such studies is often commissioned by media associations and is used to build a case for spending advertising dollars in a particular medium. An example of the results of a magazine media image study is shown in Figure 13–5.

The major difficulty in making use of media or vehicle image studies is that there is no clear-cut proof that image qualities contribute to advertising effectiveness. In other words, it might be numerically established that Publication A is 20 percent more enjoyable than Publication B, but it still is not clear whether enjoyability contributes to advertising effectiveness and, if so, to what extent. This is why publishers and media planners acknowledge the existence of vehicle image reports but tend to gravitate back to direct numerical comparisons of distribution and vehicle audience to make decisions.

Syndicated and Commercial Research Services for Print Media Research

Dozens of research companies offer services to the publishing community. These include verification of circulation figures, total audience estimates, exposure estimates, qualitative media research, and many others. Some services provide major periodic reports typically subscribed to by publishers, agencies, and advertisers. Most companies also offer special customized studies either for a single vehicle or multiple vehicles. These studies are used either internally or for sales support.

Appendix A at the end of this book features the most widely used media services: the Audit Bureau of Circulations (ABC); Simmons Market Research Bureau (SMRB); and Mediamark Research, Inc. (MRI).

Figure 13–5
A Study of Media Involvement

Contributes Most Knowledge & Usable Ideas...

Continued

Adults		Dual	Media Franchise Magazine	TV	Non
Sports	Magazines	54%	51%	46%	44%
(Personal Participation/Improving Skills)	Television	22	23	21	19
	Newspapers	11	11	11	11
	Radio	1	1	1	2
	No Opinion	12	14	21	25
Travel	Magazines	52	46	41	35
	Television	20	18	23	18
	Newspapers	23	27	23	30
	Radio	1	2	2	3
	No Opinion	4	7	11	15

"Proximity to Medium"

		Dual	Magazine	TV	Non
Medium That Best Fits Personal Needs and Lifestyle	Magazines	52%	51%	42%	49%
	Television	30	24	35	21
	Newspapers	14	16	15	14
	Radio	2	6	5	13
	No Opinion	1	3	3	4

Advertising in Medium Is Usually...

		Dual	Magazine	TV	Non
Appealing	Magazines	91%	88%	84%	82%
	Television	77	63	69	60
Annoying/Irritating	Magazines	22	22	29	23
	Television	61	63	59	63
Informative About Product	Magazines	85	81	74	67
	Television	72	60	67	57
Exaggerated/Misleading	Magazines	37	41	43	43
	Television	61	64	64	61
Believable	Magazines	79	74	71	71
	Television	59	51	56	46
Unbelievable	Magazines	23	25	29	29
	Television	46	50	48	51
Helpful As a Buying Guide	Magazines	86	81	76	67
	Television	66	57	65	53
Silly/Insulting/Juvenile	Magazines	28	24	25	29
	Television	58	60	55	61

*Less than one-half percent.
Note: In cases where percentages do not add to 100, it is due to rounding.

Continued next page

37

Figure 13–5 (continued)
A Study of Media Involvement

Advertising in Medium is Usually. . .
Continued

		Dual	Media Franchise Magazine	TV	Non
For Quality/Dependable Products	Magazines	80%	79%	71%	71%
	Television	68	62	67	51
Boring/Monotonous	Magazines	32	28	34	37
	Television	56	59	57	59
Offensive/In Bad Taste	Magazines	19	19	22	25
	Television	41	39	37	39
Confusing/Unclear	Magazines	24	23	28	29
	Television	39	39	40	41

Advertising In Medium Usually. . .

		Dual	Media Franchise Magazine	TV	Non
Makes Me Want To Buy The Products	Magazines	66%	59%	55%	45%
	Television	55	42	46	34
Keeps Me Posted On New Products	Magazines	90	89	84	81
	Television	85	78	80	72

Disposition to Seek Out the Advertising

		Dual	Media Franchise Magazine	TV	Non
There Is Too Much Advertising in Medium	Magazines	57%	49%	56%	55%
	Television	80	85	82	78
Prefer Medium To Carry Advertising	Magazines	77	73	67	57
	Television	52	46	54	35
Advertising Adds To Interest In Medium	Magazines	45	43	33	27
	Television	18	12	12	11
Advertising Detracts From Interest in Medium	Magazines	31	34	33	39
	Television	71	76	71	70
Attentiveness To Advertising In Medium (A rating of attention between 0–100, not a percent)	Magazines	61	57	48	44
	Television	50	40	43	33

Response to Advertising
Past Month

		Dual	Media Franchise Magazine	TV	Non
Shopped For Product/Service After Seeing Ad/Commercial For It	Magazines	56%	51%	36%	27%
	Television	44	32	32	24
Ordered Product/Service By Mail Or Phone After Seeing Ad/Commercial For It	Magazines	34	30	25	16
	Television	20	13	15	6

Source: Magazine Publishers of America.

Review

In this chapter we saw that:

- To evaluate print media such as newspapers and magazines, information is needed about vehicle distribution, issue audience, issue exposure, advertisement audience, and advertisement exposure.

- Vehicle distribution is measured through an audit of the publisher's books by the Audit Bureau of Circulations to determine the true circulation (sold or circulated for free).

- Issue audience, the total number of persons exposed to the circulated copies, can be measured in terms of audience size, audience composition, and extent of audience exposure.

- Issue exposure is a measure of the total number of exposures to the circulated copies; "through-the-book" estimation of readership is considered more stringent than the "recent reading" method of estimation.

- Advertisement audience is a measure of the total number of persons exposed to the advertisement space; it is not a measure of advertisement perception.

- Advertisement exposure is a measure of the total number of times each person is exposed to the advertisement space.

14 Broadcast Media Research: Network Television, Cable, and Radio

Although they share striking similarities, print media research and broadcast media research are widely different disciplines. The most significant difference is that whereas newspapers and magazines have an "issue life" and can be referred to again and again over time, messages exposed through television and radio are here one minute and gone the next. Even though it has become common for viewers to tape programs for later or repeated viewing, this distinction is still key.

Definition of Terms

Let's begin our discussion of broadcast media research by clarifying some common terms.

Media Terms

- *Broadcast vehicle:* A specific program (such as the evening news, "The Cosby Show," or a specific cartoon show) or a specific time slot.
- *Vehicle unit:* A particular installment of the vehicle or the average installment.
- *Distribution:* The number of receiving sets tuned to a particular installment or the average installment of a program.
- *Program audience:* The number of people, sets, or households exposed to a program. (This can also be expressed as a percentage of a particular group, in which case it is called a *rating.*)
- *Program exposure:* The number of times the average person is exposed to the program, summed up for all persons in the program audience. (As we will see, exposure statistics are not as useful for evaluating television and radio as they are for evaluating print media.)

- *Advertising audience:* The number of people exposed to a particular commercial time slot (also called *commercial audience*).

- *Advertising exposure:* The number of times a person is exposed to a particular commercial, summed up for all persons exposed.

Note that while issue exposure and advertisement exposure—the number of times an individual looks into a publication or is exposed to its advertising—are important in evaluating print media, these concepts are less meaningful in broadcast media research. As stated above, this is because people may skim or read a magazine or newspaper many times, but they usually tune in to see and hear programs and commercials only once.

Audience Measurement Terms

Commercial research services use standard terminology in reporting their estimates of audience size. It should be noted that use of the term *audience* necessitates that one know the number of people whose eyes were open and facing the program. Early TV meters, which are described in more detail later, measured household or TV reception only. *Vehicle (program) audience,* which involves an estimate of the number of people exposed to a program, is measured by diary, telephone coincidental, and the new people-meters, all of which yield information about the demographics of individuals who watch specific programs. Here are some of the most common audience measurement terms:

- *Rating:* The size of an audience for a radio, TV, or cable program, expressed as a percentage of a complete population group. It is important to specify which critical population is being measured—a local market area, the nation, or a specific demographic group, such as women age 25–49.

- *Share of audience:* The percentage of people tuned to the medium who are listening to or viewing a specific station or channel.

- *Average quarter hour (AQH) persons:* The number of people listening to a radio station or viewing a TV station or cable channel at a particular time. (The usual definition of a *listener* or *viewer* is one who listened to a station or watched a channel for a minimum of five continuous minutes.) *Example:* 35,000 people in market A were watching station XYZ between 5:30 and 5:45 p.m.

- *Cume persons:* The number of people who listened to a radio station or watched a TV station or cable channel at least once over a specified period for at least five continuous minutes within a quarter hour. *Example:* 50,000 people in market A watched station XYZ between 4 and 6 p.m.

- *AQH rating:* The percentage of a specific market population listening to a radio station or viewing a TV station or cable channel at a particular time. *Example:* If market A has a population of 500,000, and 25,000 are watching program B at some point during a quarter hour, the AQH rating is five (5 percent expressed as a whole number).

- *AQH share:* AQH persons expressed as a percentage of all people listening to a radio station or viewing a TV station or cable channel in a market. *Example:* If 250,000 people are viewing television in market A, and 25,000 people are viewing program B, the AQH share for program B is .10 or 10. A share figure takes into account how a program is doing against the competition in the same time period.

- *Cume rating:* The percentage of a market population that tunes into a radio station at least once during a specified period. *Example:* In a given week, 100,000 people in market A tune into station A. The cume rating for station A is .20 or 20. This figure indicates the station's reach into a specific market.

- *Exclusive cume rating:* The percentage of a market population who listened only to station A over a period of time without listening to any other radio station during that time. *Example:* If 20,000 of station A's cume audience (of 100,000) listened only to station A during a specified period, the exclusive cume rating is 20,000 ÷ 500,000 (population of market A), or 4. Exclusive cume rating is a measure of audience loyalty.

Note that the quarter-hour time units are standard time periods for measurement. Because people qualify as listeners or viewers only if they have been exposed for at least five continuous minutes in a given quarter hour, commercials are placed strategically by broadcasters within quarter hour segments. This maximizes the likelihood of five minutes of continuous listening or viewing. Even so, it is important to remember that program exposure (and especially five-minute viewing of a quarter-hour of a program) does *not* guarantee that the listener or viewer was exposed to a particular commercial.

The following are other useful measurement terms:

- *Persons Using Radio (PUR):* A combined total of all persons in the geographic area, demographic group, or time period tuned in to all radio stations. PUR may also be expressed as a rating (as a percentage of the group under study).

- *Persons Using Television (PUT):* The total of all people using television in a given group, geographic area, or time period.

- *Households Using Television (HUT):* The total of all homes using television in a given group, geographic area, or time period.

- *Gross Rating Points (GRP):* The sum of all the ratings (using the same base population) generated by each quarter-hour of programming carrying a particular commercial. This figure is used to describe the relative media "weight" of an advertising schedule. The formula for figuring GRPs is as follows:

$$\text{GRPs} = \text{AQH rating} \quad x \quad \text{Number of commercials}$$

- *Gross impressions:* The sum of all persons exposed to time periods in which each commercial in a campaign runs. Persons are represented from different time periods, but the same base must be used in computing gross impressions. The following formula is used:

$$\text{Gross impressions} = \text{AQH persons} \quad \text{x} \quad \text{Number of commercials}$$

Broadcast Measurement Methods

There are three commonly used data-gathering methods for estimating which households or receiving units are tuned to radio or network and cable television: telephone survey, diary, and electronic meter. Another method, the personal in-home interview, has been used in the past by broadcast measurement companies, but it is rarely, if ever, used today.

Telephone Survey

Data can be gathered by telephone through telephone recall surveys and telephone coincidental surveys. Telephone recall studies are used primarily to estimate network radio audiences. Coincidental surveys are conducted to measure media use at the time the telephone call is made. They are usually used to measure radio audiences.

Telephone recall surveys.

Participants in a recall survey are asked to recall what they listened to recently on radio. Usually a random sample of homes with telephones is chosen, and respondents are asked questions about in-home as well as out-of-home listening or viewing. Data are used to estimate AQH and cume persons. Although the reliability of the telephone recall technique is limited due to respondent memory and self-reporting, it is considered to be more accurate than the coincidental method. It is especially useful for capturing information from the high percentage of people who listen to the radio away from home.

Telephone coincidental surveys.

An interviewer dials a random sample of households with telephones and asks the person who answers what he or she is watching or listening to at that moment. Advantages of the telephone coincidental are that it is inexpensive and quick—results can be compiled by the next day. Though useful for measuring AQH listening or viewing, the telephone coincidental method cannot be used for measuring cume. This is because it creates only a detailed snapshot of the moment the call is made, nothing more. Another limitation is the inability of the telephone coincidental to measure away-from-home exposure.

Diaries

Diaries are used for both TV and radio research. A radio diary is usually a pocket-sized notebook, which participants are encouraged to carry and fill out wherever they go. Radio diaries are usually kept for a one-week period by a member of a randomly selected household whose demographics also are recorded. TV diaries are assigned to a TV set, not a person. Usually each quarter-hour of each day is printed in the diary for each measurement period. Information to be recorded includes the people watching the set at a specific time as well as the channel being watched. Although the diary provides information on both what was watched and by whom, its primary disadvantage is the length of time it takes—sometimes up to two months—to prepare a ratings report.

Electronic Meters

A meter is an electronic recording device attached to a receiving set that records when the set is on and to which channel it is tuned. Meters were first used to measure household radio listening, but today meters are used exclusively to estimate TV audiences. Because they were mechanical, early meters were considered to be more objective than diaries in collecting data on when and to what the television was tuned, but their biggest drawback was that they could not capture information on audience size or demographics.

A device known as the *people-meter* was adopted in the 1980s by the ratings companies in an effort to overcome this problem. The people-meter has the same ability as the meter to record what is being viewed and the duration of viewing, and in addition it provides a means for individuals to enter their demographics. This is accomplished with a series of buttons, each of which corresponds to a member of the household. An individual simply "punches in" when he or she is watching and "punches out" when finished.

Advantages of the people-meter include its ability to capture information almost instantaneously, resulting in quick turnaround for audience reports, its accuracy in measuring channel and duration of viewing, and its ability to record audience size and composition. Both of the major TV audience research companies, Nielsen and Arbitron, use people-meters in their major measured markets.

Despite the improvements the people-meter has represented to electronic audience measurement, it has been plagued by controversy since its inception. Many of its image problems resulted from initial audience estimates in 1987, which were substantially lower than previous meter and diary estimates had been. Why the 1987 ratings were so low went largely unexplained, and as a result the accuracy of those figures remains in question. An ongoing problem with the people-meter has been the cooperation rate at both the household and individual levels. Estimates of household refusals have been higher than cooperation rates in some instances. At the individual level, efforts have been made to ensure that participants are diligent in pushing their respective buttons when they should. A light flashes on some people-meters periodically to remind viewers to punch in.

Even though it is generally agreed that the people-meter is a much-needed improvement from a methodological standpoint, more advances are anticipated in the next few years. Testing is underway for a passive meter, but as yet there is not a viable alternative to the people-meter.

Scanners.

In the 1980s the major ratings services began experimenting with the use of universal product code (UPC) scanners in conjunction with people-meters. This combination of purchase and viewing data came to be known as *single-source research*. In single-source markets, households in a TV audience sample are also issued either a hand-held scanner wand for recording grocery purchases in the home, or they use an identification card at the grocery or drug store that allows their purchases to be recorded by the retailer's scanner. Information from the scanners and the people-meters is combined to evaluate the relationships between TV program exposure and product purchases and ultimately to provide ratings based on a universe of specific product buyers. The use of scanners in single-source systems is discussed in more detail in Chapter 16.

Measuring Broadcast Advertising Audiences

The present system is set up to measure *program* audiences, not *advertising* audiences. As we noted above, the format for reporting ratings information is AQH (average quarter hour) viewing, and the operational definition of a viewer is someone who views a program for at least five minutes. Obviously, since commercials run for much less than five minutes, this means that with the present rating system it is impossible to estimate either the exact size of the advertising audience or its composition. What happens in practice is that media planners make assumptions about the extent of exposure by demographic groups to commercials and during specific programs based on the program ratings.

Many media planners rely on commercial research companies who measure advertising effectiveness to estimate advertising audience in radio, network television, and cable. Companies such as Gallup & Robinson use variations of day-after-recall techniques. They phone a random sample of households and enlist individuals to view a specific upcoming program. On the following day, participants are called and, once their exposure to the program has been verified, they are asked to recall which commercials they remember having seen during the specified time period. Technically speaking, as we discussed in the previous chapter, recall is considered to be an effect of the advertising message, not the medium. Ideally, there would exist a system that could accurately estimate the audience for a specific commercial. As it is, the best the media research companies can do is report the audience for all or part of a 15-minute segment of programming. And the companies that use recall measures are measuring something entirely different from exposure—whether the message is *remembered*.

The drawbacks of using recall measures are fairly predictable: memory problems, confusion with other viewing periods, and desire to please an interviewer. The conventional wisdom on this matter is that considerably fewer people who view a segment of programming actually remember having seen commercials during that segment. Figure 14–1 is an example of recall results for a 30-second commercial aired in three different geographic areas and during three different network TV programs. Measures of advertising recall, attitude, and persuasion will be discussed at greater length in Chapter 16.

Figure 14–1
Recall Results for a 30-Second Commercial

```
                              IN-VIEW

Commercial              30" GTE CORPORATION, "Desert CC"


                                    Proved Commercial Registration*
                                        Base              PCR %

Total Sample, Men                       (142)                 46
  By Income (excl. DK/NA/Ref)
    Under $30,000                (71)              44
    Over $30,000                 (52)              46

  By Age (excl. DK/NA/Ref)
    18-34                        (98)              46
    35-49                        (44)              46

Total Sample, Women                     (165)                 50
  By Income (excl. DK/NA/Ref)
    Under $30,000                (87)              46
    Over $30,000                 (57)              56

By Age (excl. DK/NA/Ref)
    18-34                        (84)              50
    35-49                        (79)              51


30" PCR Norms                           Men               Women

All Commercials                  29               33
All Corporate                    27               32
    18-34                                 28                 33
    35-49                                 26                 31

*Proved Commercial Registration (PCR) is defined as the percent
of qualified viewers of the program who, given the brand
name/product, can recall and accurately describe the commercial
on the day following the telecast.

-----------------------------------------------------------------

               PITTSBURGH        MINNEAPOLIS         SAN DIEGO

Date           6/18              6/19                6/18
Program        Barnaby Jones     S.W.A.T.            Quincy
Time           8:18              7:14                8:15
```

Critics of the audience measurement systems say that accurate estimates of commercial audience will only be possible with the use of a "totally passive" people-meter. Present people-meters are part active and part passive. They still require that a participant push a button indicating when he or she is watching. Passive people-meters are being promised by the ratings companies, and researchers continue to search for ways to capture accurate audience information without relying on daily active involvement by members of the sample panel. Nielsen has announced plans to experiment with a "smart sensing" people-meter, in which an image recorded by a built-in sensing device is stored in computer memory. The computer then would be able to detect people in the visual field and to identify them as specific household members or guests. Figure 14–2 shows the proposed Nielsen passive people-meter system.

Figure 14–2
Nielsen Passive People-Meter System

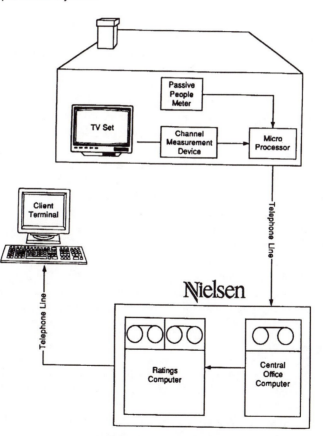

Source: ©1989 Nielsen Media Research.

Syndicated and Commercial Media Research Companies

A variety of companies provide information to advertisers and agencies who require data on television and radio audiences. The following pages contain the services and information provided by some of the largest media research firms. Notice how the sampling, data-gathering, and measurement methods differ from service to service.

Radio

Radio's All-Dimension Audience Research (RADAR).

A service of Statistical Research, Inc. (SRI), RADAR provides estimates of network radio audiences. A radio network consists of organizations that can simultaneously broadcast programs and commercial messages by way of their local affiliate stations throughout the United States. Affiliates agree to carry programs and/or commercials and then report to the network the actual carriage for each program or commercial on a quarter-hour basis. RADAR processes the carriage information and combines it with the audience data it collects itself.

Audience estimates are based on up to eight daily telephone interviews for one week of listening by a randomly selected individual at least 12 years old. A random digit dialing procedure is used to obtain a geographically disperse sample from among 38,000 central telephone operating offices in 111 area codes.

RADAR reports are contained in three volumes. Volume 1, *Radio Usage,* gives audience estimates for all AM and FM radio stations combined and also provides breakdowns of radio usage segments and demographic segments. Among the specific information summarized in Volume 1 is out-of-home radio usage and quarter-hour usage by men, women, and teens. Figures 14–3, 14–4, and 14–5 give examples of data available in the *Radio Usage* volume.

Volume 2, *Network Audiences to All Commercials,* gives audience estimates for commercials both within and outside of programs. Volume 3, *Network Audiences to Commercials within Programs,* excludes the commercials outside of programs. Figure 14–6, on page 270, gives examples of data from Volume 3.

Arbitron.

Arbitron measures local radio and TV audiences in more than 250 markets throughout the United States. Data collection is accomplished with diaries for radio and diaries, meters, and people-meters for television.

Radio audience data are published in the *Arbitron Radio Market Report.* Seven-day diaries are used in 12-week measurement periods to estimate radio audiences in about 260 markets. Eighty markets are measured year-round. Space is provided in the diary for respondents to record day, time, and location of listening and

Figure 14–3

listening levels by age and sex

Even though all groups listen to radio a great deal, audiences by age and sex vary significantly. As is seen in the charted figures, the average male, 18-34, listens to radio 17% more than does the average person (age 12+).

Older persons, age 50+, and teenagers tend to listen less than the average. However, the lowest level of 67 quarter hours of listening per week translates to an equivalent of over 2¼ hours per day.

For the heavier using groups, such as Men 18-34, usage is almost 3½ hours per day.

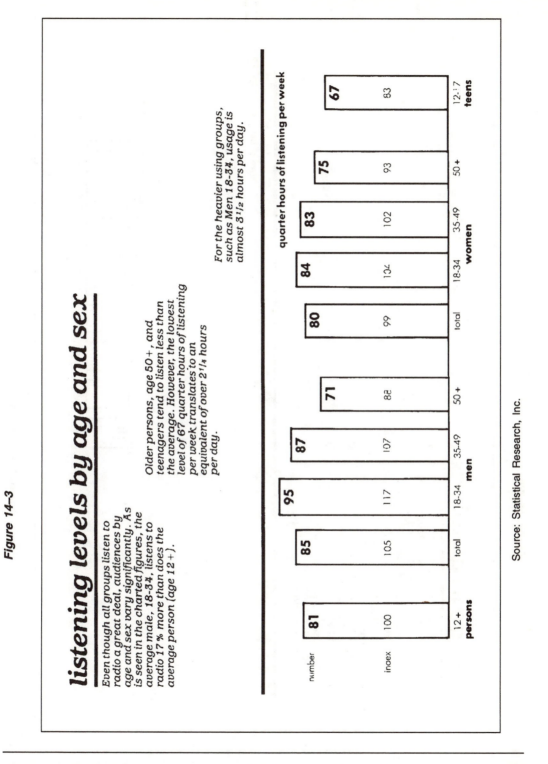

quarter hours of listening per week

	persons	total	men			women				teens
				18-34	35-49	50+	total	18-34	35-49	50+	

number: 81 (persons 12+), 85 (total men), 95 (men 18-34), 87 (men 35-49), 71 (men 50+), 80 (total women), 84 (women 18-34), 83 (women 35-49), 75 (women 50+), 67 (teens)

index: 100, 105, 117, 107, 88, 99, 104, 102, 93, 83

Source: Statistical Research, Inc.

Figure 14-4

usage in autos

The RADAR procedure separately identifies usage in autos from other out-of-home listening. Generally, the in-home portion is about 50% of all listening.

The share of usage in automobiles has increased over the past decade. Prior to the 1980's, it represented a share of between 16% and 19%.

In the most recent years, radio usage in automobiles has accounted for almost one quarter of all listening.

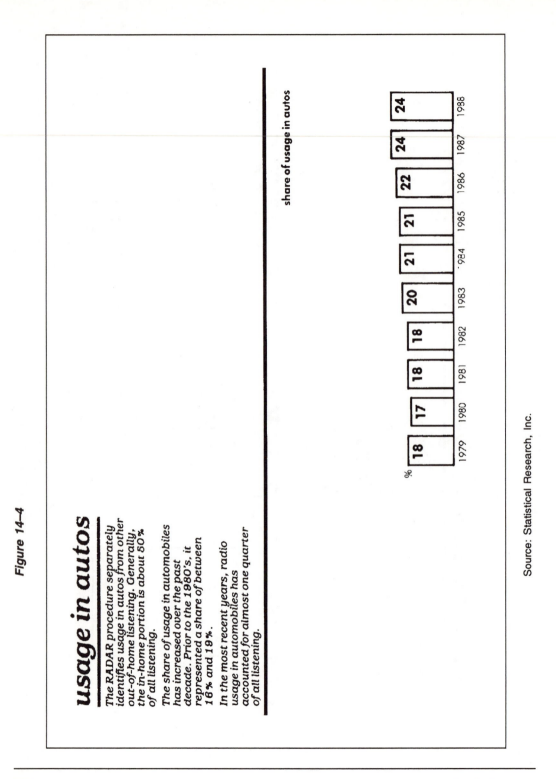

share of usage in autos

%	1979	1980	1981	1982	1983	1984	1985	1986	1987	1988
	18	17	18	18	20	21	21	22	24	24

Source: Statistical Research, Inc.

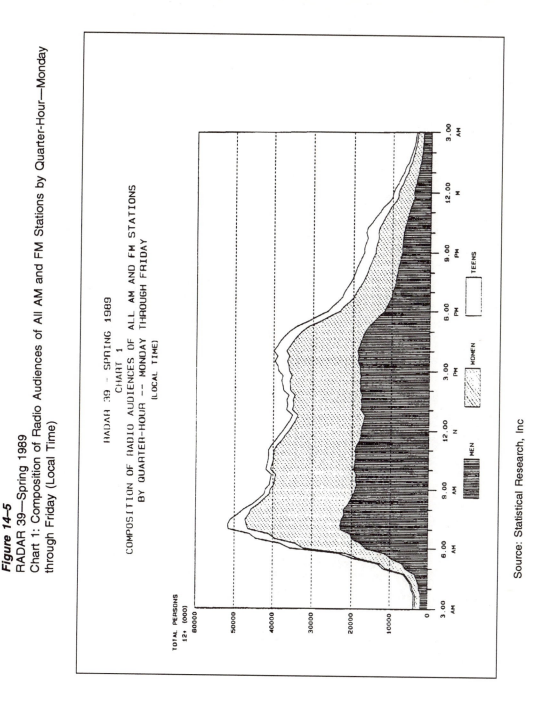

RADAR 39 - SPRING 1989
CHART 1
COMPOSITION OF RADIO AUDIENCES OF ALL AM AND FM STATIONS
BY QUARTER-HOUR -- MONDAY THROUGH FRIDAY
(LOCAL TIME)

Source: Statistical Research, Inc

Figure 14-6

RADAR 39 - SPRING 1989

AUDIENCE ESTIMATES FOR ABC ENTERTAINMENT RADIO NETWORK
AUDIENCES TO ALL COMMERCIALS
NUMBER OF PERSONS IN THOUSANDS

PROGRAM QUARTER-HOUR AVERAGES BY DAYPART

DAYPART (PER EIZ FEED TIME)	NUM OF BCST	12+	12-54	12-49	12-34	12-24	12-17	18+	25+	35+	50+	55+
MONDAY-SUNDAY												
6.00A - 12.00M	124	1672	1064	886	422	114	*	1644	1558	1250	786	608
6.00A - 7.00P	97	1931	1225	1017	478	121	*	1905	1810	1453	914	706
12.00M - 6.00A	42	141	86	81	*	*	*	139	135	116	60	55
6.00A - 10.00A	26	2362	1417	1155	528	133	*	2333	2229	1834	1207	945
10.00A - 3.00P	35	1963	1264	1051	486	112	*	1946	1851	1477	912	699
3.00P - 7.00P	36	1587	1045	880	434	122	*	1554	1485	1153	707	542
7.00P - 12.00M	27	745	489	420	223	89	*	709	656	522	325	256
MONDAY-FRIDAY												
6.00A - 12.00M	90	1852	1194	990	477	124	*	1823	1728	1375	862	658
6.00A - 7.00P	70	2152	1386	1146	547	133	*	2126	2019	1605	1006	766
12.00M - 6.00A	30	157	97	91	*	*	*	155	151	126	66	60
6.00A - 10.00A	20	2564	1591	1307	611	159	*	2529	2405	1953	1257	973
10.00A - 3.00P	25	2161	1409	1165	555	122	*	2146	2039	1606	996	752
3.00P - 7.00P	25	1810	1197	997	487	124	*	1780	1686	1323	813	613
7.00P - 12.00M	20	805	524	446	235	92	39	766	713	570	359	281
6A-10A + 3P-7P	45	2147	1373	1135	543	140	*	2115	2007	1604	1012	774
SATURDAY												
6.00A - 12.00M	22	1358	817	686	320	104	*	1331	1254	1038	672	541
6.00A - 7.00P	17	1563	920	766	347	105	*	1537	1458	1216	797	643
12.00M - 6.00A	6	138	90	80	*	*	*	137	134	127	58	48
6.00A - 10.00A	4	1853	939	720	286	46	*	1847	1807	1567	1133	914
10.00A - 3.00P	7	1824	1003	835	372	107	*	1597	1517	1252	789	621
3.00P - 7.00P	6	1303	816	722	361	144	40	1263	1159	942	581	487
7.00P - 12.00M	5	655	458	405	224	95	*	627	560	431	250	197
SUNDAY												
6.00A - 12.00M	12	916	553	483	201	64	*	889	852	715	433	363
6.00A - 7.00P	10	1018	613	535	218	68	*	992	950	800	483	405
12.00M - 6.00A	6	81	*	*	*	*	*	80	74	74	47	44
6.00A - 10.00A	2	1355	642	514	176	45	*	1341	1310	1179	841	713
10.00A - 3.00P	3	1105	663	611	184	51	*	1091	1054	921	494	442
3.00P - 7.00P	5	828	570	497	256	88	*	788	740	572	331	258
7.00P - 12.00M	3	401	243	215	112	42	40	372	359	289	186	158
ALL BROADCASTS	166	1285	817	682	322	87	*	1263	1198	963	603	468
ALL BCSTS EX 12M-6A	124	1672	1064	886	422	114	*	1644	1558	1250	786	608

PERSONS

NOTES: SEE PROGRAM LISTINGS FOR PROGRAMS INCLUDED IN AND EXCLUDED FROM DAYPARTS;
*M INDICATES NO BROADCASTS IN ONE OR MORE COMPONENT DAYPARTS.

Source: Statistical Research, Inc.

the station being listened to (see Figure 14–7). A comments section allows respondents to write what they like or dislike about their local radio stations. Entries are tabulated by Arbitron staff after being mailed back to the company. Spanish/English diaries are available to those who identify themselves as Hispanic on response to a race/ethnicity question or to those who indicate a preference.

Figure 14–7

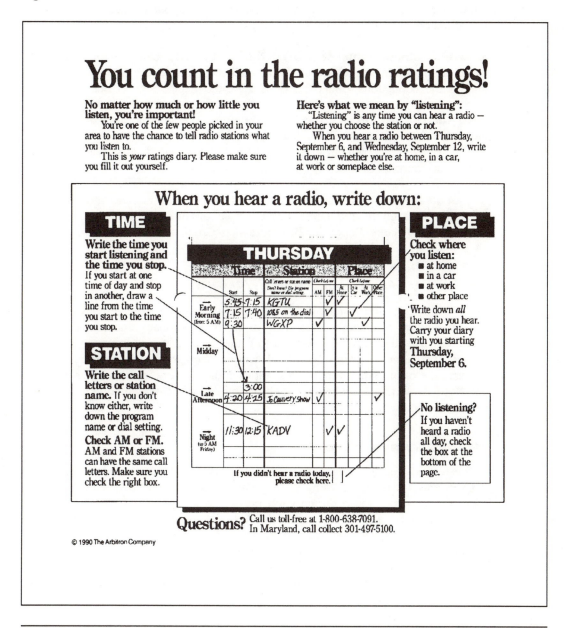

Households with telephones are the population for the diary study. A random sample of listed and unlisted telephone households are contacted and asked to participate. Diaries are distributed to all household members at least 12 years old. Sampling is done for areas designated as *metro, total survey area,* and, if applicable, *area of dominant influence.*

Metro survey area (metro). These areas generally correspond to federal government Metropolitan Statistical Areas, Primary Metropolitan Statistical Areas, or Consolidated Metropolitan Statistical Areas.

Area of dominant influence (ADI). This Arbitron designation is for TV markets based on predominance to viewing home market stations. Every county or sampling unit in the contiguous United States is allocated exclusively to one ADI.

Total survey area (TSA). The TSA represents a geographic area that includes the metro survey area and possibly other counties, depending on the extent of their diary mentions of metro-licensed stations. TSA is based on station reach into additional counties outside of the home ADI.

Radio Market Reports includes estimates of persons, ratings, and shares by quarter-hour listening and cume. An example of audience estimates from the Arbitron Radio Market Report for Baltimore Metro, ADI, and TSA is shown in Figure 14–8.

Simmons Market Research Bureau (SMRB).

SMRB uses personal and telephone interviews to estimate average daily (Monday through Friday) cumulative audiences for dayparts, formats, and networks. The "yesterday listening" technique is used to gather radio listening information, which is used in conjunction with other SMRB data on demographics and product usage. An example of an SMRB report using radio audience data is included in Chapter 13. (Note: For further explanation of SMRB sampling and data-gathering procedures, refer to Chapter 13).

Mediamark Research, Inc.

A "yesterday" recall technique is used by MRI to estimate radio audiences. Respondents are shown a listing of five dayparts and asked how much time they spent listening to a radio during each period on the previous weekday as well as "last Saturday" and "last Sunday." Names and call letters of stations also are collected. Average half-hour audiences are estimated for each daypart, and cumulative figures are provided by day, daypart, program format, and network. Cross-tabulated results appear in MRI volumes along with demographic and product usage data. Figure 14–9 gives an example. (Note: For further explanation of MRI methods, see Chapter 13.)

Figure 14–8

Target Audience
WOMEN 18-34

	SUNDAY 10AM-3PM				SUNDAY 3PM-7PM				MONDAY-FRIDAY 6AM-7PM				MONDAY-FRIDAY COMBINED DRIVE				MONDAY-SUNDAY 6AM-MID			
	AQH (00)	CUME (00)	AQH RTG	AQH SHR	AQH (00)	CUME (00)	AQH RTG	AQH SHR	AQH (00)	CUME (00)	AQH RTG	AQH SHR	AQH (00)	CUME (00)	AQH RTG	AQH SHR	AQH (00)	CUME (00)	AQH RTG	AQH SHR
WBAL METRO	1	10		.2					13	115	.4	1.5	15	95	.4	1.7	8	137	.2	1.2
TSA	1	10							15	127			16	100			9	148		
WBGR METRO	11	51	.3	2.0	11	30	.3	2.9	14	89	.4	1.6	20	89	.6	2.3	13	150	.4	2.0
TSA	11	51			11	30			14	89			20	89			13	160		
WBSB METRO	84	299	2.5	14.9	79	175	2.3	21.1	98	915	2.9	11.5	103	891	3.0	11.9	73	1054	2.2	11.2
TSA	94	337			81	179			111	1028			115	1004			82	1170		
WCAO METRO	4	26	.1	.7	5	15	.1	1.3	6	101	.2	.7	9	101	.3	1.0	5	125	.1	.8
TSA	4	26			5	15			7	113			9	113			5	137		
WCBM METRO									4	39	.1	.5	2	12	.1	.2	3	39	.1	.5
TSA									4	51			3	24			3	51		
WEBB METRO	8	40	.2	1.4					12	156	.4	1.4	14	156	.4	1.6	11	233	.3	1.7
TSA	8	40							12	156			14	156			11	233		
WFBR METRO									6	37	.2	.7	4	37	.1	.5	4	59	.1	.6
TSA									6	37			4	37			4	59		
WFSI METRO									1	13		.1		13				13		
TSA									1	13				13				13		
WGHT METRO	50	143	1.5	8.9	9	73	.3	2.4	30	542	.9	3.5	33	495	1.0	3.8	29	651	.9	4.4
TSA	50	143			9	73			30	542			33	495			29	651		
WGRX METRO	16	36	.5	2.8	21	46	.6	5.6	16	263	.5	1.9	15	234	.4	1.7	14	346	.4	2.1
TSA	26	63			34	120			31	447			33	396			27	556		
WITH METRO					4	6	.1	1.1		28				17			1	43		.2
TSA					4	6				28				17			1	43		
WIYY METRO	20	105	.6	3.6	11	48	.3	2.9	55	573	1.6	6.5	54	573	1.6	6.2	39	644	1.1	6.0
TSA	24	124			13	56			58	619			59	619			43	738		
WLIF METRO	14	46	.4	2.5	18	40	.5	4.8	49	213	1.4	5.8	35	194	1.0	4.0	31	284	.9	4.7
TSA	14	46			18	40			52	221			36	202			32	293		
WPOC METRO	32	137	.9	5.7	17	48	.5	4.5	36	309	1.1	4.2	40	298	1.2	4.6	27	363	.8	4.1
TSA	46	171			19	58			44	408			50	397			35	473		
WQSR METRO	22	92	.6	3.9	12	43	.4	3.2	31	277	.9	3.6	30	259	.9	3.5	20	326	.6	3.1
TSA	24	100			12	43			35	330			33	305			23	380		
WRBS METRO					1	10		.3	7	97	.2	.8	9	87	.3	1.0	5	106	.1	.8
TSA					1	10			7	108			10	97			5	117		
WWIN METRO	27	48	.8	4.8	30	33	.9	8.0	9	108	.3	1.1	8	108	.2	.9	10	152	.3	1.5
TSA	27	48			30	33			9	108			8	108			10	152		
WWMX METRO	65	189	1.9	11.6	37	165	1.1	9.9	115	928	3.4	13.5	108	878	3.2	12.5	81	1085	2.4	12.4
TSA	65	189			37	165			134	984			123	930			92	1145		
WXYV METRO	68	170	2.0	12.1	32	95	.9	8.5	131	790	3.9	15.4	147	768	4.3	17.0	110	881	3.2	16.8
TSA	69	178			33	99			132	801			148	779			111	908		
WYST METRO	10	10	.3	1.8	3	10	.1	.8	5	10	.1	.6	4	10	.1	.5	4	28	.1	.6
TSA	10	10			3	10			5	10			4	10			4	28		
WYST-FM METRO	10	37	.3	1.8	3	15	.1	.8	40	371	1.2	4.7	35	365	1.0	4.0	28	460	.8	4.3
TSA	10	37			3	15			41	397			35	365			28	486		
WASH METRO									1	56		.1	1	58		.1	1	115		.2
TSA									1	58			1	58			1	115		
WAVA METRO									6	133	.2	.7	7	120	.2	.8	4	145	.1	.6
TSA	8	15			4	15			22	197			20	134			13	210		
WCXR METRO																				
TSA										15				15				15		
WGAY METRO	6	9	.2	1.1	2	9	.1	.5	1	9		.1	1	9		.1	1	18		.2
TSA	6	9			2	9			1	9			1	9			1	18		
WHFS METRO	14	37	.4	2.5	7	26	.2	1.9	15	194	.4	1.8	18	156	.5	2.1	13	194	.4	2.0
TSA	14	37			7	26			16	200			18	162			13	200		
WHUR METRO	25	49	.7	4.4	9	28	.3	2.4	15	286	.4	1.8	15	261	.4	1.7	18	357	.5	2.8
TSA	25	49			9	28			15	286			15	261			18	357		

Footnote Symbols: * Audience estimates adjusted for actual broadcast schedule. + Station(s) changed call letters since the prior survey - see Page 5R

ARBITRON RATINGS

Chapter 14 Broadcast Media Research: Network Television, Cable, and Radio   **273**

Figure 14–9

REGULAR TEA 47

BASE: FEMALE HOMEMAKERS	TOTAL U.S. '000	ALL A '000	ALL B % DOWN	ALL C % ACROSS	ALL D INDEX	HEAVY (MORE THAN 3) A '000	HEAVY B % DOWN	HEAVY C % ACROSS	HEAVY D INDEX	MEDIUM (2 - 3) A '000	MEDIUM B % DOWN	MEDIUM C % ACROSS	MEDIUM D INDEX	LIGHT (LESS THAN 2) A '000	LIGHT B % DOWN	LIGHT C % ACROSS	LIGHT D INDEX
						CUPS OR GLASSES/AVERAGE DAY											
ALL FEMALE HOMEMAKERS	85323	52443	100.0	61.5	100	13508	100.0	15.8	100	15097	100.0	17.7	100	23838	100.0	27.9	100
QUINTILE I - RADIO	16633	9780	18.6	58.8	96	2447	18.1	14.7	93	2773	18.4	16.7	94	4560	19.1	27.4	98
QUINTILE II	16652	10209	19.5	61.3	100	2664	19.7	16.0	101	3194	21.2	19.2	108	4351	18.3	26.1	94
QUINTILE III	17674	11243	21.4	63.6	103	2894	21.4	16.4	103	3285	21.8	18.6	105	5064	21.2	28.7	103
QUINTILE IV	16983	10813	20.6	63.7	104	2977	22.0	17.5	111	3070	20.3	18.1	102	4766	20.0	28.1	100
QUINTILE V	17380	10398	19.8	59.8	97	2527	18.7	14.5	92	2774	18.4	16.0	90	5097	21.4	29.3	105
QUINTILE I - TV (TOTAL)	17554	10264	19.6	58.5	95	2942	21.8	16.8	106	2896	17.9	15.4	87	4425	19.4	26.3	94
QUINTILE II	17021	10137	19.3	59.6	97	2340	17.3	13.7	87	3195	21.2	18.8	106	4602	19.3	27.0	97
QUINTILE III	17138	10361	19.8	60.5	98	2758	20.4	16.1	102	2964	19.6	17.3	98	4639	19.5	27.1	97
QUINTILE IV	16802	10807	20.2	63.1	103	2783	20.6	16.6	105	3019	20.0	18.0	102	4805	20.2	28.6	102
QUINTILE V	16807	11075	21.1	65.9	107	2684	19.9	16.0	101	3223	21.3	19.2	108	5167	21.7	30.7	110
TERCILE I - YELLOW PAGES	14791	9288	17.7	62.8	102	2560	19.0	17.3	109	2497	16.5	16.9	95	4231	17.7	28.6	102
TERCILE II	14580	9421	18.0	64.6	105	2411	17.8	16.5	104	3035	20.1	20.8	118	3976	16.7	27.3	98
TERCILE III	14493	8718	16.6	60.1	98	1883	13.9	13.0	82	2618	17.3	18.1	102	4216	17.7	29.1	104
RADIO WKDAY: 6-10:00 AM CUME	46240	28371	54.1	61.4	100	7055	52.2	15.3	96	8548	56.6	18.5	104	12768	53.6	27.6	99
10:00 AM - 3:00 PM	32892	20078	38.3	61.0	99	5371	39.8	16.3	103	5691	37.7	17.3	98	9015	37.8	27.4	98
3:00 PM - 7:00 PM	31800	19780	37.7	62.2	101	5023	37.2	15.8	100	5927	39.3	18.6	105	8829	37.0	27.8	99
7:00 PM - MIDNIGHT	13867	8386	16.0	60.5	98	2012	14.9	14.5	92	2468	16.3	17.8	101	3906	16.4	28.2	101
RADIO AVERAGE WEEKDAY CUME	65084	40284	76.8	61.9	101	10571	78.3	16.2	103	11736	77.7	18.0	102	17977	75.4	27.6	99
RADIO AVG. WEEKEND DAY CUME	55042	33860	64.6	61.5	100	8980	66.5	16.3	103	9782	64.7	17.7	100	15117	63.4	27.5	98
RADIO FORMATS: ADULT CONTEMP	15021	9758	18.6	65.0	106	2108	15.6	14.0	89	2934	19.4	19.5	110	4716	19.8	31.4	112
ALL NEWS	4106	2576	4.9	62.7	102	461	3.3	11.0	69	956	6.3	23.3	132	1169	4.9	28.5	102
AOR/PROGRESSIVE ROCK	6932	4103	7.8	59.2	96	837	6.2	12.1	76	975	6.5	14.1	79	2291	9.6	33.0	118
BLACK	851	489	.9	57.5	93	*55	.4	6.5	41	*57	.4	6.7	38	*377	1.6	44.3	159
CHR/ROCK	11939	7105	13.5	59.5	97	1847	13.7	15.5	98	1920	12.7	16.1	91	3339	14.0	28.0	100
CLASSIC ROCK	2660	1592	3.0	59.8	97	*331	2.5	12.4	79	524	3.5	19.7	111	738	3.1	27.7	99
CLASSICAL	1812	1274	2.4	70.3	114	*197	1.5	10.9	69	542	3.6	29.9	169	536	2.2	29.6	106
COUNTRY	12114	7568	14.4	62.5	102	2350	17.4	19.4	123	2291	15.2	18.9	107	2927	12.3	24.2	86
EASY LISTENING	3156	2012	3.8	63.8	104	560	4.1	17.7	112	592	3.9	18.8	106	861	3.6	27.3	98
GOLDEN OLDIES	6579	4068	7.8	61.8	101	866	6.4	13.2	83	1228	8.1	18.7	105	1974	8.3	30.0	107
MOR/NOSTALGIA	3264	2020	3.9	61.9	101	423	3.1	13.0	82	749	5.0	22.9	130	848	3.6	26.0	93
NEWS/TALK	8430	5220	10.0	61.9	101	1075	8.0	12.8	81	1627	10.8	19.3	109	2518	10.6	29.9	107
SOFT CONTEMPORARY	4143	2552	4.9	61.6	100	453	3.4	10.9	69	666	4.4	16.1	91	1434	6.0	34.6	124
SPANISH	1288	631	1.2	49.0	80	*233	1.7	18.1	114	*77	.5	6.0	34	*321	1.3	24.9	89
URBAN CONTEMPORARY	4245	2346	4.5	55.3	90	586	4.3	13.8	87	655	4.3	15.4	87	1104	4.6	26.0	93
RADIO NETWORKS: ABC EXCEL	3744	2191	4.2	58.5	95	*459	3.4	12.3	77	594	3.9	15.9	90	1138	4.8	30.4	109
ABC GALAXY	2820	1679	3.2	59.5	97	*365	2.7	12.9	82	679	4.5	24.1	136	635	2.7	22.5	81
ABC GENESIS	5222	3134	6.0	60.0	98	832	6.2	15.9	101	959	6.4	18.4	104	1343	5.6	25.7	92
ABC PLATINUM	10621	6826	13.0	64.3	105	1489	11.0	14.0	89	2300	15.2	21.7	122	3037	12.7	28.6	102
ABC PRIME	13884	8640	16.5	62.2	101	1977	14.6	14.2	90	2947	19.5	21.2	120	3716	15.6	26.8	96
CBS	6438	3786	7.2	58.8	96	903	6.7	14.0	89	1132	7.5	17.6	99	1751	7.3	27.2	97
CBS SPECTRUM	9502	5583	10.6	58.8	96	1301	9.6	13.7	86	1634	10.8	17.2	97	2648	11.1	27.9	100
CONCERT MUSIC NETWORK	1584	1119	2.1	70.6	115	*181	1.3	11.4	72	443	2.9	28.0	158	495	2.1	31.3	112
INTERNET	29246	17957	34.2	61.4	100	4316	32.0	14.8	93	5088	33.7	17.4	98	8553	35.9	29.2	105
KATZ RADIO GROUP	26574	16382	31.2	61.6	100	3941	29.2	14.8	94	4679	31.0	17.6	100	7762	32.6	29.2	105
MUTUAL	5431	3413	6.5	62.8	102	752	5.6	13.8	87	1080	7.2	19.9	112	1580	6.6	29.1	104
NBC	6457	3918	7.5	60.7	99	1011	7.5	15.7	99	1212	8.0	18.8	106	1694	7.1	26.2	94
NBN	725	*430	.8	59.3	96	*66	.5	9.1	58	*116	.8	16.0	90	*249	1.0	34.3	123
POWER	4805	2766	5.3	57.6	94	604	4.5	12.6	79	853	5.7	17.8	100	1309	5.5	27.2	98
SBN SPORTS	1139	588	1.1	51.6	84	*64	.5	5.6	35	*115	.8	10.1	57	*410	1.7	36.0	129
SHERIDAN	1368	702	1.3	51.3	83	*71	.5	5.2	33	*140	.9	10.2	58	*491	2.1	35.9	128
THE SOURCE	3806	2283	4.4	60.0	98	546	4.0	14.3	91	604	4.0	15.9	90	1133	4.8	29.8	107
STRZ ENTERTAINMENT	1959	1142	2.2	58.3	95	*255	1.9	13.0	82	*309	2.0	15.8	89	578	2.4	29.5	106
SUPER	7012	4564	8.7	65.1	106	935	6.9	13.3	84	1444	9.6	20.6	116	2185	9.2	31.2	112
ULTIMATE	6674	4199	8.0	62.9	102	967	7.2	14.5	92	1288	8.5	19.3	109	1944	8.2	29.1	104
WALL STREET JOURNAL NETWORK	3708	2214	4.2	59.7	97	514	3.8	13.9	88	695	4.6	18.7	106	1006	4.2	27.1	97
TV WKDAY AV 1/2 HR:7-9:00AM	7244	4565	8.7	63.0	103	1227	9.1	16.9	107	1346	8.9	18.6	105	1992	8.4	27.5	98
9:00 AM - 4:00 PM	13251	7729	14.7	58.3	95	2391	17.7	18.0	114	1809	12.0	13.7	77	3529	14.8	26.6	95
4:00 PM - 7:30 PM	21149	12733	24.3	60.2	98	3422	25.3	16.2	102	3566	23.6	16.9	95	5746	24.1	27.2	97
7:30 PM - 8:00 PM	33293	19856	37.9	59.6	97	5469	40.5	16.4	104	5794	38.4	17.4	98	8592	36.0	25.8	92
8:00 PM - 11:00 PM	37956	22451	42.8	59.2	96	5831	43.2	15.4	97	6419	42.5	16.9	96	10200	42.8	26.9	96
11:00 PM - 11:30 PM	24664	14575	27.8	59.1	96	3666	27.1	14.9	94	4368	28.9	17.7	100	6541	27.4	26.5	95
11:30 PM - 1:00 AM	9083	5155	9.8	56.8	92	1283	9.5	14.1	89	1426	9.4	15.7	89	2447	10.3	26.9	96
TV PRIME TIME CUME	69074	42386	80.8	61.4	100	10962	81.2	15.9	100	12534	83.0	18.1	103	18900	79.3	27.4	98
PROGRAM-TYPES:DAYTIME DRAMAS	6227	3533	6.7	56.7	92	1228	9.1	19.7	125	894	5.9	14.4	81	1410	5.9	22.6	81
DAYTIME GAME SHOWS	4572	2666	5.1	58.3	95	856	6.4	18.8	119	724	4.8	15.8	89	1085	4.6	23.7	85
EARLY MORNING TALK/INFO/NEWS	7884	5224	10.0	66.3	108	1712	12.7	21.7	137	1537	10.2	19.5	110	1975	8.3	25.1	90
EARLY EVE. NETWK NEWS - M-F	12312	8149	15.5	66.2	108	2474	18.3	20.1	127	2079	13.8	16.9	95	3597	15.1	29.2	105
FEATURE FILMS - PRIME	8388	5562	10.6	66.3	108	1703	12.6	20.3	128	1620	10.7	19.3	109	2238	9.4	26.7	95
GENERAL DRAMA - PRIME	7091	4264	8.1	60.1	98	1145	8.5	16.1	102	1279	8.5	18.0	102	1841	7.7	26.0	93
PVT DET/SUSP/MYST/POL.-PRIME	11571	7076	13.5	61.2	99	2197	16.3	19.0	120	1791	11.9	15.5	87	3088	13.0	26.7	96
SITUATION COMEDIES - PRIME	10422	6631	12.6	63.6	104	1661	12.2	15.8	100	1946	12.9	18.7	105	3034	12.7	29.1	104
CABLE TV	46838	29169	55.6	62.3	101	6954	51.5	14.8	94	8666	57.4	18.5	105	13550	56.8	28.9	104
PAY TV	21734	13700	26.1	63.0	103	3283	24.3	15.1	95	4206	27.9	19.4	109	6211	26.1	28.6	102
HEAVY CABLE VIEWING (15+ HR)	21047	12760	24.3	60.6	99	3611	26.7	17.2	108	3589	23.8	17.1	96	5560	23.3	26.4	95
CABLE NETWORKS:																	
A&E (ARTS & ENTERTAINMENT)	9022	5736	10.9	63.6	103	1345	10.0	14.9	94	1661	11.0	18.4	104	2730	11.5	30.3	108
AMERICAN MOVIE CLASSICS	5154	3043	5.8	59.0	96	711	5.3	13.8	87	1024	6.8	19.9	112	1308	5.5	25.4	91
BET (BLACK ENTERTAINMENT TV)	2582	1492	2.8	57.8	94	*342	2.5	13.2	84	*359	2.4	13.9	79	791	3.3	30.6	110
CNN (CABLE NEWS NETWORK)	23650	14839	28.3	62.7	102	3274	24.2	13.8	87	4758	31.5	20.1	114	6808	28.6	28.8	103
THE COMEDY CHANNEL	2263	1328	2.5	58.7	95	*284	2.1	12.5	79	*310	2.1	13.7	77	733	3.1	32.4	116
THE DISCOVERY CHANNEL	13446	8335	15.9	62.0	101	2091	15.5	15.6	98	2671	17.7	19.9	112	3574	15.0	26.6	95
ESPN	13943	8325	15.9	59.7	97	2146	15.9	15.4	97	2660	17.6	19.0	107	3529	14.8	25.3	91
THE FAMILY CHANNEL	10636	5983	11.4	56.3	92	1666	12.3	15.7	99	1744	11.6	16.4	93	2572	10.8	24.7	87
FNN	1320	861	1.6	65.2	106	*185	1.4	14.0	89	*341	2.3	25.8	146	*335	1.4	25.4	91
HEADLINE NEWS	8691	5228	10.0	60.2	98	1233	9.1	14.2	90	1392	9.2	16.0	91	2602	10.9	29.9	107
LIFETIME	10029	6243	11.9	62.2	101	1444	10.7	14.4	91	1801	11.9	18.0	101	2998	12.6	29.9	107
MTV	8722	5198	9.9	59.6	97	1225	9.1	14.0	89	1374	9.1	15.8	89	2599	10.9	29.8	107
TNN (THE NASHVILLE NETWORK)	9443	5407	10.3	57.3	93	1490	11.0	15.8	100	1652	10.9	17.5	99	2265	9.5	24.0	86
NICK AT NITE	5881	3250	6.2	55.3	90	784	5.8	13.4	85	960	6.3	16.2	91	1512	6.3	25.7	92
NICKELODEON	8948	5522	10.5	61.7	100	1752	13.0	19.6	124	1401	9.3	15.7	88	2369	9.9	26.5	95
PREVUE GUIDE	1477	873	1.7	59.1	96	*184	1.4	12.5	79	*209	1.4	14.2	80	480	2.0	32.5	116
TBS	16718	9796	18.7	58.6	95	2971	22.0	17.8	112	2639	17.5	15.8	89	4187	17.6	25.0	90
THE TRAVEL CHANNEL	1272	868	1.7	68.2	111	*156	1.2	12.3	77	*220	1.5	17.3	98	492	2.1	38.7	138
TNT (TURNER NETWORK TV)	17288	10763	20.5	62.3	101	3125	23.1	18.1	114	3139	20.8	18.2	103	4499	18.9	26.0	93
USA NETWORK	12611	7227	13.8	57.3	93	1839	13.6	14.6	92	1849	12.2	14.7	83	3538	14.8	28.1	100
VH-1	4419	2673	5.1	60.5	98	618	4.6	14.0	88	772	5.1	17.5	99	1284	5.4	29.1	104
THE WEATHER CHANNEL	13854	8756	16.7	63.2	103	2186	16.2	15.8	100	2540	16.9	18.4	104	4021	16.9	29.0	104

Spring 1991

Television

Arbitron Television Market Reports.

Arbitron measures local TV audiences with meters and diaries. A random sample of listed and unlisted telephone numbers in local areas constitutes the Arbitron sample. A minimum of 200 households for a TV ADI is used.

One-week family viewing diaries are used to provide viewing and demographic information for diary markets (see Figure 14–10). A pre-placement letter is sent to computer-selected households informing them of their selection and upcoming interview. In a telephone interview, the Arbitron representative obtains data on VCR ownership and number of TV sets in the household. Diaries are sent for each TV set as well as for each VCR. A small cash incentive is mailed with the diary to encourage cooperation. During the week of diary keeping, an Arbitron representative contacts the household twice to assist household members and to ensure that no difficulties have developed. Special consideration is given to obtaining cooperation from minority respondents, usually in the form of increased follow-up phone calls and an increased cash incentive. English/Spanish diaries are available to respondents who desire them.

Figure 14–10

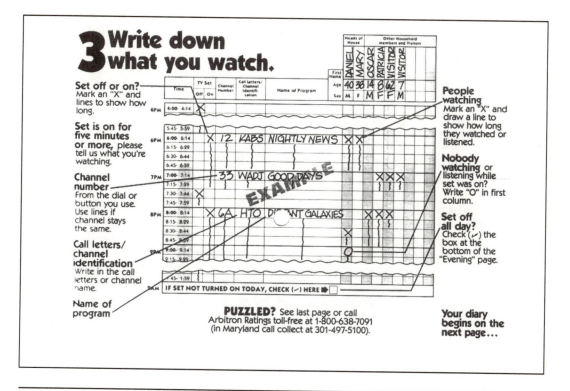

A usability edit is the first stage of dealing with the returned diaries. For a variety of reasons, ranging from the diary being kept by someone other than the respondent to a postmark before the last day of the survey week, some diaries are judged to be unusable and are excluded from tabulation. After many other checkpoints and tabulation preparation procedures, the viewing information is printed in report form in a variety of different formats. A typical page from the Television Market Report for Baltimore is contained in Figure 14–11.

The meter is attached to the television and records whether the set is on or off and the station it is tuned to. This provides the Metro and ADI TV household viewing levels for individual stations and households using television in 14 markets. The meter system consists of the meter and a minicomputer "Household Collector," which receives the metered information, checks transmission accuracy, and stores the tuning information in memory. Data collected from meters is published in *Arbitrends I Reports,* which provide overnight ratings with program titles. Weekly meter reports also are available. Meter and diary information is integrated by Arbitron to produce the *Meter/Diary Market Reports.*

A. C. Nielsen.

The A. C. Nielsen Company provides TV audience measurement in the following ways:

Information	Report	Measurement Method
National audiences	Nielsen Television Index	People-meters
Local audiences	Nielsen Station Index	People-meters, TV meters, diaries

TV meters record what is being watched, and diaries are used to measure viewer numbers and demographics. The people-meters are used to record both types of information.

Nielsen Television Index (NTI).   The NTI is based on a national sample of more than 4000 households selected randomly from throughout the United States. The NTI results in national measurement of TV audiences and is the basis for the much-publicized overnight ratings. Reports describe audiences by quarter-hour for all sponsored network programs. Measurement is by way of the people-meter, a device that sits on the TV set and contains a microprocessor to report not only what the television is tuned to but who in the household is viewing it (see Figure 14–12).

Figure 14–11

Time Period Estimates

STATION BREAK AVERAGES

TOTAL SURVEY AREA IN THOUSANDS

Monday – Friday

Figure 14–12
Nielsen People-Meter

The people-meter contains eight buttons, each of which is assigned to a specific member of the household or their guests. Visitors are instructed to push an unassigned button and then to enter their age and gender using buttons designated for the purpose. Red and green lights on the front of the box indicate presence of viewers. Green means a selected person is viewing and red indicates no viewing. A wireless remote hand-held unit may also be used to indicate viewing status.

Household cooperation rate is quoted by Nielsen as 55 percent. Each household is visited in person by trained field staff who instruct household members in using the people-meter. Households are asked to remain in the people-meter sample for two years.

Viewing data are transmitted each night by phone lines to Nielsen production facilities, where they are checked for accuracy and then analyzed. Clients of the NTI service receive reports by 3:30 p.m. the following day. A number of national reports are produced in cooperation with NTI, most notably the *Ratings Report,* called the "Pocketpiece," which is issued 52 weeks per year and includes household and person estimates for network program audiences, demographics by daypart, program averages, ratings, and shares for non-network viewing sources and VCR usage. Other NTI-based reports include *Households Using Television Summary, National Audience Demographics,* and *Program Cumulative Audiences.* Figure 14–13 shows a weekly NTI *Network Prime Report.*

For the past 35 years, Nielsen has published an annual report on TV viewing that highlights information from its regular reports and special studies. Figures 14–14 through 14–18 contain information from the *1990 Report on Television,* which updated estimates of TV penetration, average hours of TV viewing per day, and VCR usage.

Figure 14–13

Page 1

Nielsen Television Index Ranking Report
NETWORK PRIME REPORT
Current Week
01/14/91 – 01/20/91

Rank	Program Name	Net	Prog Type	(MTWRFSS)	Time	Dur	PrWk Rank	Rank	AA% (HH)	SHR	Episode Title
1	60 MINUTES	CBS	DN	S	7:36P	60	2	1	27.2	40	
2	CBS NFC CHAMPIONSHP POS(S)	CBS	SC	S	7:15P	21		2	26.2	41	
3	ROSEANNE	ABC	CS	T	9:00P	30	8	3	19.6	28	
4	MURDER, SHE WROTE.	CBS	SM	S	8:36P	60		4	18.8	27	
5	ABC NEWS SP:LINE/THE SA(S)	ABC	DN	S	8:00P	60		5	18.1	27	
6	DESIGNING WOMEN	CBS	CS	M	8:00P	30	4	6	18.0	27	
7	MURPHY BROWN	CBS	CS	M	8:00P	30		7	18.0	26	
8	MATLOCK	NBC	GD	T	8:00P	60	18	8	17.2	26	
9	ABC SPECIAL REPORT-8:00(S)	ABC	OP	W	8:00P	180		9	17.0	22	
10	IN THE HEAT OF THE NIGHT	NBC	CS	T	8:00P	60	20	10	16.1	22	
11	GOLDEN GIRLS (R)	NBC	CS	T	9:00P	30	26	11	15.8	27	
12	WHO'S THE BOSS?	ABC	CS	T	9:00P	30	62	12	15.5	24	
13	FULL HOUSE	ABC	FF	F	8:00P	30	9	13	15.4	24	
14	FAMILY MATTERS	ABC	CS	F	8:30P	30		14	15.3	25	
15	NBC NWS:AMER.AT WAR-1SUS (R)	NBC	N	W	6:50P	250	17	15	15.2	24	
16	CBS SUNDAY MOVIE (R)	CBS	FF	S	7:36P	120		16	15.1	24	THE WHEREABOUTS OF JENNY
17	EMPTY NEST	NBC	CS	S	9:36P	30	23	17	14.9	22	
18	COACH	ABC	CS		8:30P	30		18	14.8	22	
19	AMER.SUNDAY NIGHT MOVIE (R)	ABC	FF	S	8:30P	130	44	19	14.2	22	LONESOME DOVE, PT 1
20	AMER.FUNNIEST-HOME VIDEOS	ABC	CV		8:00P	30	20	20	14.2	21	
21	MAJOR DAD	CBS	CS	M	8:30P	30	47	21	14.1	21	
22	GULF WAR DAY2 8P (S)	NBC	N		8:00P	180		22	14.1	21	
23	FRESH PRINCE OF BEL AIR	NBC	CS	M	8:00P	30	37	23	13.8	21	
24	HEAD OF THE CLASS	ABC	CS	T	8:30P	30	35	24	13.6	21	
25	RESCUE: 911	CBS	N	T	8:00P	60	25	25	13.4	20	
26	NBC NWS AMER.AT WAR-4SUS (R)	NBC	CS		8:00P	30		26	13.4	20	
27	NBC MONDAY NIGHT MOVIES	NBC	GD	M	9:00P	120	19	27	13.1	21	RAIDERS OF THE LOST ARK
28	LAW AND ORDER	NBC	FF		10:00P	60	38	28	13.1	21	
29	WAR IN THE GULF-CBS-1SUS	CBS	CS	W	10:57P	303		29	12.6	19	
30	BLOSSOM	ABC	CS	M	8:00P	30	42	30	12.4	18	
31	PERFECT STRANGERS (R)	ABC	CS	F	8:00P	30	27	31	12.4	20	
32	EVENING SHADE	CBS	CS	M	9:00P	30	28	32	12.3	19	
33	NBC SUNDAY NIGHT MOVIE (R)	NBC	GV	S	9:00P	120	30	33	12.3	19	DARK SHADOWS PT.2
34	CAROL & COMPANY (S)	NBC	N		10:00P	30		34	11.7	20	
35	T.BROKAW SP-TH-10.00P	NBC	N	T	8:00P	120		35	11.6	18	
36	WAR IN THE GULF-CBS-6	CBS	FF	S	8:00P	180		36	11.5	18	
37	CBS TUESDAY MOVIE (S)	CBS	FF		9:00P	120	39	37	11.5	18	SHE WAS MARKED FOR MURDER
38	20/20 (B)	ABC	DN	F	10:00P	60		38	11.4	21	
39	CHEERS SPECIAL (RS)	NBC	CS		10:30P	30		39	11.4	20	
40	DEAR JOHN	NBC	CS		8:00P	60	48	40	11.4	18	
41	WAR IN THE GULF-CBS-12 (S)	CBS	N		8:30P	30	54	41	11.0	15	THE PRESIDIO
42	EXPOSE.	NBC	CS		8:30P	30	41	42	10.8	18	
43	GOING PLACES	ABC	CS	F	9:00P	30	45	43	10.6	18	
44	MARRIED WITH CHILDREN(R)	FOX	CS	S	8:30P	30	43	44	10.6	17	
45	TRIALS OF ROSIE O'NEILL	CBS	GD	F	10:00P	30	45	45	10.5	15	
46	DALLAS	CBS	GD		10:00P	60		46	10.3	17	
47	NBC NWS.SP:RPT.-SUN-PRI(S)	NBC	N		7:00P	60		47	10.2	17	
48	FANELLI BOYS	NBC	CS	S	8:30P	30		48	10.2	17	
49	GRAND OLE OPRY'S 65TH A(S)	CBS	GV	S	9:00P	120	51	49	9.7	16	

Figure 14-14

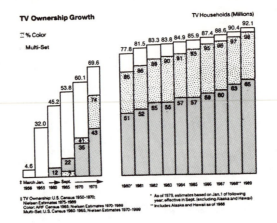

TV Ownership Growth

⊑ % Color

Multi-Set

TV Ownership: 4.6, 32.0, 45.2, 53.8, 60.1, 69.6

‡ March Jan. → Sept. →
1956 1965 1960 1965 1970 1975

‡ TV Ownership: U.S. Census 1950-1970;
Nielsen Estimates 1975-1989
Color: ARF Census 1965; Nielsen Estimates 1970-1989
Multi-Set: U.S. Census 1960-1965; Nielsen Estimates 1970-1989

TV Households (Millions)

77.8, 81.5, 83.3, 83.8, 84.9, 85.9, 87.4, 88.6, 90.4, 92.1

1980* 1981 1982 1983 1984 1985 1986 1987 1988** 1989

* As of 1979, estimates based on Jan. 1 of following
year, effective in Sept. (excluding Alaska and Hawaii)
** Includes Alaska and Hawaii as of 1988

Figure 14-15

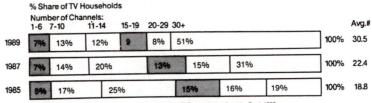

Channels Receivable Per TV Household

% Share of TV Households

Number of Channels:

	1-6	7-10	11-14	15-19	20-29	30+		Avg.#
1989	7%	13%	12%	9	8%	51%	100%	30.5
1987	7%	14%	20%	13%	15%	31%	100%	22.4
1985	8%	17%	25%	15%	16%	19%	100%	18.8

Source: NTI Audimeter Sample: Sept. each year 1985-87; NTI People Meter Sample: Sept. 1989

Figure 14-16

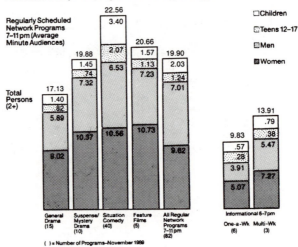

Audience Composition by Selected Program Type

Regularly Scheduled
Network Programs
7–11 pm (Average
Minute Audiences)

☐ Children
☒ Teens 12–17
▨ Men
▦ Women

Total Persons (2+)

	22.56			
	3.40			
19.88	2.07	20.66		
1.45	6.53	1.57	19.90	
.74		1.13	2.03	
7.32		7.23	1.24	
17.13			7.01	
1.40	10.57	10.56	10.73	
.82				9.62
5.89				
9.02				

General Drama (15) · Suspense/Mystery Drama (10) · Situation Comedy (40) · Feature Films (5) · All Regular Network Programs 7–11pm (82)

Informational 6–7pm

9.83: .57, .28, 3.91, 5.07
13.91: .79, .38, 5.47, 7.27

One-a-Wk (6) · Multi-Wk (3)

( ) = Number of Programs–November 1989

Figure 14–17

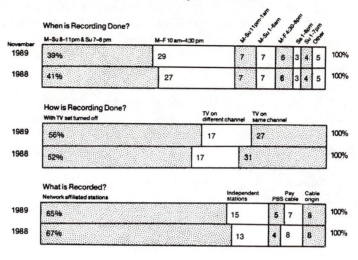

Videocassette Recorder Activity in VCR Homes

When is Recording Done?

	M–Su 6–11pm & Su 7–8 pm	M–F 10 am–4:30 pm	M–Su 11pm–1am	M–Su 1–6am	M–F 6:30–8pm	Sa 1–8pm	Su 1–7pm	Other	
November 1989	39%	29	7	7	6	3	4	5	100%
1988	41%	27	7	7	6	3	4	5	100%

How is Recording Done?

	With TV set turned off	TV on different channel	TV on same channel	
1989	56%	17	27	100%
1988	52%	17	31	100%

What is Recorded?

	Network affiliated stations	Independent stations	Pay PBS cable	Cable origin	
1989	65%	15	5	7	8	100%
1988	67%	13	4	8	8	100%

Figure 14–18

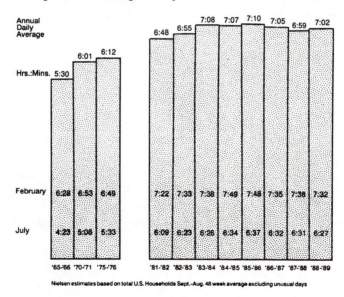

Average Hours of TV Usage Per Day

Annual Daily Average

	'65–'66	'70–'71	'75–'76	'81–'82	'82–'83	'83–'84	'84–'85	'85–'86	'86–'87	'87–'88	'88–'89
Hrs.:Mins.	5:30	6:01	6:12	6:48	6:55	7:08	7:07	7:10	7:05	6:59	7:02
February	6:28	6:53	6:49	7:22	7:33	7:38	7:49	7:48	7:35	7:38	7:32
July	4:23	5:08	5:33	6:09	6:23	6:26	6:34	6:37	6:32	6:31	6:27

Nielsen estimates based on total U.S. Households Sept.–Aug. 48 week average excluding unusual days

Nielsen Station Index (NSI).   Local markets in the United States are measured at least three times per year through the Nielsen Station Index. Time period viewing estimates and trend reports are generated for each market and can be evaluated by a variety of demographic and household statistics. Nielsen divides the country's TV markets into Designated Market Areas (DMAs), each of which includes counties in the metropolitan area of a market in which the commercial stations are estimated to have the largest average quarter-hour share of the 9 a.m. to 12 midnight household audience or in which one station in the market achieves a larger share of the 9 a.m. to 12 midnight average quarter-hour household audience than any station outside the market. Counties are assigned exclusively to one DMA.

Nielsen uses both meters and diaries to collect data for local market audience estimates. Diary samples are generated from listed and unlisted telephone households; the sample size for one all-market measurement reaches about 100,000. Participants receive a weekly diary with quarter-hour viewing sections. Demographic questions are also included. Information collected from diaries is the basis for the *Viewers in Profile* reports issued in the smaller markets. (See Figure 14–19.)

Separate meter samples are used in the larger markets, where from 300 to 500 meters are installed. The meter monitors continuously the minute-by-minute TV tuning, and data are available overnight via electronic reporting. Metered data are used in conjunction with the diary information to produce the *Viewers in Profile* reports in larger markets.

The *Viewers in Profile* reports for all markets are issued at least three times per year in November, February, and May—the "sweeps" periods. An all-DMA measurement is made in July. Some of the larger markets are measured up to seven times per year. Supplementary reports to *Viewers in Profile* include *Network Programs by DMA, Report on Syndicated Programs, Report on Devotional Programs,* and *DMA Total Activity Report,* which includes cable audiences by market.

Simmons Market Research Bureau (SMRB).

Two-week diaries of individual viewing are used by SMRB to estimate TV audiences and daypart viewing. A roster recall method uses a list of program names to measure audiences for special TV events. Data generated from the SMRB diaries include audiences for average half-hour network program audiences, cumulative audiences, and frequency of viewing. Quintile distributions of viewing by daypart also are provided. A quintile distribution divides the audience into five groups based on their viewing habits. Figure 14–20 shows an SMRB report using TV audience data. Cable and pay TV ownership and viewing are also measured by SMRB by way of personal interview. (Note: A further discussion of SMRB methods is available in Chapter 13.)

Figure 14–19

NSI AVERAGE WEEK ESTIMATES **MACON, GA**

Column groups: PERSONS (HH, 2+, 18+) | WOMEN (18+, 18-34, 18-49, 25-49, 25-54, 25-64, 50+, WKG) | FEM 12-24 | PER 12-24 | MEN (18+, 18-34, 18-49, 25-49, 25-54, 25-64) | TEENS (12-17, GIRLS) | CHILD (2-11, 6-11) | NUMBER OF QUARTER HOURS AVERAGED / WEEKS (1,2,3,4)

TIME / STATION / DAY	HH	2+	18+	W18+	18-34	18-49	25-49	25-54	25-64	50+	WKG	F12-24	P12-24	M18+	18-34	18-49	25-49	25-54	25-64	12-17	GIRLS	2-11	6-11	W1	W2	W3	W4
(total)	*10/7*	*20/5*	*16/4*	*11/3*	*10/3*	*10/3*	*9/2*	*9/2*	*9/2*	*9/3*	*9/3*	*8/2*	*12/3*	*11/3*	*12/3*	*11/3*	*10/3*	*10/3*	*10/3*	*10/3*	*7/2*	*15/4*	*11/3*				
1.00PM																											
WGXA M-F	3	3	3	3	1	2	2	2	2	1	1	1	2	3		3	3	3	3	1				20	20	20	20
WGXA SUN	4	9	8	5	1	4	3	3	1		1		2	3		3	3	3	3	1				2	2	2	2
WMAZ SUN	32	46	39	15	5	8	7	9	12	7	7	2	6	24	10	16	14	17	20	3	1	3	3	14	25	15	25
WMGT M-F	2	3	2	2		1	1	1	1	1	1	1	1									1		20	20	20	20
WMGT SUN	2																								2		
WMGT SUN	11	15	13	4	2	3	2	2	3	2	2	1	2	8	3	6	5	6	7	1		1	1	26	14	25	12
1.30PM																											
WGXA SAT	10	14	10	8	6	8	4	4	4		3	5	7	2	1	2	1	1	1	3	2	1	1	2	2	2	2
WGXA SUN	5	12	10	7	3	5	3	3	4	2	3	2	3	2		2	2	2	3			1		2	2	2	2
WMAZ M-F	46	57	51	41	18	25	16	17	21	16	10	10	11	10	4	6	5	5	7	1		5		20	20	20	20
WMGT SAT	<<																								2		2
WMGT SAT	3	3																									
WMGT SUN	2																								4		
2.00PM																											
WGXA M-F	2	2	2	2	1	2	2	2	2		1													20	20	20	20
WGXA SAT	10	15	13	9	7	9	4	4	4		4	7	8	4	1	3	3	3	3	1	1			2	2	2	
WGXA SAT	4	8	2	2																							4
WGXA SUN	7	17	11	8	4	6	4	4	4	2	3	3	5	4		4	4	4	4	2	1	4	1	4	4	4	4
WMGT M-F	2	2	1	1		1	1	1	1	1	1													20	20	20	20
WMGT SAT	<<																								7	6	6
WMGT NOR	<<																								6	6	6
2.30PM																											
WGXA SAT	5	8	7	5	4	5	2	2	2		1	3	4	2		2	2	2	2	1				2	2	2	
WMAZ M-F	44	54	48	37	16	23	14	15	19	14	9	10	11	11	4	6	5	5	7	1	1	5	2	10	10	10	10
WMGT SUN	5	6	3										3											4			
3.00PM																											
WGXA M-F	3	4	4	3	1	2	1	1	2	2	2			1										20	20	20	20
WGXA SAT	9	14	13	4	1	2	2	2	2	2	2	1	2	4	2	4	3	3	5	1				16	18	16	16
WGXA SUN	8	18	13	9	3	6	4	4	4	3	3	3	4	4		3	3	3	4	2	1	3	1	8	8	8	8
WMAZ M-F	49	66	54	42	18	26	16	18	22	16	10	13	15	12	6	8	7	7	9	4	4	7	3	20	20	20	20
WMGT M-F	1	1																						20	20	20	20
3.15PM																											
WMAZ SAT	10	12	11	5	2	3	2	3	4	2	3	1	2	6	1	3	3	4	5	1				12	13	11	
WMAZ NOR	10	11	10	5	2	3	2	2	4	2	3		1	5	1	3	3	4	5	1				12	9	11	
3.30PM																											
WMAZ SAT	6	7	7											7													2
WMGT SAT	3	4	2											2												2	6
WMGT SAT	<<																										
WMGT SUN	2	1	1											1											2		
3.45PM																											
WMGT SAT	1	3	3	1										2											7		
4.00PM																											
WGXA MON	11	16	3	3	2	2	1	1	1	1		2	4	2	1	1	1	1	1	3	2	11	6	2	2	2	2
WGXA TUE	7	9	3	1		1	1	1	1			2	4	1	1	1	1	1	1	1	1	6	4	2	2	1	2
WGXA WED	12	20	4	3	3	3					1	2	4	1	1	1	1	1	1	1	1	15	8	2	2	2	2
WGXA THU	15	24	3	3	3	3	2	2	2			3	4							3	3	18	9	2	2	2	2
WGXA FRI	9	17	4	4	3	3	1	1	1		2	3	3							1		12	5	2	2	2	2
WGXA AVS	11	17	3	2	2	2	1	1	1		1	3	3	1		1			1	2	1	13	7	10	10	9	10
WMAZ MON	25	32	24	18	8	12	6	7	8	6	7	10	10	6	1	3	3	3	4	5	4	3	3	4	4	4	4
WMAZ TUE	27	43	29	22	8	15	10	11	13	7	11	11	11	7	3	5	4	4	5	6	4	8	4	4	4	4	4
WMAZ WED	21	26	19	14	4	7	5	5	8	7	5	9	10	5	3	2	2	3	5	5	2	3	2	4	4	4	4
WMAZ THU	29	44	35	26	11	15	11	12	16	11	8	9	10	9	2	3	2	3	6	6	4	3	2	4	4	4	4
WMAZ FRI	25	38	27	20	7	10	9	11	13	10	6	8	9	7	2	3	3	5	6	6	5	4	4	4	4	4	4
WMAZ AVS	26	37	27	20	8	12	8	9	11	8	7	7	10	7	2	3	3	3	4	6	4	4	3	20	20	20	20
WMAZ SAT	5	4	4									7		4													4
WMGT MON	8	17	7	5	4	4	3	3	4	1	1	2	6	2	2	2	1	1	1	3	1	7	5	2	2	2	2
WMGT TUE	8	20	8	8	5	5	3	3	4	1	1	2	6	2	2	2	2	2	2	4	1	8	7	2	2	2	2
WMGT WED	9	20	9	5	4	4	3	3	4	1	1	2	7	4	4	4	3	3	3	1	1	7	5	2	2	2	2
WMGT THU	8	16	6	3	2	3	2	2	3	1	1	2	8	2	2	2	2	2	2	5	1	7	5	2	2	2	2
WMGT FRI	9	19	6	4	3	4	3	3	3	1	1	2	8	2	2	2	2	2	2	7	2	6	5	2	2	2	2
WMGT AVS	8	18	7	5	4	5	2	3	3		1	2	7	2	2	2	2	2	2	5	1	6	5	10	10	10	10
WMGT SAT	5	5	3	1								2		2						5						4	
WMGT SUN	2	2	1	1								2		1													2

For explanation of symbols, see page 3.
For RSE explanations, see page 2.
See Time Period for complete competitive and post 1:15AM programming.

NOVEMBER 1985

P R O G R A M   A V E R A G E S

15

Figure 14-20

AGE WITHIN HOUSEHOLD INCOME
(FEMALE HOMEMAKERS)

	TOTAL U.S. '000	UNDER $20,000 18-34 A '000	B % DOWN	C % ACROSS	D INDX	UNDER $20,000 35-54 A '000	B % DOWN	C % ACROSS	D INDX	UNDER $20,000 55 OR OLDER A '000	B % DOWN	C % ACROSS	D INDX	UNDER $20,000 35-49 A '000	B % DOWN	C % ACROSS	D INDX
TOTAL	82531	10077	100.0	12.2	100	6452	100.0	7.8	100	16499	50.8	20.0	100	4994	100.0	6.1	100
MKDAY LOCAL EVENING TV NEWS		2906	28.8	10.3	85	2291	35.5	8.1	104	8379	29.8	29.8	149	1611	32.3	5.7	95
NETWORK AFFILIATES - EARLY	28124	1947	19.3	9.9	81	1653	25.6	8.4	108	4602	27.9	23.5	117	1229	24.6	6.3	104
NETWORK AFFILIATES - LATE	19610	329	2.3	10.5	86	212	3.3	9.7	124	474	2.9	21.7	108	159	3.2	7.3	120
INDEPENDENTS - LATE	2187																

[Table continues with extensive programming data including TV EVENING NTWK 6 PM - 2 AM listings (ABC NEWS:NIGHTLINE, ABC WORLD NEWS TONIGHT, ALF, BILL COSBY SHOW, BRONX ZOO, CBS EVENING NEWS-RATHER, CHEERS, DALLAS, DESIGNING WOMEN, DYNASTY, FACTS OF LIFE, FALCON CREST, FAMILY TIES, GOLDEN GIRLS, GROWING PAINS, HEAD OF THE CLASS, HIGHWAY TO HEAVEN, HOUSTON KNIGHTS, HUNTER, KATE & ALLIE, KNOTS LANDING, L.A. LAW, MACGYVER, MAGNUM P.I., MATLOCK, MAX HEADROOM, MIAMI VICE, MOONLIGHTING, MURDER SHE WROTE, MY SISTER SAM, NBC MONDAY NIGHT MOVIE, NBC NIGHTLY NEWS, NBC SUNDAY NIGHT MOVIE, NEWHART, NIGHT COURT, OUR HOUSE, PERFECT STRANGERS, SATURDAY NIGHT, SIMON & SIMON, 60 MINUTES, SPENSER: FOR HIRE, TONIGHT SHOW, 20/20, VALERIE, WHO'S THE BOSS?); TV SHOW TYPES; and TV VIEWING SPORTS EVENTS.]

Mediamark Research, Inc.

A "yesterday" recall technique is used by MRI to estimate TV audiences. In the personal interview session, respondents are given a listing of dayparts and asked to say how much time was spent watching television in each time period on the previous weekday as well as "last Saturday" and "last Sunday." Call letters for stations viewed in the previous week also are collected. These data from the personal interview are used to estimate TV audiences by weekday and weekend average half-hours for various dayparts.

Audience estimates for specific programs are based on responses to a questionnaire that is left behind with the respondent. It contains a list of network programs, specials, and sports events, and respondents are asked to record how many times per month or week they usually watch each show. Other questions measure the degree of attentiveness while watching and whether viewing was done in-home or out-of-home. An example of a table generated using MRI TV audience estimates appears in Figure 14–21.

A special *MRI Cable Report* provides information on incidence of cable ownership and pay TV ownership (Cinemax, Disney Channel, Home Box Office, etc.), heavy cable viewing, and by 17 individual cable networks. As with other reports, the cable viewing information is cross-tabulated with demographic and product usage information.

Industry Guidelines for Media Research in Radio, Television, and Cable

In response to Congressional hearings on broadcast audience research, which revealed shortcomings in broadcast audience measurements, the Broadcast Rating Council was established in 1964. In 1982 the Council was renamed the Electronic Media Rating Council (EMRC) and included as its focus radio, television, cable, and other electronic media. The Council's credo is as follows: "Adherence by the rating services to specific minimum standards is necessary to meet the basic objectives of valid, reliable and useful electronic media audience measurement research."

Ratings companies apply to EMRC on a voluntary basis, and EMRC grants or withholds accreditation to specific services and reports after the companies agree to:

- Supply complete information to the Council
- Comply substantially with Council minimum standards
- Conduct their service as they represent to subscribers and the Council
- Submit to audits by the Council
- Pay the costs of these audits

Figure 14–21

82 HOUSEHOLD SIZE

BASE: MEN	TOTAL U.S. '000	1 A '000	1 B % DOWN	1 C % ACROSS	1 D INDEX	2 A '000	2 B % DOWN	2 C % ACROSS	2 D INDEX	3 OR 4 A '000	3 OR 4 B % DOWN	3 OR 4 C % ACROSS	3 OR 4 D INDEX	5+ A '000	5+ B % DOWN	5+ C % ACROSS	5+ D INDEX
ALL MEN	83367	8392	100.0	10.1	100	25918	100.0	31.1	100	35832	100.0	43.0	100	13225	100.0	15.9	100
MORNING NEWS/TALK/INFO:																	
FACE THE NATION CBS	2429	295	3.5	12.1	121	986	3.8	40.6	131	793	2.2	32.6	76	*355	2.7	14.6	92
GOOD MORNING AMERICA ABC	5210	412	4.9	7.9	79	1740	6.7	33.4	107	2030	5.7	39.0	91	1028	7.8	19.7	124
MEET THE PRESS NBC	3054	474	5.6	15.5	154	1384	5.3	45.3	146	800	2.2	26.2	61	*390	3.0	13.0	82
MORNING PROGRAM CBS	2009	268	3.2	13.3	133	758	2.9	37.7	121	702	2.0	34.9	81	*282	2.1	14.0	88
THIS WEEK WITH BRINKLEY ABC	5056	896	8.3	13.8	137	1936	7.5	38.3	123	1758	4.9	34.8	81	666	5.0	13.2	83
TODAY SHOW NBC	5541	677	8.1	12.2	121	2019	7.8	36.4	117	2078	5.8	37.5	87	767	5.8	13.8	87
DAYTIME:																	
ALL MY CHILDREN ABC	4292	*308	3.7	7.2	71	1070	4.1	24.9	80	1866	5.2	43.2	101	1058	8.0	24.7	155
ANOTHER WORLD NBC	1811	*118	1.4	6.5	65	583	2.2	32.2	104	764	2.1	42.2	98	*346	2.6	19.1	120
AS THE WORLD TURNS CBS	2696	*212	2.5	7.9	78	981	3.8	36.4	117	1048	2.9	38.9	90	*454	3.4	16.8	106
THE BOLD & THE BEAUTIFUL CBS	1535	*29	.3	1.9	19	483	1.9	31.5	101	823	2.3	53.6	125	*200	1.5	13.0	82
DAYS OF OUR LIVES NBC	3639	*234	2.8	6.4	64	1113	4.3	30.6	98	1679	4.7	46.1	107	*612	4.6	16.8	106
GENERAL HOSPITAL ABC	3537	380	4.5	10.7	107	904	3.5	25.6	82	1523	4.3	43.1	100	730	5.5	20.6	130
GUIDING LIGHT CBS	2283	*150	1.8	6.6	65	745	2.9	32.6	105	883	2.5	38.7	90	*504	3.8	22.1	139
LOVING ABC	1597	*90	1.1	5.6	56	*344	1.3	21.5	69	654	1.8	41.0	95	*508	3.8	31.8	201
NEW CARD SHARKS (AM) CBS	2145	*93	1.1	4.3	43	840	3.2	39.2	126	901	2.5	42.0	98	*311	2.4	14.5	91
ONE LIFE TO LIVE ABC	2972	308	3.7	10.4	103	780	3.0	26.2	84	1311	3.7	44.1	103	*573	4.3	19.3	122
THE PRICE IS RIGHT CBS	4895	508	6.0	10.3	103	1753	6.8	35.8	115	1898	5.3	38.8	90	738	5.6	15.1	95
SANTA BARBARA NBC	1789	*137	1.6	7.7	76	441	1.7	24.7	79	800	2.2	44.7	104	*411	3.1	23.0	145
SCRABBLE NBC	1609	*134	1.6	8.3	83	593	2.3	36.9	119	555	1.5	34.5	80	*328	2.5	20.4	129
SUPER PASSWORD NBC	1523	*181	2.2	11.9	118	450	1.7	29.5	95	715	2.0	46.9	109	*178	1.3	11.7	74
$25,000 PYRAMID CBS	1981	*215	2.6	10.9	108	829	3.2	41.8	135	618	1.7	31.1	72	*322	2.4	16.3	102
WHEEL OF FORTUNE NBC	4885	435	5.2	8.9	88	1871	6.4	34.2	110	2130	5.9	43.6	101	*649	4.9	13.3	84
THE YOUNG AND RESTLESS CBS	4175	*227	2.7	5.4	54	1316	5.1	31.5	101	1802	5.3	45.6	106	731	5.5	17.5	110
EARLY EVENING:																	
EVENING NEWS CBS	11781	1156	13.8	9.8	97	4424	17.1	37.6	121	4285	12.0	36.4	85	1916	14.5	16.3	103
EVENING NEWS-SUN CBS	3651	428	5.1	11.7	116	1410	5.4	38.6	124	1189	3.3	32.6	76	*624	4.7	17.1	108
NIGHTLY NEWS NBC	11637	983	11.8	8.5	85	4257	16.4	36.6	118	4612	12.9	39.6	92	1775	13.4	15.3	96
NIGHTLY NEWS-SAT NBC	8798	847	10.1	9.6	96	3440	13.3	39.1	126	3222	9.0	36.6	85	1290	9.8	14.7	92
NIGHTLY NEWS-SUN NBC	4755	654	7.8	13.8	137	1579	6.1	33.2	107	1753	4.9	36.9	86	769	5.8	16.2	102
SATURDAY NEWS CBS	3936	351	4.2	8.9	89	1530	5.9	38.9	125	1532	4.3	38.9	91	*523	4.0	13.3	84
WORLD NEWS SATURDAY ABC	4907	500	6.0	10.2	101	1535	5.9	31.3	101	1868	5.2	38.1	89	1004	7.6	20.5	129
WORLD NEWS TONIGHT ABC	13848	1291	15.4	9.3	93	4740	18.3	34.2	110	5894	16.4	42.6	99	1923	14.5	13.9	88
WORLD NEWS TONIGHT-SUN ABC	7655	873	10.4	11.4	113	2660	10.3	34.7	112	2824	7.9	36.9	86	1298	9.8	17.0	107
PRIMETIME:																	
ALF NBC	14405	1194	14.2	8.3	82	3254	12.6	22.6	73	7083	19.8	49.2	114	2874	21.7	20.0	126
AMEN NBC	4880	524	6.2	10.7	107	1881	7.3	38.5	124	1808	5.0	37.0	86	668	5.1	13.7	86
CAGNEY & LACEY CBS	9611	843	10.0	8.8	87	3040	11.7	31.6	102	4144	11.6	43.1	100	1584	12.0	16.5	104
CHEERS NBC	18472	1587	19.0	8.6	86	5181	20.0	28.0	90	8796	24.6	47.6	111	2897	21.9	15.7	99
THE COSBY SHOW NBC	26911	2321	27.7	8.6	86	7852	30.3	29.2	94	12071	33.7	44.9	104	4667	35.3	17.3	109
CRIME STORY NBC	5576	629	7.5	11.3	112	1533	5.9	27.5	88	2501	7.0	44.9	104	913	6.9	16.4	103
DALLAS CBS	9152	878	10.5	9.6	95	3628	14.0	39.6	128	3486	9.7	38.1	89	1160	8.8	12.7	80
DESIGNING WOMEN CBS	7531	690	8.2	9.2	91	2246	8.7	29.8	96	3518	9.8	46.7	109	1076	8.1	14.3	90
THE DISNEY HOUR ABC	8920	568	6.8	6.4	63	2224	8.6	24.9	80	4422	12.3	49.6	115	1706	12.9	19.1	121
DYNASTY ABC	6501	526	6.3	8.1	80	2547	9.8	39.2	126	2428	6.8	37.4	87	1000	7.6	15.4	97
THE EQUALIZER CBS	10235	979	11.7	9.6	95	3088	11.9	30.2	97	4294	12.0	42.0	98	1874	14.2	18.3	115
FACTS OF LIFE NBC	7461	586	7.1	8.0	79	2411	9.3	32.3	104	3178	8.9	42.6	99	1278	9.6	17.1	108
FALCON CREST CBS	6264	554	6.6	8.8	88	2529	9.8	40.4	130	2395	6.7	38.2	89	786	5.9	12.5	79
FAMILY TIES NBC	18729	1541	18.4	8.2	82	4846	18.7	25.9	83	8911	24.9	47.6	111	3431	25.9	18.3	115
THE GOLDEN GIRLS NBC	15176	1321	15.7	8.7	86	5743	22.2	37.8	122	6237	17.4	41.1	96	1875	14.2	12.4	78
GROWING PAINS ABC	11815	791	9.4	6.7	67	3122	12.0	26.4	85	5432	15.2	46.0	107	2469	18.7	20.9	132
HEAD OF THE CLASS ABC	8001	541	6.4	6.8	67	2293	8.8	28.7	92	3525	9.8	44.1	103	1641	12.4	20.5	129
HIGHWAY TO HEAVEN NBC	9965	905	10.8	9.1	90	3404	13.1	34.2	110	4045	11.3	40.6	94	1611	12.2	16.2	102
HOTEL ABC	4309	300	3.7	7.2	71	1618	6.2	37.6	121	1716	4.8	39.8	93	664	5.0	15.4	97
HUNTER NBC	9352	804	9.6	8.6	85	2895	11.2	31.0	100	4240	11.8	45.3	105	1414	10.7	15.1	95
KATE & ALLIE CBS	8667	650	7.9	7.6	76	3172	12.2	36.6	118	3592	10.0	41.4	96	1246	9.4	14.4	91
KNOTS LANDING CBS	7361	538	6.4	7.3	73	2512	9.7	34.1	110	3235	9.0	43.9	102	1077	8.1	14.6	92
L A LAW NBC	11529	1027	12.2	8.9	88	3613	13.9	31.3	101	4905	13.7	42.5	99	1985	15.0	17.2	109
MACGYVER ABC	10770	1046	12.5	9.7	96	3400	13.1	31.6	102	4767	13.3	44.3	103	1557	11.8	14.5	91
MAGNUM P.I. CBS	13340	1284	15.3	9.6	96	4163	16.1	31.2	100	5517	15.4	41.4	96	2376	18.0	17.8	112
MARRIED...WITH CHILDREN FOX	2778	257	3.1	9.3	92	841	3.2	30.3	97	1198	3.3	43.1	100	*483	3.7	17.4	110
MATLOCK NBC	10499	982	11.7	9.4	93	4441	17.1	42.3	136	3943	11.0	37.6	87	1133	8.6	10.8	68
MIAMI VICE NBC	12759	1266	15.1	9.9	99	3462	13.4	27.1	87	6078	17.0	47.6	111	1953	14.8	15.3	96
MON. NIGHT AT THE MOVIES NBC	8692	673	8.0	7.7	77	2893	11.2	33.3	107	3500	9.8	40.3	94	1626	12.3	18.7	118
MOONLIGHTING ABC	15034	1163	13.9	7.7	77	3912	15.1	26.0	84	7017	19.6	46.7	109	2943	22.3	19.6	123
MURDER, SHE WROTE CBS	14543	1369	16.3	9.4	94	5957	23.0	41.0	132	5517	15.4	37.9	88	1698	12.8	11.7	74
NEWHART CBS	11546	1060	12.6	9.2	91	3905	15.1	33.8	109	5037	14.1	43.6	101	1545	11.7	13.4	84
NIGHT COURT NBC	14894	1222	14.6	8.2	82	4619	17.8	31.0	100	6701	18.7	45.0	105	2351	17.8	15.8	100
OHARA ABC	5034	602	7.2	12.0	119	1453	5.6	28.9	93	2037	5.7	40.5	94	943	7.1	18.7	118
OUR HOUSE NBC	6697	507	6.0	7.6	75	2149	8.3	32.1	103	2878	8.0	43.0	100	1163	8.8	17.4	109
PERFECT STRANGERS ABC	7373	510	6.1	6.9	69	2042	7.9	27.7	89	3301	9.2	44.8	104	1519	11.5	20.6	130
60 MINUTES CBS	21127	2282	27.3	10.8	108	7798	30.1	36.9	119	8278	23.1	39.2	91	2758	20.9	13.1	82
SLEDGE HAMMER ABC	4638	486	5.8	10.5	104	1342	5.2	28.9	93	2054	5.7	44.3	103	756	5.7	16.3	103
SPENSER: FOR HIRE ABC	8077	730	8.7	9.0	90	2728	10.5	33.8	109	3516	9.8	43.5	101	1105	8.4	13.7	86
ST. ELSEWHERE NBC	7126	689	8.2	9.7	96	2061	8.0	28.9	93	3028	8.5	42.5	99	1348	10.2	18.9	119
SUN. NIGHT AT THE MOVIES NBC	11079	1041	12.4	9.4	93	3899	14.3	33.4	107	4223	11.8	38.1	89	2116	16.0	19.1	120
SUNDAY NIGHT MOVIE CBS	8393	865	10.3	10.3	102	2968	11.5	35.4	114	3180	8.9	37.9	88	1380	10.4	16.4	104
20/20 ABC	15022	1519	18.1	10.1	100	4811	18.6	32.0	103	6042	16.9	40.2	94	2650	20.0	17.6	111
227 NBC	4490	495	5.9	11.0	110	1613	6.2	35.9	116	1717	4.8	38.2	89	664	5.0	14.8	93
VALERIE'S FAMILY NBC	5306	380	4.5	7.2	71	1242	4.8	23.4	75	2467	6.9	46.5	108	1217	9.2	22.9	145
WHO'S THE BOSS ABC	14252	1041	12.4	7.3	73	4184	16.1	29.4	94	6118	17.1	42.9	100	2910	22.0	20.4	129
LATE NIGHT:																	
DAVID LETTERMAN NBC	5519	637	7.6	11.5	115	1639	6.3	29.7	96	2412	6.7	43.7	102	831	6.3	15.1	95
FRIDAY NIGHT VIDEOS NBC	2917	*293	3.5	10.0	100	730	2.8	25.0	80	1241	3.5	42.5	99	*653	4.9	22.4	141
LATE NIGHT - MONDAY CBS	4270	362	4.3	8.5	84	1419	5.5	33.2	107	1678	4.7	39.3	91	810	6.1	19.0	120
LATE NIGHT - WEDNESDAY CBS	2389	*271	3.2	11.3	113	721	2.8	30.2	97	970	2.7	40.6	94	*427	3.2	17.9	113
LATE NIGHT - THURSDAY CBS	3128	*266	3.2	8.5	84	749	2.9	23.9	77	1691	4.7	54.1	126	*423	3.2	13.5	85
LATE NIGHT - FRIDAY CBS	2308	*260	3.1	11.3	112	677	2.6	29.3	94	851	2.4	36.9	86	*519	3.9	22.5	142
NEWS NIGHTLINE ABC	6259	614	7.3	9.8	97	1977	7.6	31.6	102	2731	7.6	43.6	102	936	7.1	15.0	94
SATURDAY NIGHT LIVE NBC	5770	456	5.4	8.7	87	1536	5.9	29.4	95	2259	6.3	43.3	101	969	7.3	18.6	117
SUNDAY NIGHT NEWS CBS	3546	523	6.2	14.7	147	1456	5.6	41.1	132	1137	3.2	32.1	75	*430	3.3	12.1	76
THE LATE SHOW FOX	2465	*206	3.2	10.8	107	887	3.4	36.0	116	886	2.5	35.9	84	*425	3.2	17.2	109

Spring 1988

Results of the audit are used to make suggestions for improvement and as a basis for continued accreditation, but they are not released to the public. Appendix B at the end of the book consists of the EMRC's *Minimum Standards for Electronic Media Rating Research.*

Review

In this chapter we saw that:

- The term *audience* means the number of persons with eyes open and facing the program.
- Vehicle (program) audience involves an estimate of the number of people exposed to a program and can be measured by diary, telephone coincidental, and people-meters.
- Telephone recall studies are used primarily to estimate network radio audiences; telephone coincidental surveys measure media use at the time the telephone call is made.
- Diaries are used for both TV and radio research: for radio, a notebook is given to a person to be filled out throughout the day; TV diaries are assigned to a TV set, not a person.
- The people-meter has the advantages of capturing information almost instantaneously, recording channel and duration of viewing accurately, and recording audience size and composition.
- Single-source research is the combination of purchase and viewing data using a people-meter attached to a TV set and a scanner to record purchases at grocery or drug stores.
- The format for reporting ratings information is average quarter hour (AQH) viewing; the operational definition of a viewer is someone who views a program for at least five minutes.
- Commercial media research companies for radio include Statistical Research, Inc. (SRI), which provides Radio's All-Dimension Audience Research (RADAR); Arbitron, which measures local radio and TV audiences; Simmons Market Research Bureau (SMRB), which estimates average daily cumulative audiences for dayparts, formats, and networks; and Mediamark Research, Inc. (MRI), which estimates radio audiences cross-tabulated with demographic and product usage data.
- Commercial media research companies for television include Arbitron, which measures local TV audiences with meters and diaries; A. C. Nielsen, which provides TV audience measurement through people-meters, TV meters, and diaries; SMRB, which uses two-week diaries to estimate TV audiences and daypart viewing; and MRI, which uses the "yesterday recall" technique to estimate TV audiences.

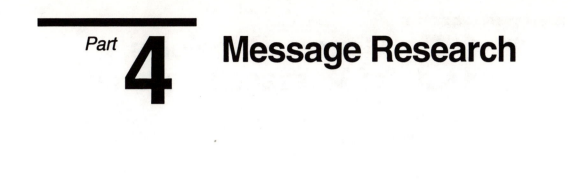

Part **4** **Message Research**

15 General Principles of Message Research

As we have seen in the last few chapters, audience or media research usually involves measurement of the number of people exposed to a vehicle or carrier of advertising, and not necessarily to the advertisement itself. In this chapter and the ones that follow, we will focus on the advertisement as the subject of study and examine the methods we might use to answer the question "Is my advertising effective?"

The terms "message research" and "copy research" are two names for the process of testing the effectiveness of the advertising message. The term "copy" dates back to pre-broadcast times when advertising was primarily made up of the printed word. The use of the term has endured, and researchers can be heard referring to even the testing of a finished commercial as "copy research." A term frequently used to describe testing of the effectiveness of the creative work done in the advertising message is "creative research." In both of these processes— message/copy research and creative research—the focus is on the message, as opposed to the market, the media being used, or the money being spent to advertise.

Three Stages of Message Research: Pretesting, Pilot Testing, and Posttesting

The researcher faces many choices when formulating a copy-testing strategy. Among these is the decision of when to test. Pretesting may involve research prior to creation of the advertising message. For example, concept testing could be employed to help determine which characteristic of a product should be empha- sized in the advertising. Should we have consumers react to storyboards of our commercials? Most often, pretest or precampaign research is conducted with rough copy, or a storyboard in the case of TV commercials. Chapter 16 describes pretest message research methods.

Pilot testing, which involves the use of "smooth" copy but on a small scale geographically, allows the advertiser to assess the effectiveness of the advertisement in a real-world situation without yet committing money to a full-blown media schedule.

Under ideal conditions, a controlled field experiment could be used as a pilot test. The controlled field experiment, as discussed in Chapter 9, has the advantages of random assignment of treatments to subjects, under natural conditions, and includes a behavioral measure, such as calling a 1-800 telephone number, sending in a business reply card, or redeeming a coupon. Examples of controlled field experiment pilot tests are the split-run capabilities offered by some magazines and newspapers, and split-sample direct mail tests. Other pilot-testing possibilities include running an advertisement once in a selected market in an attempt to gauge its effectiveness under natural conditions. These and other pilot-testing procedures will be discussed in Chapter 17.

The posttest, which in this case refers to postcampaign testing, involves measuring the effectiveness of a campaign once it is in large-scale media distribution. Posttests utilize various measures of the advertisement's effect, including recall, recognition, attitude measures, persuasion, inquiries, and sales. One common type of posttest, the tracking study, is designed to assess the impact of a campaign over time.

While posttest research is essential to the advertiser as a means of determining marketplace effectiveness, one major drawback is that it cannot provide the "why" in analyzing results. For example, sales of your product may be low, yet recall of your campaign may be determined to be high. The reason for this discrepancy is difficult if not impossible to tease out. It may be the nature of your creative work, a problem with your product, a hitch in your distribution channels, or the simultaneous marketing efforts of your toughest competitor. A larger problem associated with the use of posttesting research is the difficulty of adjusting the campaign at the late date when posttest results are in. While media placement or frequency levels might still be open to adjustment, it's generally too late to change the creative effort for the current campaign after posttesting. Obviously, lessons learned during the current campaign can be applied to future efforts. Posttest message research will be discussed in Chapter 18.

Reasons for Conducting Message Research

If we keep in mind that the primary purpose for creating advertising is to inform or persuade a particular group of consumers, then it seems prudent to consider consumer reaction to our advertising ideas before we commit all of our funds to the creative effort. Creativity for creativity's sake may win advertising awards and may impress one's advertising peers, but if it doesn't get the message across to the consumer it is a failure. Properly conducted message research can act as a preview of how the message will be received in the ultimate testing ground—the marketplace.

Specifically, researchers can test creative for a number of reasons: to determine which advertising approach or strategy is best to accomplish the marketing objective (such as use of a celebrity spokesperson, demonstration, etc.); to narrow a pool of concepts or ads from a large number to a much smaller number, or maybe even just one; to determine which elements of an ad are the most effective or noticed; to gauge the memorability of a slogan; to signal if a particular campaign is wearing out; and so on.

Issues and Problems Associated with Message Research

Over the years, message research has received more than its share of criticism from creatives, clients, and others associated with the advertising process. Some of the major issues associated with message research practices are discussed below.

Single Exposure versus Multiple Exposure

Most research suggests that a consumer must be exposed to an advertisement three or more times if it is to have its desired effect. Yet in many testing procedures, consumers are allowed to see an advertisement only once and then are asked to react to it. These "once-only" reactions then become the basis for decisions concerning the future of the advertisement. Some believe that single-exposure testing favors the more intrusive or offensive advertisements that leave a distinct impression on first viewing.

Validity of Measures of Effectiveness

The ultimate goal of most advertising is to make a sale. It would seem to follow that sales levels would be the ultimate indicator of the success or failure of an advertising campaign. However, a question of validity arises—if I measure sales, will that be a true indication of advertising effectiveness? The answer is probably not. Many factors can influence sales levels, including climate, legal developments, economic trends, competitors' marketing efforts, and so forth. Obviously, sales figures cannot be ignored, but they might not provide a complete analysis of the effectiveness of an advertising campaign. Other possible measures of advertising effectiveness are recall of an advertisement, attitude toward the advertisement, and measures of consumer persuasion or conviction. These measures are discussed later in the chapter.

Conditions of Exposure

Should message testing be conducted in a natural environment or in the laboratory? This is a question the message tester must answer. There are pros and cons to using either condition of exposure.

Natural environment. It would seem ideal for people to be exposed to advertisements in their "natural" environment so that message testers can get a true reading of their response to it. Often it is highly desirable to conduct a test under what some call "battlefield conditions"—where an advertisement must compete with other advertising and environmental stimuli, such as family members, the telephone, and mother nature. The problem with such naturalistic exposure is that its effect may be difficult to assess if a subject is not exposed to the advertisement at all, is only partially exposed, or is exposed under unfavorable conditions.

Laboratory environment. In contrast to the natural environment, over which the researcher has no influence, laboratory conditions provide for control by the researcher. Subjects in the laboratory are asked to view or read the advertisements under study. This testing environment affords assurance that subjects have seen the message, but it suffers from its artificiality. We do not normally view advertisements because someone is directing us to, nor do we necessarily pay as much attention to them in our living room as we might if we were participating in a study held in a controlled environment.

Sample considerations.

Because of time and money constraints involved with message testing, it is often impossible to obtain a perfect random sample of a client's prospects. Many tests use some type of convenience sample, such as visitors at a shopping mall or some other public place. The potential problem here lies in not getting a sample of the population in question.

In cases where small random samples of populations are used, the matter of sample error also must be taken into account. Many of the syndicated message research services interview anywhere from 100 to 400 respondents. The ability to generalize results of such a small sample to the larger population must be taken into account.

Another sample-related issue facing the researcher is whether to recruit an audience to view a program or read a magazine or to choose a self-selected audience made up of people who, on their own initiative, were exposed to the vehicle carrying the advertising. Recruited audiences are called ahead of time and asked to watch a specific program that they might not otherwise have viewed. This calls into question whether their viewing can be considered "normal" since they were requested specifically to do so.

Rough versus finished ads. Because testing of the creative effort can be conducted at any point in the production process, often it is more cost-efficient to test a rough or unfinished advertisement rather than a finished one. Examples of rough executions range from pencil sketches of print ads to storyboards or animatics (simulated commercial using storyboard frames and background music) for television.

Three basic formats for testing rough commercials on videotape are the animatic, the photomatic, and the live-action rough. The three methods have roughly the same production cost, but experts disagree over which yields results closest to the finished commercial.

Animatics use hand-drawn artwork (such as pictures of the frames from a storyboard) and camera techniques such as zooming and panning to impart a sense of motion.

Photomatics use real photographs rather than hand-drawn art, and camera techniques similar to those of the animatic to achieve motion. They are generally considered to be better "surrogates" for actual commercials than animatics unless an actual commercial is to be animated.

Live-action roughs use actors on videotape where shots of people are called for, and full normal motion is possible. A study by Gallup & Robinson has shown that live-action roughs provide effectiveness scores closest to those of the finished commercial.

One problem with using rough executions in testing is their potential lack of believability. Animatics, for example, look a lot like cartoons. Therefore they might appear frivolous or unprofessional to the average consumer, who is accustomed to seeing only finished commercials on television. An even more serious problem can result when advertisements at different stages of completion are tested against each other. Consumers might prefer a finished commercial over an animatic because it appears more polished, not necessarily because of its content.

Aided versus unaided recall.

Message testers measure recall by determining whether consumers can remember having been exposed to a message and can relate specific information about its contents. In an unaided recall situation, respondents are asked to name any advertisements they might have seen or heard in media the previous day solely from memory. With aided recall, the respondent is given either a category prompt, such as "Did you see any dishwashing liquid commercials during the program?" or a brand prompt, such as "Did you see a commercial for Lux Liquid dishwashing soap on the program?" Aided recall actually measures both recall and recognition—whether the respondent recognizes the category or brand name of a product. As you might expect, aided recall measures generally yield higher scores than do unaided ones.

Variations in testing criteria.

An advertiser who wishes to test an ad potentially has dozens, or even hundreds, of options related to any or all of the following factors:

- whether the ad is rough or finished
- whether the ad is to be placed in real media or evaluated on its own
- which program or editorial environment will be used

- whether testing should be done in a natural or laboratory environment
- whether a recruited or self-selected audience should be used
- how many times subjects will be exposed to the ad
- what measures of effectiveness will be chosen
- what level of results will be accepted for the measures chosen
- what sample of people will participate in the test

Researchers who began planning a copy research validity project quickly discovered that a complete experiment covering all aspects of copy research would involve some 6,840 design cells, or separate testing options, and would cost in the neighborhood of $2 billion![1]

Interestingly there is very little agreement among experts about which options yield the best results. The wide variety of commercial services is a testament to that fact.

Disagreement about effectiveness measures.

The subject of how to measure the effects of advertising has a long history and is still a topic of considerable debate today. Any discussion of the effectiveness of an advertisement requires appropriate qualifications, definitions, and caveats. Consider the following situations:

- Simultaneous with the June debut of your new advertising campaign for Lotsafizz soda are the coldest summer temperatures in a decade. Sales are lower than the monthly average for June. How effective was your campaign? Is it possible to separate the effects of your campaign from the effects of the weather?

- A tracking study of your Lotsafizz campaign reveals high recall of your brand name and product attributes among your target market, yet your sales are down. Was the Lotsafizz campaign successful?

After reviewing current models and measures of advertising effectiveness, researcher David Stewart found that much message research in recent years has run counter to his conclusion that there does not exist a single best absolute measure of advertising effectiveness. In fact, the nature of the advertising response function is affected by what is measured, when, and in what environment.[2] The two most frequently used measures—recall and persuasion—have been found to have an inconsistent relationship. Recall may be a necessary element of persuasion, but it is not sufficient in itself to cause a change in consumer behavior.

Stewart divides common advertising response function research into four areas: memorability measures, environmental factors, attitude measures, and action measures. Reliability and validity tests on a variety of such measures within and between each of the four major categories have shown that these measures do not necessarily have consistent, linear relationships. In other words, recall could be high, but persuasion may be low. A recent study on the effectiveness of advertising techniques reveals the most important determinant of success is a brand-differentiating message. Commercial messages that clearly stated a point of differentiation for their products had the highest persuasion scores of all commercials in a large-scale test.[3]

The ARF Copy Research Validity Project

A study conducted by the Advertising Research Foundation attempted to determine which copytesting methods and measures were good predictors of how advertising works in the marketplace. Five pairs of television commercials that had produced major sales differences in split-cable test markets were used for the study. Researchers already knew which commercial in each pair had resulted in significantly greater sales in a carefully controlled field experiment. Each pair was then tested by three on-air (viewing done in the home) and three off-air companies that used agreed-upon criteria formulated by the ARF. Measures included persuasion, salience (awareness), recall, communication, commercial reaction (liking), and commercial diagnostics (explanatory questions).

The study concluded that advertising copytesting systems work. When tested in similar market conditions, commercials that had been shown to result in greater sales for a product usually were shown to be more effective by a number of pretest copytesting methods in common use by advertisers. Among the several specific findings of the copy research validity project were:

- Top-of-mind awareness (asking which brands come to mind when given a category prompt) correctly identified the winning commercial from each pair 73 percent of the time.
- Reaction to commercials in the form of a like–dislike scale had a better prediction record than any other measure, correctly predicting the winning commercial from each pair 87 percent of the time.
- Use of a recall measure with only a product category prompt picked the winning commercial 87 percent of the time (but had a lower index of significant scores than the commercial reaction measure).
- Recall measures that used a minimum of prompting of respondents were more effective at picking winning commercials than those which used several prompts or probes.
- Communication measures of "main point" communication and playback of the ad situation and visuals predicted correctly 60 percent and 67 percent, respectively.
- Diagnostic measures, considered by many as explanatory material for other measures such as persuasion, emerged as surprisingly good predictors of winning commercials (87 percent). An example of a diagnostic item used in the study was: "I learned a lot from this advertising." Items were scored on a 5-point scale of agreement–disagreement.

The Extent of Message Research in Advertising

Research practices used in copy development, pretesting, and posttesting run the gamut from very simple, inexpensive qualitative methods to more costly evaluation procedures using real media. There seems to be no single favorite method, and each agency or advertiser has its own approach to employing preferred techniques or services. Historically, the agency has had primary responsibility for research involving copy development and most pretesting, while the advertiser has been responsible for evaluation of the advertising campaign after its placement in major media.

In 1984 the Advertising Research Foundation conducted a survey of leading advertisers and agencies to determine the extent of their use of various message research practices. The study was repeated again in 1989 with a few modifications.

In a 1988 survey by the Association of National Advertisers (ANA), corporate advertising managers were asked about their use of message research, specifically pretesting and posttesting studies, for corporate campaigns. Slightly more than two-thirds of respondents said they pretest their corporate advertising, and half of them said they did so with focus groups. Other methods used were the one-on-one interview and the splitrun. Results of the questions about pretesting are contained in Tables 15–1 and 15–2.

Table 15–1
Pretesting Advertising

There were no major changes reported in the pretesting of advertising from last year. The number of companies pretesting advertising has risen slightly, from 65.3% last year to 68.5% in 1988. (Nonmembers report somewhat less pretesting, at 57.9% of respondents.) Focus groups continue to be the most popular form, with one-on-one copy testing in second place.

	1987 Survey (72 Respondents)		1988 Survey (92 Respondents)	
	Number	Percentage	Number	Percentage
Do you pretest advertising?				
Yes	47	65.3%	63	68.5%
No	25	34.7	29	31.5
How?				
Focus group	37	51.4	49	53.3
One-on-one	20	27.8	29	31.5
Split-run	4	5.6	1	1.1
Other	5	6.9	10	10.9

Source: Association of National Advertisers, 1988.

Table 15–2
Tracking Advertising

Slightly fewer advertisers (85.6%) tracked their advertising compared to last year's 90.3%. However, these appear to be using awareness and attitude studies even more frequently than in the past—81.4% in 1988 versus 72.2% in 1987. This is certainly a more reliable measure than checking stock prices, a method which dropped in use from 5.6% last year to one holdout this year. (Non-ANA members exhibited a similar preference, with 88.9% using some form of tracking method and 77.8% using awareness and attitude studies.)

	1987 Survey (72 Respondents)		1988 Survey (97 Respondents)	
	Number	*Percentage*	*Number*	*Percentage*
Do you track advertising results?				
Yes	65	90.3%	83	85.6%
No	7	9.7	14	14.4
How?				
Awareness/attitude	52	72.2	79	81.4
Mail/phone response	19	26.4	20	20.6
Increase in sales	9	12.5	12	12.4
Stock price	4	5.6	1	1.0
Profits	—	—	—	—
Other	3	4.2	4	4.1

Source: Association of National Advertisers, 1988.

Industry Guidelines and Recommendations for Message Testing

To the extent that a company's profitability depends on effective advertising, the selection and implementation of a system for choosing among advertising alternatives is clearly a critical matter. The message-testing needs of advertisers often are quite different, and it is important that the system chosen fit those specific needs. Because of the individual considerations to be addressed by the testing methods, it is pointless to attempt a ranking. Rather, industry organizations have focused on the criteria for choosing and then using testing procedures. Two major documents have been produced to address these issues.

The ANA Document

Choosing the Best Advertising Alternative: A Management Guide to Identifying the Most Effective Copy Testing Technique was first published in 1971 by the Association of National Advertisers. In the foreword to the 1986 reprinted edition, author Joel Axelrod lamented that not much had changed since the document was originally conceived:

> It is certainly evident that the marketer who attempted to use this book to guide his/her selection process must be frustrated. Only one firm has developed a print and commercial testing system consistent with the model but there has been no validation.[4]

The ANA document recommends four steps in testing alternative advertising communications.

1. Select a single criterion measure.

Ideally, sales would be the testing criterion for effective advertising. But for reasons discussed earlier regarding uncontrollable influences on advertising, the sales criterion is not always a true reflection of advertising effectiveness. Alternatives to the sales criterion are measures of awareness, attitude change, and persuasion. Most services offer all of these measures, so the problem becomes choosing among them. The use of multiple independent criteria can result in decision-making dilemmas, as in the following example:

	Commercial A	Commercial B
Recall	20	33
Attitude change	8	2

This situation, in which one commercial scores high on recall and the other on attitude change, leaves the manager to choose one criterion over the other. If the decision about which criterion is more important has not been made ahead of time, the choice could be a difficult one. If a single measure has not been designated as the basis for acceptance, the ANA document recommends that a formula reflecting the importance assigned to each of several variables be used to make a decision. An example might be: 65 percent attitude change + 35 percent copy point recall.

2. Design the test so that the respondent is not aware that the true purpose of the interview is to assess the effects of exposure to an advertisement.

3. Expose the individual to the stimulus in a naturalistic environment, such as the home.

4. Set up multiple exposure situations. This ensures a more realistic assessment of the effects of the advertisement.

The PACT Document

In 1982, top research executives from 21 leading American agencies collaborated on a document intended to outline fundamental message-testing principles. The document, *Positioning of Advertising Copy Testing* (PACT), provides the advertising agency viewpoint on the testing controversy and takes into account both management's need for "go/no go" criteria and creatives' need for guidance. Figure 15–1 contains the nine PACT principles.

Figure 15–1
Principles of Advertising Copy Testing

PACT PRINCIPLES

The shared views of PACT Agencies on the fundamental principles underlying a good copy testing system.

Principle I

A good copy testing system provides measurements which are relevant to the objectives of the advertising.

Advertising is used (as are all marketing tools) to contribute to the achievement of marketing objectives—whether they be for a product, a service, or a corporation. The industry recognizes (as exemplified by the landmark "DAGMAR" [*Defining Advertising Goals for Measured Advertising Results:* Copyright 1961 by Association of National Advertisers] study of the ANA) that the goal of advertising is to achieve specified objectives. And it is further recognized that different advertisements can have a number of objectives. For example:

- Reinforcing current perceptions
- Encouraging trial of a product or service
- Encouraging new users of a product or service
- Providing greater saliency for a brand or company name
- Changing perceptions and imagery
- Announcing new features and benefits

To be useful, a copy test for a given advertisement should be designed to provide an assessment of the advertisement's potential for achieving its stated objectives. Indeed, advertising objectives should be the first issue for discussion when a copy testing program is to be developed or a particular method is to be selected. In recognition of the fundamental importance of these objectives, every copy testing proposal and every report on results should begin with a clear statement of the advertising objectives.

Principle II

A good copy testing system is one which requires agreement about how the results will be used *in advance* of each specific test.

A primary purpose of copy testing is to *help* in deciding whether or not to run the advertising in the marketplace. A useful approach is to specify what are called "action standards" before the results are in. Some examples of possible action standards are:

- Significantly improve perceptions of the brand as measured by ____ .
- Achieve an attention level of no lower than ____ % as measured by ____ .
- Perform at least as well as (specify execution) as measured by ____ .
- Produce negative response of no higher than ____ % as measured by ____ .

The practice of specifying how the results will be used before the results are in insures that there is mutual understanding on the goals of the test—and it minimizes conflicting interpretations of the test once the results are in.

Moreover, prior discussion allows for the proper positioning of the action standards since the copy test results are not, in most cases, the sole information source when deciding whether to use a particular advertisement. The results of any given copy test should be viewed in the context of a body of learning. Thus, prior discussion should take into account:

- How well the particular copy testing method being used relates to the objectives of the advertising
- The *range* of results which are realistically achievable for the advertising approach used and for the brand or company in question
- The entire research context (including other types of studies) for the tested ad and for similar ads

A discussion of these issues prior to initiating a copy test provides benefits for both the advertiser and the agency. It minimizes the risks which are inherent in using copy test results in a mechanistic way, isolated from other learning. It maximizes the opportunity to draw upon the learning and seasoned judgment of the advertiser and the agency as both parties reach for the best possible advertising.

Principle III

A good copy testing system provides *multiple* measurements—because single measurements are generally inadequate to assess the performance of an advertisement.

With the exception of corporate advocacy advertising, it is commonly believed that the ultimate measurement by which advertising should be judged is its *contribution* to sales. But the complexity of the marketing process (and the constraints of time and money) usually preclude rigorous testing—that is, testing which can separate out the effects of advertising from the many other factors influencing sales and thereby provide an estimate of the sales contribution of a given advertisement prior to a national launch. Nor is there any universally accepted single measurement which can serve as a surrogate for sales.

Moreover, the communications process is complex. To understand this process, and to learn from each successive test, it is necessary to use multiple measures—measures which reflect the multi-faceted nature of communications. However, the inclusion of multiple measures should not imply that all measures have equal weight in evaluating the advertising. As noted previously, in advance of each test, agreement should be reached as to the relative importance of the various measurements in judging the acceptability of the tested execution.

Principle IV

A good copy testing system is based on a model of human response to communication—the *reception* of a stimulus, the *comprehension* of the stimulus and the *response* to the stimulus.

PACT agencies view advertising as performing on several levels. To succeed, an advertisement must have an effect:

- on the "eye," on the "ear": *It must be received* (RECEPTION)
- on the "mind": *It must be understood* (COMPREHENSION)
- on the "heart": *It must make an impression* (RESPONSE)

It therefore follows that a good copy testing system should answer a number of questions. Listed below are examples of the kinds of questions relevant to these communications issues. The order of the listing does not relate to priority of importance. As discussed in the preceding principles, priorities will vary depending on the objectives of the specific advertising being tested.

- Reception
  - Did the advertising "get through"?
  - Did it catch the consumer's attention?
  - Was it remembered?
  - Did it catch his eye? His ear?
- Comprehension
  - Was the advertising understood?
  - Did the consumer "get" the message?
  - Was the message identified with the brand?
  - Was anything confusing or unclear?
- Response
  - Did the consumer accept the proposition?
  - Did the advertising affect attitudes toward the brand?
  - Did the consumer think or "feel" differently about the brand after exposure?
  - Did the advertising affect perceptions of the brand?
  - Did the advertising affect perceptions of the set of competing brands?
  - Did the consumer respond to direct action appeals?

Another area of response measurements relates to executional elements. PACT agencies agree that it is useful to obtain responses to:

- Executional Diagnostics: Questioning about consumers' reactions to the advertising execution (e.g. perceived differentiation from other advertising, reactions to music, to key phrases, to presenters or characters, to story elements, etc.) can provide insight about the strengths and weaknesses of the advertising and why it performed as it did.

PACT agencies use different measures to address the issues in these four areas. However, they are all based on the same fundamental understanding of the communications process.

Principle V

A good copy testing system allows for consideration of whether the advertising stimulus should be exposed more than once.

Extensive experimentation in the field of communications and learning has demonstrated that learning of test material is far higher after two exposures than after one—and that subsequent exposures do not yield as large an increase as that between the first and second exposure.

In light of the experimental work, PACT agencies share the view that the issue of single versus multiple exposures should be carefully considered in each test situation. There are situations in which a single exposure would be sufficient—given the objectives of the advertising and the nature of the test methodology. There are other situations where a single exposure could be inadequate—particularly for high risk situations or for subtle or complex communications or for questioning about executional diagnostics.

Principle VI

A good copy testing system recognizes that the more finished a piece of copy is, the more soundly it can be evaluated and requires, as a minimum, that alternative executions be tested in the same degree of finish.

Experience has shown that test results can often vary depending on the degree of finish of the test executions. Thus, careful judgment should be used in considering the importance of what may be lost in a less than finished version. Sometimes this loss may be inconsequential; sometimes it may be critical.

The judgment of the creators of the advertising should be given great weight as to the degree of finish required to represent the finished advertisement for test purposes. If there is reason to believe that alternative executions would be unequally penalized in preproduction form, then it is generally advisable to test them in a more finished form. If alternative executions are tested in different stages of finish within the same test, then it is not possible to insure that the results are not biased due to the varying degrees of finish.

Principle VII

A good copy testing system provides controls to avoid the biasing effects of the exposure context.

Extensive work in the field of communications and learning has demonstrated that the perception of and response to a stimulus is affected by the context in which the stimulus is presented.

In the case of advertising, it has been demonstrated, for example, that recall of the same commercial can vary depending on a number of conditions—such as, whether exposure to the commercial:

- Is off-air versus on-air
- Is in a clutter reel of commercials versus a program context
- Is in one specific program context versus another specific program context

Thus, PACT Agencies share the view that it is imperative to control the biasing effects of variable exposure contexts.

Principle VIII

A good copy testing system is one that takes into account basic considerations of sample definition.

- The testing should be conducted among a sample of the target audience for the advertised product. Limiting testing to the general population without provision for separate analysis of the target audience can be misleading.
- The sample should be representative of the target audience. To the degree that the sample drawn does not represent the target audience, the users of the research should be informed about the possible effects of the lack of representativeness on the interpretation of test results.
- The sample should take into account any geographical differences if they are critical to the assessment of the performance of a brand or service.
- The sample should be of sufficient size to allow a decision based on the obtained data to be made with confidence.

Principle IX

A good copy testing system is one that can demonstrate reliability and validity.

To provide results which can be used with confidence, a copy testing system should be:

- *Reliable:* it should yield the same results each time that the advertising is tested. If, for example, a test of multiple executions does not yield the same rank order of performance or test/retest, the test is not reliable and should not be used to judge the performance of commercials. Tests in which external variables are not held constant will probably yield unreliable results.
- *Valid:* it should provide results which are relevant to marketplace performance. PACT Agencies recognize that demonstration of validity is a major and costly undertaking requiring industrywide participation.

While some evidence of predictive validity is available, many systems are in use for which no evidence of validity is provided. We encourage the cooperation of advertisers and agencies in pursuit of this critical need.

ISSUES WHICH MERIT FURTHER EFFORT AND INVESTIGATION

PACT agencies share a view of how we can contribute to continued improvement of copy testing procedures and of how we can make full use of copy testing approaches.

To contribute to improvement in copy testing:

- We must continually examine the reliability and validity of what we do, and support industry efforts to examine these critical issues.

- We must foster an attitude of experimentation, looking for improvements in present methods and exploring the capabilities of new approaches and new learning.

To make full use of copy testing:

- We must continually demonstrate how copy tests can be used both to *learn* about how and why an ad works and to help *decide* whether to use an ad.

- We must take a leadership role in seeing that copy tests are used in a *balanced* way—to contribute to creative development and to identify effective advertising.

- We must work to insure that research results and informed professional judgment are properly *blended* in arriving at decisions about what is effective advertising.

For further information about PACT, contact:

PACT CHAIRWOMAN: Sonia Yuspeh, J. Walter Thompson Company, 466 Lexington Avenue, New York, New York 10017

PACT DEPUTY CHAIRMAN: Ted Dunn, Benton & Bowles, 909 Third Avenue, New York, New York 10022

PACT DEPUTY CHAIRMAN: Joe Plummer, Young & Rubicam, 285 Madison Avenue, New York, New York 10017

Source: PACT Agencies.

Review

In this chapter we saw that:

- Message research focuses on determining whether an advertisement is effective; its three stages are pretesting, pilot testing, and posttesting.

- Major issues to be considered in message research are single exposure versus multiple exposure; validity of measures of effectiveness; and conditions of exposure.
- The Association of National Advertisers has established guidelines for message testing: (1) Select a single criterion measure; (2) Design the test so that the respondent is not aware that the true purpose of the interview is to assess the effects of exposure to an advertisement; (3) Expose the individual to the stimulus in a naturalistic environment, such as the home; and (4) Set up multiple exposure situations.
- There does not exist a single best, absolute measure of advertising effectiveness; the two most frequently used measures—recall and persuasion—have been found to have an inconsistent relationship.

Endnotes

1. Russell Haley and Allan Baldinger, "The ARF Copy Research Validity Project," *Journal of Advertising Research,* April/May 1991, pp. 11–32.
2. David Stewart and Scott Koslow, "Executional Factors and Advertising Effectiveness: A Replication," *Journal of Advertising* 18, no. 3, 1989, pp. 21–32.
3. David Stewart, "Measures, Methods, and Models in Advertising Research," *Journal of Advertising Research,* June/July 1989, pp. 54–60.
4. Joel Axelrod, *Choosing the Best Advertising Alternative: A Management Guide to Identifying the Most Effective Copy Testing Technique,* rev. ed. (New York: Association of National Advertisers, 1986).

Chapter **16** Message Pretesting

Chapter

Message pretesting is conducted before an advertisement is scheduled in major media. It can occur at the very early stage of concept development or at the point when rough or even finished executions of advertisements are available. A distinction should be made between testing of advertising concept and testing its message. The purpose of testing a concept is to determine which is the most appropriate or best approach to emphasize. An example would be whether to stress the durability of a washing machine, its variety of washing cycles, or some other feature. The general purpose for pretesting advertising messages is to determine whether any problems are associated with the concept, strategy, or execution of the idea before committing a media budget to the advertising. Once advertising messages are placed in major media, it is too late to make adjustments. Pretesting, if conducted properly, can serve as a form of creative risk insurance for the advertiser.

Some popular methods of testing creative ideas and/or executions include the focus group discussion, the one-on-one interview, and a host of projective techniques. Mechanical devices that measure physiological responses to advertising stimuli provide another method of determining the effects of a given advertisement.

General Pretesting Guidelines

Much advertising today is not subjected to testing before it is placed in major media, despite obvious risks involved in allowing creative judgment or some other nonscientific means to determine advertising effectiveness. As we saw in Chapter 15, however, most of the top advertisers employ some form of message testing.

There exists little agreement among researchers about which method of testing is best. Much of the available comparative research is proprietary in nature and hence unavailable to those who do not own it. Most researchers do agree, however, that some general guidelines for pretesting are desirable. Below are some suggestions obtained from Advertising Research Foundation conferences and other sources.

How to Test

1. Copy research should be conducted among the target prospects for the specific brand.

Studies have shown that consumers of a particular brand often respond differently from nonprospects.

2. Copy research should be part of an integrated research plan and should be preceded by information about what to communicate to which audience.

The total research plan should address the following areas: market and motivation research, to define goals for a product at a certain point in its life cycle; concept research, to determine which characteristic of the product to emphasize; copy research, to determine the optimum execution of the chosen concept; and effectiveness testing, to track advertising performance in its natural environment over time.

3. Methods should be developed to test entire campaigns, rather than single advertisements or commercials.

When only one commercial or advertisement is tested, it is difficult to predict the impact of the total campaign in the actual market environment.

What to Measure

1. Copy research should not only test reaction to the advertising, but also to the product advertised.

Consumer evaluation of the advertisement itself can be quite different from evaluation of the product being advertised.

2. Copy research should contain diagnostic information to determine why an advertisement does or does not work.

True understanding of why an advertisement is or is not effective cannot be obtained without analyzing its individual elements.

3. Copy research methods must be validated.

Most copy testing systems assume that advertisement effectiveness in the testing situation will translate into effectiveness in the marketplace. This must be confirmed by basic research.

How to Use Results

1. Copy researchers should coordinate their efforts with those responsible for creating the advertising message.

A copy tester should work closely with creative and account service personnel to ensure proper understanding of the intended impact of the advertising and to help interpret the results of the copy testing.

2. Sales goals of the advertisers must be recognized in copy testing procedures.

Although many different phenomena can contribute to the sales figures for a given product, the copy researcher should attempt to identify the communication measures that are most relevant to sales effectiveness.

3. Copy research should lead to the development of general principles of advertisement construction.

Over time, research conducted to answer immediate questions must be synthesized to provide guidelines for future advertising development. This will require extensive record-keeping of advertisement performance both in the laboratory environment and in the marketplace.

Pretest Methods

Focus Group Discussions

As we saw in Chapter 6, the focus group method lends itself to a variety of applications in the advertising research context. Focus groups can allow extensive consumer input into the creative deliberations of the advertiser by discussing general ideas or advertising approaches, evaluating the competitors' advertising, or reacting to specific strategies or executions.

Focus groups can be used for testing of either rough or finished advertisements. Unfinished versions of magazine or newspaper advertisements can be used to test headlines or other copy elements. Storyboards, animatics, or other rough material can be used to test commercials.

Focus group interviews offer the benefit of individual as well as group reaction to the advertisement. Focus group moderators can be flexible in their line of questioning, paying special attention to key elements that seem particularly effective, distracting, offensive, or annoying. Two focus group scenarios might include:

- Presenting and discussing the current Lotsafizz advertising campaign, followed by the acted-out storyboard presentation of three new commercial ideas. The ensuing discussion compares the old with the new and includes reaction to the three new ideas.

- Evaluating several different messages used to communicate a new product feature to consumers; for example, a new carbonation process to make Lotsafizz soda more bubbly.

One-on-One Interview

An alternative to the focus group method is the one-on-one interview. Although the benefit of group interaction is not possible with this type of test, some researchers believe that individual consumers often will "open up" about their true feelings about an advertisement if they do not fear being embarrassed in front of their peers. Another advantage of the one-on-one interview is the comparative ease of recruiting a single subject versus a larger group. Much one-on-one recruiting is conducted in shopping mall settings, where researchers identify a potential subject by sight and conduct a brief interview to confirm the desired demographic profile. The subject is then escorted into a viewing room to see the advertisements to be tested, and an in-depth discussion of the person's reactions to the advertisement follows.

Telephone Interview

Several companies test advertising by interviewing respondents over the telephone. In many cases this involves recruiting audiences to watch a particular program or read a magazine and then telephoning them the next day to obtain their evaluation of advertisements. In other instances, participants in a one-on-one interview or other ad exposure situation might be re-interviewed after a period of time to measure the memorability of a commercial or attitude shift. Those who advocate use of the telephone interview emphasize the importance of the use of random sampling procedures to obtain representative samples of residents with telephones.

Large Group/Auditorium Format

Certain economies of scale can be achieved by exposing and then measuring large groups of respondents simultaneously, either by paper-and-pencil questionnaires or in conjunction with a mechanical device such as the program analyzer. (Program analyzers will be discussed later in the chapter.) Recruiting for large groups is done by issuing invitations to a program screening at a central location, via mail or by telephone. Commercials can be shown on a large screen or on individual television monitors placed around the location.

The obvious advantage of measuring large groups is efficiency and economy, while the primary disadvantage is potential contamination of results due to respondents conferring with one another or otherwise being affected by the testing environment.

Laboratory Observation

In certain situations it is possible to obtain physiological feedback resulting from exposure to advertising from a variety of mechanical devices. These machines are used in laboratory settings to insure a controlled exposure and testing environment. Those who advocate use of the laboratory and mechanical devices point to their accuracy and objectivity as main advantages. Those who criticize such an approach cite the "unnaturalness" of the laboratory setting compared with a real world environment as a major disadvantage.

Stimulus Presentation/Context

Presentation Environment

A researcher can choose from several different presentation environments for either a rough or finished ad. Simply presenting the ad alone, sometimes called a "naked presentation," has the advantages of focusing maximum attention on the ad stimulus and ensuring exposure on the part of respondents. An in-program test, on the other hand, places the ad in a real or fictitious program in the belief that exposure will be more natural. Programs can be shown in an auditorium, in one-on-one settings, or by way of videotapes that can be mailed to a sample of respondents. The print advertising equivalent of an in-program test involves the use of a real or fictitious magazine or newspaper into which test ads can be placed. When a radio or television program or a print vehicle is produced solely for the purpose of testing, it is called a test or "dummy" vehicle. ASI's *Reflections* magazine and Video Storyboard Tests' *Looking At Us* are examples of dummy publications.

Rough versus Finished Commercials

Because of the tremendous expense associated with the full-scale production of a television commercial, much discussion has centered around whether it is necessary to test a finished commercial in order to obtain an accurate evaluation. Some research purists argue that a finished commercial must be used to obtain accurate results; others maintain that pre-finished versions are suitable. The three major forms in which commercials are tested are the storyboard, the rough commercial, and the finished commercial.

The storyboard represents the artist's first rendering of the major elements of the commercial. It usually is composed of a series of illustrations or photographs that depict the visual elements. The illustrations are accompanied by dialog and sound effects information below each frame. Typically these items are mounted or drawn on poster board. In the most elementary form of testing, the board itself could serve as the visual stimulus while a narrator reads the verbal information and gestures to the individual frames. One variation of this basic method involves adaptation of the storyboard material by way of slide presentation with an audiotape of sound elements. These "animatics" are essentially the storyboard shot on videotape with a few visual and audio enhancements.

Rough commercials are simply scaled-down versions of the real thing. They involve improvised or "stock" scenery and available personnel as talent, and they use an early version of the commercial script. A photomatic uses photographs on videotape, while a live-action rough commercial involves live filming of actors. Some advertising agencies maintain production facilities that enable them to produce such rough versions of commercials in-house. Others use a production studio. It is possible to produce and test several different rough commercial arrangements in just a few days at a fraction of the cost of producing a single finished commercial. Ideally, the best rough or a combination of the best elements of several roughs can be combined to create the final, desired effect.

The finished commercial probably provides the best overall testing stimulus, but as mentioned earlier, time and money constraints often preclude the researcher from evaluating creative ideas for TV in finished form. An additional dilemma might arise if the finished commercial does not score well in testing. Should the advertiser go ahead with an expensive, but possibly ineffective commercial that has already been produced, or scrap it and go back to the drawing board?

A potential hazard exists in situations where commercial ideas in varying stages of finish are tested against each other. Some agencies will test a commercial from an existing campaign or some other commercial in finished form against a rough commercial. The danger here is that the degrees of finish might confound the results. In other words, it may be impossible to determine if viewer evaluation is a result of the commercial idea or because of how "polished" it was. As with many other situations, a well-rehearsed, slick presentation often is more credible in the eyes of viewers—despite its content—than is an awkward, first effort (most animatics, for instance, look like cartoons). The apparent solution to this problem is to test finished commercials only against finished commercials, and so forth. Every effort should be made to hold to a minimum the role that production variables play in viewers' evaluations.

Pretest Measures

Though some of the earliest copy testing methods used only recall as a measure of effectiveness, now it is typical for copy tests to include multiple measures of effectiveness. This is due in part to the lack of validity tests which relate effectiveness measures to sales. The practice of using multiple measures is also a reflection of the many and often different objectives that advertising is designed to achieve. Some advertisements are primarily informational, some are more persuasive, some use memorable music, and so forth.

Awareness

Consumer awareness can be measured for both a brand and its advertising. In some cases, the researcher is interested in whether respondents are aware of a particular campaign or slogan. In other instances the measure is intended to determine which brand or brands are named first when a product category is mentioned. One way of asking this unaided top-of-mind awareness question is as follows:

> When you think of root beer, what are all the brands you think of?

Of primary interest in evaluating responses to a top-of-mind item is the first brand name mentioned. The question can also be asked in aided fashion by calling out a list of brands and asking respondents to say whether they are aware of each.

Recall

The memorability of an ad can be calculated in a number of ways. A completely unaided approach would involve asking which, if any, commercials a respondent can recall having seen on a particular program. Use of a brand cue might ask a qualified magazine reader if she can remember having seen an ad for Honda automobiles in a given issue. In the ARF copy research validity project, the recall questions using only the product category prompt identified winning commercials more often than other methods. The question was asked as follows:

> On the show you just saw, do you remember seeing a commercial for
> a brand of _____ ? (If yes) What brand was that? _____

Communication/Playback

Whether a viewer or reader can recall specific information from an advertisement is considered an important measure of its effectiveness. Researchers use a number of approaches to determine this, including the use of questions about the main point of the commercial, or an invitation to recreate the visual and verbal elements of an ad in one's own words. In the ARF copy validity project, a main point message question like the one below was used:

> Of course the purpose of the commercial was to get you to buy the
> product. Other than that what was the main point of the commercial?

Persuasion/Conviction/Buying Attitude

While the overall rating of a brand does not necessarily reflect the effectiveness of its advertising, rating is often asked in conjunction with measures that address the persuasion power of the ad. When used before and after exposure to an ad for a brand, it can serve as a measure of how persuasive the message was. The image of the brand and the advertising can be linked in the following manner:

Based on the commercial you just saw, how would you rate the brand in the commercial on an overall basis using the following words?

- excellent
- very good
- good
- fair
- not so good
- poor

The persuasion item can take other forms, asking subjects to respond to statements such as "I definitely will buy" a particular brand, or using a market-basket question that allows a consumer to choose from among different brands of prize or gift products, or to allocate a certain amount of "prize" money to one or more brands. Again, though these types of questions do not directly address the advertising, a shift in brand preference after exposure to advertising is considered a strong positive signal about the power of the message. Though a market-basket vote is somewhat short of marketplace behavior, advocates of these measures argue that it is a closer determinant of behavior than other communication or attitude-related measures.

Reaction/Attitude toward the Advertisement

Several studies have shown that commercial preference has a strong relationship with an ad's effect on sales. Whether an ad is designed to be informative, entertaining, or persuasive, many believe that its likability is a good predictor of its success. There are numerous ways of gauging how likable an individual ad is. Two examples are offered below:

1. Please choose the statement below which best describes your feelings about the commercial you just saw.
   - I liked it very much.
   - I liked it.
   - I neither liked nor disliked it.
   - I disliked it.
   - I disliked it very much.

2. Please indicate your level of agreement or disagreement with the following statement about the ad you just saw.

"This ad is one of the best I've seen recently."

- strongly agree
- agree
- neither agree nor disagree
- disagree
- strongly disagree

Diagnostics

A category of items called diagnostics can provide explanation for other evaluative measures. These items usually take the form of statements used to describe the ad, to which a respondent replies by agreeing or disagreeing. Diagnostic items used in the ARF validity project included the following:

- The advertising tells me a lot about how the product works.
- This advertising is funny or clever.
- I learned a lot from this advertising.
- This advertising told me something new about the product that I didn't know before.
- This advertising helps me to find the product that I want.
- This advertising is enjoyable.
- I find this advertising artistic.

Ad/Ad Component Preference

In some testing situations pairs of ads are presented and respondents are asked which they like better and why. If several competing executions are to be tested, every possible two-ad combination might be presented and preferences recorded. This is known as paired comparison.

When researchers want respondents to rate portions or segments of a television commercial they can use the program analyzer (a mechanical device with buttons to record positive and negative feelings about the ad). During the viewing of a commercial, respondents simply push a green button if they like what they see or a red button if they don't. The program analyzer provides an analysis of the strengths and weaknesses of an execution based on the audience response. It can also provide a direct comparison of two executions.

Projective Techniques

Projective testing techniques allow respondents to project their feelings or opinions into the creative process. The goal of projective techniques is to present respondents with fragmentary pictures, words, or situations in the hopes that they will project their underlying feelings or motivations. Often the respondent is presented with a vague or ambiguous stimulus and asked to respond verbally or in writing. Types of projective techniques include association, completion, dialog balloons, and construction.

Association tests present the respondents with a brand name, slogan, or other word or image and then record the words or thoughts that first come to their minds. This open-ended process allows respondents to offer positive and negative word associations and to offer reasons for their responses, if desired.

In completion techniques, a researcher presents an incomplete stimulus, whether a picture, sentence, or word, and invites the respondent to fill in the details. A simple sentence-completion technique could be structured as follows:

"Most colas are _____ . Lotsafizz is _____ ."

The dialog bubble or dialog balloon provides respondents the opportunity to supply the script for a scene involving a particular product. The purpose of this technique is to present the respondent with a seemingly ambiguous and incomplete stimulus (the cartoon or illustration) and to ask how the respondent feels a certain character would reply. An example is found in Figure 6–2 in Chapter 6. The drawing was sent to two sample groups—Dallas residents who had used the *Dallas Observer* personal classified advertisements and residents who had not. Responses were analyzed to determine favorable and unfavorable attitudes toward the use of the personal classifieds.

Construction or storytelling techniques identify consumer perceptions of potential product users. The researcher presents a scene or picture and asks respondents to build a story around it or describe the personalities of the characters involved. One such research effort used samples of respondents who were given one of two brand names of a toothpaste and asked to describe a typical Friday night date with a person who used the brand. Respondents were encouraged to provide details such as the type of automobile the person might drive, the clothes he or she might wear, where the couple would go on the date, and how the evening might end.

When using projective techniques, it is important to use a stimulus that is sufficiently neutral to encourage the respondent's true projection of thoughts and feelings and not simply evoke a description of the stimulus content. Another important consideration when using projective tests is to interpret responses in as objective a manner as possible. The fact that different researchers can arrive at different conclusions after being exposed to the same consumer responses is cause for great concern among those who use such techniques. This uncertainty about how to interpret results has called into question the usefulness of projective techniques as a means of testing concepts or advertisements. At the very least, projective techniques can be used as creative tools, both for those who test advertisements and for those who create them.

Mechanical Devices

Several methods utilize laboratory apparatus to obtain physiological responses to advertising stimuli. Mechanical devices such as the eye-movement camera, psychogalvanometer, and eye pupil camera are used.

The **eye-movement camera,** used primarily for print advertisements, photographs the viewer's eye movements around a page. By charting where the eyes are drawn on first viewing the advertisement (information that is often very difficult for the viewer to articulate), the researcher can isolate the dominant element on the page. Subsequent measurements provide information about which elements cause the viewer to progress around the page, and which elements are being concentrated on or ignored. Different versions of the advertisement can be tested to obtain information on the optimal placement of its visual elements.

A recent improvement in this device allows the camera to be camouflaged in a reading lamp that is used to illuminate a viewer's reading material. With the eye-camera lamp, subjects are unaware that their eyes are being monitored and are more likely to peruse a publication or advertisement as they normally would.

The **eye pupil camera** measures changes in size of the pupil. A dilation, or enlargement, of the pupil is interpreted as a favorable response to the stimulus. A contraction, or decrease, in size of the pupil indicates an unfavorable response. Various arrangements of visual elements and color can be manipulated to obtain the most pleasing stimulus.

The **psychogalvanometer** (also called the galvanometer) is used in a laboratory setting to detect viewer arousal by measuring electrodermal response, or perspiration, with electrodes attached to the hand. When a viewer is excited, increased nerve activity results in increased sweat. One drawback of this device is its inability to distinguish between extremely positive or extremely negative reactions on the part of the respondent—both produce the same reading. Other physiological responses to advertising include muscle contraction, pulse rate, blood pressure, and brain wave activity, which can be measured by the electroencephalograph.

Another mechanical device sometimes used in conjunction with testing of an advertisement is the **tachistoscope.** This device can present an image for varying degrees of time, allowing the researcher to determine the optimal exposure duration for message effectiveness. Experiments generally yield recognition threshold levels in the range of 10 to 110 milliseconds. The underlying belief behind the use of the tachistoscope is that in order for an advertisement to be effective it must be quick, not only to gain attention but also to impart its message.

The tachistoscope may be best known for its role in experiments involving subliminal stimuli to which subjects were exposed at durations below recognition threshold. The theory behind subliminal stimulation holds that a message need not be consciously perceived to have an effect. Rather, it can be registered at a level below consciousness and produce a short- or long-term effect. For example, a widely publicized study conducted in the 1970s by Hawkins reported that subliminal messages containing the word COKE caused higher thirst ratings among respondents.[1] However, a recent replication of the study failed to confirm those results.[2]

Program Analyzer

The program analyzer is an electronic device on which audience members can press buttons to register their reaction to material shown on film or videotape. The program analyzer can be used with an entire audience or with an individual viewing situation.

This method offers several advantages over straight interview procedures. First, it allows the viewer to react to each segment of the commercial as it appears, rather than gauging overall reaction to the entire commercial. Because of this capability, the program analyzer can provide feedback on which parts of the commercial are strongest or weakest. Second, viewer reaction is anonymous, so the concern about peer disagreement that can be a factor in group discussions is not an issue.

There is a disadvantage to this method as well. The program analyzer does not provide information on the reasons for viewer reactions. It is advisable to use such mechanical measurement devices in conjunction with some form of a personal interview to capture the basis for viewers' favorable or unfavorable attitudes.

Commercial Pretesting Services

On the next pages are examples of services for testing rough or finished ads in television or print before they run in major media.

Television

Research Systems Corporation: ARS Persuasion System.

The ARS Persuasion System, offered by RSC, uses a recruited audience to test rough or finished commercials embedded in television programs. Between 800 and 1,200 men and women are invited to central locations in four metropolitan areas to view television programs. Before and after the viewing, respondents are asked to indicate from sets of competitive products which ones they would like if they were chosen as a winner of the market basket door prizes.

The ARS Persuasion measure is the percent of respondents who choose the test product after exposure to the television program and commercials minus the percent who chose the test product before exposure.

Three days after the program exposure, about 280 respondents are interviewed by telephone with questions designed to measure recall, communication, and diagnostic elements.

Gallup & Robinson: InTeleTest.

Gallup & Robinson uses at-home exposure of video cassettes with test commercials embedded in a pilot program. The InTeleTest services take advantage of the widespread use of VCRs to achieve in-home viewing.

Testing is done in ten cities with 150 respondents of each sex. Respondents are contacted door-to-door in residential neighborhoods and asked to participate in a study of a new television series. As an incentive, each respondent's name is placed in a monthly drawing for $300.

Each respondent is given an hour-long video cassette with a pilot program in which six test and six control commercials have been inserted. Commercials are rotated to avoid order bias.

Before viewing the tape, respondents fill out a self-administered questionnaire about television viewing habits and preferences. A respondent views the tape and then fills out a questionnaire about reactions to the program. The next day a G&R interviewer telephones the respondent to ask about recall of commercials, using a product category cue and six questions related to reaction to the advertising.

Respondents are later re-exposed to the commercials by viewing the end of the tape where they have been re-inserted, after which they fill out a self-administered questionnaire containing evaluative items for recognition, main point communication, brand rating, likability, and reactions to the commercial.

Video Storyboard Tests, Inc.

A special service for both production and testing of rough commercials is provided by Video Storyboard Tests (VST). VST produces the test commercials from clients' original storyboards and soundtracks. One-on-one interviews are conducted at central locations in a number of markets. Respondents are shown the commercial on a television monitor and then asked questions to measure persuasion, communications, product uniqueness, competitive strength, believability, and likes and dislikes (see Figure 16–1). VST offers norms for various product categories to which specific commercial scores can be compared. An example of norms for over-the-counter products is contained in Figure 16–2.

Print Media

Perception Research Services, Inc.

PRS evaluates print advertising with the use of an eye-tracker camera which follows a reader's eye around a printed page. Respondents, qualified by a screening interview to insure that they fit the proper demographic and product usage description, are exposed to a series of newspaper, magazine, or direct mail messages and allowed to view them as long as they wish. The eye camera records the following: length of time each ad is viewed, sequence in which ad elements are viewed, areas overlooked or quickly bypassed, copy read, and proportion of time spent with various elements of the ad. (The PRS viewing procedure is demonstrated in Figure 16–3).

A verbal interview which follows initial exposure is intended to measure recall, likes and dislikes, aesthetic appeal, main idea perceptions, purchase interest, and product image ratings.

Figure 16–1
Questions for Testing Rough Commercials

Questionnaire

The commercial you are going to see is in sketch form. We are going to make a regular commercial from it using real people.

Show Commercial and Check Below

Commercial "A" .... ( ) 7-1   "B" .... ( ) -2

1. Based on what you've seen in this commercial, how interested would you be in trying the product? (READ LIST)
   - Extremely interested ....( ) 8-1
   - Very interested ....( ) – 2
   - Somewhat interested ....( ) – 3
   - Not very interested ....( ) – 4
   - Not interested at all ....( ) – 5

2. Why do you say that? _____ 9-
   _____ 10-
   _____ 11-

3. Other than asking you to buy the product, please tell me what was the *one main idea* the commercial was trying to get across?
   _____ 12-
   _____ 13-
   _____ 14-

4. How important is this idea to you? (READ LIST)
   - Very important ....( ) 15– 1
   - Somewhat important ....( )   – 2
   - Not important ....( )   – 3

5. From what you've seen in the commercial, would you say that the product would be different from other products you've used or heard about or the same as others?
   Different .... ( ) 16-1   Same .... ( ) -2

---

6. (IF DIFFERENT) What about the commercial makes you feel that the product might be different?_____ 17-
_____ 18-
_____ 19-

7. From what you've seen in the commercial, how do you think the product might compare to other products you've used or heard about? Would you say that the advertised product might be better than, as good as or not as good as other products?
Better than ...... ( ) 20-1   As good as ...... ( ) -2   Not as good as ...... ( ) -3

8. (IF BETTER THAN) What about the commercial makes you feel that the product might be better than other products? _____ 21-
_____ 22-
_____ 23-

9. Was there anything in the commercial you found hard to believe?
Yes .... ( ) 24-1   No .... ( ) -2

10. (IF YES) What did you find hard to believe?
_____ 25-
_____ 26-
_____ 27-

11. What, if anything, did you particularly like about this commercial?
_____ 28-
_____ 29-
_____ 30-

12. What, if anything, did you particularly dislike about this commercial?
_____ 31-
_____ 32-

13. Think about the situation and characters in the commercial you just saw. In your opinion, how suitable are they for advertising ——? Would you say they are. . . (READ LIST)
Very suitable .... ( ) 33–1
Somewhat suitable .... ( ) –2
Not suitable .... ( ) –3

14. Why do you say that?
_____ 34-
_____ 35-
_____ 36-

Thank you.

Name _____

Address _____

Phone no. _____

Interviewer _____

Source: Video Storyboard Tests, Inc.

Figure 16–2
Norms and Hypothetical Scores for Rough Commercials

		Test Commercials		
Summary				
	VST-OTC Averages	**"A"**	**"B"**	**"C"**
Persuasion	26	34	12	18
Communications	69	66	72	50
Importance of Communications	50	54	26	26
Uniqueness	50	88	76	70
Competitive Strength	26	42	26	22
Positively Inclined	59	60	68	55
Negatively Inclined	37	30	34	34

Source: Video Storyboard Tests, Inc.

Figure 16–3
Eye Tracking Procedure

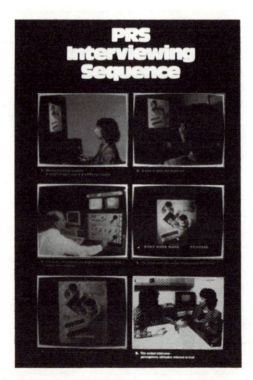

Source: Perception Research Services, Inc.

ASI: Print Plus.

ASI offers the Print Plus system via existing national magazines or in its own test publication called *Reflections*. As a control publication, *Reflections* magazine provides an opportunity for advertisers to pretest their ads.

Testing is typically done in five markets with 175 males or females, or 100 males and 100 females for a dual audience. Test magazines are placed with qualified participants who are told they are participating in a public opinion survey. In the context of a prize drawing, attitude and brand preference information is obtained before magazine placement. Respondents then read the magazine that evening.

A telephone interview is conducted the following day. Brand cues are used to determine claimed recall of ads in the magazine, and further questions measure communication of the ad message. Respondents are then asked to re-expose themselves to four of the ads, after which an adjective checklist and product interest questions are administered. A post-exposure brand preference question is re-asked in the same prize drawing context as before.

Video Storyboard Tests, Inc.

VST tests ads from black-and-white line drawings to finished color or black-and-white. Ads are placed in a version of a VST test magazine, *Looking At Us,* whose contents match the ad's degree of finish throughout.

One-on-one interviews are conducted in high-traffic shopping malls. Respondents are exposed to the magazine and then asked questions measuring recall, communications, persuasion, product uniqueness, believability, competitive strength, likes/dislikes, and reaction to headlines (see Figure 16–4). Respondents are then asked to re-focus on the test ad and are asked additional questions about their evaluation. An example of all-product norms for the VST rough print ad tests is included in Figure 16–5.

Figure 16–4
Questions for Testing Rough Magazine Ads

Questionnaire

Here is a pilot issue of a new magazine. Please go over it as you would normally look at your favorite magazine.

HAND MAGAZINE TO RESPONDENT AND CHECK:

"A" ...... ( ) 9–1   "B" ...... ( ) –2   "C" ...... ( ) –3

TAKE MAGAZINE BACK AFTER RESPONDENT HAS SEEN IT.

1. Please tell me which one story in the magazine you would like to read most?
_____ 10-

---

2. Please try to recall all the brands you saw advertised in this magazine. (DO NOT PROBE. WRITE BELOW IN ORDER MENTIONED BY RESPONDENT. IF RESPONDENT MENTIONS PRODUCT, ASK HIM/HER TO NAME THE BRAND BEFORE WRITING BELOW.)

   1. _____ 11–
   2. _____ 12–
   3. _____   7. _____
   4. _____   8. _____
   5. _____   9. _____
   6. _____   10. _____

3. Now, I'm going to read you a list of brands. Some of them were advertised in the magazine, others were not. Please tell me which ones you remember seeing even if you have mentioned them before. Did you see an ad for ... (READ LIST. BEGIN WITH ITEM CHECKED AND CONTINUE UNTIL ALL NAMES HAVE BEEN COVERED.)

Masumi fragrance ....( )13–1	Visa credit card ....( ) –5	American Airlines.......( ) –9
Beefeater gin ....( ) –2	.....................................( ) –6	Aziza eye make-up ...( ) –0
Clinique products ....( ) –3	Diamonds....................( ) –7	.....................................( ) –x
True cigarettes ....( ) –4	Palmolive soap ....( ) –8	Now cigarettes ....( ) –y

4. (ASK ONLY IF CHECKED IN Qs. 2 OR 3) Think about the _____ ad for a moment. What do you remember about it? What else? What did it show? What did it say?

   _____ 14-
   _____ 15-
   _____ 16-
   _____ 17-

   (OPEN FOLDER TO SHOW _____ AD) Now I want you to look at one of the ads you saw before. (LET RESPONDENT READ THIS AD. TAKE FOLDER BACK AND CLOSE IT.)

5. Aside from trying to persuade you to buy the product, what was the *one main idea* the advertiser was trying to get across? (DO NOT PROBE)

   _____ 18-
   _____ 19-
   _____ 20-

6. How important is this idea to you? (READ LIST)

   Very important ....( ) 21– 1
   Somewhat important ....( )   – 2
   Not important ....( )   – 3

7. Based on what you've seen in the ad, how interested would you be in trying the product? (READ LIST)

   Extremely interested ....( ) 22– 1
   Very interested ....( )   – 2
   Somewhat interested ....( )   – 3
   Not very interested ....( )   – 4
   Not at all interested ....( )   – 5

8. Why do you say that? (PROBE)

_____ 23-
_____ 24-
_____ 25-

9. From what you saw in the ad, would you say that the product advertised would be different from other products you've used or heard about or the same as others?

Different ...... ( ) 26–1   Same ...... ( ) –2

10. (IF DIFFERENT) What about the ad makes you feel that the product might be different?

_____ 27-
_____ 28-
_____ 29-

11. From what you saw in the ad, would you say that the product advertised would be better than, as good as or not as good as other products you have used or heard about?

Better than ... ( ) 30–1   As good as ... ( ) –2   Not as good as ... ( ) –3

12. (IF BETTER THAN) What about the ad makes you feel that the product might be better than other products?

_____ 31-
_____ 32-
_____ 33-

13. Was there anything in the advertisement that you found hard to believe?

Yes...... ( ) 34–1   No ...... ( ) –2

14. (IF YES) What did you find hard to believe?

_____ 34-
_____ 35-

15. What, if anything, did you particularly like about this ad?

_____ 36-
_____ 37-
_____ 38-

16. What, if anything, did you particularly dislike about this ad?

_____ 39-
_____ 40-

17. The headline of this ad was, "_____ ."
What does this mean to you?

_____ 41-
_____ 42-
_____ 43-

18. How important is this statement to you? (READ LIST)

Very important .... ( ) 44– 1
Somewhat important .... ( )   – 2
Not important .... ( )   – 3

WRITE NAME, ADDRESS & PHONE NO. ON THE SCREENER

Source: Video Storyboard Tests, Inc.

Figure 16–5
Norms for Test of Rough Magazine Ads

	Summary		
		Test Advertisements	
	VST-All Product Averages	**"A"**	**"B"**
Claimed Recall—Test Ad	68	74	64
Unaided	38	47	36
Aided	30	27	28
Proven	54	61	47
Unproven	4	2	3
No recall	10	11	14
Claimed Recall—Competitive Ad	71	68	71
Unaided	42	41	46
Aided	29	27	25
Communications	50	56	54
Importance of Communications	31	48	37
Persuasion	23	35	25
Uniqueness	30	50	48
Competitive Strength	19	28	22
Positively Inclined	63	78	67
Negatively Inclined	28	27	27

Source: Video Storyboard Tests, Inc.

McCollum Spielman Worldwide: Ad*Vantage Print.

McCollum Spielman uses a test vehicle called *Spotlight Classics* magazine to test print advertising. (See Figure 16–6.) Qualified respondents are recruited by intercept in shopping malls and invited to participate in a study for a new magazine prototype. Average test sample size is 125 subjects.

One-on-one interviews are conducted at mall research facilities. At the beginning of the interview, information on product and category usage are asked, as well as magazine readership information. Participants flip through the magazine quickly and then are asked for their initial reactions to the magazine as well as unaided brand recall questions. The latter are intended to measure "stopping power" of the ads—their ability to capture readers' attention and generate awareness.

Figure 16–6
A Test Magazine for Pretesting Print Ads

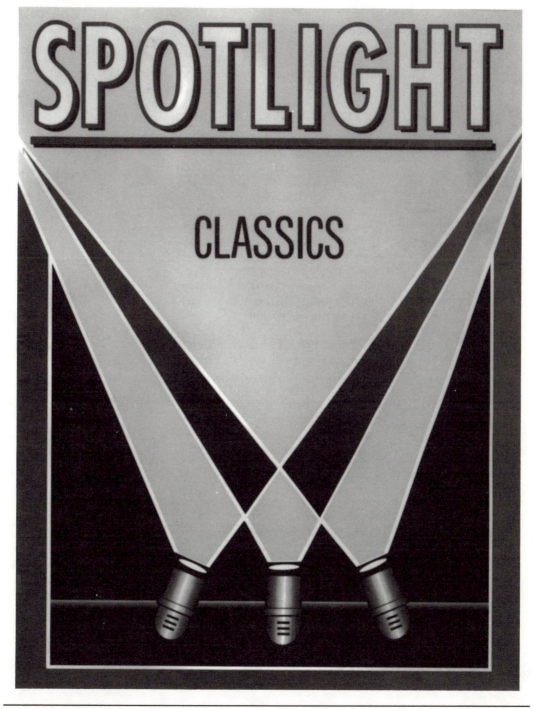

WELCOME TO THE WORLD OF SCREEN CLASSICS

This is the prototype issue of a new magazine concept called **SPOTLIGHT**.

SPOTLIGHT is being created to bring you interesting stories, features and behind the scenes information about screen classics of both television and movies. The publisher feels this magazine will motivate you to see these classics if you've missed them or interest you in seeing them again, perhaps in a new light.

Obviously this is a highly condensed version of the magazine's ultimate size, but it will provide you with a good idea of what the magazine will be like. Therefore, we are most interested in your impressions and invite you to read through it. Later we'd like to obtain your reactions to this new magazine concept.

Thanks!

_____

A second exposure opportunity allows respondents to look through the entire magazine. Detailed questions are then asked, including another unaided brand recall question, an unaided communication question, and a persuasion/attitude shift item.

After a third exposure in which respondents are asked to focus their attention on the specific test ad, tailored diagnostic questions are asked. Topics include reaction to layout, meaning of headline, what the visual was trying to demonstrate, communication, product attribute rating, likes and dislikes, message comprehension, and believability.

Review

In this chapter we saw that:

- Message pretesting is conducted to determine whether any problems are associated with the concept, strategy, or execution of the idea before committing a media budget to the proposed advertising.
- Some popular methods of testing creative ideas and/or executions include the focus group discussion, the one-on-one interview, projective techniques such as association, completion, dialog balloons, and construction, and mechanical devices that measure physiological responses to advertising stimuli.
- The Advertising Research Foundation has set down general guidelines for message pretesting. Copy research should:
  1. Be conducted among the target prospects for the specific brand.
  2. Be part of an integrated research plan and should be preceded by information about what to communicate to which audience.
  3. Be developed to test entire campaigns, rather than single advertisements or commercials.
  4. Not only test reaction to the advertising, but also to the product advertised.
  5. Contain diagnostic information to determine why an advertisement does or does not work.
  6. Be validated.
  7. Be coordinated with those responsible for creating the advertising message.
  8. Recognize the advertiser's sales goals.
  9. Lead to the development of general principles of advertisement construction.
- Commercials can be tested in the form of storyboards, rough commercials, or finished commercials; however, different commercial ideas should always be tested at a similar stage of completion.

Endnotes

1. Del Hawkins. "The Effects of Subliminal Stimulation on Drive Level and Brand Preference." *Journal of Marketing Research* 7. August 1970, pp. 322–326.

2. Beatty, Sharon and Del Hawkins. "Subliminal Stimulation: Some New Data and Interpretation." *Journal of Advertising* 18, no. 3, 1989, pp 4–8.

Chapter 17 Message Pilot Testing

Pilot testing involves running a finished or near-finished advertisement in limited or small-scale media. This phase of testing occurs between pretesting, which does not involve placement in actual media vehicles, and posttesting, which is done after the advertisement has run in full-scale media. The easiest way to distinguish pilot testing from pretesting and posttesting is to think of it like test driving a new vehicle or experimenting with a new recipe on a few friends rather than serving it at the annual office party. The pilot test is a *real world,* scaled-down advertising effort, and its results are used to help predict how that effort will perform on a larger scale.

Beyond the pretest and the posttest, the pilot test provides another layer of feedback about the effectiveness of the message. The pilot test, as opposed to the pretest, is conducted under real-world or near real-world conditions of audience exposure and selection. The major advantage of the pilot test over the posttest is the opportunity for the advertiser to make adjustments or modifications after the results are in.

General Types of Message Pilot Testing

Trial Runs in Limited Media

Placement of an advertisement in a single magazine, newspaper, TV station, or other medium can provide a preliminary indication of how effective the advertising message will be on a larger scale. A strong performance in the full run of a small-circulation magazine, for instance, might yield results that would warrant running an advertisement in larger-circulation magazines. A commercial may run on a single cable system and, depending on the results, may be extended to other cable systems, spot TV markets, and so forth.

Criteria for measuring message effectiveness in a pilot test situation can include awareness measures, attitude measures, and sales or inquiry data. In an ideal situation, a direct-response opportunity such as a toll-free number, business reply card, or order blank would allow a preliminary measure of the advertisement's effectiveness. Other more indirect or "surrogate" measures such as recall of the advertisement's copy, attitude toward the advertisement, or persuasion can be used. (See Chapter 8 for a more detailed discussion of survey measurement procedures.)

Controlled Field Experiments

Variations of the controlled field experiment are sometimes used to test advertising messages in various media. Three of these methods are split-cable transmission for television, split-run distribution for magazines and newspapers, and split-list experimentation in direct mail. All of these methods test advertising messages under naturalistic conditions (the media vehicles in question are real), and they also allow for random distribution of the test messages. What sets these methods apart from other less rigorous designs is the random assignment of experimental treatments to readers or viewers. Because of this superior design, the internal validity is very high—if one version of the advertisement performs better than another in the experiment, it is correct to assume that the differences in performance were due to the differences in the advertisements themselves and not a sample-related or environment-related factor.

Split-cable transmission.

Unlike broadcast, where a signal transmitted through the airwaves is available to anyone with the appropriate receiver, cable television operates via direct transmission to households through cable wiring. This delivery scheme makes possible the setup of a system called "split-cable," in which an area is wired so that every other household receives either an "A" or "B" signal. Advertisers are interested in this set-up because it offers a rare opportunity to expose randomly selected groups (A households and B households) of the same population (the neighborhood) to different advertising treatments under naturalistic conditions. In recent years technological improvement in cable system delivery have enabled the pioneers of single-source data systems to practice selective transmission—sending advertising messages via cable to households in specially wired neighborhoods based on the demographics of a particular household. This type of testing is done to study the different effects of the commercial messages on highly selected audiences.

The split-cable system is well-suited for testing a variety of advertising-related variables including message, frequency, and timing. Our interest at the moment is in testing one message against another in limited media, and split-cable provides us with the opportunity. Though split-cable experiments are not in widespread use today, they have been used in recent years to validate the surrogate effectiveness measures used by commercial testing services such as recall, communication, and persuasion.

Split-run distribution.

The same principles used in split-cable testing can be applied to the print media through split-run advertising. In split-run, every other copy of a certain issue of a publication contains version "A" or version "B" of an advertisement for the same product or service. Because every other copy has one or the other treatment, and because readers are unaware of the experiment, the split-run provides a highly controlled yet naturalistic testing situation.

A direct-response opportunity included as part of the advertisements being tested provides an ideal built-in measure of advertisement effectiveness. One example is a business reply card to be filled out and mailed in by the reader. By keying the reply cards in some manner, perhaps printing A or B on them somewhere, the researcher can determine immediately which advertisement pulled more inquiries, orders, replies, etc. Other direct-response opportunities that could be used in a split-run experiment are toll-free numbers, addresses, fax numbers, and coupons.

It should be noted that some definitions of "split-run" are not as rigorous as described above. Some publishers consider a split-run to be any of a number of different partial runs such as a geographic edition, a special version of a publication that goes only to affluent subscribers, or some other subset of subscribers. Of course, the population samples generated from this broad definition of split-run are not true random samples of the larger population and therefore are not necessarily representative of all readers.

Split-list experimentation.

Direct mail advertising is probably the most perfectly suited of all media for quick, efficient, and accurate testing of the advertising message. The prudent direct mail advertiser is constantly testing new ways of increasing response rates. Direct mail pieces can be tested in finished form by mailing them out to random samples of the list. A relatively small percentage of the list can be used to test two or more versions of a piece. The version that "pulls" more responses will be used in future mailings.

Effective direct response advertising relies on testing to determine the most profitable selling strategies. The difference between a response rate of 2.2 percent and 2.5 percent could easily translate into thousands of dollars of profit potential for the advertiser.

Commercial Pilot Testing Services

Print

Gallup & Robinson: Rapid Ad Measurement (RAM).

Rough or finished print ads can be tested via RAM. A schedule of test issues is provided by Gallup & Robinson, and advertisers are invited to buy ad space in one or more issues of *Time* and *People* magazines. If lead time is short, G&R offers its Tip-In service, in which the ad is carefully pasted into the copies to be tested before distribution. The Tip-In service technically is considered a pretest by our definition.

Regular readers of the two magazines in five metropolitan areas are recruited for the study. RAM samples are approximately 150 male readers of *Time* and approximately the same number of female readers of *People*. Dual sex testing can be done with *Time*.

The test copy is delivered to participants' homes and a telephone interview is conducted the following day. After readership has been established, respondents are asked if they recall ads for a list of brands and companies. A series of detailed questions about each ad recalled measures three basic levels of effectiveness:

1. Intrusiveness. Recall, referred to by G&R as Proved Name Registration, is the percentage of respondents who can accurately describe the advertisement the day after exposure.

2. Idea communication. Measures the number of respondent descriptions of their retained ideas, thoughts, and feelings about the ad.

3. Persuasion. Referred to as Favorable Buying Attitude for consumer advertising and Favorable Attitude for corporate advertising, this is intended to measure how the advertisement affected interest.

Diagnostic questions can also be asked. Figure 17–1 shows normative distributions for RAM scores from 1978 to 1990. The average Proved Name Registration, or recall, score is 19.1 for all ads tested. Figure 17–2 shows Proved Name Registration for one-page four-color ads for men and women. It is interesting to note that women's recall scores were higher than those of men.

Television

Gallup & Robinson: In-View.

In-View is an on-air test for rough or finished commercials. Commercials are accepted in animatic, photomatic, live-action rough, or finished form. Single-sex or dual-sex audiences of 100 or 150 randomly chosen subjects are selected by telephone in three metropolitan areas in the East, Midwest, and West.

Figure 17–1
Rapid Ad Measurement Scores Distribution

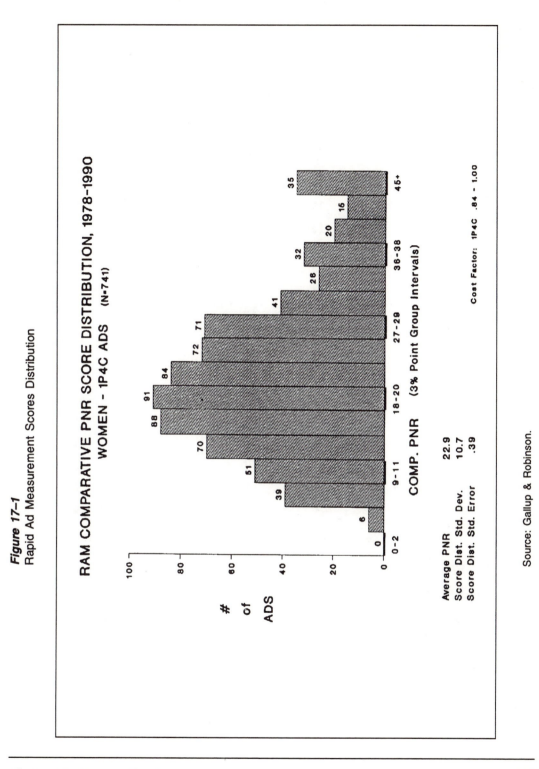

RAM COMPARATIVE PNR SCORE DISTRIBUTION, 1978–1990
WOMEN – 1P4C ADS (N=741)

Source: Gallup & Robinson.

Figure 17–2
Proved Name Registration Scores for RAM

RAM Comparative PNR Score Distribution, 1978–1990

| | NUMBER OF ADS | | | |
| | MEN | | WOMEN | |
COMP. PNR	ALL ADS*	1P4C ADS*	ALL ADS*	1P4C ADS*
45+	9	2	49	35
42–44	11	8	15	15
39–41	13	10	26	20
36–38	15	10	38	32
33–35	24	17	36	26
30–32	34	22	49	41
27–29	61	42	90	71
24–26	89	69	96	72
21–23	114	67	108	84
18–20	123	68	125	91
15–17	168	96	129	88
12–14	179	87	128	70
9–11	131	65	95	51
6– 8	72	40	80	39
3– 5	24	14	13	6
0– 2	1	1	2	0
TOTALS	1068	618	1079	741
AVERAGE PNR	18.4	19.1	21.5	22.9
SCORE DIST. STD. DEV.	8.7	8.6	11.1	10.7
SCORE DIST. STD. ERROR	.27	.35	.34	.39

*Cost Factors: All Ads .4 – 2.1; 1P4C .87 – 1.00

Source: Gallup & Robinson.

The test commercial is aired on an independent station in an hour-long prime-time former network program now in syndication. Respondents are called and invited to watch the program for the purpose of offering their opinions about the program. The day following the program, participants are phoned and asked about their evaluation of the program and which commercials they remember seeing. A category and brand cue is used. For each commercial they claim to recall, participants are asked the standard impact questions (intrusiveness, idea communication, and persuasion). Examples of In-View norms for 30-second commercials on intrusiveness and copy points are contained in Figures 17–3 and 17–4.

ASI: Recall Plus and Persuasion Plus.

ASI uses cable television transmission to facilitate in-home exposure for rough or finished commercials to a recruited audience. The standard sample consists of 200 males or females, or a total of 200 males and females for a dual-sex audience. Respondents are randomly drawn from cable television households in a minimum of two out of a dozen test cities.

For Recall Plus, respondents are contacted the day of the test and invited to preview a new television program. The test program is an unaired, 30-minute situation comedy that contains four non-competing test commercials and one non-test filler commercial.

The day following exposure to the program, respondents are contacted by telephone and asked questions about program evaluation, commercial recall using product and brand prompts, and communication. More detailed diagnostics can be collected if desired.

The Persuasion Plus service uses the Recall Plus system with the addition of brand choice measures. At the end of the recruiting interview, respondents are also asked brand usage and preference questions. A brand list is read and the respondent is asked which he or she is most likely to buy next and the brand currently used most often. Within two hours of having watched the program, respondents are re-interviewed by phone and, after the Recall-Plus questions, are invited, within the context of a prize drawing for a certain amount of a product in a given category, to select the brand they would most like to have.

A Tru-Share Persuasion score is calculated based on results obtained from the respondents who were exposed to the program and a previous test of respondents who did not view the program, but who were asked about brands they plan to buy and about which they would choose if they won a prize drawing.

Figure 17–3

Proved Commercial Registration Scores for In-View

In-View PCR Score Distribution, 1979–1988
By Sex and Commercial Length

	NUMBER OF COMMERCIALS					
	MEN			WOMEN		
PCR	60"	30"	15"	60"	30"	15"
75+	1	7	-	2	9	-
70-74	1	8	1	2	15	1
65-69	3	22	1	9	43	3
60-64	3	47	-	7	70	4
55-59	11	106	1	13	124	3
50-54	17	148	5	21	188	8
45-49	23	272	4	19	300	6
40-44	34	398	10	31	446	5
35-39	34	538	22	38	487	23
30-34	36	547	15	31	628	19
25-29	24	591	18	19	564	16
20-24	23	603	31	18	523	23
15-19	13	492	21	9	444	24
10-14	8	354	33	8	277	23
5-9	3	152	23	2	122	15
0-4	-	54	6	-	32	11
TOTALS	234	4339	191	229	4272	184
AVERAGE PCR	36.2	29.8	23.2	39.0	31.7	26.0
STD. ERROR	.85	.20	.96	.96	.21	1.17
PCR Index (30" = 100)						
Obtained	121	100	78	123	100	82
Product-Group Controlled	140	100	81	134	100	82

Source: Gallup & Robinson.

Figure 17–4
Copy Point Scores for In-View

In-View Copy Point Score Distribution, 1970–1988
(30" Commercials)

IN-VIEW COPY POINTS SCORE DISTRIBUTION, 1970–1988
(30" COMMERCIALS)

COPY POINTS PER RESPONDENT	NUMBER OF ADS	
	MEN	WOMEN
4.5 +	10	13
4.2 – 4.4	15	9
3.9 – 4.1	56	35
3.6 – 3.8	68	70
3.3 – 3.5	141	119
3.0 – 3.2	229	171
2.7 – 2.9	273	259
2.4 – 2.6	281	273
2.1 – 2.3	277	251
1.8 – 2.0	236	232
1.5 – 1.7	156	147
1.2 – 1.4	88	76
0.9 – 1.1	24	29
0.6 – 0.8	2	8
0.3 – 0.5	1	0
0.0 – 0.2	0	0
TOTALS	1857	1692
AVERAGE COPY POINTS PER RESPONDENT	2.5	2.5
SCORE DIST. STD. DEV.	.72	.72
SCORE DIST. STD. ERROR	.02	.02

Source: Gallup & Robinson.

Issues Associated with Test Markets

A number of challenges face the researcher who wishes to test advertising in the marketplace. Because pilot testing involves in-market experimentation as opposed to more controlled environments, a number of factors and influences are outside the researcher's control. Such real-world testing scenarios also involve competitive factors, retail environment factors, and climatic factors such as the weather. Since in-market testing makes use of existing local media to carry the test advertisements, certain media-related problems can arise. An Advertising Research Foundation Marketplace Testing Symposium in 1987 focused on providing guidelines for in-market testing. The following are some top-priority concerns and some suggestions for dealing with potential in-market complications.

Before the Test

Researchers must have sufficient knowledge about the methods to be employed.

If the researcher does not fully understand the pros and cons of a particular method, then the reliability, validity, and projectability could be adversely affected. It is essential that all of the setup issues involved in a marketplace test—media chosen, creative used, measurement strategies employed—be communicated properly to everyone involved in the research process. The increasing number of services and variations of methods available to the researcher have made this first guideline an increasingly difficult one to attain.

Researchers must set criteria for judging success or failure of the marketing effort.

Setting evaluative criteria is essential to determining the validity of the test marketing study. If all parties involved do not agree about what test results will constitute success or failure of the marketing and advertising program, then there is no reason to conduct the test at all. Setting quantifiable objectives for the test requires coming to agreement about overall goals in light of the measurement systems available and determining how the test market measurements would translate into sales volume, new users, or other indicators of effectiveness.

During the Test

Researchers must be able to execute all of the elements of the marketing plan for the test.

This boils down to a translation of the national marketing plan to a local market, and it involves factors of media, promotions, and retail. The ability to plan for the national marketing effort in a local test market is the prerequisite for a media schedule that utilizes the desired media options with the desired frequency; a promotional campaign in which the desired advertising and special events run on schedule; and a retail environment that is conducive to an accurate test.

Researchers must be able to monitor the competition.

This step includes searching for variables outside control of the researcher that could be used to explain overall test results and monitoring the sales levels of all competitive items. Research activities involved in this phase of the test include monitoring media plan execution for the test brand, monitoring promotions for the test brand and its competitors, assessing retail environment factors that could affect the test, and obtaining sales data for the category.

After the Test

Researchers must be able to project from a sample to a larger universe.

In this case, projection means extrapolating data from the test market to a larger geographic universe, usually the country. This issue is extremely important in view of the number of services, including single-source systems, that are limited in the media they use and in the measures they employ. The critical question of projectability based on test results must be resolved early in the planning process so markets that are for any reason considered unprojectable can be ruled out.

Researchers must be able to understand why a test succeeded or failed.

Diagnostics is a general area of research that deals with the reasons for a testing method's failure or success. Unfortunately, sometimes it is not possible to explain just why an effort failed or succeeded. After the results are in, it might be clear whether a test succeeded, but it might be difficult to determine which aspect of the plan contributed in what amount to the outcome.

Depending on the number and type of measures used in a test, the resulting data might not provide diagnostic information. An example would be a campaign including TV advertising, outdoor signs, couponing, and in-store displays that ran concurrently with a competitive effort using similar media. Sales figures alone are insufficient to explain why the campaign did not work. Research designs that include multiple treatment conditions (preferably in similar or "matched" markets) and multiple measures (including communication measures as well as sales) are preferable to "one-shot" studies involving a single dependent variable. (See Chapter 6 for a discussion of research design options.)

Review

In this chapter we saw that:

- Pilot testing involves running a finished or near-finished advertisement in limited or small-scale media; this step occurs between pretesting and posttesting.
- Pilot testing is a real-world, scaled-down advertising effort allowing the advertiser to make adjustments or modifications after the results are in.
- General types of message pilot testing include trial runs in limited media and controlled field experiments, including split-cable transmission for television, split-run distribution for magazines and newspapers, and split-list experimentation in direct mail.
- The Advertising Research Foundation has set down general guidelines for in-market testing. Researchers must:
  - Have sufficient knowledge about the methods to be employed.
  - Set criteria for judging success or failure of the marketing effort.
  - Be able to execute all of the elements of the marketing plan for the test.
  - Be able to monitor the competition.
  - Be able to project from a sample to a larger universe.
  - Be able to understand why a test succeeded or failed.

Chapter 18

Posttesting: Feedback after Media Distribution

Posttesting is the final stage of message measurement. It has been likened to a postmortem examination, conducted too late to be of much good to the patient. But the primary reason for posttesting is usually not to find ways to alter the current campaign. Rather, posttesting provides a means of recording how campaigns perform in the real world.

Advertisers naturally desire feedback on an advertisement's impact in the marketplace after major media dollars have been committed to an advertising campaign. Some advertisers spend the bulk of their research dollars on posttesting, rather than investing at least part of the budget in pretesting or pilot testing. As you learned in Chapters 16 and 17, pretesting is conducted with ideas, rough advertisements, or finished advertisements before they are placed in media. Pilot testing calls for a trial run—limited exposure in real media to integrate marketplace effects into the test design.

Posttesting is market evaluation, the measuring of advertising effects in the marketplace *after* the campaign is in place. There are two types of posttesting discussed here. The first, research that evaluates specific advertising executions in large-scale distribution, is sometimes called *ad hoc posttesting.* It analyzes a single execution or possibly a single campaign, and asks: "How effective was this execution among readers of a specific magazine or viewers of a particular television program?" An example would be measuring the effectiveness of a magazine ad appearing in *Good Housekeeping* magazine by interviewing a sample of the magazine's readers to see if they remembered seeing it and what they remembered about it.

The second type of posttesting, a *tracking study,* involves measurement of advertising and brand performance over time to monitor the success of the advertising effort over a longer period. An example might involve measurements of advertising awareness and brand attitudes during periods of advertising and non-advertising over several years. Tracking studies can involve traditional measures of advertising awareness—information and persuasion—and they can also incorporate other factors such as ad spending levels, brand sales levels, and activities of competitors. The tracking study suggests a longitudinal approach to measurement.

Reasons for Conducting Posttests

Posttesting enables the advertiser to capture data on a variety of variables as they occur in the marketplace. Some view these procedures as similar to keeping a scorecard in a bowling game or other contest. An advertiser might desire posttest data to gauge the effectiveness of a single execution or campaign. Sometimes the purpose of a posttest is to determine if a specific ad in a specific medium achieved the desired communication effects. In these cases a sample of consumers exposed to specific vehicles is interviewed and asked awareness, communication, and persuasion questions similar to those used in pretests and pilot tests.

Another use of posttesting is to record advertising effects over time. Such longitudinal research yields an "effectiveness history" of a brand. If measured at regular intervals, the variables of brand awareness, advertising awareness, sales, and other measures can be plotted to reveal trends over time.

Posttesting is also used to monitor advertising effectiveness under varying market conditions. One benefit of longitudinal research is that it indicates how a single sample of respondents, or equal samples of respondents, behave in the marketplace over time. Tracking studies can include not only information about consumer evaluation of the brand under study but also for its competitors during the same time period.

As we have seen in earlier discussions, it is very difficult to estimate with certainty the contribution that advertising makes to sales levels. Tracking does not involve experimental manipulation of market variables in an effort to isolate the effects of one variable such as advertising, so tracking data under most circumstances are correlational, not causal. In the absence of causal data, the correlation data provide the best picture available of the relationships between marketplace variables. Top-of-mind brand awareness for a given product might have suffered during a very heavy competitive marketing effort, and it might rebound afterward. The tracking of your own and your competitor's marketing moves, as well as other relevant variables such as weather, distribution problems, and media problems, can help put things into historical if not causal perspective.

Posttesting can help estimate advertising wearout. It is estimated that the average advertising campaign runs for about 18 months. One assumption behind the planning of an advertising campaign is that the impact of the advertising message will decay over time and require modification or replacement. For certain advertisements, wearout occurs more quickly than for others, but in any case it is difficult if not impossible to determine the viability of any given advertisement or campaign without regularly measuring its effectiveness.

Posttesting can measure the effectiveness of message elements. If a commercial claims a new sports drink is "lower in calories" and the "best choice for those who exercise," a tracking study can provide feedback on how the two claims fare once the campaign is running. Figure 18–1 shows hypothetical scores in relation to GRP spending levels for both claims among people who recall the commercial. In the example, it appears that advertising spending levels have little effect on the "best choice" belief, but that the "lower in calories" claim varies with advertising spending. Note that this does not necessarily mean that it is the advertising which is responsible for the success or failure of either claim in the marketplace. It could be that the "best choice" claim is a very difficult one for consumers to accept in the face of many category alternatives. The tracking information simply supplies an indication of the extent to which the message claims are known or believed, or both.

Posttesting can determine if advertising objectives have been achieved. We've discussed the importance of setting objectives for an advertising campaign. To the extent that advertising objectives were quantified, such as increasing awareness from 20 percent to 30 percent in a six-month period, then posttest research can provide feedback on whether communication or sales objectives have been met. Some advertising which is failing miserably is pulled before its intended expiration because of poor performance.

Finally, posttesting can help advertisers study the competition. Tracking studies provide a periodic report card of the relative position of all brands within a category. Again, studies can focus on the awareness of advertising for each brand or on attitudes toward the brand, or both. Results can be evaluated in terms of media spending levels, timing, patterns, or other factors.

Figure 18-1

Tracking Study Scores for Two Product Claims During and Between Advertising Flights

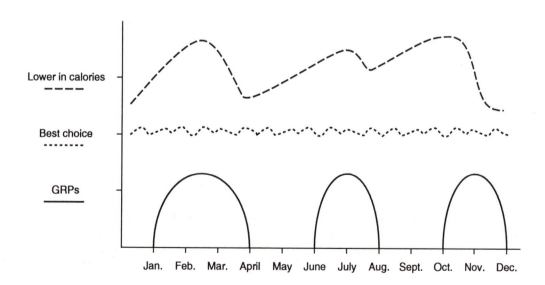

What to Measure

The ultimate goal of almost all advertising is to make a sale. However, based on what we know about the many different marketplace factors that can affect sales levels, it is both naive and inaccurate to evaluate the advertising effort according to sales levels alone. Therefore, it is common practice to take readings of multiple effectiveness variables. Some of these variables are discussed below. Awareness, recall, recognition, and attitude are measured using survey methods, while sales measures are obtained from diaries, scanner panels, or store audits.

Awareness

At the very least, an advertiser hopes that a significant percentage of the target audience is aware of a product or its advertising after a campaign is in place. When measuring awareness, the researcher has the options of asking unaided or aided questions. An example of an unaided question is: "Have you seen any commercials for laundry soap recently? Which ones?" An aided question may be; "Have you seen any commercials for XYZ laundry soap recently?" Of course, awareness measurements are taken in the absence of the advertising itself, and usually these results are viewed in conjunction with data from other tests of advertising effectiveness.

There are many different ways for researchers to ask the awareness question, beyond the use of aided versus unaided formats. Figure 18–2 gives some examples. According to British researchers Juchems and Twyman, version A is the format typically used in the United States.[1] The authors contend that version D leads to reduced "overclaiming" and provides maximum sensitivity to changes in the advertising.

Figure 18–2
Four Approaches to Measuring Awareness of a Campaign

> ***Version A***
>   (i) Can you tell me the names of any brands of (product field) for which you have seen or heard any advertising recently? Probe: Any others?
> (ii) Apart from these you have already mentioned, have you seen or heard any of these brands (show card already shown previously for brand awareness) advertised recently? Probe: Any others?
> (iii) For each brand mentioned—where did you see or hear the advertising for _____ ? Was it in newspapers, magazines, on television, poster, radio or elsewhere?

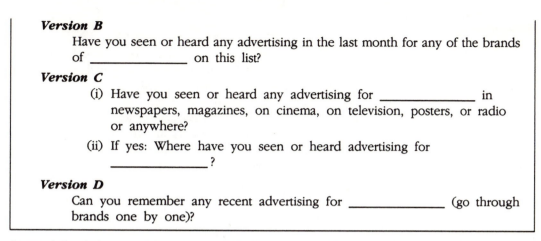

Version B

Have you seen or heard any advertising in the last month for any of the brands of _____ on this list?

Version C

(i) Have you seen or heard any advertising for _____ in newspapers, magazines, on cinema, on television, posters, or radio or anywhere?

(ii) If yes: Where have you seen or heard advertising for _____ ?

Version D

Can you remember any recent advertising for _____ (go through brands one by one)?

Source: Arthur Juchems, and Tony Twyman, "The Measurement of Advertising Awareness and Its Applications," *Journal of the Market Research Society*.

Recall and Communication

Aside from determining whether a respondent is aware of advertising for a brand, a researcher can probe deeper to determine the extent to which the person can remember the essence of the advertisement, the slogan, the main character, or some other creative element. An interviewer might ask a respondent to "describe what you remember about the commercial, what it was about." Some researchers contend that verbal recall, or "playback," of advertising elements is not a valid measure of advertising impact primarily because of the difficulty viewers have relating the elements of mood-oriented advertisements. However, many advertisers consider playback to be a valuable source of feedback on campaign memorability and impact.

One benefit of using playback as a tracking measure is the ability to follow the consumer learning process over time. Used in combination with claimed awareness figures, playback levels are an indication of how well the advertising content has been remembered. Playback data also gives the researcher an opportunity to compare the relative memorability of several executions in the same campaign. For instance, commercial A may have been running longer, but commercial B may continue to dominate even after new commercial C is introduced. Over time, this displacement of one commercial by another can be documented.

Because of the difficulty of translating recall scores into measures of advertisement exposure, playback often is considered to be a diagnostic measure, or one that is used to supplement awareness and/or recognition data. As such, playback scores can provide a rich source of feedback to the advertiser.

Recognition

Recognition measures typically ask whether respondents remember having seen an advertisement and whether they can link the advertisement with the sponsor. With print media, the actual advertisement is shown, and with television a photoscript can be used in lieu of the commercial itself. The Starch technique (discussed at the end of this chapter) is an example of a recognition test.

A major problem with recognition measurements, and the primary reason they are not in more widespread use, is that they necessitate in-person interviewing, whereas much other posttesting is conducted on the telephone. In-person interviews are more expensive, and so far most advertisers have opted for other types of measurement. Another related problem stems from a concern about validity. Are respondents in the in-person, prompted situation prone to exaggerating their reported readership of or exposure to advertisements?

Attitude Measures and Persuasion

Attitude measures in a tracking study tap consumer reaction to either the brand or its advertising. When used in conjunction with awareness and playback measures, attitude responses can serve as an additional level of information on campaign impact. Typically, attitude measures employ scaled items to measure the intensity of response. An example of a rating scale for a particular brand might be as follows:

- Excellent
- Very good
- Good
- Fair
- Poor

Measurement of the brand's consumer ratings over time, especially when considered with other tracking measures, yields a picture of consumer sentiment and brand loyalty. When a product is new, media advertising and promotions such as point-of-purchase displays can have a great effect on brand attitude, because they are the consumer's only information for evaluation. Later in the product life cycle, especially after the consumer has been exposed directly to the product, more factors come to bear on the evaluation, and it is difficult to determine to what extent each individual factor has contributed to overall brand attitude. Persuasion items, as we have seen in previous chapters, focus on favorable buying attitude and/or change in attitude before and after exposure to advertising messages.

Reported Behavior

Surveys are often used for awareness, recall, and attitude measurements, while some other method is used to measure behavior. In many cases the method of

---

choice is a diary, in which the respondent is instructed to record purchases over a period of time. Diary panels are sometimes used for several years. It is generally believed that because diaries involve self-reports of purchase behavior they are less accurate (more inflated) than mechanical recording devices.

Recorded Behavior

Some companies have incorporated electronic devices into their measurement techniques. These devices include hand-held scanner wands for use by consumers in the home and scanners at a retail outlet, for which the consumer carries an identification card to be inserted into the cash register. These devices record the Universal Product Code (UPC) marked on the product itself.

Direct Sales Measurement

Most advertisers use some method of direct sales measurement, such as warehouse removals, store audits, or store scanner data, to track sales levels over time. The information from these sources often is used as a direct or indirect measure of advertising performance, but because advertising is but one of many factors affecting sales, these figures are far from the best method of evaluating advertising. Nonetheless, many companies will change advertising if sales are down and will determine next year's advertising budget based on this year's sales.

How to Measure

Surveys

Sample surveys are used to obtain measures of awareness, recall, and attitude. They can be conducted via mail, telephone, or in person. Because recognition measures require that the respondent be presented with the advertisement, they are usually conducted in person, but it is possible to send advertisements through the mail and hold a telephone follow-up interview to determine recognition scores.

Diaries are a special type of questionnaire used in tracking surveys. Panel members record purchases or media behavior daily in their diaries and then mail them back after a specified period of time.

Scanners

Scanners can be used at home or at the retail site to record purchases. At the micro level, scanners are used by the individual consumer to record purchases of products bearing the UPC symbol. At the macro level, manufacturers obtain scanner data from the retail store as a direct measure of sales volume.

Whom to Measure

Two major decisions about whom to measure involve whether to use a panel or sample survey when tracking over a long period and how to choose individual markets to most closely represent the entire country.

As we learned in Chapter 2, the ability to project the findings from a smaller group to a larger group is directly related to how representative the smaller group is of the larger. The best way to ensure a representative sample is to randomly select it from a larger group. This is the procedure of choice for many panel and sample survey designs. In other cases, however, it is virtually impossible to select a random sample, and so compromise methods are used.

Panel versus Sample Survey Designs

Panel designs call for recruiting a sample that will be monitored continuously over time. The alternative to monitoring the same group over time is to select separate households or individual samples each time a measurement is needed.

The primary benefit of using a panel is that it makes available longitudinal data—information from a constant source (sample) over time. Panels are used to provide figures on the percentage of households buying a category or brand and the volume purchased by each household. With single-source systems, the panel is also measured for media exposure (either through diaries or people-meters). Over time, the combination of media exposure data and purchase data provide some powerful tools for analysis. Household buying behavior changes can be observed in response to changes in advertising content, weight, or other changes in the marketing mix.

The primary disadvantage of panel data stems from questions about the representativeness of the panel itself. Frequently only a fraction of the number of households approached will actually agree to participate. Cooperation rates vary and generally are not made public. Beyond the issue of representativeness is the additional concern that participants over time become more deal prone and price conscious. Some studies have suggested this may be the case.

Sample surveys call for measuring different individuals in the same manner over a period of time. This procedure prevents respondents from becoming overly sensitized, but it has a few drawbacks of its own. Of primary concern is that it is impossible to gauge the stability of attitudes if a different sample is interviewed in each wave of measurement. In other words, you can describe in the aggregate to what extent responses have changed, but you do not know to what extent individuals changed over the time period under study.

Choosing Tracking Samples

Whenever sampling procedures are used, the question of representativeness must be addressed. For tracking studies, it is necessary that the individuals or geographic areas of markets under study provide a true picture of the larger population. For a simple sample survey, the answer is to choose subjects randomly. For a panel, subjects who drop out, move away, or for any reason are no longer measured must be very carefully replaced so that the representativeness of the sample is not compromised. Recently, a major problem with the single-source data markets is that respondents cease to cooperate after about a year of measurement.

When dealing with individual markets in an effort to project to the national picture, care again must be taken to ensure that the results from a few selected markets are in fact generalizable to the entire country.

When to Measure

In addition to the decisions about what measurement techniques to use, what to measure, and how to collect the data, the issue of when to conduct the measurements must be addressed. In the case of ad hoc studies of the effectiveness of a single ad in a specific vehicle, the timing of the fieldwork is planned to coincide with the appearance of the magazine at the newsstand or the airing of the program carrying the commercial to be tested. Interviewing is usually done within 24 hours of exposure. See Figure 18-3 below.

Figure 18–3
Tracking Study Results at One-Month and Six-Month Intervals

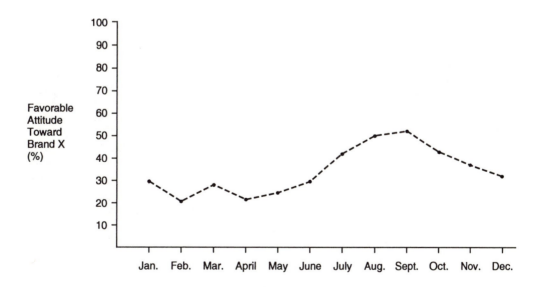

For tracking studies, the issue of timing has taken on increased importance in the past few years as studies have provided evidence to support continuous measurement practices.

Basically, the choices for when to measure boil down to: (1) "point in time" studies, which include before-and-after measurement of tracking variables as well as quarterly or other periodic measurement and (2) "continuous" measurement studies, which involve ongoing interviewing of respondents and yield a finer image of fluctuations in the measurement variables over time.

Results from the studies conducted at six-month intervals would have shown awareness levels to be fairly static, while the one-month results indicate considerable fluctuation within six-month periods. True continuous measurement often involves daily or weekly interviewing and the computation of a "rolling average" for the monthly period.

Commercial Posttesting Services

Gallup & Robinson: Magazine Impact Research Service (MIRS)

MIRS tests ads that appear in selected issues of major consumer, women's, service, and news magazines. Ads are tested in the respondent's home after natural exposure. Magazines tested include *Time, Playboy, Sports Illustrated, Business Week, Better Homes and Gardens, Bon Appetit, Cosmopolitan, Mademoiselle, Travel & Leisure, People,* and others.

A recruited sample of 150 men or 150 women, or a dual sample of 200, is taken from 10 metropolitan areas. Participants must have read at least two of the last four issues of the test magazine or a similar magazine, but not the current issue to be tested. Test magazines are delivered to respondents who are asked to read them in a normal manner that day and evening.

The day following placement, respondents are contacted by telephone and asked questions to determine readership. A list of about 15 brand/category-aided cues is read and respondents are asked which ads they remember seeing. For each ad they claim to have recalled, respondents are asked additional questions.

Results include measures of recall (proved name registration), idea communication, persuasion (favorable buying attitude or favorable attitude), responses to diagnostic questions, and verbatim remarks. A special adjusted recall score called Comparative Proved Name Registration is computed for MIRS ads to allow for different magazine issues and different ad sizes. Figure 18–4 shows MIRS Comparative PNR scores. MIRS clients also receive category norms. Subscribers to the service receive reports on five or more of their own ads as well as recall and persuasion scores for up to 25 competitors' ads.

Figure 18–4
Comparative Proved Name Registration Scores for Magazine Impact Research Service

MIRS Comparative PNR Score Distribution, 1981–1990

| COMP. PNR | NUMBER OF ADS | | | |
| | MEN | | WOMEN | |
	ALL ADS*	1P4C ADS*	ALL ADS*	1P4C ADS*
51+	5	0	12	9
48–50	0	0	7	6
45–47	3	2	14	10
42–44	5	2	10	8
39–41	6	3	28	17
36–38	5	0	46	31
33–35	16	4	72	50
30–32	34	16	128	99
27–29	78	44	246	189
24–26	144	92	458	377
21–23	317	220	643	549
18–20	475	339	709	567
15–17	770	555	692	506
12–14	1277	912	853	509
9–11	1424	847	870	485
6– 8	1317	591	767	447
3– 5	749	326	513	268
0– 2	158	52	160	71
TOTALS	6783	4005	6228	4198
AVERAGE PNR	11.7	12.5	15.3	16.5
SCORE DIST. STD. DEV.	6.2	5.7	8.5	8.3
SCORE DIST. STD. ERROR	.08	.09	.11	.13

*Cost Factors: All Ads .4 – 2.1;   1P4C .87 – 1.00

Source: Gallup & Robinson.

ASI: Print Plus

Print Plus offers advertisers the opportunity to test print ads before or after committing to a magazine schedule. A special tip-in service is available. This allows ads that do not naturally appear in a test issue to be pasted into the magazine on short notice (this is a pretest by our definition).

Posttesting can be done in current issues of general distribution magazines such as *People, Time, Newsweek, Sports Illustrated, McCalls, Better Homes and Gardens, Cosmopolitan,* or *Redbook.* Samples of 175 men, 175 women, or 100 men and 100 women for a dual-sex test are selected from at least five markets. Participants must be readers of the magazine.

Test issues are placed with participants, who are told they are in a survey of public opinion about magazines. Pre-exposure brand attitude is measured in the context of a prize drawing where a dollar amount of a product is to be awarded. Respondents are asked to read the magazine at home as they normally would, and a telephone interview is conducted the following day.

After readership is established, eight company name cues are administered, and for each ad the respondent claims to remember detailed questions are asked to determine recall and communication. Four ads are re-exposed to respondents who are asked to look at each one and then respond to a diagnostic adjective checklist and to indicate interest in the product.

A post-exposure brand preference question, again in the context of the prize drawing, is re-administered for each of the product categories.

Starch INRA Hooper: Message Report Service

Starch provides posttesting of print ads in some 700 issues of consumer, business, trade, and professional magazines and newspapers. More than 75,000 people are interviewed by Starch each year with responses to more than 50,000 ads.

Samples of at least 100 issue readers are interviewed face-to-face in 20 to 30 urban locations. After a publication has appeared and readers have had an opportunity to look through their issue, interviewing is conducted for two days for a daily publication, one week for a weekly, and two weeks for a bi-weekly or monthly publication.

No more than 90 items are evaluated by respondents in the course of a Starch interview, and different starting points in the publication are used to control for fatigue effects. Once readership of an issue has been established by allowing the participant to look at the cover or glance through the contents, the advertisement evaluation begins.

Interviewers turn the pages of the publication and inquire about each ad being studied. If a yes is given to the initial question, "Did you see or read any part of this advertisement?" follow-up questions are asked to determine observation and reading of illustrations, headlines, signatures, and copy blocks. Information from these items is used to classify readers as follows:

Noted Reader: a person who remembers having previously seen the advertisement in the issue

Associated Reader: a person who noted the ad and also read some part of it that indicated the brand or advertiser

Read Most Reader: a person who read more than half of the written material in the ad

Demographic information is collected for use in cross-tabulations of readership data. Basic Starch reports include a labeled issue with figures indicating overall readership levels and noting or reading of illustrations, headlines, signatures, and copy blocks (see Figure 18-5); a summary report listing all studied ads in each issue arranged by category and showing percentages of Noted, Associated, and Read Most Readers (see Figure 18-6); and Adnorm data including two-year averages for the publication. The norms enable an advertiser to compare readership of a specific ad in a given issue with category ads of the same size and color for other issues (see Figure 18-7).

Starch INRA Hooper: Impression Study

The Starch Impression Study can be tailored for pretesting or posttesting ads in magazines, newspaper, television, and outdoors. It is a qualitative assessment of the advertising to determine if the intended message is getting through to consumers.

Face-to-face interviews are conducted with respondents who meet criteria specified by the client. In the magazine posttesting procedure, respondents are shown an ad which has appeared naturally in a magazine. Questions posed by the interviewer are designed to elicit feedback from the respondent about the meaning of the ad and his or her level of involvement with it. Examples of specific questions and probes include:

"When you first looked at this advertisement, what was outstanding to you? Tell me more about it. What does that mean to YOU?"

"In your own words, what did the advertisement tell you about the (product, service, or company)? Tell me more about it. What does that mean to YOU?"

"What did the pictures tell you? Tell me more about it. What does that mean to YOU?"

"In your own words, what did the written material tell you? Tell me more about it. What does that mean to YOU?"

Analysts interpret responses and prepare a report on the extent to which an ad as a whole has accomplished its objectives, strong and weak points of specific ad components, normative data for comparison against other ads, and diagnostic information obtained from respondent verbatim remarks.

Figure 18-5
Basic Starch Report

Source: Starch INRA Hooper.

Figure 18–6
Starch Readership Report: Tested Ads by Category

[2A] **Ladies' Home Journal**   **STARCH READERSHIP**

November 1990
Women Readers
Total of 78 1/2 Page or Larger Ads

			RANK			PERCENTAGES		
PAGE	SIZE & COLOR	ADVERTISER	By Noted	By Associated	Noted	Assoc.	Read Some	Read Most
		COOKING PRODS./SEASONINGS						
237	1P4B	LIBBY'S PUMPKIN & PILLSBURY ALL READY PIE CRUST	8	7	64	61	47	23
239	H1/2P4B	MRS DASH SALT FREE SEASONINGS/GARLIC & HERB OFFER	45	38	51	49	34	11
241	1P4	HUNT'S TOMATO PRODUCTS	38	32	53	51	33	15
242	1/3&P4B	CRISCO VEGETABLE SHORTENING	3	5	67	63	43	17
244	H1/2S4B	NESTLE TOLL HOUSE TREASURES DELUXE BAKING PIECES	12	10	61	60	44	19
253	1P4B	SHAKE 'N BAKE COATING MIX/ OFFER	65	56	44	43	32-	11-
256	1S4	NATIONAL HONEY BOARD	12	10	61	60	44	14
269	1P4B	AUNT JEMIMA SYRUP/LITE	25	17	58	56	39-	23-
275	V1/2P4B	HEINZ CHILI SAUCE	49	44	50	48	32	8
280	M1/2S4B	BAKER'S UNSWEETENED BAKING CHOCOLATE	12	12	61	59	50	24
		COSMETICS/BEAUTY AIDS						
144	1P4B	LUBRIDERM LOTION	58	56	47	43	31-	16-
157	1P4B	CETAPHIL FACIAL CLEANSER	72	71	41	38	26	6
4C	1P4B	COVER GIRL MAKE-UP/MOISTURE WEAR	28	22	57	55	33	6
		DAIRY PRODS./SUBSTITUTES						
235	1P4B	NATIONAL DAIRY BOARD	42	44	52	48	39	19

[*] Less than 0.5%   [-] Fewer than 50 Words   [**] Not Applicable   [=] Fewer than 4 Words   [#] Page/Copy Varies
[++] Not Available   [+] All Ads for Size/Color Used as Base

Starch INRA Hooper, Inc.

Source: Starch INRA Hooper.

Figure 18–7
Starch Readership Adnorms for One-Page Four-Color Magazine Ads

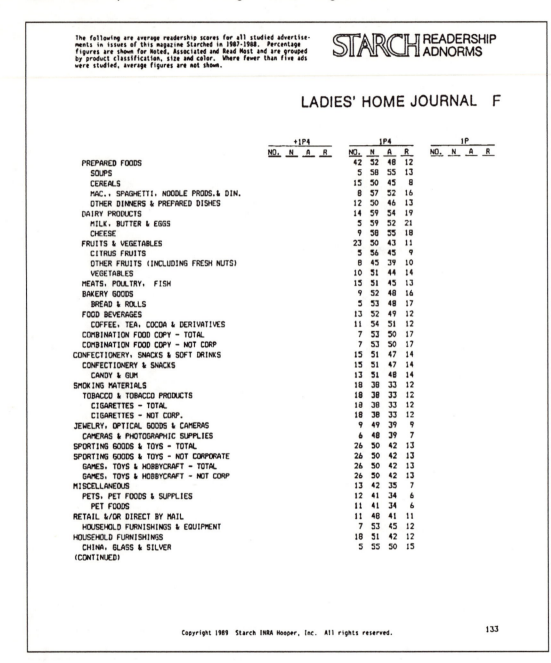

STARCH READERSHIP ADNORMS

LADIES' HOME JOURNAL   F

	+1P4				1P4				1P		
	NO.	N	A	R	NO.	N	A	R	NO.	N	A	R
PREPARED FOODS					42	52	48	12				
SOUPS					5	58	55	13				
CEREALS					15	50	45	8				
MAC., SPAGHETTI, NOODLE PRODS.& DIN.					8	57	52	16				
OTHER DINNERS & PREPARED DISHES					12	50	46	13				
DAIRY PRODUCTS					14	59	54	19				
MILK, BUTTER & EGGS					5	59	52	21				
CHEESE					9	58	55	18				
FRUITS & VEGETABLES					23	50	43	11				
CITRUS FRUITS					5	56	45	9				
OTHER FRUITS (INCLUDING FRESH NUTS)					8	45	39	10				
VEGETABLES					10	51	44	14				
MEATS, POULTRY, FISH					15	51	45	13				
BAKERY GOODS					9	52	48	16				
BREAD & ROLLS					5	53	48	17				
FOOD BEVERAGES					13	52	49	12				
COFFEE, TEA, COCOA & DERIVATIVES					11	54	51	12				
COMBINATION FOOD COPY - TOTAL					7	53	50	17				
COMBINATION FOOD COPY - NOT CORP					7	53	50	17				
CONFECTIONERY, SNACKS & SOFT DRINKS					15	51	47	14				
CONFECTIONERY & SNACKS					15	51	47	14				
CANDY & GUM					13	51	48	14				
SMOKING MATERIALS					18	38	33	12				
TOBACCO & TOBACCO PRODUCTS					18	38	33	12				
CIGARETTES - TOTAL					18	38	33	12				
CIGARETTES - NOT CORP.					18	38	33	12				
JEWELRY, OPTICAL GOODS & CAMERAS					9	49	39	9				
CAMERAS & PHOTOGRAPHIC SUPPLIES					6	48	39	7				
SPORTING GOODS & TOYS - TOTAL					26	50	42	13				
SPORTING GOODS & TOYS - NOT CORPORATE					26	50	42	13				
GAMES, TOYS & HOBBYCRAFT - TOTAL					26	50	42	13				
GAMES, TOYS & HOBBYCRAFT - NOT CORP					26	50	42	13				
MISCELLANEOUS					13	42	35	7				
PETS, PET FOODS & SUPPLIES					12	41	34	6				
PET FOODS					11	41	34	6				
RETAIL &/OR DIRECT BY MAIL					11	48	41	11				
HOUSEHOLD FURNISHINGS & EQUIPMENT					7	53	45	12				
HOUSEHOLD FURNISHINGS					18	51	42	12				
CHINA, GLASS & SILVER					5	55	50	15				
(CONTINUED)												

133

Source: Starch INRA Hooper.

Review

In this chapter we saw that:

- Posttesting is the final stage of message measurement, which provides a means of recording over time how campaigns perform in the real world.
- Reasons for conducting a posttest include recording advertising effects over time; monitoring advertising effectiveness under varying market conditions; and estimating advertising wearout.
- The variables measured in posttesting are awareness, recall, recognition, and attitudes, measured using survey methods; and sales measures, obtained from diaries, scanner panels, and store audits.
- Panel designs call for recruiting a sample that will be monitored continuously over time; sample surveys call for measuring different individuals in the same manner over a period of time.
- Measurements can be taken either at a point in time (quarterly or some other period) or continuously (daily or weekly, with computation of a rolling average).
- Four commercial posttesting services currently in operation are: Gallup & Robinson, MIRS; ASI, Print Plus; Starch INRA Hooper, Message Report Service; and Starch INRA Hooper, Impression Study.

Endnotes

1. Arthur Juchems and Tony Twyman, "The Measurement of Advertising Awareness and Its Applications," *Journal of the Market Research Society.*

19 Money Research

We have already discussed three of the four *M*s associated with advertising—markets, media, and messages. Now we turn to money, or advertising expenditure, research. We will deal with questions of *how much* money to spend, *when* to spend it, and *where* to spend it.

How *Not* to Conduct Money Research

There are many ways of making *wrong* decisions on advertising expenditure. Four of the most common are "seat of the pants," "agency recommendation," "percentage of sales," and "watch the competitor."

The "seat of the pants" procedure goes something like this. The president and the principal officers of a company sit down around a conference table and discuss and argue the question, "How much money should we spend on advertising next year?" All of them have opinions on the matter—based on their own special interests, prejudices for or against the value of advertising, desire to impress people outside the company, and so on. Sometimes an entire marketing budget has already been established and the discussion centers around what proportion of that total should go to advertising. After hours or days or sometimes months of wrangling—all based on opinions rather than evidence—some sort of compromise solution is reached. This is usually heavily weighted toward the opinion held by the highest-ranking company officials taking part and the most valuable, persistent and persuasive talkers at the table. The eventual figure bears little or no relation, to what really *should* be spent—it may be too much, in which case money is wasted, or it may be too little, in which case extra profits are lost.

"Agency recommendation," though it sometimes makes the least sense, is possibly the most often used way of deciding advertising expenditure. The advertising agency advises the client on how much to spend. If you were the agency, and your income was based on the size of your client's expenditure (usually 15 percent of it), would you recommend a small advertising budget or a large one?

Obviously, it's in the agency's best interests to recommend a high level of spending on advertising.

"Watch the competitor" is a game based on the assumptions that the leading competitors (a) are smarter, (b) have some divine guidance, or (c) have some real knowledge based on research. The advertising budget of the "watching" company is then geared to the budget of the competitor. Chances are, however, that competitors are also operating on faith and ignorance. Even if the competitors' advertising *is* based on research knowledge, what's right for one company isn't necessarily right for another. For example, advertising spending for a company that clearly leads the field in sales may be either too much or too little for companies with a smaller share of market.

The "percentage of sales" method gives the comfortable illusion that it is scientific because it is based on numbers and statistics. Sometime in the past, a company oracle may have decided that, for example, advertising should be 3 percent of gross sales income. If this policy is followed year after year, it's possible to achieve a high correlation between sales and advertising. The fallacy is that cause-and-effect is reversed—instead of advertising being a cause of sales, it ends up being an *effect* of sales.

All four of these ways of deciding how much to spend on advertising are also common in deciding which media and messages to use.

A Better Way: Controlled Field Experiments (CFX)

The most reliable method for determining advertising expenditure is the controlled field experiment, using sales (or profits) as the dependent variable. As with other advertising research methods, experts are not in complete agreement on this. However, the best support for the controlled field experiment comes from some of the largest and most profitable advertisers in the country who have adopted it, such as Ford, Curtis, DuPont, and others. It satisfies the businessperson's requirement for practical and realistic goals, and the researcher's requirement for valid and rigorous measurement.

A description of controlled field experiment design has already been given in Chapter 9. (It may be useful at this point to review that section.) Some special uses of CFX for solving problems of advertising expenditure will be discussed here—total advertising budget, spending patterns over time, market concentration, media allocation, and vehicle allocation.

Setting Total Advertising Budget

Planning a controlled field experiment on the total advertising budget should start many months before a new budget is to go into effect. Why? Because advertising's effects are usually slow to take hold, necessitating months of research before budget decisions are made.

Here is an example, using a fictitious product, Sparkle-Dent toothpaste. In the example, the main dependent variable is sales, to be determined by UPC scanning and store audits. (Sales could also be determined by using sales registration cards, pantry inventory, or surveys of reported purchase.) The researcher could also measure such things as brand awareness, knowledge, image, attitude, buying preferences, and so on. While a measure of sales alone will determine what happened, these other measures are needed to determine *why* they happened and give a better understanding of the dynamics of the advertising.

The experimental unit is *markets* (metropolitan areas) rather than individuals or small geographic tracts. The reason for this is that it is next to impossible to manipulate several variations of spending level in all media *within* a market. A whole market can be controlled and varied more precisely.

It is usually impossible in the case of an established product to completely withdraw all advertising and set up a "no advertising" control treatment. For this reason, in this example, the control treatment is the *normal* advertising budget. Spending levels will be varied above and below the normal level to answer the questions, "Should we decrease or increase the advertising budget? If so, by how much?"

This example assumes that, from pre-research planning and discussion, management has agreed to test the following expenditure levels: one-half of normal (50%), normal (100%), one-half above normal (150%), and twice normal (200%). It's possible, of course, to test any other levels that are considered practical, all the way up to ten times normal or more, if desired. This is called a one-variable experiment—only spending level is varied.

Another assumption in this example is that advertising will be varied proportionately in all media if possible. In the 50 percent treatment, for example, where the advertising is cut in half, someone might note that television makes up half the total advertising budget and perhaps it would be easier to simply cut out television. This procedure would, however, confuse the effects obtained: It would be impossible to tell if change in sales was due to budget decrease or to the cut in television advertising only, or if similar results would be obtained with decreases in other media. (To vary media allocation as well as budget level, a 2-variable "factorial design" would be used. For example, a 4 x 3 factorial design would include 12 treatments—4 budget levels for each of 3 kinds of media allocations.)

For the example we also assume that the advertising messages themselves are handled "normally" in all treatments. If both spending level and advertising messages were varied, it would be impossible to tell which factor caused any obtained change, unless factorial design is used.

In short, in an experiment on spending level alone, all other conditions (media used, messages, etc.) should be held constant.

Having made these decisions and assumptions, the details of the spending experiment can now be planned, with the following ingredients specified:

Product (fictitious):	Sparkle-Dent Toothpaste
Independent variable:	Spending level
Number of treatments:	Four (50% normal, 100% normal, 150% normal, and 200% normal), respectively, S1, S2, S3, and S4.

Primary dependent variable (M1):	Sales
Other possible dependent variables:	Awareness, knowledge, image, attitude, buying intentions (data gathered by personal interview sample survey)
Advertising timetable:	January–December 1993 (12 months)
Research timetable:	Sales: Continuing measurement for six months before, during, and six months after, respectively, T1, T2, and T3
	Surveys: Before, during, and after tests
Measurement units:	40 markets, randomly divided into four groups of 10, respectively, P1a, P1b, P1c, and P1d

The notational diagram looks like this, showing only the major components:

	T1	T2	T3
P1a	M1	S1	M1
P1b	M1	S2	M1
P1c	M1	S3	M1
P1d	M1	S4	M1

This basic plan can now be fleshed out to show more detail, in this manner:

Treatment	July 1 1992 — Pretest Period (6 mos.)	Jan. 1 1993 — Test Period (12 mos.)	Jan. 1 1994 — After-test Period (6 mos.)	June 30 1994
A (10 markets)	$: 100%	50%	100%	
B (10 markets)	$: 100%	100%	100%	
C (10 markets)	$: 100%	150%	100%	
D (10 markets)	$: 100%	200%	100%	
Sales audit	Monthly,	Continuous		
Surveys	x	x x x	x x	
	Dec. 1992	Mar. June Sept. 1993	Jan. June 1994	

Note that monthly sales figures will be accumulated, permitting detection of *when* the sales changes occur and how long after the test period they persist. For the same reason, surveys are conducted just before the test, at three-month intervals during the test, immediately after, and six months after. For other products, these time intervals might vary, depending on marketing conditions, the natural purchase cycle, and other factors.

From here on, there are many other details to be planned—the advertising agency must arrange to buy the media in the planned amounts, sales auditing and survey procedures must be scheduled, and many other coordination efforts must be carried out among the company, the agency, the research firm, and the media.

During the course of the experiment, rigorous attention must be paid to detailed execution of the plan. Analysis of the data is carried out throughout and after the experiment, resulting in a final report and a budget decision based on the results.

The bare bones of the analysis, however, are simple. The change in sales for each treatment are compared, and net sales changes—compared against the control—are computed. Then, advertising cost effectiveness, cost-per-thousand sales (CPMS), can easily be calculated, in addition to net sales, net profit, etc.

Treatment	Measurement	Change (after minus before)
A (50%)	Before and after advertising	Amount, + or −
B (100%)	Same	Same
C (150%)	Same	Same
D (200%)	Same	Same

As we have seen, advertising expenditure (the independent treatment variable) can be varied in many ways:

Thus: 50%, 100%, 150%, 200% (as in the example)

or: 0%, 100%, 200%

or: 75%, 100%, 125%

It's worthwhile to reiterate one requirement for such 1-variable experiments: *all other conditions, except the independent treatment variable, in the test markets should be maintained exactly as normal.* The money taken away or added to advertising should not be funneled into other marketing activities in those markets; local advertising by retail merchants should not be changed to compensate for the budget changes. Otherwise, the results of the experiment will be clouded. Regarding competitive advertising, there is of course no way to control this; one reason for using equivalent groups of markets for each treatment is to ensure that *fluctuations in competitive advertising and other non-controllable factors are constant for all treatments.* The time, place, and conditions of such testing are generally guarded as top secret information, to prevent others within and without the company from spoiling the results, either deliberately or accidentally.

Here is a fictitious table of results that might be obtained from the example given: (Raw scores converted to index: 100 = normal sales)

Group/ Treatment	Sales index performance After year-long test				Net sales change		
	Before 1992	1/94 1 mo.	3/94 3 mos.	6/94 6 mos.	1/94 1 mo.	3/94 3 mos.	6/94 6 mos.
P1a (50%)	100	60	70	80	− 40	− 30	− 20
P1b (100%-normal)	100	100	100	100	0	0	0
P1c (150%)	100	110	105	100	+ 10	+ 5	0
P1d (200%)	100	160	140	120	+ 60	+ 40	+ 20

The researcher can draw the following conclusions from these results:

1. Changes in advertising budget have an immediate effect which gradually decreases as the budget is returned to normal.

2. Sales are lost when advertising is decreased by 50 percent.

3. Sales do not increase appreciably when advertising is increased by 50 percent.

4. Doubling the budget produces a significant (but not proportional) increase in sales which decreases somewhat over time but is maintained significantly higher as long as six months after the change.

The rate of decay in increased sales for the doubled budget could be determined by continuing the analysis for a year or more. One could also trace the change in *profits* as well as in sales; even though sales increased significantly when advertising doubled, it's conceivable that the cost per incremental sale was excessive, resulting in *decreased* profits, along with increased sales.

Other analyses could compare the sales change with changes in awareness, knowledge, attitudes, and other dependent variables measured.

Determining Advertising Spending Pattern

The advertising spending pattern is simply the timing of advertising expenditures. Given a certain amount of money to spend over a year, say, one million dollars, an infinite number of spending patterns is possible. A few are shown in Figure 19–1.

Figure 19–1
Spending Treatment Patterns

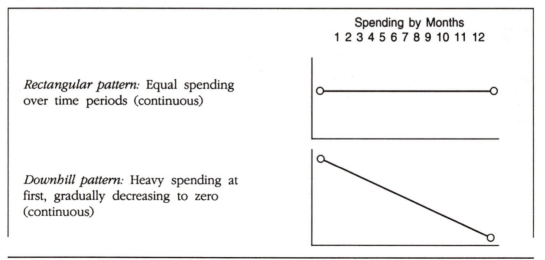

Rectangular pattern: Equal spending over time periods (continuous)

Downhill pattern: Heavy spending at first, gradually decreasing to zero (continuous)

Spending by Months
1 2 3 4 5 6 7 8 9 10 11 12

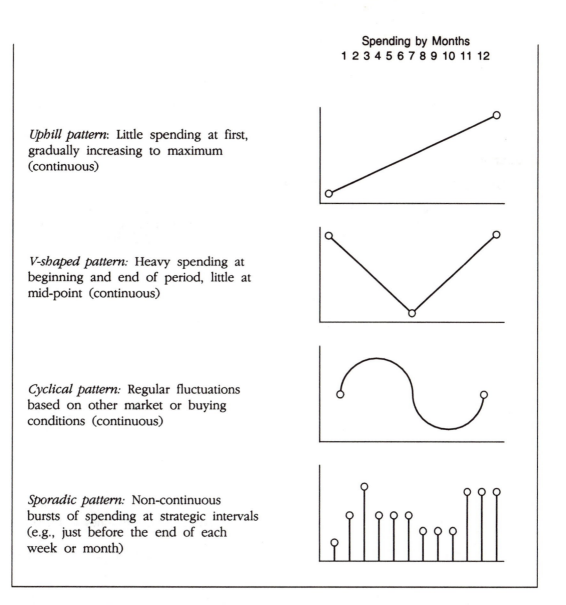

Uphill pattern: Little spending at first, gradually increasing to maximum (continuous)

V-shaped pattern: Heavy spending at beginning and end of period, little at mid-point (continuous)

Cyclical pattern: Regular fluctuations based on other market or buying conditions (continuous)

Sporadic pattern: Non-continuous bursts of spending at strategic intervals (e.g., just before the end of each week or month)

There are, of course, innumerable variations in spending patterns that might be tested—inverted V patterns, W-shaped patterns, irregular patterns based on seasonal fluctuation, and so on. The correct pattern for one product may not be appropriate for another. Some products have seasonal usage, and the variations in spending pattern might be geared to those fluctuations. Other products, such as automobiles, have annual product changes, and the advertising expenditure may be geared to introduction time.

For the advertising researcher, the major point is this: any variations in spending pattern may be tested by controlled field experiments in much the same manner as budget experiments. From a pool of markets, markets can be randomly assigned to as many groups as there are spending pattern treatments to be tested.

The pattern of spending can be an extremely important factor in the results obtained from advertising. It's conceivable that a given advertising budget might result in 50 percent fewer sales or 50 percent more sales, depending on the spending pattern.

Determining Market Allocation of Funds

For whatever reason, the researcher may decide to test whether a given advertising budget gets better results in some kinds of markets than others. Some of the variations in market allocation that might be considered are these:

1. Market size;
2. Market strength;
3. Geographical area;
4. Socioeconomic conditions.

Let's look at each.

Market size

Treatments   Large markets (over 500,000 population)
vs.
Medium-sized markets (50,000 to 500,000 population)
vs.
Small markets (under 50,000 population)

Market strength

Treatments   Strong markets (where existing share of sales is high)
vs.
Average markets (where existing share of sales is medium)
vs.
Weak markets (where existing share of sales is low)

Geographical area

Treatments   Far west
vs.
Midwest
vs.
East
(Or a comparison of the seven major census regions)

Socioeconomic conditions

Treatments   High income (high per capita income and spending)
vs.
Medium income (medium per capita income and spending)
vs.
Low income (low per capita income and spending)

There are many other ways in which different geographical locations, or markets, can vary. The important market characteristics vary from product to product, so no one style of market allocation is ideal for all products. Intensive study of other data on the product and its customers provide clues to the crucial experimental treatments.

The controlled field experiment can test these different strategies of advertising spending by allocating the same amount of money to several market conditions and measuring the results.

Determining Media Allocation

Apart from the question of overall advertising expenditure, one problem that always arises in advertising is the problem of deciding how the advertising budget should be allocated to the various media or vehicles within media. Which medium, or combination of media, would be best for placement of *additional* or supplemental advertising money?

In Chapters 13 and 14 on media research, this problem was discussed in terms of such dependent variables as circulation, audience size, and advertising exposure. Through such considerations, it's possible to narrow down the tremendous number of alternatives to a few alternatives for final experimentation. The controlled field experiment, with sales or profits as the dependent variable and expenditure per medium as the independent variable, is really the acid test of media effectiveness.

To test the relative effectiveness of incremental spending in one or other of several media, the researcher conducts *single media experiments.* To test the relative effectiveness of combinations of media, the researcher conducts *media mix experiments.* As an example, assume there is $100,000 to invest in added media— that is, $100,000 over and above the normal budget.

Single-media experiment

Treatments   Normal media usage (control)
vs.
Normal plus $100,000 radio
vs.
Normal plus $100,000 TV

---

vs.

Normal plus $100,000 newspaper

vs.

Normal plus $100,000 magazine

vs.

Normal plus $100,000 direct mail

This example contains six treatments—normal usage to serve as a control, plus five treatments consisting of $100,000 extra in each of five media. It's possible, of course, to test either one additional medium in this fashion, or as many as are available, including outdoor, skywriting, matchbook covers, or whatever. In this case, with six treatments, the researcher starts with an initial selection of 12, 18, 24, 30, or any number of markets divisible by six—the more the better—and then randomly assigns those markets to the six treatment groups as described earlier. The results of this experiment provide direct comparison of every medium with every other in terms of incremental sales and profits, and/or various survey measures of effectiveness.

A media mix experiment is somewhat more complicated, since it involves a simultaneous test of *combinations* of media at various levels. To reduce the complexity, the example below deals only with two media—newspapers and television—and two levels of additional spending in each. This produces four treatments as follows:

Constant-sum media mix

Treatments	Normal (control)
	vs.
	Normal plus $50,000 TV plus $50,000 newspaper
	vs.
	Normal plus $100,000 TV
	vs.
	Normal plus $100,000 newspaper

The term *constant sum* above simply means that some fixed amount—in this case, $100,000—is allocated among two media. To determine the best constant-sum combination of six media could require 64 different treatments ($2 \times 2 \times 2 \times 2 \times 2 \times 2$); in usual practice, owing to limitations in the number of test markets available, this number of treatments is not feasible.

Variable-sum media mix

Treatments	1. Normal (control)
	vs.

2. Normal plus $50,000 TV

vs.

3. Normal plus $100,000 TV

vs.

4. Normal plus $50,000 newspaper

vs.

5. Normal plus $100,000 newspaper

vs.

6. Normal plus $50,000 TV and $50,000 newspaper

vs.

7. Normal plus $50,000 TV and $100,000 newspaper

vs.

8. Normal plus $100,000 TV and $50,000 newspaper

vs.

9. Normal plus $100,000 TV and $100,000 newspaper

In this variable-sum example, there are two media (newspapers and television) at three different levels—zero, $50,000, and $100,000—for each, for a total of nine different treatments. This is a *variable*-sum media mix because, even though no single medium gets more than $100,000, the total spending per treatment varies from $50,000 to $200,000. The results of this experiment can determine not only which individual medium is best in comparison with the other, but also the effects of different *combinations* of media. Depending on the number of test markets available and suitable, an advertiser could theoretically test any number of media, at any number of levels; in practice, sixteen treatments becomes unwieldy to manage and is extremely expensive. It's more practical to use more markets and fewer treatments.

Determining Vehicle Allocation

Assuming it has already been decided to spend an additional $100,000 in the magazine medium, the next question is which vehicle to use. This leads to a vehicle allocation study. Should the $100,000 be spent in *Cosmopolitan, Redbook,* or *American Home?* In the case of magazines, the researcher can depart from the use of markets as the measurement units, and instead use *split-run* experimentation, in which individual subscribers are the measurement units. In the split-run technique, a listing of *individuals* is randomly divided into treatment groups. This requires that sales data be keyed to individuals rather than markets and is more feasible for some products (e.g., cars) than others. In this case, let's say that sales information by subscribers can be determined.

Single vehicle experiment

Treatments	Normal spending (control)
	vs.
	Normal plus $100,000 in *Cosmopolitan*
	vs.
	Normal plus $100,000 in *Redbook*
	vs.
	Normal plus $100,000 in *American Home*

The researcher could also conduct *constant-sum vehicle mix* and *variable-sum vehicle mix* experiments in the same manner as described previously for media experiments.

Other Advertising Expenditure Problems

This chapter has described only a few applications of controlled field experiments to problems of total advertising budget, spending patterns over time, market concentration, media allocation, and vehicle allocation. It's also possible to design experiments which test various *combinations* of those allocations simultaneously—for example, a simultaneous test of total advertising budget levels and various spending patterns. Such complex studies are relatively easy to design, but they are difficult to execute. Reasons include the limited numbers of suitable test markets, a high number of possible treatment combinations, the attention necessary for executing the details of the design, and the coordination of the efforts of the company, the advertising agency, and the media. One rule of thumb is that a controlled field experiment becomes difficult to manage when more than twelve treatments are involved. This is not to say that a large number of treatments is impossible, but only that the problems multiply much more rapidly than the number of treatments.

The controlled field experiment, with sales or profits as the dependent variable, embodies the best business and scientific approaches in advertising research today. The plan is not suitable for *all* problems concerning media or messages or money—but, where possible, it is the method of choice.

Some statisticians believe that statistical analysis of data, without conducting any additional or new research, can provide answers to many advertising problems. But many others believe that statistical analysis alone is wishful thinking. It is useful to keep in mind the general principle: only a *controlled* experiment can accurately show cause and effect. And only a *field* experiment can accurately be projected to the real world.

Review

In this chapter we saw that:

- The most valid method for determining advertising expenditure is the controlled field experiment, using sales (or profit) as the dependent variable.

- The controlled field experiment can solve problems of setting total advertising budget, determining advertising spending patterns, determining market allocation of funds, and determining media allocation and vehicle allocation.

Part 5

The Future of Advertising Research

20 Advertising Research Today

The marketing environment has been affected by significant changes in the economy, business ownership, work force, technology, social structure, media industry, and other factors. This has caused industry analysts to point to the importance of managing change as a strategy for remaining successful in the competitive world of advertising and marketing. It is impossible to discuss the "state of the art" in advertising research without acknowledging not only developments directly related to the practice of measurement, but also the more far-reaching developments and issues in the field of marketing promotion as a whole. It is these industrywide trends that determine the environment in which the advertising agency, and hence the research department, operates. Some of the factors affecting the advertising research industry are discussed below.

Shifts in Marketing Emphasis

Marketing strategies that involve mass production, mass targeting, mass media, and aggregation of data have been changed somewhat by developments in the marketplace—particularly by changing consumer needs and desires. One market researcher described traditional mass marketing of the 1950s and 1960s as follows:

> You do research to uncover the most important benefit sought by the greatest number of consumers. You create products delivering those benefits. You develop TV commercials appealing to the broadest population base and you run those commercials on network TV to reach the greatest number of viewers. You gain broadscale distribution in supermarkets across the land, and then continue to advertise and promote to reinforce consumer loyalty.[1]

While mass marketing has not disappeared, we are seeing an increasing combination of mass and "micro" marketing techniques being used. This "demassified" marketing places a premium on disaggregation rather than aggregation of data. One of the most significant effects that demassified marketing already has had on research departments is the redefinition of a database and what information is necessary to facilitate micromarketing strategies. Identifying, understanding, and effectively communicating to a particular segment may require, for instance, individual store sales information or names and addresses of individual prospects.

Social Trends

Economic and social patterns provide the backdrop against which marketers operate. The past 20 years have been characterized as "turbulent" with respect to the acceleration of change in the marketplace. Some of the changes that have had the greatest effect on marketing and advertising are described below.

A Shrinking Middle Class

As the upper class and lower class both have grown since 1975, the middle class share of income has diminished. This has resulted in decreasing possibilities for "mass markets" of homogeneous, middle-class consumers.

Women in the Workplace

More than half of the women in the United States are in the work force, a fact that is having tremendous impact on household earning potential, child-rearing, and household consumer decision making. The changing demographics of the female consumer are a challenge to the market researcher who must target her.

The Aging of America

"Baby boomers" (born between 1946 and 1964) currently account for one-third of American adults. Because of the size of this segment, it is important to study them as a market. Of interest are their changing demographics, with respect to not only age but also career interests, spending patterns, marriage and divorce, and social values. As they age, baby boomers will continue as a major marketing focus due to their changing status in the workplace and decisions in the marketplace.

Advertising Expenditures

U.S. advertising expenditures have increased steadily for the past 50 years, with the 1986 annual total exceeding $100 billion. This escalation in spending has placed unprecedented emphasis on the media planning function, which has become increasingly complex due to the availability of new media alternatives. Client companies and agencies are being held accountable for spending and placement strategies that most efficiently and effectively use the advertising dollar in a highly competitive market. Adding to the complexity of the planning process is the proliferation of qualitative and quantitative data that must be dealt with for individual media vehicles and their audiences, and the choice of various media modeling techniques and formulas for computer optimization plans. All of these factors have resulted in unprecedented attention to media research by both the advertising industry, where many agencies have media research specialists, and by the academic community, which has christened a new *Journal of Media Planning*.

Cable TV and Specialized Media

Cable television, now at more than 40 percent estimated penetration of U.S. TV households, is more of a competitor than ever for the "Big Three" networks that have dominated broadcast advertising expenditures to date. The "narrowcasting" capabilities of specialized cable channels and programming are being used in demassified marketing and can be especially attractive to the smaller advertiser. In the magazine industry, circulation figures continue to climb as specialized titles proliferate. Research on the characteristics of these specialized media and their audiences is essential for the advertiser who makes them a part of the media mix.

Computerized Media Planning

Although intuition, experience, and qualitative judgments still have a place in media planning, the availability of computerized research, frequency information, and other syndicated data and the advances in highly sophisticated media modeling programs have brought computers into the forefront of the media planning function. Research into how to best use syndicated information and modeling techniques such as optimizing programs is making the computer an increasingly valuable planning tool.

People-Meters

For years, the seemingly simple concept of "who is watching television" has been the source of ongoing controversy in the advertising industry. The practices of personal interviewing, diary, and traditional metering all were found to have their methodological drawbacks, and it was predicted by some that the introduction of the people-meter in the mid-1980s would both improve and standardize broadcast audience measurement. Unfortunately, the people-meter, which combines the traditional electronic meter components with a keypad that viewers are to punch as they enter and exit the viewing situation, was not the cure-all some had hoped. The new technology, whose initial testing often resulted in significantly lower audience estimates than had been obtained previously, still was plagued by the lingering question of how the researcher could be sure that participants were punching in and out as directed. At present, more experimentation is planned with the people-meter, and the best method of determining who watches which programs on television still eludes researchers.

Single-Source Research

The marriage of people-meter data with Universal Product Code (UPC) scanner information on purchase habits has been labeled single-source because, theoretically, an advertiser would obtain all information on target market demographics and their media-usage characteristics from a single database. Proponents of single source contend that the major advantage of the combined methodologies is the ability to make cause-and-effect statements about the absolute contribution of advertising to the consumer purchase decision. Ventures on the part of major market information vendors and other research firms to bring single-source techniques into the marketplace have met with mixed reviews. Among the major sources of concern is the reliance of single source on people-meters—TV data only. Media diaries for print and radio are proposed, but if these were used in conjunction with the meters and scanners, the specter of measurement would loom quite prominent in the household of the single-source participant. Another concern centers around the inherent limitations in using the UPC system. It is estimated that only about 35 percent of client advertising dollars are spent on products bearing the UPC. Missing from that list are big-advertising-dollar categories such as insurance, automobiles, airlines, and others.

Lack of Public Confidence in Research Methods

A variety of developments have culminated in a sometimes hostile public when it comes to participation in research studies. The growing use of the telephone for telemarketing, the introduction of computerized research and sales messages, and an increasingly wary and sophisticated consumer population have all contributed to *eroding trust in marketing institutions in general and to research specifically*. In 1987, the ARF issued a report on "Phony and Misleading Polls." The introduction to this report is shown in Figure 20-1.

Figure 20–1
ARF Report: "Phony and Misleading Polls"

ARF POSITION PAPER
PHONY OR MISLEADING POLLS

INTRODUCTION

In our information society, most Americans are asked to process large quantities of data. Our ability to quantify people's ideas and activities is basic to our marketplace and to our government. In a real sense, survey research can and has contributed to a more egalitarian and responsive social fabric.

The key factor in making this process of data-gathering a valuable tool is the quality of the work itself. Survey research is an objective process and, therefore, possesses explicit guidelines and principles. It takes place, however, in a subjective context and, therefore, is vulnerable to distortion by its producers and perceivers.

Research which is inferior, deficient, inaccurate, or misnamed threatens the entire process of marketing. It misleads the public and undermines properly conceived and executed work.

Since its founding in 1936, the Advertising Research Foundation has been dedicated to the advancement of professional standards in market research. It does this through publications, conferences, consultations, and its research councils. Two current ARF publications provide written statements of general standards for research and practical guidelines for their implementation. One of these publications is the *ARF Criteria for Marketing and Advertising Research,* originally published in 1953, updated in 1984. This document is applicable to the broad range of market research activities. The second document, entitled *Guidelines for the Public Use of Market and Opinion Research,* published in 1981, is concerned specifically with the conduct and use of public opinion polls. Hence, guidelines exist in readily available published form.

Industry standards for survey research are grounded in solid academic disciplines, including statistics with its body of principles and mathematical laws. Adherence to basic principles allows for real gains in knowledge; deviation from those principles leads to misinformation. If the principles are inadequate as an expression of the academic discipline, they should be called to account; if they are too rigorous to be practical for use in business they should be debated. But, in every case the principles and guidelines must be the focal point for judging survey research activity.

In addition to publishing general industry guidelines, the ARF seeks to identify errant practices such as the two discussed in this paper. These are examined at this time because they seem to be occurring with greater frequency and because few people seem to be able to recognize easily the ways in which they represent unprofessional work. This paper will contrast these practices to accepted industry procedures. It will note the ways in which these two practices are unacceptable and misleading.

This report is directed toward the business community, since these phony or misleading polls often occur under the auspices of persons without training in the standards that frame survey research. It is intended to reaffirm the ARF's commitment to quality through adherence to professional principles. As a business-to-business document, it is meant to alert the research community to the need for a proper response and nonresearch business professionals to the serious problems posed by these inappropriate practices.

There are two sections. The first defines each problem, provides examples, and discusses the implications of the practices. The second section points to solutions.

Review

In this chapter we saw that:

- The marketing environment has been affected by significant changes in the economy, business ownership, work force, technology, the social structure, the media industry, and other factors.

- Whereas mass marketing has not disappeared, there is an increasing development of "demassified" marketing, which places a premium on disaggregation rather than aggregation of data.

- Some of the social trends affecting advertising research in the past twenty years include a shrinking middle class, more women in the workplace, and the aging of America.

- An unprecedented emphasis on media planning has arisen from the constant growth in advertising expenditures, the proliferation of qualitative and quantitative data, and the availability of various media modeling techniques and formulas for computer optimization plans.

- The "narrowcasting" capability of specialized cable channels and programming are being used in demassified marketing and can be especially attractive to smaller advertisers.

- The people-meter has not become the cure-all that many predicted it would be by the mid-1980s, and the best method of determining who watches which programs on television still eludes researchers.

- Single-source data collection techniques have met with mixed reviews in the marketplace because of their reliance on TV data only and the inherent limitations in using the UPC system.

- Eroding trust in marketing research among consumers has stemmed from the growing use of the telephone for telemarketing, the introduction of computerized research and sales messages, and an increasingly wary and sophisticated public.

Endnotes

1. John C. Webber, "Nine Shifts Changing the Nature of Marketing Research," *Thirty-Third Annual Conference of the Advertising Research Foundation,* March 1987, p. 124.

Chapter 21

Single Source Data Systems

A new method of describing relationships among demographics, media usage, and promotions is currently under development and in limited use. Single source data, as it is often called, represents, at least in principle, a one-stop-shopping approach to marketing and advertising information about the consumer. The term single source has taken on a variety of meanings, but it involves the attempt to integrate three major classes of information:

1. product purchases at the household level

2. media exposure at the individual or household level

3. marketing activities for a brand, including in-store and in-market promotion

At the heart of single source systems is electronic measurement technology. For product purchase data, UPC scanning equipment is used at either the retail store or at the participating household. Exposure to television programs and commercials is measured by television meters or more advanced people-meters attached to TVs in each household. Both sets of electronically gathered information are transmitted to a central processing facility where the data are correlated and prepared for clients.

At a 1990 single source workshop sponsored by the Advertising Research Foundation, Joseph Russo, of Thomas J. Lipton Co., offered the following definition of single source:

> Single source data is the ongoing collection of all purchase behavior and the key elements which advertisers believe influence this behavior—advertising, promotion and merchandising—from a common buying unit (i.e., purchaser and end user) and during a common time period.[1]

While all of these classes of information are currently available from a number of sources, single source systems attempt to collect all data from the same samples of respondents at the household or individual level. Ideally, for example, the resulting data show relationships between what people watch on television, what they purchase at the store, and which promotions they might have seen. Another unique characteristic of single source is the rapidity with which the integrated information can be made available. Because much single source information is collected electronically, correlations between household television viewing patterns and store purchases are available literally overnight, and the opportunities for advertisers to respond to such information are unprecedented.

Concerns about Single Source Data Systems

Critics of single source warn that the information offered is still only correlational—not causal as some proponents claim—and that while single source represents a major step forward in highlighting relationships between advertising exposure and sales, it will not render useless all other forms of advertising research. Some of the concerns about single source are discussed below.

Reliance on Universal Product Code

Because an electronic scanning system is used, sales data are captured only for products bearing the UPC. Estimates vary as to what proportion of consumer dollars are spent on items and services other than those with the UPC, but entire categories of services such as airlines, banks, and hotels, as well as product categories such as automotive, some apparel, and fast food are not measured by the present system. A purchase diary is being used by some single source companies, but the diary poses its own problems of accuracy, as well as the potential to overload a consumer already burdened with using a television meter and a household scanner.

Limited Retail Coverage

Though single source vendors are testing their systems in various geographic locations, store scanner collection devices are not available in all grocery, drug, or other retail outlets. This limits the scope of information available. The single source companies that use the household scanner argue that their systems are not dependent on in-store scanners for the collection of individual household purchase data.

Sample Limitations

Though the number of households participating in single source panels has increased, there is still concern about the representativeness of those groups. Participation rates, suspected to be as low as 50 percent, have made some critics question whether single source gives a true picture of consumer purchase and media exposure information. Underrepresentation of African-American and Hispanic households is also of concern to advertisers.

Cost

Because of the millions of dollars in initial investment for such a high-tech venture, single source research at present is very costly. Though some users are participating at greatly reduced rates in order to test the systems, estimates are that the actual costs could be in the hundreds of thousands of dollars per brand.

Emphasis on the Short Term

Because of the almost instantaneous and frequent reporting of relationships between consumer purchases and media and market variables, users of single source systems may be tempted to emphasize promotional expenditures, which tend to manifest their results fairly quickly. The value of traditional image advertising, critics argue, involves a long-term investment, and without it consumers do not develop true brand loyalty. In other words, while a coupon promotion or other short-term incentive might trigger increased levels of purchasing, advertising that focuses on brand image contributes to purchase levels over a longer period. Some recent research has suggested that image advertising for a brand over time does make a positive contribution to overall sales, yet it is often difficult to measure its exact effect.

Limited Media Exposure Information

The original emphasis of single source systems was on measuring television exposure of household panelists and correlating that information with purchases. Though the scope of single source has expanded over the years, the only electronic measurement of media exposure still is on television. As mentioned above, some companies are supplementing media exposure information with media diaries in which participants write names of magazines, newspapers, or radio vehicles they were exposed to, but not all media exposure is measured with the same methods or standards used by the major media measurement companies. If single source is truly to be a single source of media exposure information, great strides will have to be made in this area.

Single Source Research Companies

At this writing, three of the major suppliers of single source information are Nielsen ScanTrack, Arbitron ScanAmerica, and Information Resources, Inc., InfoScan.

InfoScan

Information Resources' InfoScan system provides information on the relationship between several marketplace variables and sales of a brand or product category. The system uses combinations of four types of information: retail scanner data at the store level, household panel sales data, field survey information, and television monitoring.

Retail store sales.

Retail store UPC scanners track more than one million separate codes from thousands of grocery stores, convenience stores, drug stores, and mass merchandisers.

Consumer purchases.

A special ID card is issued to participants in the InfoScan household panel. Panel members present their cards at the checkout line, and purchases are automatically recorded and identified by individual household. This process allows demographics to be linked simultaneously with sales volume.

Trade and consumer promotion.

An IRI field staff provides a weekly report on both in-store merchandising plans (price reductions, displays, etc.) and out-of-store promotions such as couponing.

Television viewing.

A subset of household panel members is equipped with television meters that electronically measure when the set is on and which program is being watched.

Data from the four sources are combined by IRI to examine the following relationships involving advertising and promotion:

- in-store promotion activities such as features, displays, or price reductions that result in incremental sales (sales above base level)
- advertising programs that result in increases in base sales (everyday sales volume minus trade promotion)
- combinations of trade and consumer promotions that are most effective
- the number of purchases made by households which viewed different numbers of commercials for a brand

Figure 21–1 shows an example of InfoScan data that uses television viewing information from metered households and market share of three different brands derived from households using the ID card at retail stores.

Figure 21–1
Ad Exposures and Household Purchase Data from a Single Source System

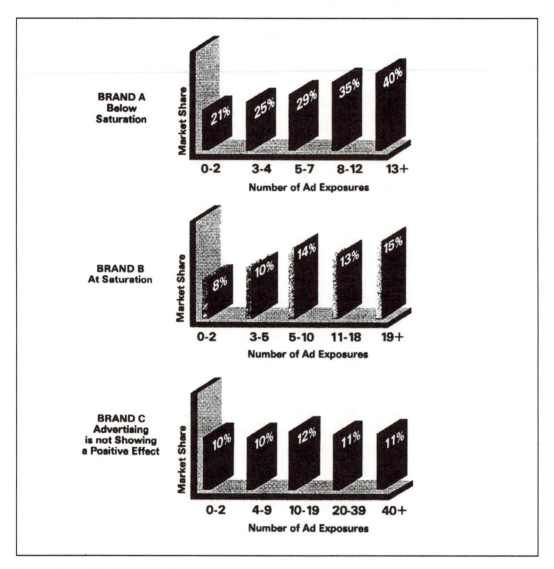

Source: Information Resources, Inc.

Note: The IRI metered household panel is divided into five groups based on viewing of programs carrying commercials for three brands. Sales data from households using ID cards when making retail purchases are used for market share for each brand.

Arbitron ScanAmerica

The ScanAmerica single source system currently uses 1,000 households in each of five markets, with a nationally projectable sample planned in the next year or two. Arbitron describes its service as a national television ratings service that uses people and in-home UPC scanner wands to measure what households are watching, who is watching in the households, and what products the household members buy.

The electronic measurement components of the system are the people-meter and the household scanner wand. Each of the ScanAmerica households is equipped with a people-meter that inserts a flashing question mark in the upper left-hand corner of the TV screen. The prompt is used to remind viewers to register by punching the appropriate assigned button on a hand-held remote keypad. As the button is pressed, the viewer's name appears on the screen. If no entries have been made for 30 minutes, the on-screen prompt reappears to remind viewers to register. In addition to measuring television viewing, Arbitron also measures exposure to other media by way of a household media diary.

A portable, hand-held scanner wand is used by household panel members to record UPC symbols of products purchased. The wand is passed over the UPC symbol. A beep and blinking light confirm the entry. When the wand is inserted into a well in the meter, product codes are transferred from the wand's memory to the meter for overnight collection. Purchase of products that do not bear the UPC are recorded in purchase diaries.

Demographic ratings from the people-meter system are available overnight, weekly, and monthly. Weekly and monthly BuyerGraphics ratings combine television viewing and product purchases or ownership as established through household questionnaires. An example of a BuyerGraphics output for automobile owners is shown in Figure 21–2. A comparison of demographic versus BuyerGraphic audiences is displayed in Figure 21–3.

Another Arbitron service called MediaWatch collects information on television advertising activity in network, spot, and cable by category and brand. The MediaWatch data can be related to sales figures from ScanAmerica markets.

Nielsen ScanTrack

Components of the Nielsen single source system are store-level sales data, household panel data, and reports on advertising and promotion activity by market. Store-level scanner sales information from 3,000 stores yields a national picture of brand and category sales by price, flavor, and type, and reports on the top 50 local markets.

A national panel of 40,000 households uses hand-held scanners to record all purchases with the UPC code. A portion of these households also are measured for television viewing with people-meters; magazine and newspaper reading is recorded with the hand-held scanners using cards with special UPC symbols.

Figure 21–2
BuyerGraphics
for Automobile
Owners

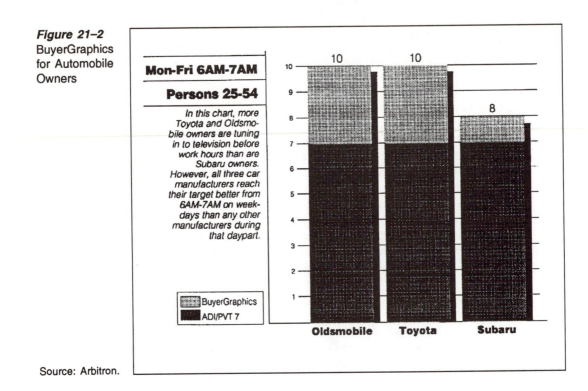

Mon-Fri 6AM-7AM

Persons 25-54

In this chart, more Toyota and Oldsmobile owners are tuning in to television before work hours than are Subaru owners. However, all three car manufacturers reach their target better from 6AM-7AM on weekdays than any other manufacturers during that daypart.

BuyerGraphics
ADI/PVT 7

Oldsmobile   Toyota   Subaru

Source: Arbitron.

Figure 21–3
Demographics
and BuyerGraphics
Compared

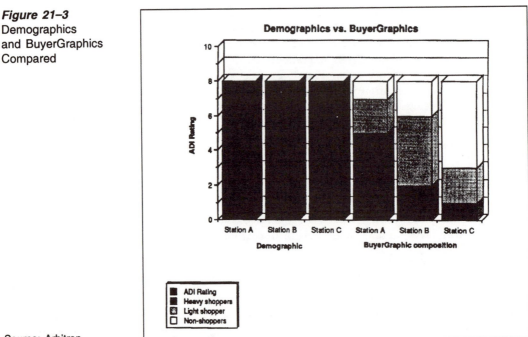

Demographics vs. BuyerGraphics

ADI Rating

Station A   Station B   Station C   Station A   Station B   Station C
Demographic   BuyerGraphic composition

■ ADI Rating
■ Heavy shoppers
▨ Light shopper
□ Non-shoppers

Source: Arbitron.

In local markets, ScanTrack participants use store ID cards to record purchases. Purchase information is combined with television advertising information gathered by the Nielsen Monitor-Plus system that tells which ads appeared in specific markets at certain times.

Sales and media exposure information from ScanTrack is correlated with the third measure—advertising and promotion variables. Nielsen records retail advertiser support (major, feature, or line ads run by local retailers in newspapers); special store display activity for brands; and retailer use of coupons in ads for various brands.

Information at the store and market levels enables clients of ScanTrack to examine such relationships as those between in-store variables and sales, in-market advertising activities and sales, and competitive analyses by product category.

Review

In this chapter we saw that:

- Single source data systems integrate three types of information:
  1. product purchases at the household level
  2. media exposure at the individual or household level
  3. marketing activities for a brand, including in-store and in-market promotion
- Because of the manner in which single source data is collected, correlations between types of information are available almost instantaneously, and advertiser response rate is enhanced.
- Critics of single source cite the following as reasons for concern over the effectiveness of the system:
  1. reliance on Universal Product Code
  2. limited retail coverage
  3. sample limitations
  4. cost
  5. emphasis on the short term
  6. limited media exposure information
- One major supplier of a single source data, Information Resources' InfoScan system, combines information from retail store sales, consumer purchases, trade and consumer promotions, and television viewing.
- Arbitron's ScanAmerica single source system uses people meters and in-home UPC scanners to measure what household members are watching on television, who is watching, and what those people are buying.
- The Nielsen ScanTrack system utilizes store-level sales data, household panel data, and reports on advertising and promotion activity as components of its single source analysis.

Endnote

1. Joseph Russo, "The Range of Possibilities," from *Proceedings of the Behavioral Research and Single Source Data Workshop,* Advertising Research Foundation, 1990, p. 11.

Advertising Research and Society

Comparative Advertising

A comparative advertisement evaluates one or more attributes of its sponsor's brand against one or more competitors. Some comparative ads are "head to head," in which the advertisement directly names or depicts the competitor. Others are more indirect; the comparison is merely implied or a "Brand X" comparison is made. The research literature on comparative advertising has taken basically three routes: (1) studies of the content and form of the advertisement, (2) studies of the effects comparative advertising has on consumers, and (3) studies that address the proper, legal use of research studies as a basis for comparative claims.

Content and Form of Comparative Advertising

Most estimates of the proportion of comparative advertising today in relation to all other advertising say that about 35 percent, or one in three, advertisements qualify as comparative. The topic of comparative advertising took on added significance in the early 1970s when the Federal Trade Commission issued a directive encouraging product comparison in the belief that consumers would be able to make more informed decisions as a result.

Most of the content studies are of print, rather than broadcast, advertising. Several studies of magazine advertising have been published, each using a content analysis method. Examination of these studies yields information about historical trends in the use of such advertising. To the extent that the researchers used comparable measurement and coding schemes, some of the studies of comparative advertising can themselves be compared.

Information Content of Comparative Advertising in Magazines

Resnik and Stern studied the advertising content of four consumer magazines during 1980.[1] Using a coding scheme that counted 14 separate informational categories,

---

they conducted a content analysis of the number of informational cues contained in each advertisement. One general finding was that comparative advertisements using a direct method of comparison were found to be more informative than those employing an indirect method.

A study by Chou, Franke, and Wilcox examined 949 full-page ads from 12 different magazines published in 1970, 1975, and 1985. The Stern and Resnik coding scheme was applied to the five research questions below:[2]

Q. Is comparative advertising more informative than noncomparative advertising?

A. Yes, significantly so. Strictly comparative advertising contained an average of 2.53 pieces of information, compared with 1.96 pieces of information for implied comparative ads and 1.39 pieces for noncomparative ads.

Q. Is strictly comparative advertising more informative than implied comparative advertising?

A. Yes. The difference was significant at the .01 level.

Q. Has the use of comparative advertising increased over time, compared with its use prior to the FTC's actions in the early 1970s?

A. Yes. Significant differences were found between "pre-FTC advocacy" (1970) and "post-FTC advocacy" (1975, 1985) advertising.

Q. Has the information content of magazine advertising increased over time?

A. Not much. The distribution of information content did not vary significantly over the years studied.

Q. Is there a relationship between the product type advertised and the use of comparative advertising?

A. Yes, if one considers comparative versus noncomparative ads. A greater than average percentage of ads for personal care items and durable goods use comparative advertising (40.0% and 31.3%), and a below average percentage of household product ads and clothing ads use comparisons (8.7% and 10.8%).

Effects of Comparative Advertising

Comparative advertising claims in magazine advertisements.

Gorn and Weinberg examined the impact of comparative magazine advertisements on consumer response to brands that were leaders in their categories and to brands that were nonleaders, or challengers.[3] Of particular interest to the researchers was the extent of perceived brand similarity between brands employing comparative advertising. This facet of consumer evaluation had not previously been studied.

The type of ad (comparative or noncomparative) and the context (leader advertisement present, leader advertisement absent) were varied in each of three

---

product categories. A study that is structured in this way is said to have a $2 \times 2 \times 3$ design. The experimental conditions repeated over each product category were:

1. Challenger advertisement—noncomparative; leader advertisement—not present

2. Challenger advertisement—comparative; leader advertisement—not present

3. Challenger advertisement—noncomparative; leader advertisement—present

4. Challenger advertisement—comparative; leader advertisement—present

Hypotheses and findings for the study were as follows:[4]

- *Hypothesis 1:* Greater perceived challenger-leader brand similarity would occur with exposure to comparative versus noncomparative advertisements. *Finding:* Type of advertisement was found to have a significant effect on both the perceived similarity of the challenger to the leader and the perceived similarity of new brands that might be introduced into the marketplace.

- *Hypothesis 2:* Greater perceived brand similarity for two hypothetical new brands would occur with exposure to comparative versus noncomparative advertisements. *Finding:* This hypothesis also was supported, as brand leader-challenger similarity was increased with such exposure.

- *Hypothesis 3:* Greater perceived brand similarity between two brands of cola would occur after exposure to a series of comparative advertisements versus noncomparative advertisements. *Finding:* Upon hearing a description of two cola soft drinks, subjects who had been exposed to a series of comparative advertisements for other product categories were more likely to perceive the two colas as similar than subjects who had been exposed to more advertisements for other products. This phenomenon was described as the cumulative impact of exposure to comparative advertisements, which results in consumer predisposition to perceive brands in other categories as similar.

- *Hypothesis 4:* Greater perceived brand similarity between two brands of deodorant (physically different—one a roll-on and one a spray) would occur after exposure to a series of comparative advertisements versus a series of noncomparative advertisements. *Finding:* As expected, the two brands of deodorant, which were described to subjects as having different physical characteristics, were not perceived to be similar. The cumulative impact did not affect judgments of similarity between products for which there was a known point of difference.

- *Hypothesis 5:* A more favorable attitude toward the challenger would occur with exposure to comparative versus noncomparative advertisements. *Finding:* This hypothesis was not supported.

The authors considered their findings as support for continued use of comparative advertising.

Consumer reaction to comparative copy blocks.

Golden examined the effects of different copy treatments for antiperspirants on consumer evaluations of the brands.[5] Only the advertisement copy—not an entire magazine advertisement—was presented. The copy varied such factors as product characteristics, brands, and copy themes.

Hypotheses and findings for the study were as follows:[6]

- *Hypothesis 1:* There will be no significant difference for ratings of purchase intention, claim believability, or advertising credibility between comparative and noncomparative advertisements. *Finding:* The hypothesis was supported for purchase intention, claim believability, and advertising credibility, although results for the latter were approaching significance.

- *Hypothesis 2:* There will be significant interaction of advertisement copy type and advertiser's competitive position for ratings of purchase intention, claim believability, and advertisement credibility. *Finding:* The interaction of advertiser's competitive position and copy type did not significantly influence purchase intention or claim believability ratings for advertisements. There did appear, however, a significant effect for the interaction of advertisement copy type and advertiser's competitive position for advertisement credibility. Interestingly, the results did not go in the direction the author predicted. It was expected that a noncomparative advertisement would be more credible than a comparative advertisement for the number-one brand, and that a comparative advertisement would be more effective for a new brand and the number-three brand. A comparative advertisement was found to be slightly more effective for the new brand, and a noncomparative advertisement was only slightly more effective for the number-one brand. The "underdog effect" did not seem to operate for the number-three brand, since the noncomparative advertisement was considerably more effective than the comparative advertisement.

- *Hypothesis 3:* There will be a significant interaction of advertising copy type and claim substantiation for ratings of purchase intention, claim believability, and advertising credibility. *Finding:* This hypothesis was not supported for purchase intention, claim believability, or advertisement credibility.

Golden concluded that advertisers who wish to use comparative advertising must look closely at competitive situations, advertising objectives, and the context of the advertisement.[7] The effectiveness of comparative advertisements is far from straightforward. Rather it is a highly complex phenomenon likely to be influenced by variables in the advertising environment. Comparative and noncomparative advertising did not appear to be significantly different in effectiveness for purchase intentions, claim believability, or advertising credibility.

Research Issues in Comparative Advertising

FTC encouragement of the use of comparative advertising has resulted in an increasingly large number of such advertisements. Comparison advertising is almost invariably initiated by a product category challenger, because the challenger has everything to gain by taking a swing at the leading brand. The advertising typically uses one or two types of data to support the comparative claim: (1) data that are objective and easy to prove or refute, such as the highway miles-per-gallon rating, and (2) subjective consumer product test results, which usually are the result of some type of consumer survey research.

The appropriateness, accuracy, truthfulness, and validity of such supporting data was the subject of an article by Buchanan, who put forth a five-part "test" for the targets of comparative advertising and for those who contemplate using it.[8] The questions in the test all involve investigating the basis on which a comparative claim is made. Buchanan's suggestions are based on laws, guidelines, and court decisions.

Question 1: Did anyone actually compare anything?

If brand A reports that a greater percentage of consumers prefers it to brand B, the suggestion is that consumers made some sort of direct comparison of the brands in question. Often this is far from the case. Any number of different research methods and techniques have been used to establish consumer "preference."

In the "cola wars," market share figures were used as the basis for a consumer preference claim. Greater market share was construed to equal greater consumer preference for Coke over Pepsi. But, as Buchanan notes, market share is not equivalent to brand preference.[9] A variety of separate factors such as scale of production, advertising effort, and order of market entry also may affect market share.

Another example of inferred preference was used by Body on Tap shampoo. The advertisers claimed in a TV commercial that: "In shampoo tests with over 900 women . . . Body on Tap got higher ratings than Prell for body, higher than Flex for conditioning, and higher than Sassoon for strong, healthy looking hair." The basis for the comparison was a "blind monadic" test—one in which unlabeled products were evaluated by subjects who receive only a single brand. So actually, no direct comparison was ever made between any of the brands of shampoo. According to Buchanan, results of a blind monadic test do not sufficiently substantiate a preference claim, and, if possible, subjects should be allowed to test all products and reveal any preferences.[10]

Question 2: Who participated in the product test?

This is a question of sampling procedure, and it is an unfortunate fact that many preference claims are based on the results of studies conducted with samples of questionable integrity. Obviously, improper sampling methods can lead to results that are due as much to sample bias as to actual consumer brand preference. According to Buchanan, if the sample used by the challenger brand differs from the category customer profile, and the difference affects the results of the claim, grounds may exist for a successful challenge of the claim in court.[11]

Question 3: Did you measure preference or choice?

This ultimately is a question of validity. When subjects choose between brand A and brand B in a blind taste test, are they really stating a preference? If they do not perceive a difference, but choose one brand anyway, does such a choice constitute a real preference? The fact is that even in direct comparison tests, the choice of one brand over another may reflect either preference or random guessing.

Buchanan suggests that one approach to overcoming the limitations of tests intended to discriminate between two brands is the "triangle test," wherein subjects taste three samples, two of which are identical, and try to identify the one that differs from the other two. Another possible solution is to have subjects complete repeated paired comparisons of the same two brands. If they are consistent in their judgments, then a strong likelihood exists that their choices were based on actual preference.[12]

Many soda and cigarette campaigns have been based on single paired comparison tests only, and many of them are amazingly close to a 50–50 split. Figures such as these could simply reflect random choices on the part of subjects.

Question 4: Are you inducing parity?

Parity, or equivalency, between two brands is present in the following situations:

1. Subjects cannot discriminate between two brands.
2. Subjects can discriminate but have no preference for one or the other.
3. Subjects can discriminate, but half prefer brand A and half prefer brand B.

Product tests resulting in parity must be used to substantiate such a claim. According to Buchanan, a number of techniques can be used to induce parity, including selection of subjects who may be light users of a product and hence have little ability to properly discriminate between brands. They may be oblivious to slight differences in formulation, and the results might therefore suggest a parity situation erroneously.[13]

Question 5: Is your claim consistent with the test results?

This question addresses the issue of "fudging" the facts, or put another way, making the data support an *a priori* conclusion no matter what the outcome of the test. Buchanan offers the example of a cigarette campaign in which Triumph claimed that: "An amazing 60 percent said the 3-milligram Triumph tastes as good as or better than 8-milligram Merit."[14] In fact, subjects had been asked to rate both cigarettes on a 5-point scale ranging from "much better tasting than Merit" to "much worse tasting." One in four (24 percent) of subjects had responded that the two brands tasted about the same. This information when coupled with the 11 percent who said Triumph was "much worse tasting than Merit" and the 29 percent who said Triumph was "somewhat worse tasting," resulted in 64 percent of the subjects reporting that Merit tasted as good as or better than Triumph. This finding is totally at odds with the impression the Triumph advertisement left with the consumer. An injunction was issued against the Triumph advertisement on the grounds that more than one in three consumers in a communications test said the advertisement implied that "Triumph was better tasting than Merit" and thus left an incorrect impression.[15]

Advertising and Its Effect on Alcohol Consumption

One of the hottest regulatory issues in advertising in the 1990s is whether alcohol is an appropriate product category to advertise in the mass media. In 1988, the Surgeon General appointed an alcohol advertising/promotion advisory panel that offered several recommendations for marketing alcoholic beverages in the United States. Among these recommendations were eliminating the tax deductibility of advertising for alcoholic beverages and banning sponsorships of sporting events by alcohol marketers. Though these were merely recommendations, there exists a swell of public support for such measures.

At the heart of the debate over restrictions on alcohol advertising is the question of whether the advertising of alcoholic beverages contributes to increased consumption, illegal drinking by minors, or alcoholism and alcohol abuse due to overconsumption. Two studies, one in the United States and the other in Canada, are representative of the types of methodologies and the findings in this area.

Findings of Two Studies of Alcohol Advertising

No empirical evidence was found to attribute increases in Canadian alcohol consumption to advertising.

Two Canadian researchers gathered data across 10 provinces during a 24-year period from 1951 to 1974.[16] Per capita consumption of beer, wine, spirits, and total alcohol were the dependent variables measured. Dozens of independent variables were used (see Table 22–1). These were divided into controllable, semi-controllable, and noncontrollable variables. Included in the controllable marketing variable list were such factors as print and broadcast advertising, taxes, minimum drinking age, and number of liquor stores. Those factors considered noncontrollable included disposable income, religious factors, ethnicity, broken homes, and average age of the population.

Table 22–1

List of Variables Investigated

Dependent Variables

Var. 1: Per-capita consumption of beer
Var. 2: Per-capita consumption of wine
Var. 3: Per-capita consumption of spirits
Var. 4: Per-capita consumption of total alcohol

Independent Variables

Controllable Marketing Variables

Var. 11: Print advertising
Var. 12: Broadcast advertising
*Var. 13: Price index
*Var. 14: Relative (to income) price index
*Var. 15: Tax index
Var. 16: Number of liquor stores
Var. 17: Provincial minimum drinking age
Var. 18: Introduction of the breathalyzer

Semicontrollable Nonmarketing Variables

Var. 19: Number of dwelling starts per 1,000 population
Var. 20: Number of immigrants per 1,000 population
Var. 21: Unemployment rate
Var. 22: Provincial-income-tax level
*Var. 23: Welfare financial assistance index
*Var. 24: Minimum-wage-rate index
Var. 25: Ratio of homes owned to rented

Noncontrollable Nonmarketing Variables

Var. 26: Per-capita disposable income
Var. 27: Percent of population urban
*Var. 28: Population reproductivity factor
*Var. 29: Religious factor 1: liberal/Protestant
*Var. 30: Religious factor 2: fundamentalist/nonsacramentalist
*Var. 31: European ethnicity factor
*Var. 32: Broken-homes factor
Var. 33: Proportion of population in school
Var. 34: Average number of hours worked per week
Var. 35: Strike effect on striking provinces
Var. 36: Strike effect on other provinces
Var. 37: Proportion of population aged 15 to 29

* Composite or "index" variables—that is, a combination of a group of original variables. We created these indices using principal-components analysis.

Source: Bourgeois, J.C. and J.G. Barnes. "Does Advertising Increase Alcohol Consumption?" *Journal of Advertising Research*, Vol. 19 No. 4, pp. 19-29.

Using a series of mathematical models for determining the effects of each variable on consumption of beer, wine, spirits, and total alcohol, the researchers found that more variance in per capita consumption is explained by the noncontrollable variables than is explained by the controllable variables.[17] The study offered little support for the claim that per capita consumption levels of alcoholic beverages in Canada are influenced by volume of advertising for those products.

The presence of price advertising has no significant effect on beer consumption.

Some states have prohibitions against price advertising for alcoholic beverages. The assumption seems to be that advertising of alcoholic beverages for discount prices would result in greater consumption. In 1975, administrative rules by the Michigan Liquor Control Commission prohibited truthful price advertising for beer. After a document was issued by the Michigan attorney general in 1982 declaring the rules unconstitutional, the Liquor Control Commission ceased enforcement. But in May 1983, a county circuit court judge reimposed the rules, and restrictions resumed in June 1983.

The enactment of the rules on beer advertising, their subsequent repeal, and eventual reinstatement provided a situation in which effects of the presence and absence of the advertising restrictions could be assessed. Using information about the number of retail outlets that placed local advertising during the time periods studied and total brewed beverage sales for that same period, Wilcox discovered the following:[18]

1. The presence of price advertising appeared to have no significant effect on sales of brewed beverages.
2. A significantly higher percentage of retail stores engaged in local advertising during the nonrestrictive period.

Table 22–2 contains results of Wilcox's study. He concluded that total prohibition of price advertising is an unnecessary restriction in a free enterprise economy, as it limits the ability of retailers to implement competitive strategy.

Twenty-year correlational study finds mixed results.

Franke and Wilcox examined advertising expenditures of the alcoholic beverage industry and per capita consumption of beer, wine, and distilled spirits in the United States over a 20-year period.[19] Advertising media expenditures studied included network and spot television, network radio, magazines, newspaper supplements, and outdoor billboards. Personal income, consumption trends, and seasonality also were examined.

Table 22–2

Total Sales of Brewed Beverages

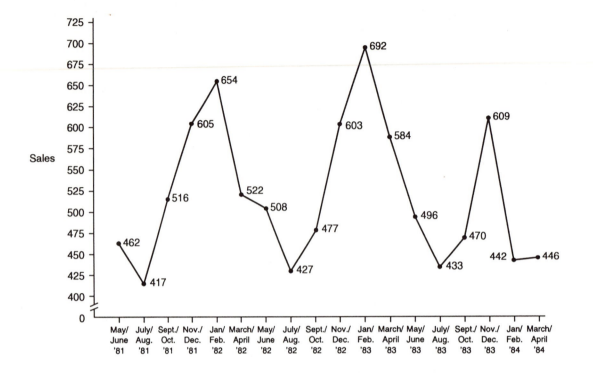

Source: Wilcox, Gary. "The Effect of Price Advertising on Alcohol Sales.' *Journal of Advertising Research,* Vol. 25 No. 5, pp. 33–38.

Models were used to determine which variables were significant predictors of consumption. Among the major findings were:[20]

1. Total advertising was not significant in the beer consumption model. Aggregate beer advertising had no relationship with levels of primary demand for beer.

2. Total wine advertising, linear trend, and fourth-quarter seasonality explain 92 percent of the variation in per capita wine consumption from 1970 to 1984 (previous data not available). Much of the relationship between total advertising and consumption was due to spot TV expenditures.

3. Total distilled spirits advertising, personal income, trend, and seasonality accounted for 99 percent of the variance in per capita distilled spirits consumption.

Thus, advertising and consumption levels in the United States were found to be significantly related for wine and distilled spirits, but not for beer. The significance levels, however, are very slight. To put this into perspective, the authors projected that a 10 percent increase in average annual advertising expenditures would be associated with an annual increase in per capita wine consumption of 2.7 ounces, or about one-third of an ounce of alcohol. The authors cite this finding as significant but not substantial. They also caution that the results are correlational, and not necessarily causal.

Subliminal Advertising

For the past three decades, a considerable volume of writing has been published on the topic of subliminal communication. Made popular by the books of Wilson Bryan Key, the notion of subliminal communication is predicated on the belief that messages can be sent and received at a level below the threshold of consciousness.[21] The literature of subliminal communication in advertising can be divided into professional and consumer opinion, claims and assertions by critics, and actual research studies on the effectiveness of subliminal techniques.

Professional and Consumer Opinion

The public not only is aware of subliminal techniques, but individuals have also formed opinions about them. Interestingly, the greatest percentage of respondents said they first learned about subliminal advertising in a high school or college course. According to a study by Zanot, Pincus, and Lamp, half of those who were aware of subliminal techniques judged such practices to be unacceptable, unethical, or harmful.[22] (See Table 22–3.) Consumers also seem to stop short of endorsing subliminal techniques as effective in positive activities like self-improvement programs.

In a study by Block and Vanden Bergh, a sample of 330 consumers interviewed by telephone reported skepticism toward the efficacy of subliminal communication for losing weight, stopping smoking, and improving study habits.[23]

Communications professionals as a group are much less willing than the public to recognize subliminal techniques as either widespread or significant. A survey of 100 art directors revealed that 96 percent of those responding denied ever using subliminal methods, and nine out of ten said they didn't know anyone who did use them.[24] After studying marketing failures of a range of subliminal communication products and reviewing the research literature, a trade publication writer concluded that communication professionals were "still laughing" at subliminal advertising tactics.[25] Researcher J. Steven Kelly terms the subliminal issue a "challenge to advertising ethics," but his research fails to support the existence of subliminal effects with a print advertising experiment.[26]

Table 22-3
Block and Vanden Bergh Study

First Learned of Subliminal Advertising Through . . .		
Category	n	%
Education	24	13.5
Television	17	9.6
Magazine	12	6.7
Acquaintance	12	6.7
Book	9	5.1
Newspaper	8	4.5
Other	8	4.5
	90	50.6

How Often Do You Believe Subliminal Advertising Is Used?		
Category	n	%
Always	24	13.5
Often	66	37.1
Sometimes	42	23.6
Seldom	12	6.7
Never	1	.6
Don't Know	18	10.1
No Response	15	8.4
	178	100.0

Source: Zanot, Eric, J. David Pincus and E. Joseph Lamp. "Public Perceptions of Subliminal Advertising." *Journal of Advertising*, Vol. 12, No. 1, 1983, pp. 39–45.

Claims by Advertising Critics

Foremost among those who have brought subliminal advertising tactics to the public plane of discussion is Wilson Bryan Key. The titles of three of his books, *Subliminal Seduction, Clam-Plate Orgy,* and *Media Sexploitation* suggest an emphasis on use of sexual "embeds," as he calls them, to manipulate consumer behavior. Key has studied numerous examples of print advertising and presents a series of nationally published advertisements in which he asserts to have uncovered a range of craftily airbrushed stimuli such as phallic symbols, sexually oriented words, and people involved in an orgy.

Noticeably absent from Key's books is substantial empirical proof that the embeds have their desired marketing effect. In fact, it was the writings of Key and others that prompted Moore to write: "Whether or not erotic imagery has been deliberately planted is not relevant to a consideration of the imagery's alleged effects."[27] Attempts to make the distinction between the presence of subliminal messages and the effects of such messages have been frustrating for Vokey and Read, who concluded that neither the media nor the public "appreciate the methods and distinctions necessary for scientific investigation."[28]

Research Evidence

In 1957, James Vicary reported that brief film exposures of the messages "eat popcorn" and "drink Coca-Cola" during a movie in Fort Lee, New Jersey, resulted in patrons' increased purchases of those refreshments.[29] Subsequent attempts to replicate Vicary's results failed. Post-Vicary research has taken a variety of directions, but most fails to support beliefs of purported influence on consumer behavior.[30]

In a test of televised messages for food products, DeFleur and Petranoff reported that while communication is possible with subliminal devices, persuasion is ineffective.[31] In one of the only exceptions to this genre of nonsignificant findings, Silverman reported changes in pathological behavior with institutionalized subjects who briefly saw visual stimuli appealing to their unconscious wishes.[32]

At least two studies have dealt specifically with Key's assertions that the presence of sexually oriented embeds in print advertising enhances those advertisements' evaluation and effectiveness. Kilbourne, Painton, and Ridley showed undergraduate students a pair of Marlboro cigarette advertisements, one of which contained an embed of male genitalia, and a pair of Chivas Regal whiskey advertisements, one of which contained the image of a nude female.[33] The Chivas Regal advertisement resulted in statistically significant differences on cognitive, affective, sexual, and behavioral variables, but the Marlboro advertisement did not. Both the Marlboro and Chivas Regal advertisements containing embeds yielded higher galvanic skin response results than the non-embedded versions.

In a study by Gable et al., results were mixed.[34] Four pairs of black-and-white photos, with one of each pair containing a sexual embed, were presented to 500 undergraduate students who then were asked which version they preferred. It is not clear which specific embeds were used. Curiously, each photo was coded with either a letter "M" or "P," as cues for the researchers for which was the embedded and which the non-embedded version. In three of the four cases, no photo preference was shown. In the fourth pair, statistically significant differences were obtained in favor of the embedded photo, a finding that was deemed a "chance occurrence" by the authors.

Review

In this chapter we saw that:

- A comparative advertisement evaluates one or more attributes of its sponsor's brand against one or more competitors, either head to head or indirectly.

- Research on comparative advertising includes studies of content and form of advertisements, studies of the effects comparative advertising has on consumers, and studies that address the proper, legal use of research studies as a basis for comparative claims.

- In the early 1970s, the Federal Trade Commission issued a directive encouraging product comparison in the belief that consumers would be able to make more informed decisions as a result.

- The effectiveness of comparative advertisements is far from straightforward, and advertisers who wish to use comparative advertising must look closely at competitive situations, advertising objectives, and the context of the advertisement.

- A comparative advertisement usually uses one of two types of data to support the comparative claim: data that are objective and easy to prove or refute, and subjective consumer product test results.

- Bruce Buchanan has established a five-part test to evaluate the appropriateness, accuracy, and validity of supporting data for a comparative advertisement:

  1. Did anyone actually compare anything?
  2. Who participated in the product tests?
  3. Did you measure preference or choice?
  4. Are you inducing parity?
  5. Is your claim consistent with the test results?

- One of the hottest current regulatory issues is whether alcohol is an appropriate product category to advertise in the mass media; results of research studies have had mixed results.

- Subliminal communication, the belief that messages can be sent and received at a level below the threshold of consciousness, has been widely studied; communications professionals as a group are much less willing than the public to recognize subliminal techniques as either widespread or significant.

Endnotes

1. Robert Harmon, Nabil Razzouk, and Bruce Stern, "The Information Content of Comparative Magazine Advertisements," *Journal of Advertising* 12, no. 4, 1983, pp. 10–19.

2. Linly Chou, George Franke, and Gary Wilcox, "The Information Content of Comparative Magazine Ads: A Longitudinal Analysis," *Journalism Quarterly* 64, no. 1, 1987, pp. 119–124.

3. G. J. Gorn and C. B. Weinberg, "The Impact of Comparative Advertising on Perception and Attitude: Some Positive Findings," *Journal of Consumer Research* 2, 1984, pp. 719–727.

4. *Ibid.*

5. Linda Golden, "Consumer Reactions to Explicit Brand Comparisons in Advertisements," *Journal of Marketing Research* 16, 1979, pp. 517–532.

6. *Ibid.*

7. *Ibid.*

8. Bruce Buchanan, "Can You Pass the Comparative Ad Challenge?" *Harvard Business Review* 63, no. 4, August 1985, pp. 106–113.

9. *Ibid.*

10. *Ibid.*

11. *Ibid.*

12. *Ibid.*

13. *Ibid.*

14. *Ibid.*

15. *Ibid.*

16. J. C. Bourgeois and J. G. Barnes, "Does Advertising Increase Alcohol Consumption?" *Journal of Advertising Research* 19, no. 4, August 1979, pp. 19–29.

17. *Ibid.*

18. Gary Wilcox, "The Effect of Price Advertising on Alcoholic Beverage Sales," *Journal of Advertising Research* 25, no. 5, October/November 1985, pp. 33–37.

19. George Franke and Gary Wilcox, "Alcoholic Beverage Advertising and Consumption in the United States, 1964–1984," *Journal of Advertising* 16, no. 3, 1987, pp. 22–30.

20. *Ibid.*

21. Wilson Bryan Key, *Subliminal Seduction* (New York: Signet Books, 1974); *Clam-Plate Orgy and Other Subliminals the Media Use to Manipulate Your Behavior* (Englewood Cliffs, N.J.: Prentice-Hall, Inc., 1980); *Media Sexploitation* (New York: Signet Books, 1977).

22. Eric Zanot, J. David Pincus, and E. Joseph Lamp, "Public Perceptions of Subliminal Advertising," *Journal of Advertising* 12, 1983, pp. 39–45.

23. Martin Block and Bruce Vanden Bergh, "Can You Sell Subliminal Messages to Consumers?" *Journal of Advertising* 14, 1985, pp. 59–62.

24. Jack Haberstroh, "To Tell the Truth: Subliminal Seduction," *Research in Action* 9, 1985, pp. 10–14.

25. "Subliminal Ad Tactics: Experts Still Laughing," *Marketing News* 15, March 1985, pp. 6–7.

26. J. Steven Kelly, "Subliminal Embeds in Print Advertising: A Challenge to Advertising Ethics," *Journal of Advertising* 8, 1979, pp. 20–24.

27. Timothy Moore, "Subliminal Advertising: What You See Is What You Get," *Journal of Marketing* 46, 1982, pp. 38–47.

28. John Vokey and J. Don Read, "Subliminal Messages—Between the Devil and the Media," *American Psychologist* 40, 1985, pp. 1231–1239.

29. The Vicary study was discussed in several publications, including Vance Packard's *The Hidden Persuaders,* New York: McKay Co., 1957.

30. Stephen George and Luther Jennings, "Effect of Subliminal Stimuli on Consumer Behavior: Negative Evidence," *Perceptual and Motor Skills* 41, 1975, pp. 847–854.

31. Melvin DeFleur and R. M. Petranoff, "A Televised Test of Subliminal Persuasion," *Public Opinion Quarterly* 23, 1959, pp. 168–180.

32. L. H. Silverman, "The Reports of My Death Are Greatly Exaggerated," *American Psychologist* 31, 1976, pp. 621–637.

33. William Kilbourne, Scott Painton, and Danny Ridley, "The Effects of Sexual Embedding on Responses to Magazine Advertisements," *Journal of Advertising* 14, 1985, pp. 48–55.

34. Myron Gable, Henry Wilkens, Lynn Harris, and Richard Feinberg, "An Evaluation of Subliminally Embedded Sexual Stimuli in Graphics," *Journal of Advertising* 16, 1987, pp. 26–31.

Attitudes Toward Advertising in General

Anderson, Engledow, and Becker summarized conclusions from public opinion polls about advertising during the period from 1965 to 1975. Among their major generalizations were:[1]

1. Attitudes toward advertising are composed of several dimensions. One method used to separate these complex attitudes is to measure various aspects of the economic versus social characteristics of the advertising.

2. Various groups in the population feel differently about advertising. More educated groups have been more critical of advertising than less educated ones. Various dimensions of the advertising may be evaluated differently by different groups: Some feel positively about the economic functions of advertising but negatively about its social function.

3. Attitudes toward advertising were more favorable in the past than in more recent times. Attitudes have become more negative over time.

The authors conducted a survey of two random samples of readers of *Consumer Reports* magazine in 1970 and again in 1976. They used a questionnaire originated by Bauer and Greyser in 1968.[2] Among their conclusions were that advertising in the second study (1976) was considered to be:[3]

- Less essential
- More insulting to the intelligence
- Unchanged in the effect on price
- More able to persuade people to buy things they do not want
- Presenting a less true product picture
- Contributing less to the standard of living
- Contributing less to better products

Overall attitude toward advertising was measured separately on a 7-point scale. In 1970 it was 4.38, but it dropped to 3.75 by 1976, reflecting a lower overall evaluation of advertising over time. A regression analysis revealed that social issues were most important in predicting overall attitude in 1970, and economic dimensions became more important in 1976.[4]

The authors pointed out two important matters when interpreting the data: (1) readers of *Consumer Reports* are a highly educated, high-income group and are not representative of the population at large, and (2) Americans' evaluations of institutions other than advertising had likewise eroded over time. This unfavorable view toward social institutions in general, they hypothesized, could be attributed to increasing cynicism on the part of the public (see insert below).[5]

> By cynicism, we mean the tendency to mistrust the motives of other people, particularly authority figures (e.g., advertising spokespeople). This is in contrast to the skeptic, who may initially disbelieve what is said but who retains an open mind and the possibility of being persuaded.
>
> It does not require a gigantic inductive leap to see how this cynical mind-set affects receptivity to advertising in general and certain kinds of advertisements in particular. There is some compelling evidence gathered by the 4As and others that bolster this point.
>
> In the 1968 book Advertising in America, sponsored by the 4As, we see the following:
>
> - 43% of Americans agree that advertising insults the intelligence of the average consumer.
> - 41% of Americans agree that advertising presents a true picture of the product advertised.
>
> There is plenty of cynicism about advertising in these figures. In the '70s, Dunn and Bartos came up with comparable figures in their excellent study of advertising. Even higher figures were found in Europe in 1980 by Marplan, and finally, in the national probability sample by Diagnostic Research in 1983, the figures showed marginally more cynicism about advertising— that it insults intelligence and does not present a true picture.
>
> In a 1988 study . . . Diagnostic Research found across five product categories with 1,000 respondents, up to 45% said, "The people who paid for this ad think I'm dumb."
>
> Interestingly, depending upon the creative treatment, the number of people who felt they were advertised to as "dummies" changed. The point is, insulting consumer intelligence is transparent to the audience. And the study found that among the people who felt they were treated as advertising dopes, there was a significantly higher percentage of people who thought the company who paid for the ad was "just fair or poor," as compared to "excellent or good."
>
> This means more advertisers must begin to regard their markets as smarter than they do—or suffer the consequence in building less desirable brand images. Such a thing can be dangerous in an age of price promotions and limited brand loyalties.

Advertising Age Study

A 1983 study commissioned by *Advertising Age* showed that advertising received high scores from consumers on quality, accuracy, and creativity. Consumers gave advertising poor scores for honesty and trustworthiness. The study was conducted by Selection Research Inc., and used a national stratified random sample of 1,250 adults. Surprisingly, 53 percent of respondents said they would like their children to work in the advertising business. Nine out of ten respondents agreed that advertising is an important part of the American economy and the American way of life and that advertising is a highly professional business or occupation.[6]

Gallup Polls

Periodically, the Gallup organization poses questions about advertising to a probability sample of American adults. Here is an example of the results obtained in a 1986 poll of 2,000 adults responding to the following statement: "Having commercials on TV is a fair price to pay for being able to watch it." Of the sample, 75 percent agreed, 20 percent disagreed, and 5 percent said they didn't know.[7]

A 1987 ARF study (cited in Chapter 20) found that public trust is eroding for marketing activities in general and for survey research in particular.

Miscomprehension of the Advertising Message

It would seem obvious that not every advertising message is understood in either a complete or perfect manner by those who are exposed to it. As with interpersonal communication, it is possible for a recipient to be exposed to an advertisement through mass communication yet fail to come away with the message its sponsor intended.

This phenomenon of confused or otherwise imperfect communication—the miscomprehension of the advertising message—became the focus of considerable research in the early 1980s. One reason for the keen interest was the fact that comprehension has long been considered an antecedent of higher-level effects such as attitude change or persuasion. These factors form the building blocks of models of communication effectiveness.

Studies of miscomprehension attempted to determine to what extent advertising messages are misunderstood, whether the medium in which the message appeared had significant effects, and whether advertising messages were any more misunderstood than other media forms such as newscasts or entertainment programs. One major measurement issue arose from this genre of research: What type of question format is best for accurately estimating levels of miscomprehension? In other words, should guessing the answers to comprehension questions be taken into account, and what are the effects of miscomprehending the questions themselves?

AAAA Study

One of the first large-scale studies of the miscomprehension of televised messages was conducted in 1979 by Jacoby and Hoyer for the American Association of Advertising Agencies. Sixty different 30-second communications that had been broadcast on television in 1978–79 constituted the message treatments. Specifically, the treatments included:[8]

- *Advertisements:* Image and product/service
- *Noncommercial advertisements:* "Cause" (With cause advertisements, the source stands to benefit if the recipient engages in the desired action— such as donating to the United Negro College Fund.)
- *Public service advertisements:* (In the case of public service announcements, the viewer stands to benefit.)
- *Program excerpts:* Speeches/editorials and entertainment/information

It is interesting to note that program excerpts were condensed to 30-second segments in order to standardize the length of the treatment stimuli. Therefore, subjects viewed only a fraction of a TV program but were allowed to view entire advertisements.

The 2,700 subjects ranged in age from 13 to over 65. They were chosen by convenience method at shopping mall sites in 12 major U.S. cities. Each subject viewed two 30-second messages. A six-item miscomprehension quiz consisting of true/false questions was administered after exposure to each communication. Viewers were asked to answer true or false based on what was presented or implied in the 30-second message. Research questions for the study and selected findings are discussed below.

Does miscomprehension occur?

Only 16.8 percent of viewers answered all six questions correctly for either of the 30-second messages they viewed (see Figure 23–1). This means that in 83.2 percent of the cases, viewers miscomprehended at least some portion of the test communication. Only 3.5 percent of viewers scored correctly on all six answers for both of their test messages.[9]

Overall, only 29.6 percent of the 32,400 questions posed were answered incorrectly.[10] For reasons to be discussed later, it is believed that this estimate is below the actual miscomprehension rate. At least some degree of miscomprehension was associated with each communication tested.

What is the typical range of miscomprehension?

The most miscomprehended message had a 50 percent degree of inaccuracy, while the least miscomprehended message had an 11 percent degree of inaccuracy.[11]

Figure 23–1
Results from Miscomprehension Study

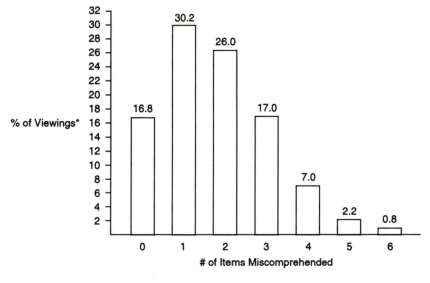

* Base = 5,400 Viewings

Source: Jacob Jacoby and Wayne Hoyer. "Viewer Miscomprehension of Televised Communication," *Journal of Marketing* 46, Fall 1982, p. 17.

Is advertising less miscomprehended than nonadvertising?

Program excerpts were associated with a significantly higher rate of miscomprehension than commercial and noncommercial advertisements. However, these differences are relatively small. Using the middle 50 percent of responses, the miscomprehension levels are as follows:[12]

Program excerpts	27–38%
Commercial advertising	22–34%
Noncommercial advertising	22–35%

See Table 23–1 for more details.

Are there demographic differences associated with miscomprehension?

Only age and education were significantly related to miscomprehension. Both younger and older viewers were more likely to miscomprehend the test communications. Miscomprehension also tends to decrease slightly as amount of formal education increases.[13]

Table 23-1
Miscomprehension of News Programming

Miscomprehension Rates Associated with News-Oriented Televised Communications*

Nature of the Communication**	% Miscomprehension
Local editorial (Indianapolis ABC affiliate)	50.00%
Local news (Indianapolis ABC affiliate)	43.00%
President Carter's Press Conference on China (January 1979)	35.00%
President Carter's State of the Union Address (January 1979)	34.00%
"Meet the Press"	31.00%
Local news (Indianapolis NBC affiliate)	30.00%
Republican response to State of the Union Address (January 1979)	27.00%
National network news (CBS—Cronkite)	27.00%
National network news (NBC—Brinkley)	26.00%
Average % miscomprehension	33.67%

* Taken from Jacoby, Hoyer and Sheluga 1980, p. 68–69.

** Except as indicated, all test communications had actually been broadcast during November and December of 1978.

Source: Jacob Jacoby and Wayne Hoyer. "Viewer Miscomprehension of Televised Communication," *Journal of Marketing* 46, Fall 1982, p. 20.

Methodological issues.

Several methodological issues surfaced during and after the course of the investigation. Two of the most troubling were the decision to use a 30-second excerpt of a 30-minute or one-hour entertainment program as a test message and the decision to use all true/false statements as test items.

The researchers defended their decision to use 30-second excerpts on the basis that it would be difficult or impossible to compare the evaluation of a 30-second commercial with a 30-minute program. Viewer attention span and memory were cited as reasons for standardizing the duration of the test communications. The researchers recognized, however, the difficulty of generalizing to an entire program based on a 30-second excerpt.

The more serious problem lay in the area of measurement and the choice of all true/false test items. Educational testing researchers have determined that true/false items result in guessing on the part of respondents who do not know the correct answer. Given a 50–50 rate of success with merely a guess, it then follows that a higher percentage of correct scores would result. Furthermore, researchers for the AAAA study reported that respondents fared much worse when the true/false statements were false; that is, they had less difficulty identifying a true statement about the test communication content than they did if a false statement was offered.

Schmittlein and Morrison estimated that if proper adjustments are made to account for guessing and yea-saying, the actual average percentage of miscomprehended televised messages was 46 percent, significantly higher than the averages reported in the AAAA study.[14] Gates further tested the two types of recognition measures—true/false and multiple choice—and reported that while subjects find multiple choice easier to answer, significant miscomprehension rates occurred with both question formats.[15]

Review

In this chapter we saw that:

- Consumer attitudes toward advertising vary across the dimensions of economic class and level of education; in general, attitudes toward advertising and marketing in general have become more negative over time.

- Better educated persons are more critical of advertising than others.

- While ads are rated high on quality, accuracy, and credentials, thay rate low on honesty and trustworthiness.

- No advertising message is understood completely or perfectly by those who are exposed to it; the phenomenon of miscomprehension of the advertising message has become the focus of considerable research.

- Studies of miscomprehension have attempted to determine to what extent advertising messages are misunderstood, whether the medium in which the message appeared had significant effects, and whether advertising messages were any more misunderstood than other media forms such as newscasts or entertainment programs.

- Five out of six viewers will miscomprehend some part of a television message. Youngest and oldest viewers miscomprehend more often, as do those with less education.

Endnotes

1. Ronald Anderson, Jack Engledow, and Helmut Becker, "How Consumer Reports Subscribers See Advertising," *Journal of Advertising Research* 18, no. 6, December 1978, pp. 29–34.

2. Raymond Bauer and Stephen Greyser, *Advertising in America: The Consumer View* (Boston: Harvard University, Graduate School of Business Administration, Division of Research, 1968).

3. Anderson, *op. cit.*

4. *Ibid.*

5. From "Cynicism and Creativity," Donald Kanter, *Marketing & Media Decisions,* April 1988, p. 152.

6. Nancy Millman, "Consumers Rate Advertising High," *Advertising Age,* October 24, 1983, pp. 1, 18.

7. Gallup Poll, December 1986.

8. Jacob Jacoby and Wayne Hoyer, "Viewer Miscomprehension of Televised Communication: Selected Findings," *Journal of Marketing* 46, Fall 1982, pp. 12–26.

9. *Ibid.*

10. *Ibid.*

11. *Ibid.*

12. *Ibid.*

13. *Ibid.*

14. David Schmittlein and Donald Morrison, "Measuring Miscomprehension for Televised Communications using True-False Questions," *Journal of Consumer Research* 10, September 1983, pp. 147–156.

15. Fliece Gates, "Further Comments on the Miscomprehension of Televised Advertisements," *Journal of Advertising* 15, no. 1, 1986, pp. 4–9.

A Codebook of Variables for the Stewart and Furse Study of Commercial Content*

Information Content

(D001) **Price:** Refers to the amount the consumer must pay for the product or service; this may be in absolute terms, like a suggested retail price, or relative terms, like a 10 percent off sale.

(D002) **Value:** Refers to some combination of price and quality or quantity, as in more x for the money, better quality at a low price, the best value for the dollar.

(D003) **Quality:** Refers to how good the product or service is; may refer to craftsmanship and/or attention during manufacture, use of quality (better, best) ingredients or components, length of time to produce or create the product.

(D004) **Economy/savings:** Refers to saving money or time either in the original purchase or in the use of the product relative to other products in the category.

(D005) **Dependability/reliability/durability:** Information concerning how long the product will last without repair, service records, and so on.

(D006) **Sensory information** (taste, fragrance, touch, comfort): Information concerning a sensory experience: "smells April fresh," "tastes homemade," "feels silky smooth," "smooth taste," "luxurious comfort."

(D007) **Aesthetic claims** (styling, color): Information concerning appearance, classic beauty, and so on of the product either when purchased or when prepared in final form.

(D008) **Components, contents, or ingredients:** What went into the making or manufacture of the product—for example, "contains lanolin," "made with pudding." These contents should be in the product purchased, not ingredients added to the product by the consumer in preparation for use.

(D009) **Availability:** Any information concerning the place(s) the consumer may purchase or otherwise obtain the product—for example, "available in supermarkets," "look for it in the dairy section." May also refer to places where the product is not available—for example, "not available in all areas."

(D010) **Packaging:** Information about the packaging of the product—for example, "look for the package with the red spoon," "look for our special two in one package," "the package is reusable," "in the convenient one serving package."

(D011) **Guarantees or warranty:** Refers to any information concerning the presence of a guarantee or warranty, including but not restricted to money back offers, offers to repair or service the product in the event of problems, or offers to replace the product if the consumer is dissatisfied or has a problem.

* David Stewart and David Furse, *Effective Television Advertising* (Lexington, Mass.: Lexington Books, 1986), pp. 131–145.

(D012) **Safety:** Information concerning the safety of the product—for example, "has a built-in cut-off switch," "nontoxic," "won't harm delicate hair."

(D013) **Nutrition/health:** Information concerning the nutritional or health-related characteristics of the product—for example, "fortified with vitamin D," "the formula doctors recommend," "relieves iron-poor blood."

(D014) **Independent research results:** Information offered about tests of the product or of product users that were carried out by an identified individual or organization other than the company manufacturing or distributing the product, such as Underwriter's Laboratory, a leading university, or the U.S. government. Such tests may concern objective product characteristics ("lasts twice as long") or may be related to user preferences ("preferred by two-thirds of the people surveyed").

(D015) **Company-sponsored research results:** Information about tests of the product or users of the product that were carried out by the company manufacturing or distributing the product—for example, the Pepsi challenge.

(D016) **Research results from unidentified source:** Information about tests of the product or users of the product when the source of the test results is not identified.

(D017) **New uses:** Refers to any information about a new way to use an established product—for example, "use X brand paper cups for sorting and storing nut and bolts," "new recipes," "use Y baking soda to deodorize refrigerator."

(D018) **Company image or reputation:** Refers to any information about the image or reputation of the company that manufactures or distributes the product—for example, "we've been in business longer than anyone else," "we try harder," "the other guys," "babies are our business."

(D019) **Results of using (either tangible or intangible):** Any information concerning the outcomes associated with the use of the product. These outcomes may be in a positive form—"gives hair bounce," "makes you feel healthier,"—or a negative form—"won't yellow floors."

(D020) **User's satisfaction/dedication/loyalty:** Refers to any information concerning users' satisfaction, preference for the brand, or length of time consumer has used the advertised product—for example, "I'd never give up my Tide," "I've always used . . . ."

(D021) **Superiority claim:** Information that claims the advertised product is better than competitive products or an older version of the advertised product in some particular way(s).

(D022) **Convenience in use:** Information concerning the ease with which the product may be obtained, prepared, used, or disposed of.

(D023) **Special offer or event:** Information concerning special events such as sales, contests, two-for-one deals, premiums, or rebates to occur for a specified limited time.

(D024) **New product or new/improved product features:** Refers to any information concerning a new product introduction, new components, ingredients, features, or characteristics of an existing product or an improvement (qualitative or quantitative) in any feature, component, ingredient, or characteristic of an existing product—for example, "new and improved," "now with 50 percent less sugar," "new, milder . . . ," "new, stronger . . . ," "now with built-in flash."

(D025) **Use occasion:** Information that clearly suggests an appropriate use occasion or situation for the product—for example, "buy film for the Christmas season," "enjoy Jello at a birthday party," "the beer for special occasions."

(D026) **Characteristics or image of users:** Refers to any information concerning the type(s) of individual(s) who might use the advertised product—for example, "for the young at heart," "for the busy career woman."

Brand and Product Identification

(D027)   **No product:** No product is identified in the commercial.

       Single product: A single product is the focus of the commercial.

       Multiple products: The commercial presents two or more distinct product lines—for example, Keebler Cookies, Keebler Crackers.

(D028)   **Double-branded product:** Does the product have two brand names—for example, Keebler Rich 'n Chips, Canon AE1, Ford Fairmont?

(D029)   **Identification of company manufacturing and/or distributing the product:** Is the company manufacturing or distributing the product identified in the commercial, either as part of the brand name (Ford Fairmont) or explicitly ("another fine product from General Foods")? (Note: Do not include copyright identifiers as company identifiers.)

(D030)   **Visual brand sign-off:** Is the brand name, package, or other obvious identifier of the product visible as the commercial ends?

(D031)   **Auditory sign-off:** Is the brand name repeated within the last 3 seconds of the commercial?

Congruence of Commercial Elements

Brand Name Reinforces Product Message

(D032)   1. Brand name provides no product information (Tide, Duz, Cheer, Gleem);

       2. Brand name reinforces a product benefit somewhat (Dove, Caress, Life-saver Radial, Firestone 721 Tires, Anyday Panty-liners);

       3. Brand name states exactly (or almost) what product is or will do (Bonz Dog Biscuits) or is by strong reputation clearly identified with the product category or particular benefit (Kodak Instamatic Camera).

Setting

(D033)   Setting not related to normal product use or purchase (for example, car on top of mountain peak);

(D034)   Setting unrelated to product use but somehow relevant to product performance (for example, demonstration of Timex watch strapped to bottom of speedboat, pick-up truck driving up a pile of boulders);

(D035)   Setting directly related to normal product use or purchase situation (for example, car in showroom, driveway);

(D036)   No setting.

Visual Devices

(D037)   **Scenic beauty:** Does the commercial present striking scenes of natural beauty (mountains, flowing streams) at some point?

(D038)   **Beauty of one or more principal characters:** Does the commercial present one or more strikingly beautiful people?

(D039)   **Ugliness of one or more principal characters:** Does the commercial present one or more strikingly ugly characters?

(D040)   **Graphic displays:** Does the commercial use graphic displays or charts as part of its presentation? Such graphics may be computer generated.

(D041)   **Surrealistic visuals:** Does the commercial present unreal visuals, distorted visuals, fantastic scenes like a watch floating through outer space?

(D042) **Substantive supers:** A superscript (words on the screen) used to reinforce some characteristic of the product or a part of the commercial message—for example, "50% stronger," "3 out of 4 doctors recommend."

(D043) **Visual tagline:** A visually presented statement of new information at the end of the commercial; for example, the screen shows the name of participating dealers or another product that was not the focus of the commercial shown. Corporate logos or slogans do not qualify.

(D044) **Use of visual memory device:** Any device shown that reinforces product benefits, the product name, or the message delivered by the commercial—for example, time release capsules bouncing in the air, the word *Jello* spelled out with Jello Gelatin, piece of sun in Polaroid commercials.

Auditory Devices

(D045) **Memorable rhymes, slogans, or mnemonic devices:** Nonmusical rhymes or other mnemonics (memory aid devices) may be incorporated in lyric of a song, but must also stand alone, apart from music—for example, "You're in good hands with Allstate," "Get a piece of the rock".

(D046) **Unusual sound effects:** Out of place, unusual, or bizarre use of sound—for example, the sound of a jackhammer as someone eats a pretzel.

(D047) **Spoken tagline:** A statement at the end of the commercial that presents new information, usually unrelated to the principal focus of the commercial—for example, "And try new lime flavor too."

Promises, Appeals, or Selling Propositions

(D048) **Attributes or ingredients as main message:** A major focus of the commercial is to communicate something about how the product is made (for example, care in manufacturing) or ingredients (for example, the only toothpaste with stannous fluoride).

(D049) **Product performance or benefits as main message:** A major focus of the commercial is to communicate what the product does (for example, shinier tub, fresher breath, whiter teeth) or how to use it.

(D050) **Psychological or subjective benefits of product ownership:** A major focus of the commercial is to communicate hidden or nonprovable benefits of having/using the product (for example, "you'll be more popular, sexier, more confident").

(D051) **Product reminder as main message:** The product or package is the primary message rather than any specific attribute or benefit of use.

(D052) **Sexual appeal:** Main focus of commercial is on sexual cues.

(D053) **Comfort appeals:** Main focus of commercial is on cues appealing to creature comforts (soft chairs, cool climate).

(D054) **Safety appeals:** Main focus of commercial is on cues appealing to being free from fear or physical danger.

(D055) **Enjoyment appeals:** Main focus of commercial is on cues about enjoying life to the fullest, having good food and drink, and so on.

(D056) **Welfare appeals:** Main focus is on caring or providing for others (for example, gift giving).

(D057) **Social approval:** Main focus of commercial is on belonging, winning friends, obtaining approval of others.

(D058) **Self-esteem or self-image:** Main focus of commercial is on feeling better about oneself, improving oneself, being a better person.

(D059) **Achievement:** Main focus of commercial is on obtaining superiority over others, getting ahead, winning.

(D060) **Excitement, sensation, variety:** Main focus of commercial is on adding excitement, thrills, variety to life, avoiding boredom.

Commercial Tone or Atmosphere

(D061) **Cute/adorable**

(D062) **Hard sell**

(D063) **Warm and caring**

(D064) **Modern/contemporary**

(D065) **Wholesome/healthy**

(D066) **Technological/futuristic**

(D067) **Conservative/traditional**

(D068) **Old fashioned/nostalgic**

(D069) **Happy/fun-loving**

(D070) **Cool/laid-back**

(D071) **Somber/serious**

(D072) **Uneasy/tense/irritated**

(D073) **Relaxed/comfortable**

(D074) **Glamorous**

(D075) **Humorous**

(D076) **Suspenseful**

(D077) **Rough/rugged**

Comparisons

(D078) **Direct comparison with other products:** A competitor is identified by name. May also be a direct comparison with an old version of the product advertised.

(D079) **Indirect comparison with other products:** A comparison is made between the advertised product and a competitor, but the competitor is not named.

(D080) **Puffery, or unsubstantiated claim:** Product is declared best, better, finest without identification of dimension or attribute.

Commercial Structures

(D081) **Front-end impact:** The first 10 seconds of the commercial creates suspense, questions, surprise, drama, or something that otherwise gains attention.

(D082) **Surprise or suspense in middle of commercial:** Something surprising, dramatic, or suspenseful occurs in the middle of the commercial.

(D083) **Surprise or suspense at closing:** Commercial ends with a surprise, an unexpected event, suspense, or drama.

(D084) **Unusual setting or situation:** Product is in setting not normally associated with product purchase or use—for example, a car on top of a mountain, a contemporary wine in ancient Greece.

(D085) **Humorous closing:** Commercial ends with a joke, pun, witticism, or slapstick.

(D086) **Blind lead-in:** No identification of product until the end of the commercial.

(D087) **Message in middle (doughnut):** Music and/or action at the start and close of commercial with announcer copy in the middle—for example, Green Giant commercials.

Commercial Format

(D088) **Vignettes:** A series of two or more stories that could stand alone; no continuing storyline but several independent stories (which may convey the same message). Multiple interviews would be an example. Has no continuity of action.

(D089) **Continuity of action:** Commercial has a single storyline throughout with an obvious beginning, middle, and end; a common theme, character, or issue ties the whole commercial together from beginning to end. This may be an interview with a single individual, slice of life, or any other format that involves continuity of action.

(D090) **Slice of life:** An interplay between two or more people that portrays a conceivable real-life situation. There is continuity of action.

(D091) **Testimonial by product user:** One or more individuals recounts his or her satisfaction with the product advertised or the results of using the product advertised—for example, Bill Cosby for Jello Pudding, Henry Fonda for Life Savers.

(D092) **Endorsement by celebrity or authority:** One or more individuals (or organizations) advocates or recommends the product but does not claim personal use or satisfaction—for example, Karl Malden for American Express.

(D093) **Announcement:** Commercial's format is that of a newscast or sportscast, sales announcement.

(D094) **Demonstration of product in use or by analogy:** A demonstration of the product in use—for example, a man shaving in a commercial for shaving lather, women applying makeup, no pantylines in pantyhose commercial. A demonstration of the use of the product, benefit, or product characteristic by an analogy or device rather than actual demonstration, as in the case of dipping chalk into a beaker of fluoride to demonstrate how fluoride is to be absorbed by teeth.

(D095) **Demonstration of results of using the product:** Demonstration of the outcome of using the product—for example, shining floors, bouncing hair.

(D096) **Comedy or satire:** The commercial is written as a comedy, parody, or satire. Not only is humor an element of the commercial, but also the commercial is written to be funny.

(D097) **Animation/cartoon/rotoscope:** The entire commercial or some substantial part of the commercial is animated; for example, the Green Giant opening is always a cartoon followed by real life in middle or the Keebler Elves. A rotoscope is a combination of real life and animation on the screen at the same time—for example, the Trix rabbit.

(D098) **Photographic stills:** The use of photographic stills in part of the commercial. These may be product shorts, settings, or models.

(D099) **Creation of mood or image as dominant element:** An attempt to create a desire for the product, without offering a specific product claim, by appealing to the viewer's emotional/sensory involvement. The primary thrust of the commercial is the creation of a feeling or mood.

(D100) **Commercial written as serious drama:** The commercial is written as a stage play, melodrama, or tragedy.

(D101) **Fantasy, exaggeration, or surrealism as dominant element:** The use of animation or other visual device instead of a realistic treatment to suspend disbelief or preclude literal translation on the part of the viewer.

(D102) **Problem and solution (before/after presentation):** An attempt to define or show a problem, then indicate how the product eliminates or reduces the problem—for example, "ring around the collar."

(D103) **Interview (person on the street or elsewhere):** An interview (questions and answers) is a primary vehicle in the commercial for Rolaids, "How do you spell relief?"

(D104) **Camera involves audience in situation:** Use of camera as eyes of viewer. Camera creates participation in commercial.

(D105) **New wave (product graphics):** Use of posterlike visuals, fast cuts, high symbolism as in Diet Pepsi, RC 100, Lincoln-Mercury (Lynx), Magnavox (with Leonard Nimoy).

Production Characteristics and Quality

(D106) **Number of word in commercial:** The average 30-second commercial has 60 to 70 words in it. Does the commercial clearly have fewer than this number (*few*), about this number (*average*), or obviously more than this number (*many*)? Words in songs count as words. For commercials longer or shorter than 30 seconds, use the ratio of length of commercial to 30 seconds to determine number of words. Codes: 1 = no words, 2 = few, 3 = average, 4 = many.

(D107) **Visual pace of commercial (number of camera cuts):** The average 30-second commercial has 6 to 8 camera cuts. Indicate whether the commercial has a *fewer, average, many more* scene changes. For commercials longer or shorter than 30 seconds, use the ratio of length of commercial to 30 seconds to determine the number of scene changes. Codes: 1 = fewer, 2 = average, 3 = many.

Music and Dancing

(D108) **Music:** Is music present in the commercial in any form?

(D109) **Music as major element:** Do the lyrics of the music used in the commercial carry a product message—for example, "Have it your way . . ." "I'm a Pepper . . ."?

(D110) **Music creates mood (versus background only):** Music contributes to the creation of a mood or emotion—for example, suspense, sensuality.

(D111) **Dancing:** Do cast members dance in the commercial?

(D112) **Musical and dance extravaganza:** Is there a large cast (more than five) that engages in singing or dancing during a significant portion of the commercial, like in the Pepper commercial?

(D113) **Adaptation of well-known music:** Is music recognized popular, classical, country and western tune—for example, "Anticipation"?

(D114) **Recognized continuing musical theme:** Is music clearly identified with brand or company—for example, "I'm a Pepper"?

Commercial Characters

(D115) **Principal character(s) male:** The character(s) carrying the major on-camera role of delivering the commercial message is a male. Incidental, background on-camera appearance is not applicable.

(D116) **Principal character(s) female:** The character(s) carrying the major on-camera role of delivering the message is a female. Incidental, background on-camera appearance is not applicable.

(D117) **Principal character(s) child or infant:** The character carrying the major on-camera role of delivering the product message is a child or infant.

(D118) **Principal character(s) racial or ethnic minority:** One or more of the principal on-camera characters is black, Hispanic, Oriental, or of some other clearly identifiable minority. Must be delivering a significant portion of message, not just cameo, background, or incidental appearance.

(D119) **Principal character(s) celebrity:** The character(s) delivering the major portion of the message on camera is well known either by name or face. Celebrities may be athletes, movie stars, or well-known corporate figures (but not simply the identified head of a corporation).

(D120) **Principal character(s) actor playing role of ordinary person:** Must be delivering the major portion of the message.

(D121) **Principal character(s) real people:** Are one or more of the principal characters identified as real people (as opposed to actors playing a role)? This may take the form of a hidden camera or interview.

(D122) **Principal character(s) creation:** The principal character is a created role, person, or cartoon figure—for example, Ronald McDonald, Pillsbury Doughboy.

(D123) **Principal character(s) animal:** Is one or more of the principal characters an animal (either real or animated)?

(D124) **Principal character(s) animated:** Is one or more of the principal characters animated (cartoon figures)?

(D125) **No principal character(s):** No central character or set of characters delivers a major portion of the commercial message, although there may be characters performing roles on camera relevant to the message.

(D126) **Characters identified with company:** Is one or more of the characters in the commercial symbolic of or well identified with the company manufacturing and/or distributing the product? The character may be real, created, or animated but should be identified with the company, not a specific product—for example, Keebler Elves, Green Giant.

(D127) **Background cast:** Are there people in the commercial other than the principal characters, people who serve as scenery or background—for example, people walking by, people sitting around a bar. These people are only incidental to the commercial message—that is, not active in making a product claim or demonstrating a product benefit.

(D128) **Racial or ethnic minority character in minor role.**

(D129) **Celebrity in minor role (cameo appearance).**

(D130) **Animal(s) in minor role.**

(D131) **Created character or cartoon characters in minor role.**

(D132) **Real person in minor role (not professional actors):** May be actual consumers (specifically identified) or employees.

(D133) **Recognized continuing character:** Is one or more of the principal or minor characters in the commercial recognized as a part of a continuing advertising campaign? Is the character associated with the product by virtue of previous appearances in commercials for the product?

(D134) **Presenter/spokesperson on camera:** Is the audio portion of the commercial message delivered by voice-over announcer (person not on camera), character(s) on camera, or a combination of both? Codes: 1 = voice-over only, 2 = voice-over and on-camera characters, 3 = no voice-over, entire audio message delivered by on-camera characters.

Commercial Setting

(D135) Is the commercial setting, or a significant part of it, indoors or in other humanmade structures (for example, a kitchen, garage, office, stadium, airplane)?

(D136) Is the commercial setting, or a significant part of it, outdoors (mountains, rivers, backyard, garden, or other natural setting)? Do not include unnatural environments such as stadium or home driveway.

(D137) There is no particular setting for the commercial; the setting is neutral, neither indoors nor outdoors.

Commercial Approach

(D138) **Rational/emotional appeal:** A fairly straightforward presentation of the product's attributes and claims is a rational appeal. An emotional appeal does not appeal to reason but to feelings. Is the commercial primarily making a rational or an emotional appeal to the audience? Codes: 1 = more rational, 2 = balance of rational and emotional appeals, 3 = more emotional.

(D139) **Positive or negative appeal:** A positive appeal to buy or use the product is based on what it will do for the consumer, the benefit offered, how the user will be better off. A negative appeal is based on what will happen to the consumer if he or she does not buy the product or what will not happen if the product is used (for example, wax floors won't yellow). Is the commercial making primarily a positive appeal (emphasis on how the product will help you, make you better, healthier) or negative appeal (emphasis on what will happen if you do not use the product, like cavities, or if you use competitor's product)? Codes: 1 = more negative, 2 = balance negative and positive, 3 = more positive.

(D140) **Brand-differentiating message:** Is the principal message of the commercial unique to the product being advertised, or could any product make this claim? The commercial must make it clear that the message is unique; that is, the commercial must explicitly indicate the uniqueness or difference of the product. Dichotomous items are coded as follows: 1 = present, 0 = absent.

Created Variables

Research: Coded as present if any research is presented in the commercial—that is, if independent research (D014), company-sponsored research (D015), or unidentified research (D016) is present.

Total information: The sum of D001 to D026; the number of different pieces of information presented in the commercial.

Total propositions: The sum of D048 to D050; the number of different major appeals made in the commercial.

Total psychological appeals: The sum of D052 to D060; the number of different psychological appeals made in the commercial.

Total emotional content: The sum of D061 to D077; the number of emotions evoked by the commercial.

Timing and Counting Items and Product Category Identifiers

(X01) **Type of commercial**
   1. Animation
   2. Storyboard on film
   3. Live

(X02) **Length of commercial (seconds)**

(X03) **Times brand name mentioned (number)**

(X04) **Time until product category identification (seconds)**

(X05)	**Time until brand name identified (spoken or written) (seconds)**
(X06)	**Time until product or package is shown (seconds)**
(X07)	**Time actual product is on screen (seconds)**
(X08)	**Time package is on screen (seconds)**
(X09)	**Times brand name or logo is shown on screen (number)**
(X10)	**Time brand name or logo is on screen (seconds)**
(X11)	**Principal message presented in first 10 seconds**
(X12)	**Number of vignettes**
(X13)	**Number of on-screen characters (0–9)**
(X14)	**Product category**

Appendix B

EMRC Minimum Standards for Electronic Media Rating Research

Introduction

The Electronic Media Rating Council, Inc., (EMRC) believes that adherence to the following minimum standards is necessary to meet the basic objectives of valid, reliable and useful electronic media audience measurement research. Acceptance of Electronic Media Rating Council minimum standards by a rating service is one of the conditions of accreditation by the Electronic Media Rating Council, Inc. These are intended to be minimum standards and neither they, nor anything in EMRC Procedures, shall prevent any rating service from following higher standards in its operations.*

The minimum standards listed herein are divided into two groups:

A. Ethical and Operational Standards

These standards govern the quality and integrity of the entire process by which ratings are produced.

B. Disclosure Standards

These standards specify the detailed information about a rating service which must be made available to users, to the Electronic Media Rating Council, Inc., and its audit agent, as well as the form in which the information should be made available.

A. Ethical and Operational Standards

1. Each rating service shall try constantly to reduce the effects of bias, distortion and human error in all phases of its activities.

2. Appropriate quality control procedures shall be maintained with respect to all external and internal operations which may reasonably be assumed to exert significant effects on the final results.

   Quality control shall be applied but not necessarily limited to sample selection, sample implementation, data collection, data editing, data input, tabulation and printing. It shall include (where relevant) periodic independent internal verification of field work and periodic accuracy checks of meter performance and computer accumulations of base data.

3. The sample design for audience surveys (sample frame and sampling plan) must, to a reasonable degree, accurately reflect the statistical population targeted for measurement. In each rating report the statistical (target) populations to which measurements are projected must be clearly defined. In instances where the

---

*In this document, all references to "rating services" are intended to mean "electronic media rating services." Source: Electronic Media Rating Council.

sample frame may exclude part of the "target" population such deviations shall be described clearly.

4. All field personnel (including supervisors) shall be furnished with detailed written instructions and manuals covering all steps of their work. Such personnel shall be thoroughly trained to assure that:

   a. They know the responsibilities of their positions.

   b. They understand all instructions governing their work.

   c. They will deviate from such instructions only when justified by unusual conditions and that any such deviations will be reported in writing.

   d. They recognize and will avoid any act which might tend to condition, misrepresent or bias the information obtained from respondents.

5. To improve quality of performance, interviewers and other personnel shall be informed that their work will be periodically checked by internal quality control procedures and by EMRC auditors. Every effort shall be made to avoid divulgence to such persons of the checking procedures and the personnel, times and places selected for checking.

6. Detailed written instructions shall be maintained to insure uniform procedures in editing operations. Any editing changes in diaries or questionnaires (additions, deletions or changes) shall be made in an easily identifiable manner so that such editing changes can be checked or audited. Any routines for editing by computer shall be clearly documented.

7. Each rating service utilizing computer systems for processing audience data shall establish procedures to insure that:

   a. The operations to be performed by the computer system are documented in sufficient detail to specify for each computer program at least: the objective of the program; the input data to be used; the editing and processing steps to be performed; and the output data.

   b. The computer programs and data are diligently protected from unauthorized manipulation.

   c. Changes in any computer program are documented in enough detail to identify what is being changed, the reason for the changes, tests performed to confirm the effect(s) of the changes, and the effective data of the changes.

8. The anonymity of all personnel in any way concerned with sample respondents or households shall be preserved.

9. If respondents have been led to believe, directly or indirectly, that they are participating in an audience measurement survey and that their anonymity will be protected, their names, addresses, and other such identifying information shall not be made known to anyone outside the rating service organization, except that such information may be provided to:

   a. The audit firm of the Electronic Media Rating Council, Inc., in the performance of an audit.

   b. The Electronic Media Rating Council, Inc., when such disclosure is required in a hearing before the Electronic Media Rating Council, Inc.

   c. Another legitimate market research organization, for methodological purposes only, at the discretion of the rating service.

10. Experiments in methodology shall not be conducted in conjunction with regular syndicated surveys unless previous independent tests have indicated that the possible effect on the audience data reported will be minimal and unless full disclosure is made as provided in B-2 below.

11. Rating services shall take adequate steps to avoid including in audience measurement samples any station or network principal or employee or any member of their households because of the possibility of conscious or unconscious bias in the reporting of their media behavior.

12. In the event that a rating service has identified an attempt to bias measurement results by a respondent's submission of fabricated information, it will do whatever may be necessary to identify and eliminate such cases. In the event that such cases have been included in published data, the service will attempt to assess the effect on results and will notify users should this prove to be of practical significance.

B. Disclosure Standards

General

A concise description of the survey methodology shall be included in each rating report. This description shall include—but is not to be limited to—a description of the survey technique used, a delineation of the area or areas for which ratings were reported, the sampling procedures used, periods during which the viewing or listening data were obtained, criteria for reporting stations, a statement as to whether weighting and/or adjustment factors have been used, and a statement as to whether special interviewing and/or retrieval techniques have been used. Additional details regarding procedures used in sampling (including the selection of samples, callback procedures, substitution procedures), weighting, area determination, etc., shall be provided subscribers in methodological supplements which shall be updated periodically to reflect current policy and practice.

Specific

1. Each report shall include statements calling attention to all omissions, errors and biases known to the rating service which may exert a significant effect on the findings shown in the report.

2. Each rating report shall point out changes in, or deviations from, the standard operating procedures of the rating service which may exert a significant effect on the reported results. This notification shall indicate the estimated magnitude of the effect. The notice shall go to subscribers in advance as well as being prominently displayed in the report itself.

3. Each rating report shall show the number of different households (or individuals or other sample units) initially selected and designated to provide audience information and the number among these that provided usable rating data utilized for that specific rating report. If any of the usable interviews or responses have not been included in the final rating report, that fact and a description of the procedure by which the responses used were selected shall be included in the report.

4. Each rating report shall indicate the sample base for the reporting of any separate audience data (households or persons, geographic breakdowns such as Metro and Total Area and demographic, tabulations based on age, sex, ethnic origin, etc.). This information is to be provided on a basis of in-tab and (where appropriate) effective sample sizes.

5. Geographic areas surveyed shall be clearly defined in each rating report and the criteria and/or source used in the selection of the survey area shall be given. (Thus, if the area surveyed is the Metro area as defined by the U.S. Census, the report should so state.)

6. The rating service shall show in a prominent place in each report a comparison of the geographic distribution of sample data with universe data as obtained from primary sources. In the case of individual local reports, the data shall be shown in each report according to counties or reasonable county groupings. In the case of services using continuing samples, the above information shall be published in each report but need be updated only semi-annually.

7. Each rating report shall state that the audience data obtained from the samples used in audience measurement surveys are subject to both sampling and non-sampling errors and shall point out the major non-sampling errors which are believed to affect the audience estimates.

8. With respect to sampling error:

   a. Each rating report shall contain standard error data relevant to the audience estimates contained therein. Such data shall be presented whether or not effective sample sizes are shown.

   b. The report shall also contain a non-technical explanation of the meaning and use of standard error, as well as a clear guide to how the data may be applied to any given estimate contained in the report.

   c. The method used to develop standard error estimates as well as the formulas used to compute the standard errors shall be fully disclosed. The service shall provide a basis for calculating sample errors for other audience estimates commonly calculated from data published in its reports, although this material may be included in a methodological supplement rather than the report itself.

   d. In order that the Electronic Media Rating Council can verify the accuracy of the standard error and effective sample size approximations contained in a rating report, rating services will be requested periodically to provide a sample of standard errors and effective sample sizes calculated by appropriate standard error formulas, so the EMRC can compare these results with results obtained by applying the approximation formulas given in rating reports.

9. All weighting or data adjustment procedures utilized by a rating service in the process of converting basic raw data to rating reports shall be clearly stated. If this detailed information is not available in each report, the user's attention shall be directed to the appropriate reference material which shall describe procedures and the reasons for such adjustments or weighting.

10. If a rating service establishes minimum requirements for the issuance of a rating report or for reporting stations, or demographic or geographic breaks, the service shall indicate the minimum number of sample returns required for each category.

11. If the rating service becomes aware that a station has employed special non-regular promotional techniques that may distort or "hype" ratings and/or exhortation to the public to cooperate in rating surveys, the rating service shall publish a description of this effort in the appropriate report.

12. If a rating service has knowledge of apparent rating distorting influences such as community power outages, catastrophes or transmission failures, the rating service shall indicate in its reports that such conditions existed during the survey period.

13. With respect to accreditable, but presently non-accredited surveys conducted by a company which produces a rating service(s) accredited by EMRC:

   a. Efforts must be taken by the company to disclose fully that these other (non-accredited) services are, in fact, not accredited by the Council. To avoid subscriber confusion, the minimum requirement is: (1) the report covers for non-accredited services be distinctively different from those used on accredited service(s) and (2) each non-accredited report must carry prominently (on the outside front cover, the inside front cover or the opposite page) the statement:

> (a) "This service is not part of a regular syndicated rating service accredited by the Electronic Media Rating Council and _____ has not requested accreditation _____ service does provide one or more syndicated services which are accredited by the EMRC."

b. Surveys executed by a rating service for a specific client or clients shall clearly show that the report is of a special nature and not part of a regular accredited syndicated rating service. Such report shall show the name of the client or clients and shall be easily distinguishable from accredited rating reports by use of distinctive report covers.

c. The EMRC accreditation symbol will not be used on any reports which are not an integral part of a service accredited by and subject to audit by EMRC.

14. The rating service shall permit such CPA firm(s) designated by the Electronic Media Rating Council for the purpose of auditing to review and/or audit any or all procedures or operations that bear upon the development and reporting of audience estimates.

15. Although the anonymity of all personnel concerned with sample respondents or households shall be preserved (as required by A-8) the EMRC audit form will have the right to check with such personnel and any other appropriate persons as part of the auditing process. (The audit firm will in its audit reports maintain the anonymity of such personnel.)

16. Interviewer and supervisor records shall be maintained at least eleven months by the rating service to show: Name; Date of Work; Time; Type of Work; Location of Work; Manner of Payment (e.g., full-time staff, part-time staff, hourly, per interview, conditions, if any, under which bonuses are paid, etc.).

17. Each rating service shall maintain, for at least eleven months from the end of the period covered by the report, all diaries, interviews, tape records and/or other primary sources of audience data. These shall include material actually used in the preparation of published rating reports as well as material collected but not used. In addition, each service shall maintain records of:

a. All attempts to place diaries or meters, or to obtain interviews or whatever other form of cooperation is required for the research technique used.

b. All unsuccessful attempts to obtain information, including—but not limited to— refusals, not at home, cases requiring further discussion and/or correspondence (e.g., with another member of the household), busy signals (phone), and returns from postal authorities.

c. Actual or assumed reasons for non-cooperation.

d. Which cooperating sample members are original sample selections, and which are first, second, third, etc., substitutions.

18. Returned diaries or questionnaires not put into tabulation for any reason (incomplete, late, poor quality, wrong area, etc.) shall be marked to indicate the reason for rejection and filed as provided under B-17.

19. Each service shall keep for a period of two years, documentation of errors of any type in published figures. Included in such documentation shall be: the length of time the error affected published figures; the effect of the error in absolute and relative terms; its cause; the corrective action taken; and the disclosures, if any, made to subscribers (copies of notices, etc.). If no disclosure was made, the record should indicate the reason underlying this decision.

20. Rating service edit manuals will be made available to subscribers at service headquarters where raw data is made available for inspection.

Additional Recommended Standards

In addition to adherence to the Minimum Standards, EMRC requests that accredited rating services, insofar as possible, observe the "Recommended Standards for the Preparation of Statistical Reports in Broadcast Audience Measurement Research" and "Standard Definitions of Broadcast Research Terms," both published by the National Association of Broadcasters but also endorsed by the Electronic Media Rating Council and the Advertising Research Foundation.

Appendix **C**

SMRB Reports
and ABC Forms/Definitions

Introduction

The Simmons Market Research Bureau, Inc., (SMRB) and Audit Bureau of Circulations (ABC) produce forms and standards such as those shown on the following pages.

In the case of the ABC, it is important to understand definitions for various terms that are commonly used in the reports. A list of such terms is reproduced below.

Exhibit 1
Commonly Used Terms in Audit Bureau of Circulation Reports

Arrears	Subscribers whose names are retained on an active subscription list after period for which they have paid has expired.
Association Subscription	Subscription received because of membership in an association.
Back Copies	Copies of periodicals of date prior to current issue.
Free Publication	One which is distributed mainly free of charge to recipients.
Gift Subscription	Subscription paid for by someone other than the recipient to be used as a gift and not to promote the business interest of the donor.
Official Organ	A periodical which is owned by an association organized for other purposes than to publish the periodical or which is appointed as the publication of an association in return for special privileges.
Paid Subscriptions	A classification of subscriptions paid for in accordance with the standards set by ABC rules.
Paid Subscriber	Purchaser of a publication on a term contract whose subscription qualifies as paid circulation in accordance with the rules.
Premium	Anything, except periodicals, offered to the subscriber either free or at a price with his own subscription, either direct, through or by agents.
Returns	Copies returned to publisher by dealer or other distributor for credit.
Total Paid	Total of all classes of a publisher's circulation for which the ultimate purchasers have paid in accordance with the standards set by ABC.
Unpaid Copies	Copies distributed either entirely free or at a price inadequate to qualify them as paid in accordance with the rules.

Source: Audit Bureau of Circulations.

Following are examples of two prototype forms published by the ABC.

Exhibit 2
ABC Prototype Magazine Publisher's Statement

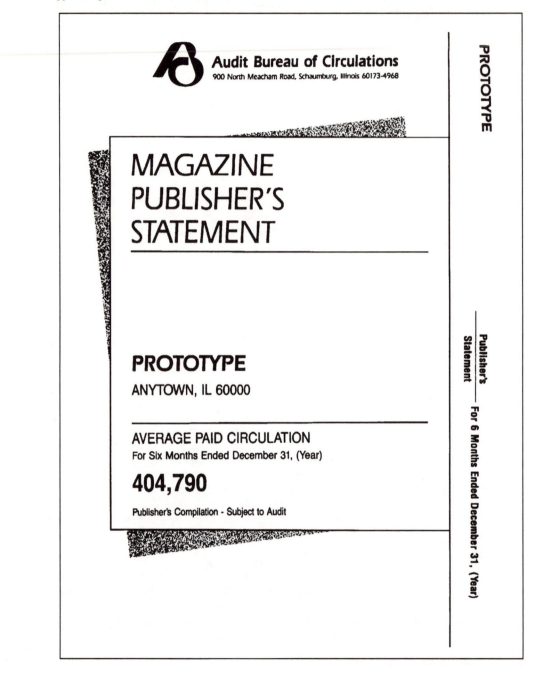

Audit Bureau of Circulations
900 North Meacham Road, Schaumburg, Illinois 60173-4968

PROTOTYPE

MAGAZINE PUBLISHER'S STATEMENT

PROTOTYPE

ANYTOWN, IL 60000

AVERAGE PAID CIRCULATION
For Six Months Ended December 31, (Year)

404,790

Publisher's Compilation - Subject to Audit

Publisher's Statement

For 6 Months Ended December 31, (Year)

Exhibit 2 (Continued)

PROTOTYPE

CLASS, INDUSTRY OR FIELD SERVED: Travel, customs of people, products and related human interest, subject to geographical and sociological nature.

1. AVERAGE PAID CIRCULATION FOR 6 MONTHS ENDED DECEMBER 31, (YEAR)

Subscriptions:	295,069
Single Copy Sales:	109,721
AVERAGE TOTAL PAID CIRCULATION	404,790
Advertising Rate Base	400,000
Average Total Non-Paid Distribution 12,050	

1a. AVERAGE PAID CIRCULATION of Regional, Metro and Demographic Editions

Edition & number of issues	
Eastern (6)	149,772
Central (6)	161,916
Western (6)	93,102

2. PAID CIRCULATION by Issues

Issue	Subscriptions	Single Copy Sales	Total Paid	Issue	Subscriptions	Single Copy Sales	Total Paid
July	285,960	116,637	402,597	Oct.	301,738	105,764	407,502
Aug.	297,181	107,749	404,930	Nov.	290,590	109,495	400,085
Sept.	300,315	102,700	403,015	Dec.	294,630	115,979	410,609

ANALYSIS OF TOTAL NEW AND RENEWAL SUBSCRIPTIONS

Sold during 6 Month Period Ended December 31, (Year)

3. AUTHORIZED PRICES

(a) Basic Prices: Single Copy: $1.50.	
Subscriptions: 1 yr. $12.00; 2 yrs. $22.00; 3 yrs. $30.00	19,431
(b) Higher than basic prices:	None
(c) Lower than basic prices: 1 yr. $7.00, $8.00, $8.99; 2 yrs. $13.99	78,924
(d) Association subscription prices	None
Total Subscriptions Sold in Period	98,355

4. DURATION OF SUBSCRIPTIONS SOLD:

(a) One to six months (1 to 6 issues)	660
(b) Seven to twelve months (7 to 12 issues)	85,669
(c) Thirteen to twenty-four months	1,021
(d) Twenty-five to thirty-six months	143
(e) Thirty-seven to forty-eight months	9,100
(f) Forty-nine months and more	1,822
Total Subscriptions Sold in Period	98,355

5. CHANNELS OF SUBSCRIPTION SALES:

(a) Ordered by mail and/or direct request	68,501
(b) Ordered through salespeople:	
1. Catalog agencies and individual agents	8,644
2. Publisher's own and other publisher's salespeople	590
3. Independent agencies' salespeople	14,100
4. Newspaper agencies	None
5. Members of schools, churches, fraternal and similar organizations	6,317
(c) Association memberships	None
(d) All other channels, See Par. 11(a)	203
Total Subscriptions Sold in Period	98,355

Exhibit 2 (Continued)

6. USE OF PREMIUMS:

(a) Ordered without premium...	92,434
(b) Ordered with material reprinted from this publication, See Par. 11(b)............	2,891
(c) Ordered with other premiums, See Par. 11(c)...................................	3,030
Total Subscriptions Sold in Period..	96,355

ADDITIONAL CIRCULATION INFORMATION

7. POST EXPIRATION COPIES INCLUDED IN PAID CIRCULATION (PAR. 1):

(a) Average number of copies served on subscriptions not more than three months after expiration 12,060

8. COLLECTION STIMULANTS: See Par. 11(d)... 1,804

9. BASIS ON WHICH COPIES WERE SOLD TO RETAIL OUTLETS:

Fully returnable..	93.15%
Nonreturnable..	6.85%
	100.00%

10. U.S. PAID CIRCULATION BY ABCD COUNTY SIZE based on October, (Year) Issue

May, Year issue used in establishing percentages.
Total paid circulation of this issue was 0.67% greater than average total paid circulation for period.

County Size	No. of Counties	% of U.S. Population	Subscription Circulation		Single Copy Circulation		Total Circulation	
			Copies	% Total	Copies	% Total	Copies	% Total
A	177	41%	106,572	36.57	39,397	40.57	145,969	37.57
B	408	30%	90,690	31.12	33,871	34.88	124,561	32.06
C	496	15%	52,572	18.04	14,867	15.31	67,439	17.36
D	1,993	14%	41,585	14.27	8,973	9.24	50,588	13.01
	3,074	100%	291,419	100.00	97,108	100.00	388,527	100.00
Alaska-Hawaii Unclassified	27		1,483		891		2,374	
TOTAL U.S.	3,101		292,902		97,999		390,901	

COUNTY SIZE GROUP DEFINITIONS BY THE A.C. NIELSEN COMPANY

A—All counties belonging as of June 19, 1981 to the 25 largest SCSAs or SMSAs according to the 1980 Census of Population.
B—All counties not included under A that are either over 150,000 population or in SCSAs or SMSAs over 150,000 population according to the 1980 Census of Population.
C—All counties not included under A or B that are either over 40,000 population or in SMSAs over 40,000 population according to the 1980 Census of Population.
D—All remaining counties.

11. EXPLANATORY:

Latest Released Audit Report Issued for 12 months ended June 30, (Year).

Variation from Publisher's Statements

Audit Period Ended	Rate Base	Audit Report	Publisher's Statements	Difference	Percentage of Difference
6-30-(Year)	400,000	403,384	402,833	+551	+0.14
6-30-(Year)	375,000	394,666	396,709	−2,043	−0.51
6-30-(Year)	(a)	381,446	385,207	−3,761	−0.98
6-30-(Year)	350,000	373,611	372,912	+699	+0.19
6-30-(Year)	350,000	358,402	359,601	−1,199	−0.33

(a) Effective 1/1/(Year) changed from 350,000 to 375,000.

(a) Par. 5(d): Represents subscriptions sold through Prototype catalogs, hobby shops and libraries.

(b) Par. 6(b): A book, with no advertised or stated value, titled Prototype's Greatest Articles which consisted of articles reprinted from previous issues was offered in connection with a 1 year subscription at $12.00.

(c) Par. 6(c): A dufflebag, with no advertised or stated value, was offered with subscriptions sold at basic prices.

(d) Par. 8: A Sweepstakes Collection Contest was conducted during the period covered by this statement in which prizes were offered to subscribers who paid in full.

(e) During the period covered by this statement a Sweepstakes was run in which prizes worth $10,000.00 were awarded.

Total expirations during 12 months May 1, (Year) - April 30, (Year)	236,219
Total renewals of these expirations	171,602
12-month renewal percentage	72.85%

102

Exhibit 2 (Concluded)

12. GEOGRAPHIC ANALYSIS OF TOTAL PAID CIRCULATION for the October, (Year) issue

Total paid circulation of this issue was 0.67% greater than average total paid circulation for period.

STATE	Subs.	Single Copy Sales	TOTAL	% of Circ.	% of Pop.
Maine	2,144	619	2,763		
New Hampshire	2,016	588	2,604		
Vermont	1,037	352	1,389		
Massachusetts	6,750	2,512	9,262		
Rhode Island	1,087	432	1,519		
Connecticut	4,907	1,345	6,252		
NEW ENGLAND	**17,941**	**5,848**	**23,789**	**6.99**	**5.45**
New York	18,594	6,688	25,282		
New Jersey	8,834	3,121	11,955		
Pennsylvania	15,153	4,502	19,655		
MIDDLE ATLANTIC	**42,581**	**14,311**	**56,892**	**14.56**	**16.24**
Ohio	14,500	4,017	18,517		
Indiana	7,598	2,178	9,776		
Illinois	17,086	3,531	20,617		
Michigan	12,654	3,882	16,536		
Wisconsin	8,402	2,189	10,591		
EAST N. CENTRAL	**60,240**	**15,797**	**76,037**	**19.45**	**18.48**
Minnesota	8,018	1,916	9,934		
Iowa	6,341	1,345	7,686		
Missouri	5,470	1,630	7,100		
North Dakota	1,393	356	1,749		
South Dakota	1,287	317	1,604		
Nebraska	2,344	507	2,851		
Kansas	3,914	973	4,887		
WEST N. CENTRAL	**28,767**	**7,044**	**35,811**	**9.16**	**7.59**
Delaware	857	248	1,105		
Maryland	5,013	1,638	6,651		
District of Columbia	426	338	764		
Virginia	5,520	2,376	7,896		
West Virginia	1,994	580	2,574		
North Carolina	5,889	1,586	7,475		
South Carolina	2,616	941	3,557		
Georgia	5,106	1,753	6,859		
Florida	10,803	5,289	16,092		
SOUTH ATLANTIC	**38,224**	**14,749**	**52,973**	**13.56**	**16.31**
Kentucky	3,186	774	3,940		
Tennessee	4,383	1,420	5,803		
Alabama	3,012	899	3,911		
Mississippi	1,729	735	2,464		
EAST S. CENTRAL	**12,290**	**3,828**	**16,118**	**4.12**	**6.47**
Arkansas	2,060	447	2,507		
Louisiana	3,733	1,374	5,107		
Oklahoma	4,922	1,553	6,475		
Texas	16,243	6,845	23,088		
WEST S. CENTRAL	**26,958**	**10,219**	**37,177**	**9.51**	**10.48**
Montana	1,479	491	1,970		
Idaho	1,587	503	2,090		
Wyoming	1,056	330	1,386		
Colorado	5,470	2,222	7,692		
New Mexico	1,964	753	2,717		
Arizona	4,047	1,452	5,499		
Utah	1,685	886	2,551		
Nevada	1,371	610	1,981		
MOUNTAIN	**18,639**	**7,247**	**25,886**	**6.62**	**5.02**

STATE	Subs.	Single Copy Sales	TOTAL	% of Circ.	% of Pop.
Alaska	815	436	1,251		
Washington	6,272	2,549	8,821		
Oregon	3,353	1,252	4,605		
California	36,154	14,264	50,418		
Hawaii	668	455	1,123		
PACIFIC	**47,262**	**18,956**	**66,218**	**16.95**	**14.84**
Miscellaneous					
Unclassified					
UNITED STATES	**292,862**	**97,999**	**390,961**	**100.00**	**100.00**
U.S. Circ. Percent of Grand Total				**96.93**	
Poss. & Other Areas	284	38	322	0.08	
U.S. & POSS., etc.	**293,146**	**98,037**	**391,223**	**96.01**	
Canada	**7,438**	**6,327**	**13,765**	**3.38**	
Newfoundland	99	22	121	0.88	
Nova Scotia	250	266	516	3.75	
Prince Edward Island	31	26	57	0.42	
New Brunswick	130	152	282	2.05	
Quebec	849	634	1,483	10.77	
Ontario	3,446	2,499	5,945	43.19	
Manitoba	298	223	521	3.78	
Saskatchewan	347	202	549	3.99	
Alberta	874	1,011	1,885	13.69	
British Columbia	1,078	1,267	2,345	17.04	
Northwest Territories	23	13	36	0.26	
Yukon Territories	13	12	25	0.18	
CANADA	**7,438**	**6,327**	**13,765**	**100.00**	**100.00**
Foreign	873	1,236	2,109	0.52	
Unclassified					
Military or Civilian Personnel Overseas	241	164	405	0.09	
GRAND TOTAL	**301,738**	**105,764**	**407,502**	**100.00**	

10a. CANADIAN PAID CIRCULATION BY ABCD COUNTY SIZE based on October, (Year) issue:

County Size	No. of Counties	% of Canadian Pop.	Subscription Circulation Copies	Subscription Circulation % Total	Single Copy Circulation Copies	Single Copy Circulation % Total	Total Circulation Copies	Total Circulation % Total
A	56	62%	4,382	58.91	4,198	66.35	8,580	62.33
B	57	18%	1,416	19.04	1,013	16.01	2,429	17.65
C	46	9%	909	12.22	648	10.24	1,557	11.31
D	106	11%	731	9.83	468	7.40	1,199	8.71
TOTAL CANADA	**265**	**100%**	**7,438**	**100.00**	**6,327**	**100.00**	**13,765**	**100.00**

EXPLANATION OF ABCD COUNTY SIZE

A—All counties which are, in whole or in part, within the boundaries of Census Metropolitan Areas.

B—All remaining counties which are, in whole or in part, within the boundaries of Census Agglomerations of 25,000 population or over and other counties containing a place of 25,000 or more population not officially designated as Census Agglomerations.

C—All remaining counties which are, in whole or in part, within the boundaries of Census Agglomerations of less than 25,000 population and other counties containing a place of 10,000 or more population.

D—All remaining counties.

We certify that to the best of our knowledge all data set forth in this Publisher's Statement are true and report circulation in accordance with Audit Bureau of Circulations' Bylaws and Rules. 0-0000-0

PROTOTYPE MAGAZINE, published by Prototype, Inc., 125 Main St., Anytown, IL 60000.

JOHN DOE   MARY ROE

Circulation Manager   Publisher

Date Signed, January 30, (Year).

Revised on September 5, 1989.

Exhibit 3
ABC Prototype Controlled Magazine Publisher's Statement

This form, printed on desert sand paper, is used by consumer magazines having less than 70% of their total distribution as paid circulation.

Audit Bureau of Circulations
900 N. Meacham Road
Schaumburg, IL 60173-4968

PROTOTYPE MAGAZINE
Controlled
Magazine Publisher's Statement
Analyzed Non-Paid and Paid Circulation
For 6 months ended December 31, 19--

Publisher's Compilation - Subject to Audit

Field Served:

Publisher's Definition of Individual Recipients	Method of Circulation

PROTOTYPE MAGAGINE

Publisher's Statement —— For 6 Months Ended December 31, (Year)

1. Average Analyzed Non-Paid Circulation   Averages for Period   % Total

  1a. Direct Request from Recipient
     Written . . . .
     Telemarketing . . . .
     Total . . . .

  1b. Other than Direct Request from Recipient
     Directories, See Par. 16(a) . . . .
     Lists, See Par. 16(b) . . . .
     Other Sources, See Par. 16(c) . . . .
       Total . . . .

  1c. Non-Paid Bulk, available for pickup at designated locations
     See Par. 16(d) . . . .

  Total Average Analyzed Non-Paid Circulation . . . .

2. Average Paid Circulation

  Subscriptions: Individual . . . .
                   Association, See Par. 16(e) . . . .
                   Bulk, See Par. 16(f) . . . .
  Single Copy Sales: . . . .

  Total Average Paid Circulation . . . .

Advertising Rate Base and/or Circulation Guarantee . . . .
  Average Non-Analyzed Non-Paid Circulation . . . .

Exhibit 3 (Continued)

PROTOTYPE MAGAZINE

3. **AVERAGE ANALYZED NON-PAID AND PAID CIRCULATION** of Regional, Metro and Demographic Editions

Edition	Direct Request	Other Than Direct Request	Non-Paid Bulk	Total Non-Paid Circulation	Total Paid Circulation	Edition	Direct Request	Other Than Direct Request	Non-Paid Bulk	Total Non-Paid Circulation	Total Paid Circulation

4. **ANALYZED NON-PAID AND PAID CIRCULATION** by Issues and Non-Paid Removals & Additions

	Direct Request	Other Than Direct Request	Non-Paid Bulk	Total Non-Paid	Non-Paid Removed	Non-Paid Added	Paid Circulation Subs.	Single Copy
July								
Aug.								
Sept.								
Oct.								
Nov.								
Dec.								

5. **ANALYSIS OF NON-PAID CIRCULATION** served for the _____ Issue

(Format is at option of publication — must be consistent with statement of recipient definition)

5a. **ANALYSIS OF PAID CIRCULATION** served for the _____ Issue

(Format is at option of publication — must be consistent with statement of recipient definition)

Exhibit 3 (Continued)

6. **ANALYSIS OF NON-PAID CIRCULATION** (Excluding Non-Paid Bulk) to Defined Recipients by Age of Source Data

for the _____ Issue

| | Qualified Within | | | | | | |
SOURCE	1 Year	%	2 Years	%	3 Years	%	Total	%
Non-Paid Circulation:								
Direct Request from Recipient:								
Written								
Telemarketing								
Other than Direct Request from Recipient:								
Directories								
Lists								
Other Sources								
Total Non-Paid Circulation (Excluding Non-Paid Bulk)								
Percent								

7. **ANALYZED NON-PAID AND PAID CIRCULATION BY ABCD COUNTY SIZE** based on _____ Issue

Analyzed non-paid circulation of this issue was _____% greater/less than the average for period.
Paid circulation of this issue was _____% greater/less than the average for period.

County Size	No. of Counties	% of U.S. Population	Non-Paid (Excluding Bulk)	Non-Paid Bulk	Total Non-Paid	%	Total Paid	%
A	177	41%						
B	408	30%						
C	496	15%						
D	1,993	14%						
	3,074	100%						
Alaska-Hawaii	27							
Unclassified								
TOTAL U.S.	3,101							

ANALYSIS OF THE SALES OF TOTAL NEW AND RENEWAL PAID SUBSCRIPTIONS

Sold during 6 Month Period Ended December-31, (Year)

8. AUTHORIZED PRICES:

(a) Basic Prices: Single Copy:
  Subscriptions: ....
(b) Higher than basic prices: ....
(c) Lower than basic prices: ....
(d) Association subscription prices: ....
  Total Subscriptions Sold in Period ....

9. DURATION OF SUBSCRIPTIONS SOLD:

(a) One to six months (1 to 6 issues) ....
(b) Seven to twelve months (7 to 12 issues) ......
(c) Thirteen to twenty-four months...............
(d) Twenty-five to thirty-six months..............
(e) Thirty-seven to forty-eight months ....
(f) Forty-nine months and more.................
  Total Subscriptions Sold in Period............

10. CHANNELS OF SUBSCRIPTION SALES:

(a) Ordered by mail and/or direct request ....
(b) Ordered through salespeople:
  1. Catalog agencies and individual agents .....
  2. Publisher's own and other publisher's salespeople ....
  3. Independent agencies' salespeople.........
  4. Newspaper agencies ....
  5. Members of schools, churches, fraternal and similar organizations ....
(c) Association memberships ....
(d) All other channels ....
  Total Subscriptions Sold in Period...........

11. USE OF PREMIUMS:

(a) Ordered without premium ....
(b) Ordered with material reprinted from this publication ....
(c) Ordered with other premiums ....
  Total Subscriptions Sold in Period............

ADDITIONAL CIRCULATION INFORMATION

12. POST EXPIRATION COPIES INCLUDED IN PAID CIRCULATION (PAR. 2):

Average number of copies served on subscriptions not more than three months after expiration ......

13. COLLECTION STIMULANTS:

14. BASIS ON WHICH COPIES WERE SOLD TO RETAIL OUTLETS:

Fully returnable ....
Nonreturnable................................

Exhibit 3 (Concluded)

15. **GEOGRAPHIC ANALYSIS OF TOTAL NON-PAID AND PAID CIRCULATION** for the _____ Issue

Analyzed non-paid circulation of this issue was _____ % greater/less than the average for period.
Paid circulation of this issue was _____ % greater/less than the average for period.

	Non-Paid Circ. (Excluding Bulk)	Non-Paid Bulk	Total Non-Paid Circ.	Paid Sub. Circ.	Paid Single Copy Circ.	Total Paid Circ.	% of Pop.
Maine							
New Hampshire							
Vermont							
Massachusetts							
Rhode Island							
Connecticut							
NEW ENGLAND							5.45
New York							
New Jersey							
Pennsylvania							
MIDDLE ATLANTIC							16.24
Ohio							
Indiana							
Illinois							
Michigan							
Wisconsin							
EAST N. CENTRAL							18.40
Minnesota							
Iowa							
Missouri							
North Dakota							
South Dakota							
Nebraska							
Kansas							
WEST N. CENTRAL							7.56
Delaware							
Maryland							
District of Columbia...							
Virginia							
West Virginia							
North Carolina							
South Carolina							
Georgia							
Florida							
SOUTH ATLANTIC							16.31

	Non-Paid Circ. (Excluding Bulk)	Non-Paid Bulk	Total Non-Paid Circ.	Paid Sub. Circ.	Paid Single Copy Circ.	Total Paid Circ.	% of Pop.
Kentucky							
Tennessee							
Alabama							
Mississippi							
EAST S. CENTRAL							6.47
Arkansas							
Louisiana							
Oklahoma							
Texas							
WEST S. CENTRAL							10.48
Montana							
Idaho							
Wyoming							
Colorado							
New Mexico							
Arizona							
Utah							
Nevada							
MOUNTAIN							5.02
Alaska							
Washington							
Oregon							
California							
Hawaii							
PACIFIC							14.94
Miscellaneous							
Unclassified							
UNITED STATES							100.00
U.S. Circ. Percent of Grand Total							
Poss. & Other Areas							
U.S. & POSS., etc.							
Canada							
Foreign							
Unclassified							
Military or Civilian Personnel Overseas							
GRAND TOTAL							

16. **EXPLANATORY:**

Latest Released Audit Report Issued for 12 months ended June 30, 19--.

(a) Par. 1: Directories, averaging _____ copies per issue, represent _____

(b) Par. 1: Lists, averaging _____ copies per issue, represent names supplied by _____ .

(c) Par. 1: Other Sources, averaging _____ copies per issue, represent _____

(d) Par. 1: Non-Paid Bulk circulation, averaging _____ copies per issue to _____ .

(e) Par. 2: Association subscriptions, averaging _____ copies per issue, represent _____

(f) Par. 2: Bulk subscription sales, averaging _____ copies per issue, represent _____

We certify that to the best of our knowledge all data set forth in this Publisher's Statement are true and report circulation in accordance with Audit Bureau of Circulations' Bylaws and Rules.

04-0000-0

PROTOTYPE MAGAZINE, published

Circulation Manager   President

Date Signed,

PAC-4

The SMRB provides information in the form of charts such as the following. A brief description of how the numbers should be read and interpreted is provided along with the sample chart.

Exhibit 4
SMRB Chart: Education of Household Head (Males)

	TOTAL U.S. '000	GRADUATED COLLEGE				ATTENDED COLLEGE (1-3 YRS.)				GRADUATED HIGH SCHOOL				ATTENDED HIGH SCHOOL (1-3 YRS.)			
		A '000	B % DOWN	C % ACROSS	D INDX	A '000	B % DOWN	C % ACROSS	D INDX	A '000	B % DOWN	C % ACROSS	D INDX	A '000	B % DOWN	C % ACROSS	D INDX
TOTAL	84064	18858	100.0	22.4	100	13492	100.0	16.0	100	31518	100.0	37.5	100	9764	100.0	11.6	100
AMERICAN BABY	393	**110	0.6	28.0	125	**45	0.3	11.5	72	**160	0.5	40.7	109	**26	0.3	6.6	57
AMERICAN HEALTH	789	*260	1.4	33.0	147	*150	1.1	19.0	119	303	1.0	38.4	102	*39	0.4	4.9	43
ARCHITECTURAL DIGEST	928	555	2.9	59.8	267	241	1.8	26.0	162	*112	0.4	12.1	32	**9	0.1	1.0	8
BABY TALK	306	**90	0.5	29.4	131	**45	0.3	14.7	92	*123	0.4	40.2	107	**8	0.1	2.6	23
BARRON'S	1026	502	2.7	48.9	218	215	1.6	21.0	131	247	0.8	24.1	64	**47	0.5	4.6	39
BETTER HOMES AND GARDENS	4769	1512	8.0	31.7	141	889	6.6	18.6	116	1738	5.5	36.4	97	356	3.6	7.5	64
BON APPETIT	982	492	2.6	50.2	224	*192	1.4	19.6	122	254	0.8	25.9	69	**38	0.4	3.9	33
BRIDE'S	*244	**98	0.5	40.2	179	**50	0.4	20.5	128	**81	0.3	33.2	89	**15	0.2	6.1	53
BUSINESS WEEK	4237	2012	10.7	47.5	212	1007	7.5	23.8	149	1034	3.3	24.4	65	*121	1.2	2.9	25
CAR AND DRIVER	3653	908	4.8	24.9	111	644	4.9	18.2	114	1523	4.8	41.7	111	336	3.4	9.2	79
CHANGING TIMES	1331	540	2.9	40.6	181	*278	2.1	20.9	131	373	1.2	28.0	75	**74	0.8	5.6	48
COLONIAL HOMES	524	*184	1.0	35.5	158	**76	0.6	14.5	91	*202	0.6	38.5	103	**17	0.2	3.2	28
CONDE NAST LIMITED (GROSS)	5817	2020	10.7	34.7	155	1409	10.5	24.2	151	1848	5.9	31.8	85	404	4.1	6.9	60
CONDE NAST PKG. WOMEN(GROSS)	1797	753	4.0	41.9	187	435	3.2	24.2	151	493	1.6	27.4	73	**82	0.8	4.6	39
CONSUMERS DIGEST	1775	558	3.0	31.4	140	455	3.4	25.6	160	657	2.1	37.0	99	**62	0.6	3.5	30
COSMOPOLITAN	1706	682	3.6	40.0	178	378	2.8	22.2	138	494	1.6	29.1	78	**98	1.0	5.7	49
COUNTRY LIVING	1901	486	2.6	32.4	144	*279	2.1	18.6	116	543	1.8	37.5	100	**90	0.9	6.0	52
CREATIVE IDEAS FOR LIVING	281	**73	0.4	26.0	116	**76	0.6	27.0	169	**112	0.4	39.9	106	**21	0.2	7.5	64
CYCLE	1583	*232	1.2	14.7	65	*306	2.3	19.3	121	705	2.2	44.5	119	*191	2.0	12.1	104
CYCLE WORLD	1739	*290	1.5	16.7	74	359	2.7	20.6	129	743	2.4	42.7	114	*215	2.2	12.4	106
DIAMANDIS MAG NETWORK(GROSS)	15035	3629	19.2	24.1	108	3137	23.3	20.9	130	6070	19.3	40.4	108	1374	14.1	9.1	79
DIAMANDIS MTRCYCL GRP(GROSS)	3322	522	2.8	15.7	70	445	4.9	20.0	125	1448	4.6	43.6	116	406	4.2	12.2	105
DISCOVER	1979	679	3.6	34.3	153	492	3.7	24.9	155	621	2.0	31.4	84	**116	1.2	5.9	50
EBONY	3620	533	2.8	14.7	66	613	4.6	16.9	106	1474	4.7	40.7	109	571	5.8	15.8	136
ELLE	333	*153	0.8	45.9	205	**105	0.8	31.5	197	**57	0.2	17.1	46	**17	0.2	5.1	44
ESQUIRE	1740	639	3.4	36.7	164	251	1.9	14.4	90	613	1.9	35.2	94	*163	1.7	9.4	81
ESSENCE	1139	*142	0.8	12.5	56	*284	2.1	24.9	156	451	1.4	39.6	106	*205	2.1	18.0	155
FAMILY CIRCLE	2117	569	3.0	26.9	120	429	3.2	20.3	127	753	2.4	35.6	95	230	2.4	10.9	94
THE FAMILY HANDYMAN	2554	333	1.8	13.0	58	709	5.3	27.8	173	1043	3.3	41.3	110	244	2.5	9.6	82
FIELD & STREAM	7921	1138	6.0	14.4	64	1561	11.6	19.7	123	3587	11.4	45.3	121	1044	10.7	13.2	114
50 PLUS	359	**76	0.4	21.2	94	**98	0.7	27.3	171	*165	0.5	46.0	123	**10	0.1	2.8	24
FINANCIAL WORLD	640	283	1.5	44.1	196	**94	0.7	14.7	92	239	0.8	37.3	100	**15	0.2	2.3	20
FLOWER AND GARDEN	621	**228	1.2	36.7	164	**84	0.6	13.5	85	*154	0.5	24.8	66	**100	1.0	16.1	139
FOOD & WINE	728	390	2.1	53.6	239	*147	1.1	20.2	126	**138	0.4	19.0	51	**29	0.3	4.0	34
FORBES	2212	1346	7.1	60.8	271	435	3.2	19.7	123	364	1.2	16.5	44	**54	0.6	2.4	21
FORTUNE	2522	1508	8.0	59.8	267	468	3.5	18.6	116	438	1.4	17.4	46	**71	0.7	2.8	24
GQ/GENTLEMEN'S QUARTERLY	3124	963	5.1	30.8	137	787	5.9	25.2	157	1037	3.3	33.2	89	*259	2.7	8.3	71
GLAMOUR	503	*183	1.0	36.4	162	**113	0.8	22.5	140	*142	0.5	28.2	75	**36	0.4	7.2	62
GOLF	1915	704	3.7	36.8	164	427	3.2	22.3	139	652	2.1	34.0	91	**99	1.0	5.2	44
GOLF/SKI (GROSS)	2690	1027	5.4	38.2	170	461	3.4	23.0	144	879	2.8	32.7	87	*109	1.1	4.1	35
GOLF DIGEST	2696	952	5.0	35.8	160	739	5.5	27.4	171	802	2.5	30.2	81	*138	1.4	5.1	44
GOLF DIGEST/TENNIS (GROSS)	3372	1253	6.6	37.2	166	883	6.6	26.2	164	1028	3.3	30.5	81	*175	1.8	5.2	45
GOOD FOOD	300	**44	0.2	14.7	65	**75	0.6	25.0	156	**106	0.3	35.0	93	**44	0.5	14.7	126
GOOD HOUSEKEEPING	2942	843	4.5	28.7	128	692	5.1	23.5	147	1044	3.3	35.6	95	*208	2.1	7.1	61
GOURMET	694	280	1.5	40.3	180	*184	1.4	26.8	167	**177	0.6	28.4	76	**31	0.3	4.5	38
HARPER'S BAZAAR	305	**116	0.6	38.0	170	**41	0.3	13.4	84	**112	0.4	36.7	98	**7	0.1	2.3	20
HEALTH	691	*177	0.9	25.6	114	*117	0.9	16.9	106	309	1.0	44.7	119	**42	0.4	6.1	52
HEARST GOLD BUY (GROSS)	4302	1491	7.9	34.7	155	667	5.0	15.5	97	1507	4.8	35.0	93	381	3.9	8.9	76
HEARST HOME BUY (GROSS)	2651	905	4.8	34.1	152	461	3.4	17.4	109	985	3.1	37.2	99	*138	1.4	5.2	45
HEARST MAN POWER (GROSS)	9771	2034	10.8	20.8	93	1805	13.4	18.5	115	4362	13.8	44.6	119	1088	11.1	11.1	96
HEARST WOMAN POWER (GROSS)	7438	2330	12.4	31.3	140	1598	11.9	21.5	134	2640	8.4	35.8	95	493	5.0	6.6	57
HOME	793	375	2.0	47.3	211	*150	1.1	18.9	118	206	0.7	26.0	69	**30	0.3	3.8	33
HOME MECHANIX	2158	335	1.8	15.5	69	422	3.1	19.6	122	1022	3.2	47.4	126	272	2.8	12.6	108
THE HOMEOWNER	810	*164	0.9	20.2	90	*144	1.2	20.5	128	389	1.2	48.0	128	**47	0.5	5.8	50
HG (HOUSE & GARDEN)	1134	307	1.6	27.1	121	301	2.2	26.5	166	371	1.2	32.7	87	*103	1.1	9.1	78
HOUSE BEAUTIFUL	625	233	1.2	37.3	166	*107	0.8	17.1	107	220	0.7	35.2	94	**30	0.3	4.8	41
INC.	1273	751	4.0	59.0	263	267	2.0	21.0	131	*210	0.7	16.5	44	**23	0.2	1.8	16
INSIDE SPORTS	2621	497	2.6	19.0	85	418	3.1	15.9	100	1130	3.6	43.1	115	346	3.5	13.2	114
JET	3355	324	1.7	9.7	43	516	3.8	15.4	96	1229	3.9	36.6	98	780	8.0	23.2	200
LADIES' HOME JOURNAL	1561	415	2.2	26.6	119	316	2.3	20.2	127	631	2.0	40.4	108	**103	1.1	6.6	57
LIFE	5254	1723	9.1	32.2	143	1022	7.6	19.1	119	1740	5.5	32.5	87	525	5.4	9.8	84
LOS ANGELES TIMES MAGAZINE	1405	689	3.7	49.0	219	296	2.2	21.1	132	318	1.0	22.6	60	**39	0.4	2.8	24
MADEMOISELLE	*241	**106	0.6	44.0	196	**75	0.6	31.1	194	**47	0.1	19.5	52	**12	0.1	5.0	43
MCCALL'S	1346	331	1.8	24.6	110	*284	2.1	21.1	132	437	1.4	32.5	87	*142	1.5	10.5	91
MCCALL'S/MRK MOTHER (GROSS)	1556	360	1.9	23.1	103	314	2.3	20.2	126	558	1.8	35.9	96	*153	1.6	9.8	85
MCCALL'S/MRK MOTH/HOM(GROSS)	1662	396	2.1	23.8	106	337	2.5	20.3	127	600	1.9	36.1	96	*155	1.6	9.3	80
MONEY	3541	1705	9.0	47.9	213	748	5.6	21.0	131	919	2.9	25.8	69	*134	1.4	3.8	32
MOTHER EARTH NEWS	959	*273	1.4	28.5	127	*293	2.2	30.6	191	307	1.0	32.0	85	**25	0.3	2.6	22
MS.	**114	**57	0.3	50.0	223	**6	0.0	5.3	33	**40	0.1	35.1	94	**0	0.0	0.0	0
MUSCLE & FITNESS	2063	456	2.4	21.9	98	345	2.6	16.6	104	1006	3.2	48.3	129	*198	2.0	9.5	82
NATIONAL ENQUIRER	6947	813	4.3	11.7	52	1189	8.8	17.1	107	2580	8.2	37.1	99	1347	13.8	19.4	167
NATIONAL GEOGRAPHIC	12314	4715	25.0	38.3	171	2463	18.3	20.0	125	3903	12.4	31.7	85	888	9.1	7.2	62
NATURAL HISTORY	694	324	1.7	46.7	208	**111	0.8	16.0	100	*225	0.7	32.4	86	**31	0.3	4.5	38
NEW WOMAN	**92	**26	0.1	28.3	126	**21	0.2	22.8	143	**22	0.1	23.9	64	**6	0.1	6.5	56
NEW YORK	700	437	2.3	62.4	278	**68	0.5	9.7	61	*171	0.5	24.4	65	**24	0.2	3.4	30
THE NEW YORKER	1022	623	3.3	61.0	272	*109	0.8	10.7	67	253	0.8	24.8	66	**19	0.2	1.9	17
NEWSWEEK	9572	3835	20.3	40.1	179	1940	14.4	20.3	127	2912	9.2	30.4	81	596	6.1	6.2	54

What the numbers mean:

1. It is estimated that male readership of *Bon Appetit* magazine is 982,000.

2. Of that figure, it is estimated that 493,000 readers of *Bon Appetit* are male household heads who have graduated college.

3. This accounts for 2.6 percent of all U.S. male household heads who have graduated college.

4. 50.2% of all *Bon Appetit* readers are male household heads who have graduated college.

5. If the 50.2% is compared with the 22.4% of all (total) magazine readers who are male household heads who have graduated college, an index of 224 results (50.2 + 22.4 × 100 = 224).

The readership of *Bon Appetit* by male household heads who are college graduates is 124 percent higher than the average percentage of all college graduate male household heads who read magazines (which is 22.4 percent and represents the average of 100).

Index

About the Authors

Jack Haskins is an advertising and marketing research consultant, based in Cape Canaveral, Florida. He was previously Director of Communications Research and Professor at Indiana University, Syracuse University, and the University of Tennessee. Earlier in his career, he was Manager of Advertising Research at the Ford Division of Ford Motor Co.

Alice Kendrick is Associate Professor in the Center for Communications Arts at Southern Methodist University. Professor Kendrick has been involved in research projects for a number of companies, including The Richards Group, Pilgrim's Pride, Sheraton Hotels, and the American Lung Association.

TITLES OF INTEREST IN MARKETING, DIRECT MARKETING, AND SALES PROMOTION

For further information or a current catalog, write:

NTC Business Books
a division of *NTC Publishing Group*
4255 West Touhy Avenue
Lincolnwood, Illinois 60646-1975 U.S.A.